# Virtual Reality Usability Design

The development of effective and usable software for spatial computing platforms like virtual reality (VR) requires an understanding of how these devices create new possibilities (and new perils) when it comes to interactions between humans and computers. *Virtual Reality Usability Design* provides readers with an understanding of the techniques and technologies required to design engaging and effective VR applications.

The book covers both the mechanics of how human senses and the mind experience immersive virtual environments, as well as how to leverage these mechanics to create human-focused virtual experiences. Deeply rooted in principles of human perception and computational interaction, the current and future limitations of these replacements are also considered.

Full of real-world examples, this book is an indispensable guide for any practising VR developer interested in making efficient and effective interfaces. Meanwhile, explorations of concrete theory in its practical application will be useful for VR students and researchers alike.

# Virtual Reality Usability Design

David Gerhard
Wil J. Norton

## CRC Press
Taylor & Francis Group
Boca Raton London New York

CRC Press is an imprint of the
Taylor & Francis Group, an **informa** business

First edition published 2023
by CRC Press
6000 Broken Sound Parkway NW, Suite 300, Boca Raton, FL 33487-2742

and by CRC Press
4 Park Square, Milton Park, Abingdon, Oxon, OX14 4RN

*CRC Press is an imprint of Taylor & Francis Group, LLC*

**Library of Congress Cataloging-in-Publication Data**

Names: Gerhard, David, author.
Title: Virtual reality usability design / David Gerhard, Wil Norton.
Description: Boca Raton : CRC Press, 2023. | Includes bibliographical references and index. | Summary: "The development of effective and usable software for spatial computing platforms like Virtual Reality requires an understanding of how these devices create new possibilities (and new perils) when it comes to interactions between humans and computers. Virtual Reality Usability Design provides readers with an understanding of the techniques and technologies required to design engaging and effective VR applications. The book covers both the mechanics of how human senses and the mind experience immersive virtual environments, as well as how to leverage these mechanics to create human-focused virtual experiences"-- Provided by publisher.
Identifiers: LCCN 2022033995 (print) | LCCN 2022033996 (ebook) | ISBN 9781032198699 (hardback) | ISBN 9781032191324 (paperback) | ISBN 9781003261230 (ebook)
Subjects: LCSH: User interfaces (Computer systems) | Haptic devices. | Virtual reality. | System design.
Classification: LCC QA76.9.U83 G45 2023 (print) | LCC QA76.9.U83 (ebook) | DDC 005.4/37--dc23/eng/20220830
LC record available at https://lccn.loc.gov/2022033995
LC ebook record available at https://lccn.loc.gov/2022033996

ISBN: 978-1-032-19869-9 (hbk)
ISBN: 978-1-032-19132-4 (pbk)
ISBN: 978-1-003-26123-0 (ebk)

DOI: 10.1201/9781003261230

Typeset in Latin Roman
by KnowledgeWorks Global Ltd.

*Publisher's note*: This book has been prepared from camera-ready copy provided by the authors.

*To Diane and Arthur*

# Contents

# I

## Understanding Virtual Reality and Users

# CHAPTER 1

# What Makes Virtual Reality Remarkable?

## 1.1  DEFINING VIRTUAL REALITY

Virtual reality (VR) is a medium that seeks to replicate the many sensations we humans experience when we interact with the physical world. Because it seeks to replicate reality, VR is defined by its resemblance to the physical world—while other computer interfaces may use audio output and visual display to represent digital information to the user, VR uses these technologies to "trick" the user into feeling as if the digital world is somehow real. The "virtual" part of *virtual reality* refers to that the world displayed on a VR device is of our own creation, as opposed to the physical world. However, by this logic, any fictional world is *virtual*, be it expressed through literature, visual arts, television, or video games. For a display to be considered virtual reality, the world displayed must be interactive, convincing, and similar to the physical world in terms of form, not just content.

There's a wide diversity of definitions for the term virtual reality, but most people have an intuitive sense of what counts as virtual reality and what does not. Different virtual reality systems support the simulation of different senses at different levels of accuracy, and the applications (or **experiences**) supported across these systems vary widely in the accuracy of their own simulation. Regardless, these systems are still all considered to belong to the category of VR—therefore any definition of the term must be abstract enough to allow for this variety.

Any definition for virtual reality requires us to first take a step back and define **reality**. A common sense definition of reality might refer to the world around us; the space and time that we live in—the place and experiences that we call "the real world." In a more general sense, however, reality refers to that set of things we can independently and objectively agree upon, and specifically the set of things which is not somehow "fake." Reality is often thus defined in a negative sense, and we seek to exclude the false from the real by experimenting to determine the objective and the independent. When discussing virtual reality, however, a much more succinct definition of reality is available—"reality" is the physical world in our immediate vicinity that we can experience with our senses; the virtual version of reality, then, exists

DOI: 10.1201/9781003261230-1

when we block out the sensations from the physical world and replace them with sensations from some virtual world, such that we might believe these new sensations, even if only subconsciously. Although a variety of media exist which attempt to block out and replace the physical world (big screen TVs and loud radios are examples), virtual reality equipment distinguishes itself from other media by attempting to produce a complete illusion of another physical place, from the perspective of and tied to the perceptions of a single user. Two people cannot share the same experience of reality, since we are looking at the world with different eyes from different perspectives. Similarly, no two people can experience the same virtual reality at the same time, since the world is presented to each user through their own apparatus, with their own personal illusions.

Notice the use of the word illusion in this last sentence. The objects and worlds you interact with in a virtual reality system aren't part of the physical world—they're a simulation, despite how much they may replicate their physical counterparts. This is the meaning of the word **virtual** in the context of virtual reality—the simulation seems like a reality but isn't. The word "virtual" originally comes from the Latin "virtus" meaning "excellence" or "potency." Other words with a similar origin are "virtuous" and "vertical," both suggesting a sense of aiming towards perfection. Over time, the meaning of the word "virtual" progressed from "representing the best example of an effect" to "capable of producing an effect" and then "capable of imitating an effect" and finally to the connotation it has today: "being something in essence or effect, but not in reality." Another sense of the word virtual is "almost a particular thing or quality." For example, we say that something is "virtually non-existent" if it's almost gone. When used in this sense, "virtual" can be replaced by "almost" with little to no loss of meaning. In the case of virtual reality, the simulation presented is "almost reality" to the mind—for a simulation to be considered virtual reality, the mind has to interpret it as if it were a physical reality. If our mind interprets a simulation as if it were a physical space we could interact with, then for all practical purposes it's almost reality—virtual reality.

So, back to the definition—for an electronic system to count as virtual reality, it has to be capable of creating the illusion for the user that they are in a different physical place. No matter how high definition your TV is, it will never feel like you're anywhere but your living room. Virtual reality systems are different—in order to make it look like you're in a physical space, a VR system must be able to block out and replace what you can see in any direction. Often, this is done with a head-mounted display that tracks the position of your head to detect the direction of your gaze and replaces your field of view with a render of the virtual world from your point of view. Not only must this display change the rendered image when you move your head and look around, it must update this view so rapidly that you don't notice the change at all. Indeed, as we will discuss later in the book, if the display does not refresh fast enough, it can cause a form of disorientation that is similar to seasickness.

### 1.1.1  Vision and other senses

Although visual replacement is usually what people think about when they consider a VR headset, sight isn't the only way that people receive information from their environment—what we feel, hear, taste, and smell all tell us the information about the physical space we occupy. In fact, humans have many more "senses" than the five just mentioned that provide our brain with information about our surroundings as well as our own bodies—the internal tension of our muscles, our sense of balance, and the system that allows us to feel acceleration and motion, just to name a few. Providing any non-visual sense with information that adds to the illusion of a physical place could also be considered virtual reality. For much longer than we've had optical displays in virtual reality headsets, we've been able to generate "virtual" audio that convincingly replicates the experience of listening to sound in a physical space— if you closed your eyes, you'd believe you were on a busy city street or listening to a performance in a concert hall[1]. Is this, then, a virtual reality device? By our definition, it is—if you close your eyes, the equipment gives you the illusion that you are somewhere else. However, since vision is such a major component of our sensation of the world around us (for those of us with typical vision), and since stereophonic headphones have been around for decades, we don't typically imagine being pulled into a virtual world when we put on our headphones for the train ride home. When people talk about a virtual reality system, at minimum we are usually discussing a system that gives the visual illusion that the user is in another place. This is the lowest bar for something to be considered a virtual reality system in the public discourse—of course, a system that can simulate additional senses is even better, and in fact most VR systems also provide audio simulation as well.

### 1.1.2  Interactions

The emergence of VR as a medium presents new, unique ways of interacting with computers. Being able to digitally generate and display content that a user's mind may interpret as a three-dimensional space introduces new ways to create and improve the way we interact with the digital world, for training, entertainment, employment, productivity, and even for therapeutic experiences. As our computing technology becomes more and more advanced, VR presents a way to merge our interactions with computers with our familiar interactions with the world around us. Even so, the existence of VR as a medium is not a guarantee that such software will be more useful, entertaining, or easier to interact with. Applications running on virtual reality systems are just like any other computer application—their actual usefulness depends on the experience, knowledge, skills and choices of the developers. This book attempts to explain the basic skills and knowledge needed to effectively develop applications involving virtual environments. Much as someone developing a physical product must practice industrial design to create a useful and elegant object to meet

---

[1]Although stereo sound by itself is engaging, it is often insufficient to convince a listener that they are somewhere else. In Chapter 4 we discuss audio technologies like HRTF and Ambisonics that are very convincing.

the user's needs, someone developing a virtual reality application must also have a solid knowledge of interaction design.

This book assumes you already have some knowledge regarding basic programming and computer graphics principles or that you have supplemental texts for these matters. Although it is not necessary to have any prior computer science knowledge to read this book, an elementary understanding of these fields is a requirement for anyone looking to develop virtual reality applications. This first chapter serves as a general introduction to the scope of virtual reality and attempts to explore some of the unique strengths and challenges of this medium. We start the chapter with a general discussion of terminology for different types of virtual environments and discuss some of the historical developments and uses of virtual reality systems. We talk about the specific problems virtual reality is well suited to address in human computer interaction (HCI), discuss some of the current applications of the technology, and try to imagine a few future use cases for virtual environments. Finally, we finish the chapter with a short discussion on why interaction design is an essential part of the development of any virtual reality application.

## 1.2   VIRTUAL ENVIRONMENTS

If virtual reality equipment creates the illusion that a digital world occupies physical space, the digital world displayed is referred to as a **virtual environment**. A virtual reality system obscures the physical environment, using displays or other equipment to block sensations from the physical world, while simultaneously providing new inputs to the occluded senses.

It is possible to provide simulated sensory input without first blocking out physical sensory input. **Mixed reality** (MR) equipment allows a user to experience elements from a virtual environment while allowing them to still receive stimuli from the physical environment, although in this case the virtual environment and the physical environment must be aligned. If VR is when the environment displayed to a user is purely virtual and physical reality is when the environment is entirely physical, then MR includes everything in between.

> **Overlapping with the real**
> The Milgram Kishino continuum, described below, applies primarily when considering different levels of augmented reality, where the virtual world is well aligned with the physical world the user is in. When the virtual world is not aligned with the physical world, each sense must be occluded as much as possible, and the goal at that point is to remove or isolate distractions from the physical world, rather than considering a continuum between them.

The Milgram Kishino Virtuality Continuum describes the spectrum of mixed reality, shown in Figure 1.1. Any device capable of generating a virtual environment could be described as being somewhere along this continuum.

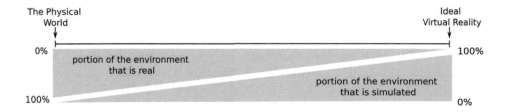

Figure 1.1: The Milgrim Kishino Virtuality Continuum.

On this continuum, "ideal" virtual reality is at the extreme right end—meaning that no stimuli from the outside world reach the user. Almost no practical VR system exists that fits this definition—even in a high-quality virtual reality headset, the user might still be able to hear sounds from the real world or see between the headset and their nose. A device that would qualify as pure virtual reality on the spectrum is at the very least more than a few years past today's technology and may never be practically achievable. Despite the way the continuum defines VR, we'll use the term "virtual reality" to refer to systems that don't quite meet the bar set by Milgram and Kishino—if the intention of a system is to replace outside inputs with simulated ones, we'll call it a virtual reality system (even if it doesn't quite achieve this goal).

On the extreme left hand of the continuum is the physical world — the unmediated experience of the physical environment around us. Everything in between this and ideal virtual reality can be considered to be a form of MR.

MR is a broad category. Although some devices are marketed generally as "Mixed Reality," it is also common to hear other, more specific terms being used. Although the Milgram Kishino continuum is well recognized in academia, there is some ambiguity about where exactly certain classifications belong on the continuum. Some common descriptions for various parts of the continuum are as follows:

- **Extended Reality** (XR) – A catch-all term that refers to any application that includes some form of digital world. This category includes both VR and MR.

- **Augmented Reality** (AR) – Often used in marketing as a synonym for MR. In academia, AR often refers to applications where digital elements do not seem to be placed in the "real world," but are simply overlaid.

- **Augmented Virtuality** (AV) – Used to describe applications for "VR devices" where physical objects are used to replicate difficult-to-simulate parts of the virtual environment. For example, an augmented virtuality tennis application may have VR visuals, but use a physical tennis racket-shaped controller to enhance the realism.

Figure 1.2 shows these various classifications labelled on the Milgram Kishino continuum.

Although this book primarily refers to designing interactions for virtual reality, many of the same design considerations that apply to the applications we discuss are equally valuable when developing MR or AR software. These mediums all relate

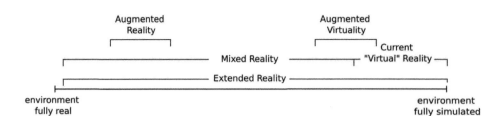

Figure 1.2: Portions of the Milgram Kishino Continuum and how they relate to common spatial computing categorizations.

in that to some degree; they involve or display a world that has similar sensory properties as physical three-dimensional space and as such may be referred to under the blanket term of **spatial computing** technologies. Since all of these mediums are defined by the use of a virtual environment, many of the chapters related to general interaction and interface design for virtual environments are applicable for technologies at any point on the continuum. Further, while most of our case studies focus on virtual reality applications, we have included a few examples showing how the same principles can be applied to mixed reality cases as well. The appendix further suggests resources that include more information on MR design outside of the scope of this book.

The Milgram Kishino continuum is a good basis for high level of comparisons between systems, but there are lots of ambiguities in how it compares systems. What if one system only simulates audio, but another only presents a visual display—which one simulates a higher portion of the environment? As there is no easy way to define if the audio or visual sense represents "more" of the real environment, it might make more sense to consider a specific system on several different continua, separated by the sense being simulated. A MR system might overlay virtual graphics over the real world (falling somewhere near the middle of the continuum for vision), but might not provide virtual sound at all (and would therefore be at the extreme left of the continuum for audio). Even this definition of the reality continuum is not necessarily useful for determining how much of the world has been replaced with simulated stimuli—as the middle 4 percent of the human field of view contains 90 percent of the total resolution of the eye, a continuum that says a headset with a display encompassing only this portion of vision is only 4 percent simulated is not an accurate measure of how much of an environment we have replaced—and neither is a continuum that places this display at the 90 percent simulated mark. A large portion of Chapter 2 and lesser portions of subsequent chapters in the first half of this book are dedicated to describing more objective measures of where a system truly fits between virtual and physical.

## 1.3 THE ORIGINS OF VR

One of the first recorded depictions of virtual reality in a form that we'd recognize today was in a 1949 novel. *Pygmalion's Spectacles* by Stanley Grauman Weinbaum is regarded as the first instance of fiction describing what we would now call "virtual reality." The story is about a man possessing a pair of eyeglasses capable of seeing into a false world as convincing as the physical one. In Weinbaum's novel, the titular spectacles were of supernatural origin, but it was not long before the fictional narrative exploring the concept of virtual reality took on a technological nature. Science fiction stories began depicting similar realities generated by electronic devices.

In almost every fictional depiction of virtual reality devices, the common ground between the systems described is that they are able to support simulations that look and act just like the physical world. Ever since science fiction planted this image in the minds of the general public, the work of countless researchers and engineers has brought us virtual reality devices that come closer and closer to achieving this goal. Eyesight could be considered our "dominant" sense—if the information we see disagrees with what we hear, feel, or smell, we tend to trust our eyes. It makes sense then that many of the earliest virtual reality advances were focused on providing input to the eyes that better replicated the way we see three-dimensional space. People had been able to create paintings to depict the visual world since prehistoric times, but even when we developed the technology required to perfectly capture a scene in time (photography), a flat photograph still wouldn't fool anyone into thinking they were actually looking through a window. There are two major reasons why no static image on a flat plane can seem fully three dimensional:

1. **Perspective** – In the physical world, even the slightest rotation or translation of our head allows us to see new sides of objects and causes the sides we do see to distort in very specific ways, according to the laws of perspective. In order for a scene to seem three dimensional, we would have to be able to track the user's head movements, as well as update the image to match the changing position of the user's head.

2. **Stereospsis** – The pupils of our eyes are separated by a small distance, varying between 3 cm and 5 cm from person to person. This causes our eyes to each receive a slightly different perspective of a scene. One flat image from a single perspective isn't enough to emulate stereospsis.

## 1.3.1 Prehistory: 1800s

Out of these problems, stereospsis was the easiest to address. The stereoscope, a device that was capable of displaying a separate image to each eye, had been invented by Sir Charles Wheatstone, in 1832. Stereoscopes saw further improvements throughout the 19th century—by 1850, over 250,000 stereoscopes had been sold. Although they had began to decline in popularity by the 1870s, stereoscopes continued to get better at depicting stereoscopic scenes—with the advent of the camera, a likeness of the physical world could be depicted by taking two separate images, with one taken from a position 5 cm to the right of the other. A stereoscopic image generated by this method would look quite similar to standing and looking at the subject of the photograph in real life—as long as the user didn't move their head. Stereoscopes survived the 19th century to live on today—not only is stereoscopy a key feature in modern

VR headsets, but modern stereoscopes, like the Viewmaster, still sell well despite remaining relatively unchanged since Sir Charles' original device. Both an early and a modern stereoscope can be seen in Figure 1.3.

Figure 1.3: Left: an early 19th century stereoscope (*Auckland Museum CC BY*). Right: a modern Viewmaster stereoscope, circa 1970 (*Jamiecat CC BY 2.0*).

The second major hurdle in making an image seem three dimensional, tracking head movement and changing perspective, took longer to solve. Early pioneers created devices that tried to emulate the physical world without the use of head tracking. For these devices to be convincing, the user had to remain stationary and their view had to be locked in place. Although the visual sense had yet to be perfected, some inventors still tried to add the support for the simulation of more senses in their "virtual worlds." One of the most ambitious simulators from the pre-head tracking era was Morton Heilig's *Sensorama* (shown in Figure 1.4). In addition to coloured stereoscopic film, a *Sensorama* booth included a seat that would move, fans to simulate wind, and even scents to match the film. Of course, the user still wasn't able to move their head, or else the lack of a change in perspective would make it apparent they weren't in a physical place.

### 1.3.2 Early Prototypes: 1960s

It wasn't until 1968 that head tracking and perspective tracking were achieved in a virtual reality system. In that year, Ivan Sutherland and three students at MIT's Lincoln Laboratory developed the *Sword of Damocles*, the direct ancestor of today's VR **head-mounted displays** (HMDs). Ivan Sutherland had been involved in research related to virtual reality for several years prior to the invention of the *Sword of Damocles* and had come up with much of the early theory of VR, including his definition of the Ultimate Display (discussed more in Chapter 2)—research that laid the groundwork for the *Sword of Damocles*. The headset was tracked via a combination of mechanical linkages and ultrasonic sensors to determine the head rotation and position of the user. Cathode ray tubes near the user's eyes projected stereoscopic vector graphics and would update appropriately when the user's head moved (the

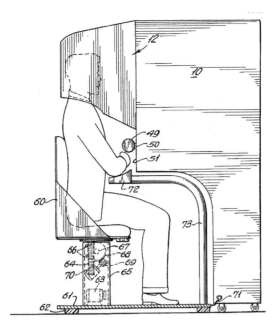

Figure 1.4: The patent drawing for Sensorama (1962).

user was still able to see the room at the same time as the vector graphics, so the *Sword of Damocles* could be considered a mixed reality headset). Due to its weight, the headset had to be suspended by a mechanical arm from the ceiling of the laboratory. With the exception of motion controls, the *Sword of Damocles* was capable of all of the same functions as the first wide-selling consumer VR headsets of the 2010s were—without, of course, the accompanying tracking accuracy or resolution.

**Ivan Sutherland – The Father of Computer Graphics**

Ivan Sutherland may be an important figure in the history of virtual reality development, but his work in VR only represents a small fraction of the overall impact he had on the field of computer science as a whole.

Sutherland's research for his PhD involved his development of *Sketchpad*, an interface which allowed users to make engineering drawings on a computer with a stylus. What made this really impressive was that *Sketchpad* was made in *1963*—before consumer text-based computers even existed! Sketchpad was not only the first computer-aided drafting (CAD) program to exist, but also the first program to use a graphical user interface (GUI). Interacting with *Sketchpad* had more in common with an iPad (2010) than the computers of the day, which for the most part still used punch cards as input.

Sutherland was given the A.M. Turing Award for his work developing *Sketchpad*. After completing his PhD, Sutherland would continue to be responsible for many more important breakthroughs across various fields of computer science.

VR would continue to be developed after the *Sword of Damocles*, primarily within universities and government institutions. Due to the prohibitive expense of equipment at the time, most applications of the technology were exclusive to research, but other uses would begin to emerge. One of the biggest applications for virtual reality in the 1970s was in training applications, particularly in the military. Flight simulators further developed virtual reality technology, and the military also started developing AR displays for jet pilot helmets. As a result of all the interest in virtual reality, headsets continued to get lighter and became capable of supporting better graphics and higher resolutions.

Aside from the continued development of head-mounted displays, researchers continued to innovate new ways to experience virtual environments. Research into haptic technology, allowing a user to move around their hand and feel force feedback, began as early as 1967—with the GROPEHaptic project. Although the GROPEHaptic also had to be mounted to the ceiling for tracking, later haptic technologies followed a similar path as HMDs, freeing themselves from the ceiling by becoming lighter and cheaper. By the 1980s, Scott Fisher and other members of the Virtual Environment Workstation Project at NASA's Ames Research Center had done a work on developing a space station maintenance simulator that included tracked haptic gloves and an HMD. In fact, by around this time, both HMDs and tracked gloves had matured to the point where they were being sold on the commercial market.

### 1.3.3  The first consumer generation: 1990s

The first wave of consumer VR equipment was marked by the founding of VPL research in 1984. Standing for "Virtual Programming Languages," VPL was founded by Jaron Lanier and would eventually develop and sell the DataGlove (a tracked glove), the EyePhone (an HMD, not to be confused with another important innovation in consumer electronics), and the DataSuit (a full body tracking garment). The EyePhone 1 cost around $9,400 and was only capable of refreshing the display at a rate of around six or seven frames per second. Although the device did see sales, they were primarily in industry—product developers and architects found the device useful for viewing designs before prototypes were made. VPL continued to operate until they shut down in 1990.

However, the 1990s saw a multitude of new VR companies established. By 1995, even Nintendo had developed a VR console, the Virtual Boy. Despite the relatively low prices of virtual reality equipment during the 90s wave, the limitations of these devices prevented them from ever truly catching on with the public. VR consoles had low frame rates, small fields of view, and in the case of the virtual boy, only supported graphics in two colours—black and red. Nintendo discontinued the Virtual Boy by 1996, after a disappointing 770,000 worldwide sales. Meanwhile, fiction kept on depicting VR systems that were capable of supporting simulations that looked just like the real world, in novels like Neal Stephenson's *Snow Crash* and William Gibson's *Neuromancer*. When you consider the dissonance between the VR systems of fiction and the actual implementations of the time, it's no wonder consumers of 90s VR were disappointed.

While consumer VR went silent, VR researchers and enthusiasts continued to develop the technology. Advancements in graphical quality and resolution in other fields allowed VR system prototypes to solve many of the issues present in early consumer models. The advent of mobile computing lead to smaller and smaller devices that were capable of better and better performance. The rise of the internet lead to wide-scale discussion and dissemination of virtual reality research—virtual reality flourished, outside of the public view.

### 1.3.4   The Second Consumer Generation: 2010s

In 2012, Palmer Luckey launched the crowdfunding campaign for the Oculus Rift, a headset he had been developing on his own for several years. By the time it was released to the public in 2016, the Oculus Rift (Figure 1.5) had a resolution of 1080 × 1220 pixel resolution, which was impressive for the time, and a frame rate of 90Hz—additionally, it originally cost $600, inexpensive compared to similar devices of the past (for reference, the VPL EyePhone cost upwards of $250,000). The combination of leading-edge hardware and a consumer-friendly price point, as well as the key feature of head-tracked field of view, was enough to capture the imagination of the public. Over 2.5 million units of the Oculus Rift were sold by 2017. Other companies began producing similar VR headsets, like the HTC Vive and Playstation VR, and these devices also saw similar commercial success—as of 2019, Playstation VR had sold 7 million units worldwide.

Figure 1.5: Palmer Luckey wearing the Oculus Rift (2016).

Since then, VR technology has continued to be developed. The second wave of consumer VR devices generated more interest in research and development of VR devices, and affordable headsets allowed a much wider audience to have access to the technology.

Prior to the second wave, the majority of VR research and development was focused on improving the hardware of VR systems to a point where the technology would be useful. In the early stages of VR, a system would be made to forward the state of VR, in which case the software would usually be simple tech demos or be custom made for a very specific purpose (such as military training). In the current state, consumer VR equipment is capable of running any manner of programs—although many of the existing programs for second wave consoles could be categorized as entertainment, VR has the potential to be a great medium for solving lots of different problems. In the next section, we explore why VR is such an exciting medium for human–computer interaction, by framing it as one of the many stages of how people have interacted with the digital world.

## 1.4  A SHORT HISTORY OF HUMAN COMPUTER INTERACTION

Both the methods through which humans have interacted with computers and the tasks people have used computer for have changed significantly since computers were first invented. The earliest practical computers, electromechanical devices such as Herman Hollerith's census tabulators (1884), used punch cards for input. The holes in punch cards would be used to encode data, which would then be tabulated by the machine and displayed on dials to an operator. Although the Hollerith machines represented a large increase in efficiency over the census tabulating methods of the time, they were still cumbersome to use. Data first had to be translated to the format of the punch cards using a separate punching device and a translation table. After the cards were fed into the machine, the output on the dials would have to be read and added by hand to a running total. Not only did data have to be manually processed by humans in order for the machine to understand it, but the output from the machine had to be further processed in order to create the total! People interacted with a Hollerith machine in a machine-centred fashion—it was up to the user to translate inputs to the machine's language and to translate outputs back to a human usable format.

Computers continued to evolve in terms of processing power, speed, and range of function over time, and incremental progress was made in human computer interaction as well. However, it wasn't until 1946 that an important leap in providing input to computers was made—the keyboard. Typewriters had existed as a commercial product since 1867, so by 1946 people had grown accustomed to using them for writing text. When John Presper Eckert and John Mauchly were developing a computer that required text input at the University of Pennsylvania, they decided to use a teletype machine (seen in Figure 1.6) to punch their cards. The end result, the *Electronic Numerical Integrator and Computer*, allowed operators to skip the step of translating instructions into punched holes—instructions could be entered in digits and English. By this time, computers had also gained the ability to print out their output, using primitive displays or ticker tape. Now, humans were able to "speak to" computers in a way that was more familiar—written language.

Figure 1.6: A teletype unit, similar to the one that would have been used with the ENIAC (*Eric Fischer CCBY2.0*).

Communicating with computers via written language was the most common method of interaction for a long time. Command line interfaces (CLIs) were the sole method of interaction in the most successful personal computers of the early 1970s. Although these command line interfaces were easy to use for a large amount of tasks involving a computer, they did have their shortfalls. While text input was useful for things like word processing and programming, using it for drawing graphics or moving files could be slow and taxing. Further, by the 1970s, computers were no longer exclusively used by computer scientists and researchers. While computer scientists were content with learning verbose technical commands to communicate with their computers, these same commands were frustrating for laypeople. The solution was to introduce a new method that people and computers could use to communicate: the GUI.

The first GUI was developed by Ivan Sutherland for his doctoral dissertation, *Sketchpad*, which allowed users to draw and see shapes on a screen using a stylus. A second important invention followed the GUI—the mouse and pointer. The Xerox Alto (1974), the first personal computer to support a GUI-based operating system, was also the first personal computer to come with a mouse. Software developers designing for GUIs now had the freedom to use **interaction metaphors**, the process of making one task a metaphor for another, in order to make it easier for newcomers to understand how to operate computers. The interaction metaphor you are likely most familiar with is the **desktop** metaphor, developed for the Alto at Xerox PARC and made widely available in the Apple Macintosh (shown in Figure 1.7). Prior to computers, people would commonly keep physical files in manila folders and were used to rearranging their papers on the top of their physical desk—the desktop. When Jef Raskin was designing the interface of the Apple Macintosh, he used the metaphor of the traditional physical file system to make it easier for users to grasp how directories and digital files worked. On the Macintosh, files would be represented by little icons that looked like pages of paper and directories would instead become "folders." If no programs were open, the user would see the desktop—a space where "folders" and "files" could be dragged around and rearranged with the mouse like their physical counterparts. By changing the way users interacted with the computer to be more like how they interacted with the world, Jef Raskin made it easier for new users to figure out how to navigate the file system—after all, they had been doing it in the physical world their whole lives.

Figure 1.7: The Apple Macintosh (1984), one of the first personal computers to use the desktop interaction metaphor. *Marcin Wichary CCBY2.0.*

The development of HCI reveals a pattern—people have difficulty formatting their inputs and reading outputs in the way the computer requires it to be done, so they change the interface to the computer to better align with human needs. This brings us to VR—which, in essence, is just another interface for computers. Like the keyboard, the GUI, and the mouse before it, VR represents a leap in bringing the way we input and receive information from computers closer to the way we interact with the physical world. Just as these prior inventions made computers more accessible for the public by making the operation of computers similar to the way we conduct other tasks in the physical world (typing, organizing files, and pointing), VR does this as well—by making the way we interact with computers match the way we move and occupy physical space.

## 1.5   WHAT VR CAN DO FOR HUMAN–COMPUTER INTERACTION

In an human–computer interaction context, "Virtual Reality" refers to a set of outputs and inputs for computers that approximate the sensations of interacting in a physical reality. As VR is a categorical term, discussing the HCI impacts of virtual reality is different than discussing the impact of the invention of the mouse. Although the computer mouse exists in several different brands and forms, all mice appear very similar in function—all are moved on a surface to move a cursor, have (at least) two buttons, and allow for scrolling. A mouse may have more features than this (for example, more buttons along the side to bind hotkeys too), but those are often unrelated to its function as a mouse. In contrast, when you talk about a "virtual reality system," the exact features supported by the hardware are ambiguous. It's probably safe to assume that a VR system supports a head-mounted display, but not all head-mounted displays support the same visual simulation. A **degree of freedom**, when used in regard to a VR headset, refers to an axis on which the headset display updates with movement. The x, y, and z axis represent the three translational degrees of freedom, while rotation around each of those axes (pitch, roll, and yaw) represent the three rotational degrees of freedom—all of these degrees are shown in Figure 1.8. A 6-DOF display updates accordingly when the headset is moved in any of these ways. While some headsets are able to simulate accurate changes in perspective for both head rotation and translation (displays with six degrees of freedom or **6-DOF** tracking), many VR devices exist that only update properly for rotational movement of the head (**3-DOF** tracking).

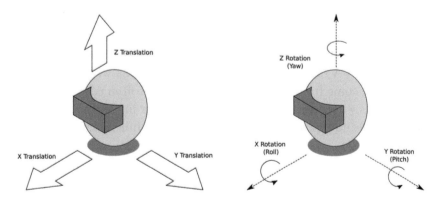

Figure 1.8: The six possible degrees of freedom a headset can move in.

Outside of the visual realm, a VR system may support motion controls with tracked hands, or it may not. A VR system could include audio or haptic feedback, both, or neither.

Each of these features could also vary greatly in quality—it's impossible for us to assume the features that any one virtual reality system could have. In order to broadly discuss how VR might impact HCI, we'll examine VR from mostly a theoretical perspective—all that we'll assume for now is that VR systems utilize some technology to simulate a virtual environment for at least one of the user's senses. When we do mention features of theoretical VR systems, we'll discuss the power of these specific features—VR systems that do not support these features will likely not have the same benefits for interaction. However, the features that we explicitly mention in this section are ones that typically exist in current consumer VR systems, and we envision that such features will only continue to improve over time. If VR ever becomes like the mouse, where every system shares a common set of features, we can say with near certainty that the features mentioned below will be included.

We've broken the ways VR could impact HCI into two major categories. The first category includes the HCI implications of using VR *to make interacting with computers more like interacting with the physical world.* Just as the keyboard made text input similar to writing on a typewriter, and the desktop made arranging file systems similar to organizing papers, we'll detail the ways in which VR will make interacting with computers even more similar to interacting with the physical world (as well as the benefits of this). Although we discuss these aforementioned implications in the context of VR, many of these HCI impacts have been seen before in mice, GUIs, and other products that mimic familiar interactions. However, the same is not true for the second category of VR's HCI effects—these benefits are unique to VR and are unrelated to mimicking real-world interactions. Instead, we care about the raw capabilities of the computer and what it can do to us—*how we can benefit from "fake" versions of the physical world.* Together, these categories encompass many of the reasons why VR has the potential to be such a beneficial technology.

### 1.5.1 Making Interacting with Computers More Like Interacting with the Physical World

VR is often lauded as a fix to many problems with existing computer interaction,and we list some of the potential benefits here. It should be noted, however, that not all opportunities offered by VR systems are net positives, and as with any new technology, the changes that come from new ways of doing things often come with trade-offs. Each of these benefits will be discussed in more detail later in this text, at which point we will also highlight and discuss the potential trade-offs inherent in these advances.

*Benefit 1: VR Applications Could Be Easier to Learn.*  Skimming through our short history of human computer interaction makes it apparent that computers used to be a lot harder to use—punch cards took a lot of training to learn how to use, and command line interfaces were intimidating to new computer users. We think of computers now as quite easy to use, but many people still have difficulty interacting with computers. You may recall learning to type—as natural as typing may seem to an experienced user, you might remember how difficult and slow it felt to first try typing while growing up. The keyboard was easier to learn than punch cards as it mimicked the operation of a typewriter, but a lot of this ease relied on the user already knowing how to type. However, VR is even easier to learn than modern desktop computing.

Since a virtual environment resembles the physical world, VR applications allow us to interact with the computer in the same way we interact with a physical world—a skill we know very well. Unlike a keyboard, which was initially easy only for those who had the prerequisite experience (using a typewriter), VR uses a prerequisite metaphor everyone is familiar with (the physical world). In a VR system that supports hand tracking, a user can reach out and press buttons or keys, pull levers, or perform other tasks in the same way that they would in the physical world. Of course, in order for it to be easy for someone to learn how to interact with a VR application, we have to make the actions match physical equivalents they've already learned to do. If you've never pressed a button in real life, we can't assume pressing one in VR would be intuitive—but most people do have experience with buttons. If we utilize physical metaphors that are common to most users, there would be no need to learn how to operate a VR interface—the user would already know from their prerequisite experience. Just as keyboards made computers accessible to a larger audience and GUIs made computers accessible to an even larger audience beyond that, VR has the potential to make it so that even more people can benefit from computing, by lowering the knowledge barrier to entry.

*Benefit 2: VR could reduce the ergonomic stress of interacting with computers.* When personal computers were invented, few people imagined how much we'd use them. Computers are helpful for completing tasks more efficiently, but weren't initially designed with ergonomics in mind. Extended use of computer keyboards has been shown to cause pain in the wrists, arms, and neck; repetitive use of a mouse can cause carpal tunnel syndrome; looking at a screen for hours a day can cause eye strain and sleep problems; and even sitting at a desk for extended periods can cause heath issues as well. Sitting for extended periods has become more and more common as computer use has increased, and with it, the health problems associated with sitting have increased as well. Sitting for long periods has been linked to increased risks of cancer, heart disease, and back problems. These problems aren't due to computers, per se—they're due to the way computers have been designed to be used. Computers only evolved to the form they are in today due to manufacturing constraints, performance requirements, and the occasional HCI concern addressed after the fact. It doesn't help that most people aren't terribly concerned about the ergonomics of the computer they're purchasing—they're more concerned about what the computer can do. Similarly, people weren't trying to think of a more ergonomically friendly method of computer interaction when they came up with VR—the ergonomic benefits of VR were an unintended side effect. Regardless, VR-based interaction presents a solution to many of the ergonomic problems caused by current computer interaction systems. Users of VR interact with the computer in the same way they interact with the physical world—by standing, reaching, grabbing, and poking, using their entire body. Many of the ergonomic problems attributed to modern computing come from the fact that using a computer requires us to perform movements that evolution left us ill suited for. Our spine shapes evolved to support us while standing, while computers require us to spend our time sitting. Our wrists evolved to perform a wide range of tasks, not to perform the same motion thousands of times a day in order to click a mouse. VR allows us to interact with computers through actions that better match the ones we evolved to perform—simply because the virtual world that a VR user interacts with is similar to the physical world we evolved in. VR is not a universal solution to computer-based ergonomic problems—some of the problems caused by modern computers, like repetitive actions and starting at artificial light for long periods of time, are still present in VR. Further, there are some ergonomic problems that are unique to VR. For example, wearing a heavy headset has been shown to cause neck discomfort and strain (although lighter headsets have helped to reduce the impact of this). We'll discuss more ergonomic considerations for designers of VR applications later in the book. However, by moving to an interaction model closer to the way we interact with the physical world, the adoption of VR as a computing interface has the potential to eliminate a large portion of the ergonomic issues caused by modern computing.

*Benefit 3: VR provides new ways of interacting with content.* The introduction of the GUI and mouse was particularly impactful in computing because these new ways of interacting with content on the computer allowed for easier ways to perform tasks. Creating an image for a manufacturing blueprint would have been extremely tedious on a command line interface (CLI), but on a GUI, drawing such an object would have been a lot easier. CLIs weren't usually used as an alternative to hand-drawn engineering drawings, but once GUIs were invented, computer-aided drafting surpassed hand-drawn drafts as the dominant method of blueprint production. Developing new ways to interact with the computer made it possible to perform tasks on a computer that weren't possible before, in addition to making existing tasks easier. Similarly, VR creates even more ways to interact with computers—allowing us to perform some existing tasks more efficiently, in addition to making the range of tasks we can use computers for even larger. Interaction with digital 3D objects is possible on desktop computers, but isn't ideal—it's often difficult to determine the orientation of an object in space or to visualize it as a 3D object without the help of (often cumbersome) 3D view port controls. In VR, we can see these objects in three dimensions, not just a 2D projection—modelling or evaluating 3D CAD models could be much less cumbersome than it is on a 2D screen. The inclusion of allowing movement in the digital space allows for new possibilities—instead of watching a video to learn dance steps, a user could follow outlines for foot placement within a virtual environment, making learning techniques easier. As the amount of ways we can interact with a computer increases, the range and effectiveness of the tasks we can perform with it increase as well—different inputs are better suited for different tasks.

*Benefit 4: VR is more suitable for displaying certain content than 2D screens.* We've just discussed how it's easier to create 3D content within a 3D environment, but 3D interfaces are also more suitable for displaying 3D items. VR is well suited for displaying 3D content, especially where it may be vital or otherwise difficult to understand how a three-dimensional object fits into a larger object or world. For example, it may be easier to grasp how a 3D part fits into a mechanical assembly if you are able to see it in a 3D environment—there's no ambiguity over where the part attaches or exists within relation to the the other parts, in contrast to when the 3D environment is projected onto a 2D screen. If an image of a 3D object is projected onto a 2D screen, shading and shadow can provide some insight about the depth and relation of the object to 3D space, but examples like common optical illusions show that the depth of a 3D object on a 2D plane can be ambiguous. One such ambiguous shape is shown in Figure 1.9.

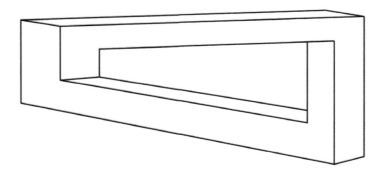

Figure 1.9: A shape that presents depth ambiguities when viewed in a 2D projection.

VR may still allow for some spatial ambiguity, but the addition of a third visual dimension reduces the number of possible visual ambiguities. Further, just as we can display a projection of 3D content on a 2D screen, we can display a projection of 4D (or even higher dimensional) geometry within a virtual environment. Of course, we'd be losing some information in showing the 4D object on a display that supports fewer dimensions than the shape has, but with a 4D shape, there's a larger degree of dimensional separation (and therefore ambiguity) when displayed on a 2D screen rather than a 3D interface.

*Benefit 5: VR maps physical motion to real-world motion.* In desktop computing, the actions we perform with the mouse or keyboard often map only indirectly to the motions on screen. For example, the plane in which the screen resides is usually (but not always) orthogonal to the plane in which we move the mouse—we look at the screen and we move the mouse on our desk. Whenever we're using a mouse, we implicitly have to translate the movement on one plane to the other—taking a little bit of cognitive load. With motion controls, motion is one to one—pointing occurs on the same plane as the motion. This removes the cognitive load associated with this translation and even makes pointing in VR a little bit faster (under certain conditions discussed in later chapters).

## 1.5.2   Making Worlds That Feel Physical By Using Computers

The previous five benefits of VR mentioned above can be viewed as the most recent steps in the history of human–computer interaction that we briefly discussed—making the form computers better match the needs of humans. These previous benefits are all due to how VR changes the way a computer is communicated with—because of either the way we provide a VR system with input or interpret its output. These benefits look at the VR output/input system as a replacement for other computer output/input systems. However, the output displayed on a VR device can be though of from a different perspective—instead of using a VR system to replace computer interactions, we can use it to replace interactions in the physical world.

Not everything is practical or possible to do in the physical world. Flight simulators, an early use case of VR, are a good example of this: although it's possible for a rookie to learn to fly using real planes, this would be an expensive (and dangerous) approach. Using VR, a novice can learn the controls for a plane in an environment that replicates much of the stimuli present while physically flying, but without the risk. VR is particularly useful for training due to the sense of **presence** it supports—users of a VR device are likely to instinctively interpret their surroundings as a physical environment (even if they know it isn't real). Because of presence, people are more likely to be mentally or emotionally affected by content if it's displayed in VR compared to other mediums. Training someone in a VR simulation causes both more accurate reactions in training compared to other non-physical mediums, and similarly, VR training carries over better to an actual scenario than other non-physical mediums. Due to the realistic physical interpretations VR invokes in a user's mind, it is useful for applications like exposure therapy. Curing someone's fear of heights by taking them to the edge of an actual roof may be dangerous, but a virtual roof can give similar benefits without the risk. The fear need not even be physical—studies have shown that many people become nervous while speaking to virtual crowds. Finally, the (relative) lack of expense of VR equipment makes many things possible for entertainment or leisure that would otherwise be too dangerous or costly for many. Simulations of hang gliding, visiting exotic locations, and scuba diving are all free assuming you have a VR system and do a good job approximating many of the sensations experienced in the real activity.

## 1.6 WHERE INTERACTION DESIGN FITS IN

Hopefully the previous few sections have given you a general understanding of how VR fits in to the history of human computer interaction and where VR may take HCI in the future. However, we've spoken a lot about the hardware advances of VR, and some specific use cases of such technology, but relatively little about VR software itself.

Any medium is only as good as the content available for it—a lack of desirable media for a platform is part of why Laserdisc lost out to VHS, why the Philips CDI flopped, and why a lot of people weren't overenthusiastic when modern VR emerged—the content available was lacking. No matter how much potential VR hardware has, it is squandered unless the software running on the platform is effective and was made with an understanding of the limitations of the user and the hardware.

Regardless of how well implemented an application's backend is, the interface is a bottleneck for the usefulness of any program. The user only sees the interface, and if the interface is designed in a way that makes it impossible to use certain functions of the software, the end result is the same as if those functions didn't exist. VR is a unique case when it comes to interface design—a VR experience isn't like a typical web or desktop interface, but it's not quite physical either. In order to be effective, a VR interface must successfully blend cues from the physical and digital worlds to accomplish a task. In order to design a spatial interface, we can borrow from traditional UI design as well as from industrial design. We can take design cues from older, physical design disciplines, such as architecture, or from newer fields, like web design. In VR, an interface may be visible or the program might be making decisions using the users' input (say, motion) without them even knowing. In this sense, a VR application can have an interface, or a traditional interface may be completely absent—although in either case, the user is still **interacting** with the experience. Over the first half of the book, we'll continue to discuss how the user interprets VR experiences, with a few case studies on how to use this knowledge to design effective VR applications. The second part of the book takes this knowledge and applies it to many different types of interfaces—both those that have been traditionally developed for computer applications or physical products and those that are only possible through the use of VR. By the end of the book, you'll have the tools you need to understand how good interaction design can make VR experiences enjoyable, effective, and easy to use.

# CHAPTER 2

# Making the Virtual Seem Real

## 2.1   THE FEELING OF BEING THERE

At a mall in an unnamed town in the Midwest, an interested but cautious consumer approaches a kiosk with trepidation. A sign beckons them to "Try the exciting immersive new technology of *Virtual Reality!*". They reflect on the virtual reality (VR) trends of the 1990s, remembering that the technology wasn't really that great, and although computer technology has improved significantly since then, they can't imagine how strapping a smartphone-sized screen to their head could provoke either excitement or immersion. After all, they have a phone. They have played games on their phone. It can't be that much better.

So they surreptitiously circle the kiosk for 20 minutes, hoping to watch someone else try it; eventually, a new shopper wandering the mall is drawn into the flashy advertising. Here, now, our sceptic will see how people really react to this new VR. The new volunteer dons the headset, immediately takes two steps back, looks up, and says "... woah..." They then proceed to waive their arms around wildly, step forward with caution, and whirl around in fear. They are behaving as if this new VR really is exciting—as if it really is immersive. Our sceptic decides to give it a try.

They approach the kiosk and don the headset, and to their amazement, they are teleported across reality to a new world filled with monsters; they grab a weapon leaning against the wall beside them, and they dive into the fray.

Many people trying VR for the first time will remark on how "real" the virtual world feels. This realism is one of the major characteristics of VR and a key component in many of its emerging use cases, which are already far beyond the confines of gaming and entertainment. The success of VR-based training, treatment, and teaching largely depends on the whether or not the experience is "real enough" to convince the brain to modify itself as a result of the stimuli it is experiencing.

### 2.1.1   Realism in Digital Media

Picture for yourself the most realistic and most believable digital environment you can imagine. What would it be like? For example, imagine a digital forest rendered

DOI: 10.1201/9781003261230-2

with such fidelity that you can watch the wind gently rustle the leaves of each tree. If you close your eyes, you can hear each bird and insect as if you were actually in the woods. You can feel the breeze on your arm as you hold your hand to block out the bright sun shining through the canopy, and you can smell the freshness of the damp earth beneath your feet. To replicate this virtual environment "perfectly," the software simulating this forest would require detailed data and physics calculations that can mirror the mechanics of the real world, down to the movement of individual leaves on a tree; although it is probably not necessary to simulate the movement of sap within the tree.

If this scene were displayed on a television, however, no one would be tricked into thinking it were real. It might be a recording of a real scene, but even at such a high level of representational detail, even if the TV could somehow display smells and weather effects, it would be impossible to mistake the simulation for an actual forest, because most of your sensory processes would still tell you that you are sitting on a couch in your living room, "watching" a forest, rather than walking through one. For this simulation to be "realistic," distractions and sensations from the real world must be removed, as much as possible, so that other sensations can be replicated in their place. This is the twofold role of virtual reality: exclude the real world so it can be replaced by the virtual world.

A virtual reality hardware system, such as a VR headset, is able to support more realistic content than a TV screen can because it is capable of blocking sensations from the real world and providing more realistic simulated data to more senses. However, even though VR systems have the potential to more realistically represent a virtual world, it is possible to imagine a traditional software experience that might be more immersive than one in VR. A VR game that poorly represents audio, makes mistakes on depth rendering, or has poor performance may feel less "real" than our perfectly simulated forest projected on a flat screen. In fact, depending on the content and presentation, a well-written book can draw the reader into a more complete feeling of "immersion" than a poorly developed software experience. Figure 2.1 presents this simple idea visually: the **realism** of a simulation can be compared as a simple sum of the realism of each aspect of that simulation. We will develop more concrete and informative analysis than the abstract measure of "realism" and build more comprehensive comparisons between simulations; but for now this is a reasonable heuristic: a simulation can be very good at one thing, but unless it is also good enough at the other aspects of simulation, it will not be immersive.

At this point, you may be able to infer that, from the perspective of human sensation, the "realism" of a given simulation is related to both the number of senses the system simulates and how realistically each of these sensations is simulated. A perfectly realistic simulation would require every human sense to be simulated with perfect accuracy. However, accurately simulating the sensations of a given world can be a difficult task in practice, and in reality there are tricks and shortcuts that can be used to create a believable experience without having to simulate every sense.

The first half of this book covers the theory required for an understanding of how to accurately simulate human senses. The current chapter covers the basics of the psychological theory behind the "reality" of virtual reality—why a good VR

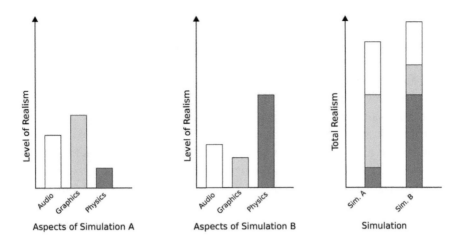

Figure 2.1: Comparing the realism of two different simulations by adding the levels of realism for each aspect of the simulations.

experience can make a user feel as if they are genuinely in a different location, a feeling called **presence**. We begin with a discussion of the concept of presence in a more precise manner. Following that, we explore two psychological effects that combine to contribute to the feeling of presence—namely, the place and plausibility illusions. Finally, we end the chapter with a discussion of how to measure these illusions in VR experiences and provide some tools and examples to help developers construct the sensation of presence within VR projects.

## 2.2  IMMERSION

VR experiences are capable of inducing a stronger sensation of "being there" than many other artificial media. Although VR users may instinctively try to reach out and touch a virtual table, TV viewers rarely make the mistake of reaching out to grab something shown on the television. This feeling of being in a real environment requires a medium that is capable of displaying a set of sensations that the brain could mistake for a physical space.

**Immersion** occurs when a sensory input is replaced with a reasonable virtual simulation of that sense—the sensory unit of the body responsible for interpreting this now-virtualized input has been immersed. Looking at a small black and white TV far away has low immersion; looking at a head-tracked VR display has much higher immersion.

**What do you mean by the word "Immersion"?**
The interpretation of the terms "presence" and "immersion" can be inconsistent across the literature, when talking about VR. Some researchers use the terms

as we have defined them in this book, while others may reverse their definitions or use them to refer to different scopes entirely. For example, people often talk of being immersed in a good book or a TV show, and by this they mean they are fully invested in the narrative. People also refer to video games as immersive if they can imagine themselves in the scenario being generated—to avoid confusion, we will use the term "narrative engagement" to describe these situations. However, throughout this book, when we use the term, we are referring to the ability of displays to replicate the range and field of real-life sensory input. If you find yourself encountering these terms elsewhere, don't assume that they are being used the way they are in this book, but seek out the definitions presented by the authors.

Mel Slater has been researching presence in VR since 1992—the date of his first conference proceedings on the experience of presence in virtual reality. Since then, his work has focused on investigating the sensation of presence in virtual reality, along with its applications. Mel Slater's work on defining the aspects that make up presence has resulted in one of the most widely accepted definitions for these terms. His distinction of the various phenomena responsible for presence is the basis of the definitions put forward in this book.

While a television screen can show a flat image, VR displays support stereoscopy, which is the ability to present a slightly different image to each eye. Since the fields of view of our two eyes overlap, the brain can interpret the slight differences between them as a proxy for the distance from the object being observed. A flat screen does not provide this depth information, but other signifiers like occlusion, shading, size, and brightness can lead to a passable illusion of depth in two dimensions. A stereoscopic display results in the brain receiving an image that is more closely aligned to the expectations of reality, and therefore more convincing and engaging. A 3D TV or movie theatre provides such an experience, but only to a small subset of the user's complete field of view. If the screen could be enlarged, then the experience would be better, but the screen and the scene it displays are also fixed in space and unresponsive to the user, meaning that if the user looks away, they won't see the screen anymore—instead, they might be met with a quizzical expression from their seat neighbour. Additionally, if the user moves their head from side to side, they might expect the perspective to change, but since the TV does not have information about the location or direction of the user's view, it cannot change what it is showing. If, however, the view itself can be made to move with the user such that their vision is replicated stereoscopically regardless of where they look, then the experience is even more convincing and engaging and closer to the way visual stimuli are processed in the real world, than images on a TV ever were. This is why current VR hardware is more like a pair of goggles than a TV screen—it can move with the user.

In order to understand how to replace a human sense input with appropriate information from a virtual world, we must first have an understanding of the processes by which humans use senses to perceive the world. A detailed discussion of the various sensation categories available to humans will be presented in later chapters, but a generalized abstract model of human sensation will be sufficient for our discussion of immersion. The process of human perception, whether from the real world or a virtual reality simulation, encompasses several layers of processing from the point where the human receives the sensation to the point where their mind interprets it. Figure 2.2 presents an abstract model of this process in a flowchart.

First, **sensation** is the physical act of a user's sensory organs receiving information from a display[1]. All of the information we have about the world comes from sensations received from our surroundings. Sensation consists of the reception, processing, and interpretation of some form of outside energy. For example, sensory cells in the eye—rods and cones—send signals to the nervous system when they are stimulated by associated frequencies of electromagnetic energy. Our ears respond to mechanical energy created by pressure differences in the air and convert those pressure waves to nerve impulses that are interpreted as sounds. Any differences we experience between sensations of the same type—for example, seeing one object as blue and another as red—are due to differences in the characteristics of the energy being received.

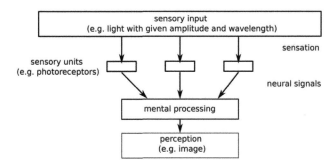

Figure 2.2: A flowchart depicting an abstract model for perception.

## 2.2.1  Displays

In the physical world, sensory stimulus comes from objects around us. Waves of energy created, reflected, or otherwise changed by objects in a person's physical environment result in the sensation of the world. For a virtual environment to be sensed by the user, it must first be rendered into physical energy corresponding to the sense being replaced. We use the term **display** to refer to any device that converts digital information into stimuli that can be sensed by the user. Displays exist for many types of stimuli—for example, a monitor is a display that outputs visual stimuli, while speakers generate auditory stimuli. Under this definition, a computer-controlled

---

[1]Since vision is such a predominant sense, much of the language of sensation is inherited from visual terminologies, like the word "display." A sensory display is any device used to replicate the stimulus to trigger a sense. Headphones can be considered an auditory display, in this sense of the word.

heater could be considered a display—it uses digital values to control the heat energy in a given area. The act of translating a digital representation to a physical stimuli by a display is referred to as **transduction**.

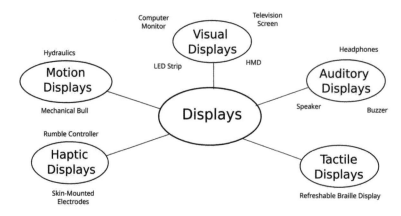

Figure 2.3: Different types of displays.

## 2.2.2 Sensory Inputs and Sensory Units

We define **sensory input** as the physical energy that the human body receives from the outside world (either from the real world or from a display) and that subsequently gives rise to sensation. A sensory input usually consists of a wave of a particular type of energy with a particular set of characteristics (amplitude, frequency, and phase) that correlates with or is a proxy for some real-world event. The term "input" considers this energy from the perspective of the user—energy that is considered a sensory input is the input to the sensation/perception process. A signal intended to stimulate a sensory input is the *output* of a display.

Sensory inputs are received and registered by **sensory units**, individual biological sensors that trigger a neurological signal when activated by a specific type of energy with specific characteristics. Sensory units are usually the size of individual cells, and we have a lot of them—there are over 120 million individual sensory units just in the eyes. The sense of sight, then, refers to a complicated system of different types of sensory units sensing many types of sensory inputs, which is integrated into a coherent concept by the brain.

**Sensory Abilities and Immersion**

Differing sensory abilities can also influence the immersion felt by the user of a simulation. Consider a user without the use of vision. One could argue that the blind user does not have the same visual immersion as a seeing player would, as they cannot see the world being simulated. However, it could be said that their visual experience of the VR game is more realistic than the seeing player—the seeing player can detect inaccuracies between the sensory inputs and the real world, but to the blind player, the visual simulation seems perfectly accurate. This is somewhat facetious; however, this technique has been used to increase immersion, by removing sources of incorrect information rather than trying to accurately simulate everything. A simulation of the inside of a room temperature room with a carpeted floor will be immersive if you are currently in such a room in the real world. The simulation will succeed in many sensorimotor contingencies, including your expectations of wind speed, humidity, and other meteorological factors. The fact that you experience no weather in VR is fine as long as you *expect* to experience no weather. See "overlapping domains" in Chapter 9.

The *senses* most people are familiar with are groups of many sensory units that sense related types of inputs. In this book, to avoid ambiguity, we will refer to groups commonly considered "senses" as **sensory categories** to emphasize that they are in fact categories of sensory units, and not really a single sense. The "sense" of sight, for example, is a collection of many different abilities including differentiating colour, motion, edges, patterns, faces textures, occlusion, depth, etc.

Each individual ability is distinct even though they all deal with visual energy, and we know this because there are individuals who have otherwise normal sight but are unable to distinguish faces, for example. More detail on the separation of a sense into sense inputs will be discussed in Chapters 4 and 5.

## Generalized Immersion Process Flowchart

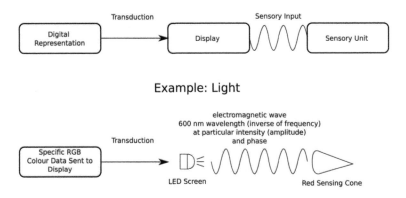

Figure 2.4: How information travels from a digital simulation to a sensory unit.

The second level of the abstract model of perception, the mental processing of signals from sensory units, is where signals are combined and interpreted. Continuing from the example of colour, a single red-sensing cone (a sensory unit) may send a signal, indicating that it has received electromagnetic radiation (the sensory input) with a wavelength that we interpret as red. If a second sensory unit, a green cone, sends a signal, the two signals may be combined at this mental processing level to indicate that the colour being sensed is actually yellow.

A single type of sensory unit responds to a certain type of sensory input. The total set of variances in stimuli that result in varying outputs from a sensory unit can be considered the **sensory range** of the said unit. If a sensory input is within the range of a particular sensory unit, that unit will respond by sending a sensory signal to the perceptive processes of the user. People are only capable of sensing stimuli when its energy characteristics fall within the appropriate sensory range. For example, most people can hear only sounds with frequencies between 20 Hz and 20,000 Hz—it's not that sounds with other frequencies don't exist; they simply fall outside of our sensory range. Ranges can also differ from user to user—the upper limit of frequencies we can hear tends to decrease with age or with exposure to excessive noise levels. Even if a sound falls within our frequency range, we still may not hear it—its intensity has to be above a certain value to be heard. Intensity and frequency characteristics are separate dimensions of sensory range for sound receptors in the ears.

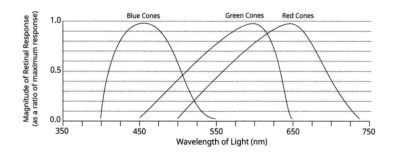

Figure 2.5: The sensory range of wavelengths by photoreceptor. Note that the response is not uniform across the range—a photoreceptor reacts more strongly to wavelengths in one part of the field than another.

In addition to the range of inputs it is able to respond to, a particular sensory unit is also limited by the area of the environment it is able to sense inputs from. The **sensory field** is the physical area around the body from which a sensory input is capable of receiving stimuli. For example, an individual cone reacts to electromagnetic energy hitting it, and due to the shape and structure of the eye, that energy can only come from a small set of directions outside the eye. Similarly, a specific touch receptor under the skin will give a sensation only when triggered by physically proximate contact with the skin.

Complete details of the limits and ranges of each of our senses are described in Chapters 4 and 5. For now, this is a sufficient background to build up a model of immersion relating to sense inputs replaced by a display, in what range, and by what quality of virtual sensation.

### 2.2.3 Quantifying Immersion in terms of Sensory Inputs and Units

We previously described immersion as the act of providing an appropriately simulated sensory input to a user. A system that is capable of correctly simulating a larger portion of the sensory input, or to a higher degree, will be more immersive with respect to that sensory input than a system that simulates a smaller portion.

We use the terms sensory range and sensory field to define the scope of a particular sensory unit, as described above. The range is related to the qualities or energies of a signal, and the field is related to the direction or scope of signal. Combined, they describe the possible conditions under which that input will be activated. It follows that these two parameters can also be used to describe what portion of the set of possible sensory inputs a simulation system is able to replicate.

To talk about the capabilities of a VR device on a system level, it helps to consider sensory field and range at a system level. Although these terms have been introduced at the level of an individual sensory unit, it is also possible to use the metrics of sensory range and field to describe the capabilities of groups of the same type of sensory unit or differing sensory units belonging to the same sensory category.

We can also specify the sensory field of a group of sensory units. For example, although people are capable of hearing sounds which originate kilometres away, the range of the sensation will be modified by the distance travelled, with farther signals becoming quieter or band limited to lower frequencies. The direction of the sound won't change, however, and therefore the portion of the (perceived audio) field that it takes up will be the same. Similarly, when considered together, the photoreceptors in the eyes are able to capture sensory information from a complete visual field 210 degrees wide. While the actual portion of the environment in the sensory field of a group of units exists in three dimensions, the field maps to the near-2D area over which the sensory units are grouped. Light hits our cones the same way regardless of how far that light has travelled to get there, whereas if the same light emanates from a spot slightly above or to the right of the original source, it is received in a different portion of the eye.

Now consider a VR hardware system that is able to display visual information on a screen with a horizontal field of view of only 100 degrees. Comparing the displayed field to the 210 degrees that can be perceived by the eyes, we can say that we are simulating 48% of the visual field[2]. The portion of the sensory field that is simulated via a display is referred to as the **displayable field**. For a given VR device, a developer is able to project stimuli covering only that device's displayed field.

Sensory range is similar to the sensory field, in that it can be extended to describe groups of sensory units. In the case of a group of sensory units, the sensory range refers to the range of values to which the group is able to elicit a response. In the same manner as the displayable field, the **displayable range** of a particular display or system can be described as the percentage of the range of a sensory unit or group

---

[2]This assumes a uniformly quantified field of vision, while in truth the majority of our sensory acuity is within the fovea which takes up only 5 degrees of our visual field. Weighted for acuity, a virtual display that reproduces 100 degrees would simulate approximately 99% of our field of view. Further details of the specifics of visual acuity are presented in Chapter 4.

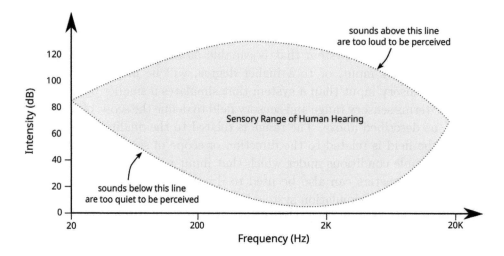

Figure 2.6: Sensory range for hearing, in frequency and amplitude.

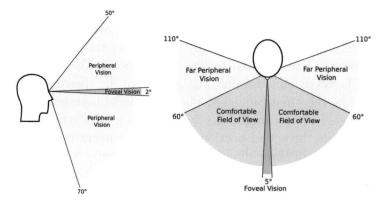

Figure 2.7: Total sensory field for vision.

that the display can output. Continuing with our example of the visual field, the displayable range of an head-mounted display (HMD) that is able to generate wavelengths between 500 and 600 nm would be 42% of the range of human vision. The displayable range is only relevant in the context of the maximum perceptible range by the user. While a display might be able to generate stimuli beyond the sensory range of a typical human, this is not relevant in the discussion of immersion, as immersion is only meaningful if the human user can perceive it.

We can specify a sensory range provided by giving the highest and lowest values that the sensor can output (absolute) or by giving the difference between the highest and lowest simulated values as a ratio over the difference of the highest and lowest senseable values (relative). For example, a speaker could be described as having an absolute sensory range of 300 Hz to 3,000 Hz or a relative sensory range of 13.5% of the total sensory range. In reality, human sensitivity varies widely within this range, but for the purposes of our discussion of immersion, this is a sufficient generalization.

This percentage specification of displayable sensory range has two significant drawbacks. First, the percentage only specifies what fraction of the possible sensory range is supported, but not where that supported field lies. A system capable of simulating light with low-to-moderate intensity may be more useful, but would have the same percentage specification as a system that simulates moderate-to-high intensity light. Second, the way that we perceive differences in the value of a stimulus may make it more important to simulate stimuli in one portion of the range than another. The perception of many senses tends to follow a logarithmic relationship— the difference between the magnitude of two stimuli has to be larger for us to notice the difference as the magnitudes get larger. If the percentage of the field that is capable of being supported starts at a lower magnitude, the user will likely perceive the range as covering a larger variety of stimuli than if it started at a higher magnitude. We will discuss logarithmic perception in later chapters, although at this point, it is enough to understand that a percentage covering lower magnitudes is *perceived* as covering a larger range than one covering higher magnitudes.

The second important metric of sensory range is the **resolution** available from the display. The term "resolution" is most often used when talking about visual displays, but it applies to displays for other sensory information as well. The resolution of a display is a metric of how small the differences between the discrete steps it is capable of outputting are. Resolution can also be given as a function of the range of a display over its levels of **quantization**, which is the number of discrete steps that can be displayed within a continuous range of values.

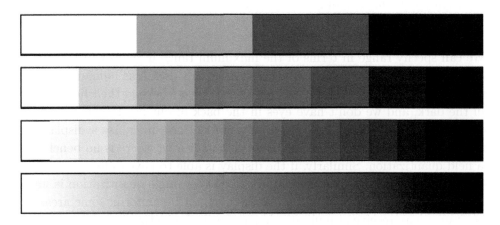

Figure 2.8: These four greyscale gradients each have a brightness value from 0 (black) to 1 (white), but differ in quantization. From top to bottom, the gradients include 4, 8, 16, and 256 greyscale values.

The energy characteristics of any sensory stimuli we receive from the natural world are best represented as continuous values. However, computers can only store information in discrete steps. Any output from a display will have to be specified by a computer, using numbers that follow a set of discrete steps. The amount of discrete values that a display is capable of outputting is defined by its quantization level. For example, many computer displays use 32-bit colour values. The "32-bit" specification refers to the number of bits used to represent the colour values—a 32-bit colour display can represent $2^{32} = 4,294,967,296$ different colours. Imagine if a display had 4-bit colour—that is, only $2^4 = 16$ different colours could be shown. Even if the range of colours was the same, the 4-bit display would be limited to making images with only 16 colours, which would not be as immersive a display as one that could replicate 4 million colours. The ability of a display to replicate the real world is not just dependent on the bounding values of its range, but on how many values lie between them as well (the quantization).

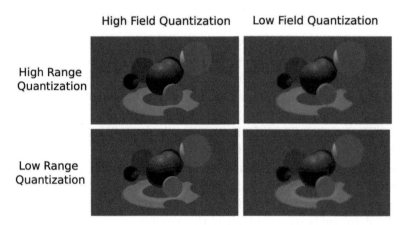

Figure 2.9: These images show the effects of decreasing both range and field quantization. Although this example is visual, range and field quantization apply to all sorts of sensory input.

We can specify range in terms of the maximum range humans can perceive, and the same for field. Simulating beyond these limits isn't useful, as humans cannot perceive beyond certain range values and cannot see objects beyond their field—we can't see in the dark, and we don't have eyes in the back of our head. The same human-imposed boundary exists for both types of quantization—if we use a display with a higher resolution than the eye is capable of distinguishing, there is no benefit to the extra field quantization. Similarly, if the display is able to have differences in brightness levels imperceptible to the human eye, the extra range quantization is wasted.

Note that the quantization of a a display may not be uniform: some areas of the field or range may receive stimuli at a higher level of quantization than other areas. For example, a visual display may have a higher pixel density in the centre of the screen than closer to the edges, matching the distribution of sensory units within the eye. In many cases, varying the field quantization across the display can be more efficient than having the highest quantization in all areas.

**Beyond the Current Set of Senses?**
We know we can simulate senses beyond the levels we are used to experiencing in physical reality—for example, we know that humans are able to perceive

strong gravitational fields from multiple directions, if there were such a place that we could find such fields. As such, since a fully immersive VR system must simulate sensations of gravity, it must be able to simulate them even outside the bounds which we are accustomed to. What if we were able to simulate a sense beyond what we could experience in physical reality? Likewise, we know that there are animals that have different senses than we do—dogs can smell much better than we can, and birds can sense magnetic fields. How might we represent these sensations to humans who do not have the ability to perceive them?

### 2.2.3.1  Isolation and Immersion

So far, immersion has been discussed in the context of a sense input receiving information either from the real world or from the virtual world. We have an assumption, therefore, that the digital stimuli of a virtual world would completely replace the physical stimuli of the real world. In practice, however, it's rare that a user of a VR system is completely deprived of outside stimuli. Some hardware displays for some sense inputs may be capable of blocking outside sensory input while providing simulated input, but many still let the user perceive stimuli other than what is generated by the display. For example, open-backed headphones play audio but do not block sounds from the real world. A user of a VR system containing such headphones would be receiving sensory input from both the real and the virtual worlds. Noise-cancelling headphones are able to measure and cancel sound from the physical environment. The result is that the user would experience the simulated auditory input without the distraction of non-simulated auditory input.

We define the sensory field from which non-simulated stimuli is blocked as the **isolated field**. Similarly, the **isolated range** is the portion of the sensory range blocked by the VR system for a particular sensory unit or group of units.

Immersion requires the replacement of external stimuli with simulated stimuli—as such, the portion of the sensory field that receives information from both external and simulated stimuli cannot be considered fully immersed. We refer to this portion of the sensory field as the **integrated field**, as sensory input from the virtual world is integrated with sensory input from the real world to form the user's perceptual model of a space. An **integrated range** similarly exists for the portion of the sensory range where both virtual and real input are able to be sensed by the user. Next, the portion of the sensory field that neither blocks real-world stimuli nor presents simulated stimuli is referred to as the **imposed field** . Here, the user experiences unaltered sensations from the real world. Similarly, the imposed range is the portion of the sensory range that receives real-world input unaltered. Finally, the **void field** represents the portion of the sensory field that blocks real-world stimuli, but does not present simulated stimuli—it can be described as the inactive portion of the user's sensory field whenever a VR headset is donned.

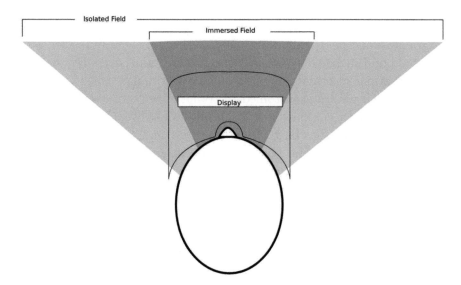

Figure 2.10: An HMD as shown above isolates much of the user's vision (the isolated field) and displays an image to a portion of that isolated area (the immersed field).

Combined, these four categories cover the entirety of a user's active sensory field (or range). As an example, an HMD may block most of the light across the users' field of view (isolated) and display images only in a portion of the users' field of view (immersed), but some light may shine in on the edges (imposed). The portion of the sensory field that is isolated from light is the isolated field, and the portion of the sensory field that is presented with stimuli from the VR display is the display field. An augmented reality headset is specially designed to allow the user to see the virtual world superimposed upon the real world, and the portion that shows both the real world and the virtual world together is the integrated field. Virtual reality headsets typically do not have any integrated field, since the point is to remove yourself from the real world.

As another example, consider headphones that block a certain range of frequencies and volumes of sound. This is the isolated range. The frequencies and volumes that the headphones can produce, then, are the immersed range. If the headphones can make a noise they cannot block, this is the integrated range, and any noises they can block that they cannot make are the void range. If you were wearing these noise-cancelling headphones and your friend came up to you and yelled in your ear, you would hear it, even if modified by the headphones, because of bone conduction and imperfections in noise-cancelling technology. If the sound is loud enough, it would be considered part of the imposed range because it is not blocked by the headphones or produced by the headphones.

## 2.2.4 Sensorimotor Contingencies

So far, we've referred to immersion as the ability to replace sensory input from the external environment with sensory input from displays. The more accurate the

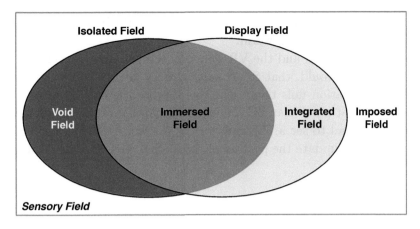

Figure 2.11: The immersion state of various sensory fields. The same definitions also apply to sensory ranges.

simulated sensory input being displayed is, the more immersive the system is. However, it is not enough merely to display a believable world—the user must be able to interact with it in a believable way. In order to reinforce the accuracy of the displayed sense, the sensory input must change responsively based on the actions of the user.

A user's actions can have a wide variety of effects on the range and field of sensation. For example, turning your head will cause you to see a different portion of the environment—even though you still see only 210 degrees around you at any one time. People and other sensory creatures exhibit behaviour (both conscious and unconscious) that is intended to make it possible to extract more information from the environment, especially when information is sparse, noisy, or ambiguous. A common example of this is a dog tilting its head when it is confused about a sound it is hearing—it is trying to get a different sensory perspective on what it is experiencing. Whenever we make a motor action that is intended to increase or otherwise modify sensory acuity, we call that a **sensorimotor contingency** (SC): "sensorimotor" because the sensation and the motor movement are tied together, one influencing the other, and "contingency" because our brains are attempting to invoke an if-then situation to gain more information about the world.

It is critical to support SCs (or, alternatively, discourage them—more on this later) in VR. A person may tilt their head or reach out to touch an object to gain more information, but if, as a result of this action, the world around them shifts, or the object disappears, not only will they not get more information about the sense being investigated, they will also be reminded that they are in a simulation.

SCs often affect sensory fields across several categories. For example, moving the head affects the way sounds are heard; what is seen and from what perspective; and even what parts of the face a wind may be blowing against. In the real world, SCs are a subconscious and reliable way to gather information about the world—if we turn our head, we see a different part of the room. In VR, this is not a given. It is up to the developer of the VR application to ensure the portion of the virtual environment received by the user's sensory units matches what would be expected had the SC been carried out in the physical world.

If we perform an action and the VR system alters what we perceive in the same way a physical world would, that SC is *supported* by the system. If we perform an action and the simulation fails to present the appropriate response, the simulation does not support that particular SC. Figure 2.12 shows an example of a SC, where a user turns their head to see a different part of the world. To support this SC, the VR system must also update the portion of the virtual environment displayed to the user.

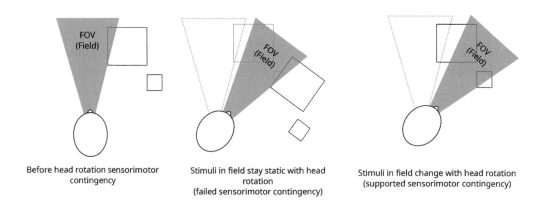

Figure 2.12: Turning your head should result in a change in the portion of the environment that you can see.

Determining whether or not a SC in VR is supported requires first identifying whether the action that would cause the contingency is supported. If a particular action makes the user perceive an appropriate change in sensory inputs, this is a **valid sensorimotor action**. In order to support a valid sensorimotor action, two steps are required on an implementation level.

First, we must be able to identify, in real time, the user's physical action—we can't update the view to respond to a user's rotation if we can't measure how far the user's head has turned. Although a computer may be able to simulate an environment, we also must track what portion of that environment is within the user's sensory field, which requires a representation of the sensorimotor action within the simulation itself. For any sensorimotor action to be valid, we require hardware capable of measuring that action. If a user is holding a VR-tracked hand controller, they can make valid sensorimotor actions with their hands, but not with their feet.

Second, we must determine what the appropriate change is to the sensory inputs of the user and update them accordingly. The accuracy of the updated inputs is directly dependent on the quality of measurements gathered in the recording step, which is contingent on the quality of tracking available in the VR hardware being used. Because this can vary from device to device, supporting SCs across different hardware platforms can be challenging. Additionally, the accuracy and immersion of the resulting sensory input change are also dependent on the hardware being used to display the input. What this means is that the believably of any VR experience is dependent not just on how well it can display information to the user but also (and just as important) on how well it can track the user's movements and actions.

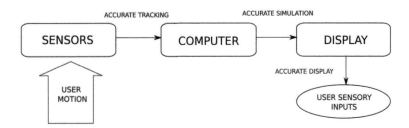

Figure 2.13: Accurate tracking, accurate simulation, and accurate display are all required for valid sensorimotor actions, which lead to higher levels of immersion.

Although actions can lead to increased information via changes to sensory inputs, it should be clear that these changes to sensory inputs are not usually the reason actions are performed—if you perform an action in real life, you're likely trying to achieve some extrinsic purpose. When you hold a football and move your arm to throw it, you expect the football to move with your arm. If a VR football can be grabbed and then subsequently thrown in an appropriate manner, this is a **valid effectual action**—the user's action has resulted in a meaningful change to the simulation, in this case the movement of the football. The act of throwing a football is not a SC—you are not doing it to gain information about the world; you are doing it to move the football; however, it is a sensorimotor action—if the football or your hand were to move in a way that was different from your expectations, your mind would instantly draw your attention to this fact and you would begin to investigate why. Is my arm tired? Is the football heavier than I expected? Is gravity suddenly different? The results of an action must be in line with expectations in order to be characterized as a valid effectual action.

Every action in the real world is both valid in an effectual capacity, in that it results in changes to the world, including changes to the position of your own body, and valid in a sensorimotor capacity, in that it results in changes to what our senses perceive. Simulated actions must address these independently, and a simulated action qualifies as a **valid action** only if it is both a valid effectual action and a valid sensorimotor action—this relationship of the sets is shown in Figure 2.14.

Both valid sensorimotor and valid effectual actions can contribute to building presence. Sensorimotor actions, if valid, will always increase the amount of presence felt—the immersed sensory inputs are being accurately updated for a sensorimotor action, so the simulation is in line with the world being experienced. Effectual actions can cause changes that the user is able to perceive—we're allowing the user to give input to move the football—but can also be effectual by causing changes that are visible only to the back end of the simulation. In both cases, if the effectual action

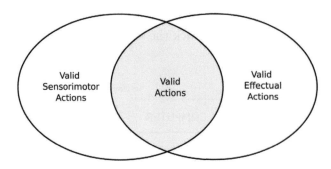

Figure 2.14: Valid actions are both valid sensorimotor actions and valid effectual actions.

eventually results in an accurate change corresponding to the user's action, presence can be increased.

It's important to note that a valid sensorimotor action within a simulation may be made invalid if a real-world stimulus impinges on the simulation. For example, if a user bumps into a virtual wall, it may be difficult or impossible to make them "feel" that wall in the real world. Likely, it would be difficult or impossible to prevent the user from passing through the virtual wall by continuing to walk in the physical world. This situation, being able to keep walking when you see yourself collide with a wall, is an invalid sensorimotor action. The reverse situation is also an invalid sensorimotor action—the user running into a wall in the physical world that is not present in the simulation. In either case, the sense of touch conflicts with the rest of the sensory inputs from the simulation—we see a wall we can't feel or feel a wall we can't see. This reminds us that different senses are immersed to different degrees—visual sensory inputs may be immersed, while touch and other kinematic sensations are integrated—it is difficult or impossible to isolate the sense of touch without putting the user in a large empty room.

**Effectual actions without sensorimotor actions**
In a system incapable of simulating all SCs, valid effectual actions may be implemented without a corresponding valid sensorimotor action. Systems without haptic simulation are a good example of this—there are many experiences where you can "grab" an object, altering its effectual position and orientation in virtual space, but you don't "feel" the contours of the object or the texture of its surface. While technologies may not yet be available for simulating all sensory inputs affected by a particular sensorimotor action, this does not mean that a sensorimotor action that approximates pieces of the SC is not useful—pressing a button that causes the hand to execute a similar motion to grabbing is not a valid sensorimotor action for grabbing, but comes closer to

replicating the feeling than pressing a button that does not mimic that action. Our experience of SCs is not static, either, and so over time we may adapt to simple button presses or vibration motors giving our brains the hint that the thing we just did had the effect we were expecting.

## 2.3  PRESENCE

When someone uses a VR system, they are moving into and perceiving events from the virtual world as displayed on the headset, at the same time as they exist in the real world. Because most virtual reality headsets block light[3], while wearing the headset, the user is unable to see[4] objects in the real world. Given enough time and distraction, users will forget that the real-world objects exist or lose their place in the real world, and as a result a VR user may find themselves bumping into furniture while they play. What is a little more surprising is that players may also behave in a way that shows that they actually believe, at some level, that the virtual world actually exists—VR users may try to lean against a virtual wall or set their controllers down on a virtual table, often leading to a sudden loss of balance.

VR users are aware that the virtual environment they are in is not physically real—after all, they only put on the headset moments ago. So why do they choose to rest their real body against a virtual wall? Although a user may be aware that the objects they are interacting with are purely virtual, if the hardware and software used are sufficiently successful at replicating even a portion of the sensations of a physical space, the user's mind will unconsciously shift to thinking of the virtual world as its current location. This mental interpretation of the user as existing within the virtual environment is what causes the user to assume, at least subconsciously, that a virtual wall is real. The phenomenon of the mind interpreting the virtual world as its current location is known as **presence**. Presence can be thought of as the feeling of "being there" and is in contrast to the concept of "emplacement," which is the term used for the physical location of the user's body in the real world.

The human mind is constantly confirming and strengthening the experience of presence based on sensory stimuli from different experiences. This process is primarily subconscious, and we are only reminded of it when we experience something that does not correlate with our expectations of reality. When we are startled or surprised by an unexpected noise or movement in the corner of our eye, this is our brain making us aware of any slight deviations in our expectations of reality.

A goal for the VR developer could be (and often is) to maximize the experience of presence as derived from the virtual world. Often, this means making the virtual environment as reminiscent of the real world as possible—but this doesn't mean that

---

[3]The exception is augmented and mixed reality headsets, which intentionally do not block light and other information-bearing energy from the physical world.

[4]VR tends to prioritize vision above other senses; the reader should not forget that this biasing towards "typical" vision may have an excluding effect on people with vision impairments. See Chapter 11 for a discussion on the implications of VR on issues of accessibility and inclusion.

the content of the environment can't be fantastical. Instead, if the basic low-level interactions of the virtual environment are predictable and consistent with reality, then the user will feel that they are there regardless of the believability of the content. This is the essence of presence—to make the user's mind accept the virtual environment as its actual location, overriding the conscious knowledge of their emplacement: that they have not left the room they are in. It is important to note that it is *the mind* that interprets presence and not *the user*—in other words, presence occurs subconsciously, and it would be inappropriate to describe it as a "belief." Additionally, the feeling of presence can be forced on to a user. A user can know that the experience is virtual, but if the virtual experience is consistent and succeeds in excluding contrary stimuli, then their mind will shift into an interpretation of the simulated environment as their current "physical surroundings." The user can, however, actively seek out interrupting stimuli from the real world by reaching out to touch an object or even by removing the VR headset, but this must be active. The user's knowledge that these surroundings are virtual is separate from their subconscious interpretation of being present in the virtual world. The user's emplacement may contain stimuli that detract from their virtual presence, but if the VR hardware is sufficiently immersive and the VR software is created according to the appropriate design principles, then the experience will be convincing.

### 2.3.1   The Relationship between Immersion and Presence

Presence is the mind's reaction to immersion. Since immersion is the degree to which we replace sensory inputs with hardware and software, the immersion experienced will be similar from individual to individual, to the degree that their human senses are similar (see the box in Section 2.2.2 on page 30, "Sensory abilities and immersion"). If two people have fundamentally similar senses, they should experience fundamentally similar levels of immersion when those senses are isolated and replaced by the same VR system. At the same time, presence exists only within the mind of the user, and thus, the degree to which it is felt is widely variable from person to person. Presence can even vary between separate sessions of the same experience, whether due to the user's state of mind, the novelty of the experience, or any combination of other internal factors. To what degree people feel presence differs from person to person, but presence is activated in a similar manner for all individuals—by immersing sensory inputs and simulating SCs with valid actions.

Before considering the mental processes and illusions that make up the experience of presence, it helps to be clear about what does *not* have an effect on presence.

The nature of the **content** of a VR experience has no direct influence on the feeling of presence—the user's mind can interpret anywhere as its actual surroundings as long as sensory inputs are immersed and simulated as they would be if the environment were physical. For example, consider a virtual waiting room in a virtual department of motor vehicles. Even though this may be a very boring experience to partake in, as long as the sensory inputs are simulated accurately, it will feel "real" and presence will be maintained. A virtual environment can produce a large degree of presence and make you feel like you're somewhere else and yet have very uninteresting content. The presence induced by a VR simulation comes from the form, not the content—it is the accuracy of the simulated environment, not the type of environment, that makes it feel real.

Similarly, the user's level of **focus**—their conscious attention—has no relation to presence. As long as the user has some sensory inputs immersed properly, they'll have some degree of presence—it doesn't matter if they're consciously daydreaming or deeply focused on the virtual task. One exception to this is if the user's focus is drawn by an *imposed* sensory input—like wind from the real world or the texture of the real floor. A sensory input that is in the user's conscious attention has a proportionally higher influence on the degree of presence experienced. If properly simulated, the immersion of the conscious input will help in establishing presence, while if improperly simulated, presence may severely weaken. Once this input leaves the user's conscious attention, however, it is entirely possible for the sense of presence to be regained by performing other supported sensorimotor actions.

**Emotional involvement** is a specific type of user focus that can have a powerful effect on the user's experience of a simulation, but it *does not* affect presence in the way that the term is defined here. Rather, levels of presence can influence emotional involvement.

Although content, user focus, and emotional involvement carry no direct bearing on presence, they are able to make a simulation feel more "real." They are outside the scope of unconscious presence, but they are still important factors when designing a VR experience and will be revisited in more detail throughout the book.

## 2.4 COMPONENTS OF PRESENCE

In the same way that immersion is difficult to define, so is presence. Presence is the feeling of "being there," in the simulation rather than in the real world experiencing the simulation.

A pair of easier-to-define components of presence can be helpful in discussing its application with regard to VR. Both of these components of presence are considered "illusions"—the user's mind interprets something within the virtual environment as real despite the fact that it is not.

### 2.4.1 The Place Illusion and How to Maintain It

The way the brain processes a VR environment is closer to how it processes the real world than how it processes other digital media. Despite the fact that everything you see in VR is really just an image a few centimetres away, the brain reconciles parts of the image as objects many metres away. Only if you really concentrate on it are you able to think of the "world" as a series of pixels. Even when a glitch occurs, our brain doesn't suddenly notice that everything is a flat screen—our knowledge of the environment being false does nothing to stop our brain from perceiving VR worlds in the same way that we perceive the physical world.

The phenomena of our brain's tendency to *interpret the virtual environment as a physical place* are what we refer to as **place illusion**. If a simulation immerses the appropriate sensory inputs, place illusion cannot be avoided—the mind will interpret the simulated information coming from that sense the same way it interprets information from a physical environment, as long as SCs are supported.

Place illusion can be broken when a sensorimotor action is performed and the output is not what it would be in the physical world, either due to that action not being supported by the hardware or a failure to include the appropriate response via software. For example, if a user rotates their head while the visual display is frozen, it is immediately apparent to their mind that they are not in a real environment. Their brain has to re-evaluate the information from the senses, concluding that it must be looking at a projection onto a screen—if it were a real environment, the eyes would have sensed movement.

Place illusion is not broken if the user only performs supported SCs. If the user wears a headset that tracks rotation, but not translational movement, the brain will fulfil place illusion as long as the user limits their actions to solely rotational movement. As soon as the user attempts the unsupported SC of moving forwards, the fact that the view doesn't adapt to the user's new position makes it apparent that what they are seeing is not aligned with the real world. This can also happen in 3D moves where the camera position is fixed—the user may shift their position but this does not alter the perspective of what they are looking at, which can break the illusion.

It is important to clarify that place illusion, like presence, is not affected by conscious belief. As much as you assure yourself that a simulation is not real, your brain interprets it as a physical space if it looks sufficiently like one—whether or not you feel as if "you're in it" is another matter entirely. Similarly, as much as you consciously try to treat a simulation as real, your brain cannot help but interpret a failed SC as something fake. In this latter case, your conscious belief is affected by place illusion, but on the other hand, believing in the illusion does not make it more real.

When applying the concept of place illusion to sensation and perception, we generally describe it as being independent for different sensory categories. Place illusion can be held or broken for different sensory input groups—the brain can believe what it sees but not what it feels, at the same time. Similarly, having a conversation with someone in the same physical room as you while you're playing a VR experience won't stop your visual processing system from interpreting the simulation as a physical place.

Place illusion is boolean for each sensory input being considered—it's either broken or maintained. However, the more sensor inputs that are subject to the place illusion, the higher the feeling of presence.

Since the user is processing these inputs from a viewpoint inside a virtual space, their brain tells them "we must be there." Not every sensory input is of equal value in the place illusion functions—stereoscopy, ocular parallax, and properly spatialized audio are more important for current displays than olfactory inputs, for example.

If the physical world matches the simulated world in some input, place illusion may occur "for free" in some contexts. If the user is in a room with heavy carpeting, for example, and the virtual experience also has heavy carpeting, then most aspects of the user's sensation of the carpet from the real world will align with their expectation of the virtual carpet, reinforcing place illusion. Similarly, a user's sense of gravity rarely requires isolation and display in order to maintain place illusion—in fact it is difficult or impossible to isolate the user's sense of gravity from the 1g towards the centre of the earth that we feel in the real world. This only matters in a VR environment where microgravity is expected (or where gravity is expected from a different direction) that the user will have gravity-specific place illusion broken.

### Renovating the Physical World to Match the Virtual One

Part of the appeal of virtual reality is the ability to simulate things we can't do or don't have access to in reality, so cases where many of the sensory inputs from the outside world match the desired simulated inputs can be rare. A developer with a higher budget could get around simulating inputs by changing the physical world to match the desired inputs. While some inputs, such as haptic sensations, are very difficult to simulate, they may be somewhat feasible to implement via a mixed reality approach of building walls or adding props. Due to the cost and lack of adaptability inherent in modifying a physical space to match the virtual world, this approach is rarely seen outside of costly training simulators.

While the previous two examples were passive (make the simulated world match the real world when it is difficult or impossible to isolate the user from the real world), it is also possible to actively match the real world with the virtual world to increase immersion. **Augmented virtuality** is a portion of the Milgram-Kishinko continuum (see Chapter 1) where most of the perceived world is virtual but some aspects are real. We can make this more active by creating real-world representations of virtual objects, in an attempt to get the maximal amount of benefit from replicating parts of the virtual environment in the physical world with the least amount of work. If you know that a user of your VR experience will spend most of their time in-game holding a specific type of gun in their hand, it would add to their place illusion if the controller they were holding in the real world was actually shaped like the handle of this gun, with the same weight and texture.

Of course, the opposite is possible as well—constructing the virtual model of the gun in such a way that it appears in-game to have the same texture, shape, and weight as the part of the controller that the user is holding will also increase the place illusion. This may, however result in some pretty odd-looking firearms, and if all objects in VR start to look like the handheld controllers that shipped with the headset, this can start to be less believable in other ways.

If the sensations we expect from the simulated world line up with the sensations we perceive from the real world, this is just as convincing as using hardware and software to artificially replicate SCs. Of course, taking this approach is quite limited and will only work in situations where the virtual and the real are in alignment—if someone uses a VR headset outside, the ground will feel "right" if the simulation presents grass, but "wrong" if the simulation presents hardwood.

It's much more common, however, for users to have an absence of sensation in the physical world for an active sense, and we can use this knowledge to our advantage when planning the simulation. If a sword in VR is held an inch away from our throat, it feels precisely the same as if there were no sword at all. The threat of the virtual sword is real, right up until it should be touching us and yet we feel no pain—as each SC fails, place illusion is broken. In real life, a sword held an inch away from the throat and one where the tip just touches the throat beget very similar levels of terror—in VR, the sword that "touches" the throat but produces no pain is instantly *less* intimidating, instead convincing us that we can't be harmed by this threat.

In order to have the brain react as if something were there, it is critical to ensure that if the same situation were to occur in real life, we'd experience the same active response from the SCs that are supported by the VR system and no response from the SCs that wouldn't be affected by the situation.

When no change in perception occurs from executing a SC in the physical world, it's easy to match that by having no change in perception occur in the virtual world. If you walk around in a completely dark room, your view doesn't change even though your head is moving. This idea can lead us to another interesting way to increase the cumulative place illusion from many sensory inputs—making the user unable to expect a SC or rather removing the SC from their frame of reference entirely.

Imagine a user who moves about the real world regularly bumping into furniture and thereby breaking place illusion. I see no chair, yet I feel a chair: something is wrong! At the same time, imagine the VR experience displays furniture not in the real world that the same user can pass their hands through. I should feel a table, yet I feel no table: something is wrong! We could prevent both of these failed SCs, which serve to break place illusion, by preventing the user from moving about in the real world. If the user was seated and their hands were fixed to the arms of the chair, they would not be able to reach out to touch a virtual table that isn't there or a real chair that is. We could either invent a narrative conceit that requires the user to hold onto the arms of the chair or, in extreme circumstances, the user's arms could even be physically tied to the chair. Putting aside how invasive and inappropriate this would be, the result is an increase in place illusion, because fewer SCs are being broken.

By fixing the user's arms to their chair, the user is prevented from being able to perform the SC that was unsupported by the system. Even though the SC is still unsupported, the user is not in a position to break that SC and therefore does not lose place illusion as a result of the unsupported SC. Discouraging the user from performing actions that would break place illusion is a good way to direct players towards more presence. For example, if you have a game where users have to navigate a maze, but you don't have any way to make them feel the sensation of touching the walls, you can discourage them from reaching out to touch the walls by placing a threat on the wall, like a trap, an enemy, a spinning saw blade, or poisonous slime. Combined with an in-game consequence (like losing a life or losing points) this may serve as a sufficient deterrent, although the curious user may still reach out to touch the threat and break presence as a result.

### Sense Suppression

Another option for eliminating broken place illusion for a sensory input is to suppress the user's expectation that they can use that sensory input entirely.

We present the following thought experiment: suppose a VR system exists that has the ability to temporarily suppress the user's memory (of course, such technology would have *much* more important applications than VR). In theory, this system would be capable of making us forget that the sensation of touch exists. Note that forgetting "the sensation of touch" isn't just forgetting what things feel like, but forgetting that you can feel things entirely. Assuming we had managed to make it so that the user was unable to remember that the sensation of feeling things existed, touching something in VR and not feeling it would not break any SCs. Despite no change in perception being simulated (no textures were output as sensory inputs), there was no change in perception expected to begin with, so place illusion is maintained. The user's expectation of what constitutes a physical environment has been altered.

If you used such a device to suppress the user's knowledge of *all* of their senses, you've removed the user's expectations entirely.

One could even make the argument that this would be a first-order system (see Chapter 1)—there's no difference between the simulation and the *user's expectation* of a physical environment, although its practical usage would be severely limited—maybe it's better if we leave this as a thought experiment.

## 2.4.2 The Plausibility Illusion and When it Breaks

The **plausibility illusion** is the false belief that the virtual environment holds a consequence for the user—it occurs on a higher cognitive level than the place illusion, but is still a subconscious process. A user can still "know" that the simulation is not real, but if they instinctively dodge a virtual punch or catch a virtual ball, then the plausibility illusion is in effect.

The plausibility illusion involves tricking the user into thinking that what occurs in the simulation holds real consequence to their person. It can be described as the illusion that a virtual cause carries a real effect. Consider the mental calculation that a user makes when a baseball bat is swung at their head in VR. If plausibility illusion is present, they will instinctively assume that the virtual stimuli carry real consequences and conclude that if they don't duck, the effect will be a head injury. If the scenario is not plausible, the user will have no reason to react and the bat will pass harmlessly through their virtual avatar. Of course, they may lose points or lose a life in-game, and these are genuine consequences, but these do not relate to plausibility illusion because they involve a conscious calculation ("I should avoid getting hit so I don't have to start this level again") rather than a subconscious reaction ("duck!").

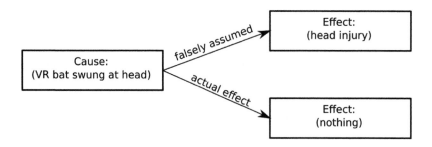

Figure 2.15: Plausibility illusion: the user subconsciously believes the false effect and acts accordingly.

### 2.4.3 Building Plausibility

The place illusion occurs when the user believes that what they see is where they are. Plausibility illusion is when the user believes that what they see can have an effect on them. Therefore, to build plausibility, we must present the user with actions that appear to have real consequences. Valid actions must be supported in order to build plausibility—if an object exists in the simulation that appears to be interactable, then when the user reaches out to grab it, it should appear to be grabbed by the user's hand. Every action the user performs that reinforces plausibility improves presence, and every action that breaks plausibility reduces presence.

It must be noted that if the plausibility illusion breaks for a specific action, it can be difficult to reinstate the illusion for that action. A virtual table appears in front of a user. While the user does not interact with the table, place illusion is not affected; however, when the user reaches out to interact with the table and their hand passes through it, then the next table they see will not seem nearly as physical. If the user's expectations of cause and effect are revealed to be false, the mind will update their mental model accordingly. The key to building strong plausibility illusion is to affirm the user's sense of cause and effect whenever we can, remove opportunities for interactions that may lead to failed SCs, and prolong the amount of time before the user's perceptions don't match the VR.

The rubber hand illusion is a good example of how to gradually build a strong plausibility illusion. In a classic psychological experiment, a participant was placed at a table and a fake rubber hand was placed in their field of view. The goal of the procedure is to trick the subjects into reacting when the false hand is threatened. The false hand is placed in a position near their real hand, and their real hand is obscured from view. The user sees the rubber hand, remembers their real hand, and knows they are different. The researchers then perform an action on the false hand and the real hand at the same time. A researcher would tap the index finger on the rubber hand at the same time they tap the same finger on the real hand. The user sees the touch on the false hand and feels the touch on their real hand. This begins to build the illusion that the real hand and the false hand are the same and that the hand the user sees is their own.

If the user moved their hand and saw the rubber hand stay still, the illusion would be broken. But as the researchers obscured their actual left hand from the field of view, the user could only rely on two senses to determine where their real hand is—touch and proprioception.

The researchers continued incremental parallel interactions with the fake hand and the real hand, and over time, the mind begins to map the location of the left hand to the false rubber hand on the table. The participant still remembers that the hand is fake, but subconsciously, the brain is beginning to map the two experiences into one. The illusion is strengthened by performing more touch-sight mapping over the next few minutes of the experiment. All of the sensory information received by the user suggested that the touches to the rubber hand on the table are genuinely felt by the participant.

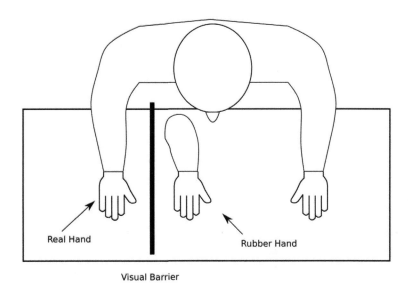

Figure 2.16: The set-up for the rubber hand illusion—through haptic reinforcement, the participant establishes plausibility that the rubber hand on the right of the screen is in fact their real hand.

In the conclusion of the procedure, the researchers surprise the subject by taking a knife and suddenly stabbing the rubber hand on the table. Universally, the user reacts as if their own hand was stabbed. They immediately pull back and experience anxiety, fear, and adrenaline. The user knows the hand is fake, but still *responds as if it is real*. The creation of the plausibility illusion takes time and effort, but can be very effective.

Maintaining plausibility illusion is like playing a game of poker—when the system can cause a user to feel an actual effect that matches a virtual cause, this builds a reputation that the effect is real. This reputation is then useful when you want to present a virtual cause whose effect you cannot actually generate. If the user believes that the effect will be real, they will respond appropriately. If not, they will call your bluff and the illusion will be broken. If you can bluff a user into responding as if the virtual was real before you have to reveal that the effect cannot occur—like backing away before the sword touches their throat—this builds further the credibility of the scenario and improves the experience for the user. Keep in mind: *the user wants to be bluffed.* Users who use virtual reality are entering into a bargain, where the developer promises to try to trick them and the user agrees to allow themselves to be tricked. The user's subconscious did not agree, however, and so it is towards the user's subconscious where we must focus much of our effort.

Although the examples used to illustrate plausibility illusion so far involve the user expecting a physical consequence, plausibility illusion can also apply to emotional and behavioural consequences. Speaking to a simulated crowd in VR may induce the same level of anxiety felt when speaking to a real crowd, for example.

While physical plausibility illusion is often limited by the capabilities of the hardware running the simulation, behavioural consequences (and therefore behavioural plausibility illusions) exist entirely in software. Believable interactions with virtual characters require subtlety and nuance in the way they are presented, with each interaction reinforcing cause and effect. If I ask this character a question, I expect the effect to be an answer. If they answer in an awkward or predictable manner, this can undermine plausibility.

One way to build the strength of plausibility is to mimic the cause and effect of the physical world as closely as possible—doing so will invoke an "if that's true..." mentality. If several things in the simulation seem to work in the same way they would in the physical world, the user is likely to expect that other interactions are similarly supported.

Breaking plausibility illusion is especially dangerous to presence because it directly reminds the user that they are in a simulation. When plausibility illusion is broken, a user is more likely to attempt to break place illusion as well by using the unsupported SCs at their disposal. If a user sees some glitch in the way their sword moves and suddenly is reminded that what they are experiencing is merely a game and is not happening in the physical world, they might want to assure themselves of this by trying to peak at the gaps in the simulation in order to confirm their situation. If we don't let plausibility illusion be broken, we're keeping the user's attention on the SCs that they *can* confirm, which reduces the likelihood of them trying to find cracks in the simulation.

## 2.5   OTHER SENSATIONS OF REALITY WITHIN VR

Place and plausibility illusion are the two major components that make up presence, the unconscious mental feeling of existing within a virtual world. This feeling of presence is integral to what makes VR unique as a medium—it has the capability to make a user's mind assume that they are located within the virtual environment. However, presence and the two illusions that comprise it occur on a lower level of conscious awareness. The player may be experiencing very convincing plausibility and place illusions, but still be actively thinking about how the experience is not real. In theory, if a simulation *was* capable of maintaining perfect plausibility and place illusions, there would be no way for the user to distinguish it from a physical world, and their recent memory of donning the VR equipment would be the only evidence that the experience wasn't real. However, a perfect simulation like this is not the only time that a user's conscious mind is acting out decisions as if a simulation is real.

One of the theories of heightened presence is the **response-as-if-real** theory. It states that the combination of convincing plausibility illusion and convincing place illusion increases the likelihood that a person will respond to a situation simulated by an immersive system as if it were real. If place illusion is maintained, particularly over multiple senses, the user's mind interprets the simulation as a physical environment within which they are present (that they are *there*). If plausibility illusion is maintained, the user believes what they are seeing is capable of causing consequences to them (that *they* are there). The combination of the two means that the user believes that they are present within an environment that is "real"—that is, an environment that carries consequence. People feeling this level of presence act within the virtual environment in similar ways to the real environment. At this level of presence, people will try to lean on virtual walls, set objects down on virtual surfaces, or feel the fear of heights at the edge of a virtual cliff. This level of presence is something that players adapt to—the aforementioned examples are much more commonly seen when observing players new to VR. As one uses VR more and more often, a higher level of plausibility and place illusion must be sustained in order to make these mistakes—the expectations of cause and effect of reality have been altered by acclimation to the cause and effect the experienced user is familiar with in VR.

Another sensation that is often associated with the sense of presence is **embodiment**: the sense of inhabiting a body or feeling like virtual limbs belong to the user. Embodiment can be considered a specific subset of presence with regard to the body and is discussed in more detail in Chapter 7.

We've discussed the different illusions and mental states that contribute to presence—plausibility illusion and place illusion. However, all of this discussion so far is only useful for describing sensations of existing within a virtual world on a low cognitive level. Is it possible to believe consciously that a virtual world is real? Likely not for a very long time—the user would not only have to be in a simulation capable of perfectly replicating the sensory inputs of the physical world, but would also have to be in the simulation long enough to forget that it isn't real. However, examples where people interact with the virtual environment as if it is real show that it *is* possible to forget, at least subconsciously, that this virtuality is fake for a short amount of time. By extension, if someone forgets that the simulation is fake for longer and longer amounts of time, we get closer to the possibility of consciously thinking of the simulation as the "real world."

## 2.6  MEASURING PRESENCE

The ability to generate high levels of presence in a VR experience is useful in plenty of applications. For training or evaluation purposes, it may be useful to have users react as they would in a real situation. Games and entertainment in VR try to make the user feel as though they exist in the narrative world of the experience, which is that is easier to achieve when the user subconsciously considers themselves to be within the virtual world. Even tools or visualizers built to be used in VR, such as drawing or sculpting tools, can benefit from presence—the user is focusing on the task in the virtual environment, and so it is worthwhile to reduce their presence in the physical world as much as possible.

Whatever sort of application you're thinking of developing, the components of presence are likely to be important to the usability of the application. VR is beneficial for many experiences, but particularly effective for experiences that require spatial interactions that are not possible in the physical world. The smoother we can make the transition into VR and the more present the user can feel in this new reality, the better an experience they will have. For this reason, it would be useful for developers to be able to measure the *degree of presence* being felt by the user.

Unfortunately, few quantitative measures of presence exist, due to the nature of the phenomena. Since presence is a quale, the way that it feels may never be able to be objectively described, and not only do different people feel presence to different degrees when exposed to the same stimuli, the same person can feel different degrees of presence given the same stimuli if they are in a different emotional or cognitive state. Although quantitative measures of presence may be difficult or impossible to achieve, *qualitative* indicators of what parts of an application generate less or more presence can still be of use to developers. One qualitative way to measure presence is through the use of questionnaires. The Witmer and Singer Presence Questionnaire, one choice of instrument to measure an individual's degree of presence, has been used in many training situations to assess the degree to which the simulation is invoking the feeling of presence in the user. In this questionnaire, the user is asked to rate statements from 1 to 5, including how much agency they felt, how accurately they were able to interpret cause and effect, and other such questions prompting a non-explicit comparison between the simulation and the real world. The questions included in this questionnaire are reproduced in Figure 2.17 for reference.

Several studies have been run that suggest higher presence correlates with increased performance within a simulation. Although some of these studies used the Witmer and Singer questionnaire, many of these use quantitative physiological reactions and performance-related statistics to measure presence. It's important to note that none of these methods directly measure presence, but instead measure reactions due to emotional state changes as a result of presence and, as a tertiary method, are not reliable except for making general observations about the relative degree to which presence is felt. Physiological reactions used in some studies to measure presence include change in heart rate, change in skin temperature, and change in skin conductance level, all of which were found to have their own advantages and disadvantages. Heart rate, the most common of the physiological reactions used for the measurement of presence, is often chosen due to its ease of measurement and the fact that it correlates closely with excitement, fear, and several other reactions that presence causes. Change in skin temperature is a less sensitive physiological reaction invoked by fear (and, therefore, presence in some scenarios), but it responds slower than change in heart rate. Change in skin conductance level is another alternative, which involves being measuring the sweat produced by the user in response to fear,

- How much were you able to control events?

- How responsive was the environment to actions you initiated or performed?

- How natural did your interactions with the environment seem?

- How much did the visual aspects of the environment involve you?

- How natural was the mechanism which controlled movement through the environment?

- How compelling was your sense of objects moving through space?

- How much did your experiences in the virtual environment seem consistent with your real-world experiences?

- Were you able to anticipate what would happen next in response to the actions that you performed?

- How completely were you able to actively survey or search the environment using vision?

- How compelling was your sense of moving around inside the virtual environment?

- How closely were you able to examine objects?

- How well could you examine objects from multiple viewpoints?

- How involved were you in the virtual environment experience?

- How much delay did you experience between your actions and expected outcomes?

- How quickly did you adjust to the virtual environment experience?

- How proficient in moving and interacting with the virtual environment did you feel at the end of the experience?

- How much did the visual display quality interfere or distract you from performing assigned tasks or required activities?

- How much did the control devices interfere with the performance of assigned tasks or with other activities?

- How well could you concentrate on the assigned tasks or required activities rather than on the mechanisms used to perform those tasks or activities?

Figure 2.17: The Witmer and Singer Presence Questionnaire.

and is even more difficult to accurately measure with a strong reading. These are few physiological metrics that correlate to unconscious reactions that suggest presence. What metric(s) to choose for a particular study depends highly on the measurement technology available, as well as the use case.

It follows that the more real a virtual environment seems—or, more accurately, the degree to which a user feels present within the environment—the more the physiological responses to the simulation resemble the physiological reactions that would occur in the real world. Knowing this, it is worthwhile to take baseline measurements of these physiological reactions in real scenarios to compare with the VR equivalents. This enables us to more authentically assess the relative presence felt by users. Of course, in situations where VR is being used as a substitute for a more dangerous real-world activity, such baseline measures may not be ethical.

It is important to think about the situations in which these metrics are at all useful for determining the level of presence felt by participants. First, these physiological presence measurements are a powerful tool for developers to get an idea of how users experience presence and what types of experiences in what circumstances can invoke this sensation of presence.

Further, the magnitude of one's physiological response is not necessarily proportional to any objective level of presence felt by the user—two users may feel equally present in one scenario, but User A's heart rate may increase more noticeably than User B's or vice versa. This discrepancy is due to natural variations in heart rate, as the same heart rate variations would occur in a real scenario. Although direct measurement of the increase in heart rate isn't a direct measurement of the increase in presence, an increase in heart rate does indicate that presence is felt—as long as the heart rate would have increased in the real-world scenario. We could more accurately gauge a user's level of presence if we were to measure their heart rate in the real-world scenario and then also measure their heart rate in the virtual scenario—the closer the heart rate is in the simulated test, the higher level of presence the user is feeling. Of course, there is also the possibility that the heart rate generated by a virtual scenario could even be greater than the heart rate in the actual scenario. This would suggest that heart rate and presence may only be loosely correlated; however, further study is necessary to determine if this could occur. Another drawback of these physiological measurements of presence is that they are only really able to measure presence through one emotional response; heart rate, for example, is a reasonable indicator of presence in horror experiences, but may be more tenuously related to presence in other scenarios.

## 2.7 SUMMARY

A major reason for VR's potential as a medium is that it is capable of presenting a digital world as an immersive space. When appropriately constructed to support SCs and valid actions, our minds may interpret the virtual world as if it were real. Generating this sensation of presence is an art, not an exact science, but does also require realism from the VR hardware and software, in the form of immersing sensory inputs and supporting SCs with valid actions. We've gone into a lot of detail over the abstract way in which presence is generated, but there's still some detail missing if you were to actually go about creating a simulation to try to maximize the presence felt by a user. What do we actually have to do for individual sensory inputs to match reality? How do you determine what inputs should be affected by a sensorimotor contingency? In order to understand the answers to these questions, we'll have to stray from the general and take a more concrete look at the human sensory process, starting with the next chapter.

# CHAPTER 3

# Sensation and Perception

## 3.1  PROVIDING THE PERCEPTION OF A VIRTUAL WORLD

It can be difficult to simulate a sensorimotor contingency accurately enough for a user to perceive the information as belonging to a physical world. People have evolved to be perceptive of their environment and acquire practice in observation using their senses every day. As a result, users are very adept at being able to tell the difference between fake and real sensory inputs when something is simulated in a way that isn't quite accurate. In the real world, we are constantly sensing the environment. Even a task as simple as making a cup of tea would involve a dizzying amount of effort to convincingly replicate in a simulation. First, you'd have to worry about all the visual aspects of the simulation—a cup would have to be displayed with the same colours we can see in the real world, and you'd have to be able to see the slight reflections of the table in the cup's china sides[1]. You'd have to simulate the steady rise in pitch of noise created by the steam as the kettle comes to a boil, and the movement of hot air past your skin as steam rises from the water you pour over the tea bag. The kettle's mass would also have to be accurately simulated: it would have to feel lighter as you pour water from it. You'd need to find some way to replicate the smooth texture of the cup, as well as the way it gradually warms the joints in your hand as you hold it to your face. Most importantly, you'd have to simulate the taste of the subtle hints of the herbs involved in the tea! Any single error and the user is reminded that they are in a simulation. In the real world, making tea is a trivial task—in the virtual world, it's a Herculean feat.

### 3.1.1  Reasons for Replicating Real-World Sensation

"Realism-focused" applications like the environment described above represent only a subset of the applications that could be used on a virtual reality (VR) platform—those that are made with the primary intention of replicating a real-life experience or environment. In many cases, replicating reality may not be the primary purpose of a VR application—instead, the application may be designed to entertain a user, allow

---

[1]Physical rendering such as this reflection is an entire discipline outside of the scope of this book—we recommended reading *Computer Graphics: Principles and Practice* if you're interested in learning more.

DOI: 10.1201/9781003261230-3

them to accomplish a task, view a particular object or set of data, or some other purpose. Regardless of the type of application, there is merit in providing accurate sensation to the point where it allows the application to fulfil its goals. All tasks require sensory information—for example, a 3D modelling software must provide its users with accurate visual information about the model they are working on (including the depth of the model), a music editing program must provide clear and properly spatialized audio, and the word processor must give feedback on where key boundaries are in order to allow for touch typing (in a traditional desktop implementation, the physical keyboard supports this role, but in VR, tactile feedback may need to be provided through other means). As such, some understanding of what an accurate sensation should be for a given environment is required for all VR applications. In many cases, the application may not necessitate perfectly accurate sensation. However, some base level of accuracy in the sensation provided is beneficial for any VR environment—many negative health effects attributed to VR such as simulator sickness and eye strain arise from a difference between the sensation we expect and the sensation that we experience within a VR simulation. Because VR sickness is most commonly associated with movement through a virtual world, an in-depth discussion of the causes and effects of VR sickness is presented in Chapter 10.

## 3.2 THE PERCEPTUAL PROCESS

You've likely seen an optical illusion like the one shown in Figure 3.1. In addition to being entertaining, optical illusions are a good demonstration of the difference between **sensation** arising from the environment and the final **perception** of the environment. In this image below, the subject of the image seems to be two faces if you consider the black portion to be the foreground and a vase-like shape if you take the white area to be the foreground. The subject of the image seems to change when you decide what portion to focus on, but the actual image remains the same. The reception of the image in your eye is the *sensation* of the image—receptors are activated by the light that reflects from the image into your eyes. The actual input a user receives from the physical world is registered by receptors as sensation. Whether you interpret the faces or the vase as the foreground is your *perception*. The final perception of a stimulus refers to the way that you experience it in your mind. Perception, as evidenced by this illusion, can be ambiguous for a given sensation—this image can be interpreted either as faces or a vase, two different perceptions arising from the same sensation.

In the physical world, sensation comes from energy that is emitted and altered by objects in the world around us. It is this energy that our sensory receptors respond to, resulting in sensation. Stimuli from a display can provide the same sensation as a given natural stimuli if it can generate the same response in the same receptor. This was the core of our discussion on immersion in Chapter 2: a sensory unit (a sensory receptor) is immersed for the full sensory field and sensory range if the display can cause the receptor to have the full set of responses that it would have to physical stimuli. In this case, the sensations the VR system can simulate match the set of

Figure 3.1: A common optical illusion with an ambiguous foreground and background.

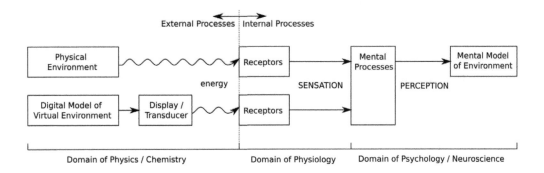

Figure 3.2: Process of how a real or virtual world results in a mental model of that world.

energy characteristics that the receptor is capable of responding to in real-world stimuli.

However, people do not experience raw sensations—every piece of information we receive about our environment is filtered and compared with the other sensations our receptors emit in order to result in our final perception. As shown in Figure 3.2, the process by which we build a mental model of an environment (real or virtual) can be split into **external processes** (the generation of sensory energy outside of the human body) and **internal processes** (the interpretation of received sensory energy inside the human sensory systems and mind). For the most part, VR developers are able to control only the external processes, by designing displays and determining the virtual environment they should display to the user. Chapter 2 discusses a very high level model of the external processes—from the energy source to the sensory unit (receptor). However, as the end goal of the system is to result in a mental model of an environment within the user's mind, it is necessary for a developer to "reverse engineer" elements of the human sensory process. The study of **physiology** allows us to understand what information receptors are capable of receiving, as well as important qualities such as the quantization of the receptor detection range and the receptor field—it is these metrics that inform the design of displays and virtual environments.

To understand the functions that map receptor signals to a final perception of an environment, we study **psychology** and **neuroscience**.

**Interfacing With the Internal**

We mentioned that VR developers are currently only able to control external processes—that is, the processes that deliver stimuli to human sensory receptors. However, as biotechnology advances, it may become possible to interact with internal systems—such as stimulating muscle fibres with implants to generate haptic sensation, or even delivering electrical impulses directly to sensory nerves, tricking the brain into "sensing" that which is not there. It may be possible that in the far future, sensory processes could be bypassed entirely and an intended perception could be written directly to the brain, using brain–computer interfaces—discussed in another box later in this chapter. Of course, using computers in this way has serious safety and ethical issues, but that hasn't stopped the idea of neurally stimulated VR to enter the public imagination through science fiction depictions such as *The Matrix*.

### 3.2.1  Hardware and Software Requirements for Accurate Sensation

The perceptual process as introduced above can also be thought of in terms that developers may be more accustomed to—a split between responsibilities of hardware and software. The diagram shown in Figure 3.3 is nearly identical to the diagram of the sensory process shown in Figure 3.2, but it has been bent into a U shape, to better illustrate how external processes map to the internal processes.

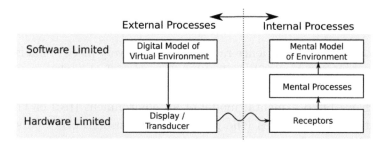

Figure 3.3: U-diagram mapping external process steps to internal process steps.

For every sensory unit that receives information from a virtual environment, two tasks must be completed for the simulation of stimuli to be accurate:

- First, the hardware we are using must be capable of outputting (displaying) stimuli with the required characteristics in order to result in a target perception.

- Second, we must know how to determine and model the required stimuli in software.

Both tasks require a knowledge of what sorts of information the individual senses require and what qualities of this information (sensation) result in the desired perception.

## 3.2.2  Alternative Paths to Perception

In the physical world, what we sense is often what we perceive. We assume (mostly correctly) that our perception of the environment around us matches the reality of the environment. However, perception does not always match reality—a VR head-mounted display (HMD) is one of the best examples of this. Although an HMD is really only displaying pixels on a flat screen a few centimetres away from the face, the user *perceives* this light to be coming from objects in a three-dimensional environment that are located much further away. Using a display to create the effect of the perception of a desired space is much cheaper (in both effort and currency) than building the desired space physically, but in terms of vision, both methods can result in the same or similar perception, depending on the fidelity of the display. Thus, one of the main advantages of VR is that we can generate the perception of certain scenes for the user with fewer resources than would result in the same perception in a physical world.

Because of the differences between the sensation of stimuli and the perception of the objects associated with the stimuli, VR developers can make more realistic or effective simulations given an understanding of these perceptual "shortcuts." Perception may involve combining multiple sensations to get a more accurate interpretation, altering how we perceive sensation from one sensory unit to better match information coming from another or even mentally "filling in" blank spots in the sensory field with assumed information.

A VR developer has to be aware of how sensations are processed before being perceived. Immersing a sensory input allows the developer to change the sensation received by the user, but what the user is consciously experiencing is the perception of that sensation. Of course, the best way to ensure that a user perceives a virtual environment the same way they perceive the real one is to provide the identical sensation; but this only matters within the bounds what the user can perceive to be identical. Although it is not always possible (or practical) to simulate an input identical to the physical world, two different stimuli received at the sensory inputs of a user can have the same perceptual result. For example, you don't need thousands of trees to simulate the sound of a forest of leaves rustling in the wind—we can generate sounds from a speaker that approximate this sensation. With careful application of speaker placement and reliable reproduction of recorded or simulated trees, the result will be indistinguishable.

There are two ways to replicate the perception of the physical environment for fewer resources than a full reproduction would necessitate, owing to the shortcuts our brain takes to process the world. They are as follows:

1. Providing the same *sensation* from a simpler source. Two sensations can be exactly the same at the sensory input, even if they come from different sources,

and thus, we can often provide the same stimuli from an electronic display as would arise in the real world. Take audio for example: although there are millions of sounds in the world, they can all be reproduced in a single ear by altering two variables—the amplitude and frequency of the pressure of air entering the ear. If we have an electronic source that is able to vary these parameters over the full range of human hearing, we can match the sensation reaching the ear—the air pressure—to the sensation generated by any natural source. A pair of headphones can be a lot cheaper than hiring an orchestra to follow around your user and, if used correctly, may sound very similar.

2. Providing the same *perception* from a simpler sensation. Two identical sensations in the same context will result in the same perception for a single user[2], but two different sensations can also result in the same perception. Perception differs from sensation due to influences belonging to two primary categories. The first of these categories, **internal conversions**, includes internal mechanisms within the user's mind that may alter the perception of a stimulus from its accurate interpretation, but will still result in the same perception. The second category, **perceptual context**, includes external information or interfering stimuli that change how we perceive a specific sensation. Context capable of altering perception includes not only the background stimuli present at the moment of interest but also all stimuli previously encountered that may affect the relative perception of the target stimuli. While both internal conversations and context may cause stimuli to be perceived "inaccurately," internal conversations will skew the perception of the stimulus in the same way every time, while the effects of context on perception will differ from moment to moment.

The "scale" in which a sensation exists may be different from the scale at which we perceive it, as a result of internal conversions. Take, for example, the loudness of a sound. A sound is generated with an intensity—this value specifies the amplitude of the sound wave (how much the pressure of the air differs about a stasis pressure). Intensity diminishes with distance, as the sound wave loses energy. Sound waves further away reach the ear with lower intensities, while sounds made close by retain a larger fraction of their initial intensity. Although how "loud" we *perceive* a sound to be is strongly influenced by intensity, it's not a proportional relationship—a sound that is twice as intense is not necessarily perceived as twice as "loud" (this is, in fact, rarely the case) shown in Figure 3.4. The scale of perceived vs. actual intensity, described by **Fetchner's law**, is actually logarithmic, as will be discussed in more detail in Section 3.4—we internally convert intensity to a completely different scale to obtain our perception of loudness. Further, the function that gives us "loudness" is not dependent on intensity alone—frequency, duration, and other sounds we heard recently all change our perception. Finally, the context of the sound can also alter our perception of its loudness. A ship's horn, far away, may be perceived as louder

---

[2]Except in the case of optical illusions or other ambiguous situations.

than a nearby dog's bark, even though the sensation of the intensities of those sounds may be reversed.

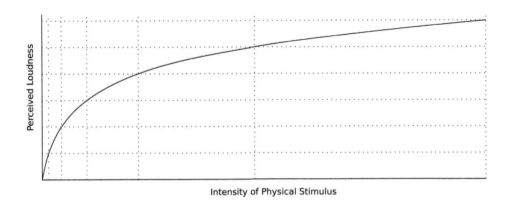

Figure 3.4: Fetchner's law: all else being equal, perceived loudness increases as the log of the intensity of the stimulus.

Context, meaning in this case, other sensations experienced (either concurrently with the sensation in question or at any time in the past) can also affect how we perceive something. We consider objects to be "heavy" or "light" dependent on objects we've lifted in the past, a bath seems extra hot when you get in from the cold, and a toothpaste tastes rather odd after drinking a glass of orange juice—all thanks to context.

As developers, we can take advantage of the effects context has on perception. Consider a hypothetical HMD that can only display a mid-range of colours—very bright and very dark colours cannot be displayed. Suppose we wanted to display an environment consisting of a very dark room using this system. Considering just the range of brightness supported by the display, any room we'd render wouldn't be very dark—this limit is imposed by the **output sensory range** of the system. However, if we displayed something with colours at the brighter end of the range prior to showing the room (rendered with the darkest colours of the range), it would seem darker in comparison. By changing the context (showing a bright loading screen before), we force the user's mind to perceive the room as darker than the system's output sensory range is capable of. We call the range that we are able to reach through perceptual tricks the **output perceptual range**.

Further, our perception of one sensory input can be altered by the sensation of sensory inputs in other categories entirely—for example, the location that we think a sound is coming from can be influenced by the objects in our visual field, as seen in ventriloquism. These other stimuli aren't changing the inputs we receive; they're only changing the information the brain considers in order to determine what is going on. These quirks can be exploited by VR developers—for example, the result of sound being influenced by vision means that we don't need to simulate as many positions for sounds if we can use the graphics to influence the perceived position.

**Are You Seeing What I'm Seeing?**

We can all agree that two different observers receive the same sensation from the same stimulus, if they perform identical sensorimotor contingencies in identical positions. It's also true, as discussed above, that no two people "perceive" sensory input in exactly the same way—although relationships like the intensity of a stimulus perceived tend to be proportional among people. Things like the perceived intensity are easy to query people on—asking them to assign intensity to a numerical scale, for example. But we can't be sure that people perceive everything similarly. This is true for many perceived qualities that we can't easily assign values to—like what the colour "red" looks like. You were taught what "red" was by being shown red objects—any object that primarily reflected light with a wavelength of 625–740 nanometres was in this category. This is the characteristic received as part of the sensation of red—but how can we be sure that what someone else perceives as "red" isn't what you perceive as "green"? We can't say for sure if you see the colour red differently than we do, but it certainly is possible for people's perceptions of wavelengths to be different. An experiment performed in 2009 to fix colour blindness in squirrel monkeys revealed some interesting information about how our minds interpret colour. Male squirrel monkeys, which are usually red–green colour blind, were given gene therapy to provide them with a third receptor. Experiments showed that the treatment was a success, as the monkeys were now able to distinguish between red and green stimuli. The monkeys being able to perceive new colours in the spectrum suggests that the perception of wavelengths is not hard coded into our biology, instead differing from person to person—thus, it is likely that the same colour is internally "seen" differently by different individuals.

## 3.3 A SENSORY VIEW OF THE HUMAN BODY

The body is capable of sensing many different types of stimuli. The human sensory system contains many different types of receptors, each capable of detecting different forms of physical stimuli. Individual receptors respond to stimuli fitting a narrow range and field: for example, a "red-sensing" cone (a photoreceptor) responds to light with wavelengths between 564 and 580 nm, originating from an area less than 1 degree of arc in width. However, when we look around at our environment, we are unable to mentally separate what input is coming from which cone—it is all fused into one complete picture in the mind. However, we are able to mentally separate the image of our environment from the sounds we hear in it, the tactile sensations we receive from it, the temperature on our skin, and so on. Although these final mental products cannot be consciously separated into the input from each individual receptor, they are separable from each other—these products, which we perceive as final sensations, are referred to as **sensory modalities**. As these receptors all respond to different characteristics of the same type of stimuli, they are considered part of the same sensory modality. Many modalities are associated with a certain sensory organ that contains many receptors belonging to that modality—the traditionally quoted "five senses" each have an organ dedicated to them. **Sensory systems** are categories grouping the biological components responsible for a particular sensation—although many sensory systems consist of a single modality, some contain more, such as the somatosensory system as shown in Figure 3.5.

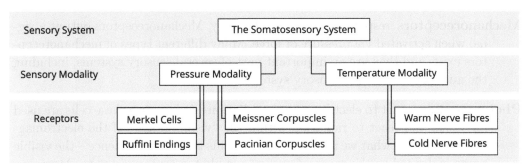

Figure 3.5: A flowchart depicting the categorical relation between sensory systems, modalities, and receptors, with the visual and somatosensory systems shown as an example.

What level of sensory abstraction that a VR developer should be considering is task dependent. For example, a hardware developer working on a VR headset may be concerned with the receptor level—selecting actuators able to stimulate specific receptors. Alternatively, a software developer deciding between user interface alternatives might be more concerned with the modality or system level—secondary layers that combine many receptors into a single modality "image."

Chapter 4 and Chapter 5 discuss various sensory systems and modalities in detail, from a black box model, as to be most useful to the developer. This model focuses primarily on the inputs of the sensory system (individual sensory units and the sensory characteristics they respond) and the functions that map inputs to the output perception, but abstracts the actual internal mechanisms of how these perceptions are generated.

## 3.3.1 Receptors

The smallest component in any given sensory system is the **receptor**. In Chapter 2, we referred to receptors as sensory units—an abstraction useful when talking about immersion quantification. Receptors are cells or structures in the body that are capable of detecting sensations.

Receptors can be broadly placed into two broad categories: **exteroceptors** and **interoceptors**. Exteroceptors are receptors located on the outside of the body or located within a sensory organ that accepts stimuli from outside of the body. For example, while photoreceptors within the retina are located *inside* the eye, they respond to external stimuli that pass through the lens of the eye and therefore are exteroceptors. Interoceptors respond to stimuli from within the body—sensations such as limb position or internal cramps. For the VR developer, exteroceptors are both easier to provide sensation to and usually more useful—in most cases, we are interested in simulating an outside world instead of sensations arising from within the body.

There are many different types of receptors in the human body. Each respond to different types of energy. As such, it is common to classify receptors based on functionality.

**Mechanoreceptors** respond to mechanical energy. Mechanoreceptors output a signal when activated via pressure or force. Many different types of mechanoreceptors exist, and they are an important part of several sensory systems, including the auditory and somatosensory systems.

**Photoreceptors** react to electromagnetic radiation—in humans, these cells are used for vision and react to radiation within the "visible range" of the electromagnetic spectrum (what we refer to as light). This is not a coincidence—the visible range is defined as the range of energy our photoreceptors react to. Many animals have photoreceptors that react to radiation beyond the visible range—if we had these photoreceptors, our definition of the visible range would likely change. Human photoreceptors are located within the eye, concentrated in the retina. Photoreceptors transduce light into neural signals via changes in the photoreceptor's membrane potential—the difference in voltage between the interior and exterior of the cell. This occurs due to a reaction between the photons that make up the electromagnetic stimulus and specialized proteins residing within the photoreceptor. Different types of photoreceptors react to different conditions—the strength of responses to certain wavelengths, light levels, response times, and other characteristics vary across several receptor types.

**Chemoreceptors** transduce chemical stimuli into neural signals. Chemoreceptors are primarily associated with the modalities of taste and scent, but some internal chemoreceptors respond to levels of certain chemicals in the blood, the amount of carbon dioxide in the lungs, and other internal sensations. Many chemoreceptors react to specific characteristics of molecules (such as functional groups), and not the molecule as a whole. The perceptions of taste and smell arise from signals from a large combination of different chemoreceptors—the vast majority of molecules will activate several different types of chemoreceptors. Chemoreceptors can be categorized into distance chemoreceptors—which detect chemicals in a gaseous state—and direct chemoreceptors—which detect aqueous chemicals (those which react with water). The chemoreceptors involved in olfaction are **distance chemoreceptors**, while those involved in gustation are **direct chemoreceptors**.

**Thermoreceptors** respond to changes in temperature and are located within the skin. Two basic types of thermoreceptors exist: cold-sensitive receptors and heat-sensitive receptors. The stimulation of these receptors are separate, so it is possible to receive both hot and cold signals at the same time.

**Nociceptors** are a category of receptors that respond to potentially damaging stimuli—they result in the sensation of pain. The actual method of transduction varies between different nociceptors—some are actually subcategories of mechanoreceptors, chemoreceptors, and thermoreceptors with extreme thresholds, while others respond to actual damage to receptor cell. Nociceptors are embedded throughout the skin, as well as in most organs.

## 3.4   QUANTIFYING STIMULUS

### 3.4.1   Terminology on Stimulus Intensity

How loud is that music? How bright is a light? How heavy is that weight? All of these questions are asking about the **intensity** of a stimulus—and all of them could be answered correctly in two ways. When the intensity of a stimuli is mentioned, it's unclear what we're referring to—how heavy something feels, to us (**perceived intensity**), or the actual weight (**absolute intensity**).

All stimuli are a form of energy. In the case of vision, we're sensing electromagnetic energy. With sound, the energy is a mechanical pressure that vibrates the cilia in our ears. We sense temperature through thermal energy on our skin, and scent and taste are forms of chemical energy. The intensity of a stimuli is the amount of energy reaching the sensor.

Usually, the term intensity is used to refer to the actual magnitude of a particular aspect of a stimulus. This may or may not be close to the intensity it is perceived as by an observer. We usually refer to this perceived quality with different names for each sensory modality—such as loudness or heaviness—but when there isn't a specific name, we'll call it "perceived intensity," which is different from the intensity of the signal itself.

It is also sometimes useful to differentiate between the **source intensity**, which is the intensity of a stimulus at the point it is generated, and **received intensity**, which is the intensity of the stimulus by the time it reaches us, as seen in Figure 3.6. All external stimuli diminish over distance as they reach us (except the ones we are in direct contact with), so it's important to remember that source and received intensity will differ for stimuli from a physical environment.

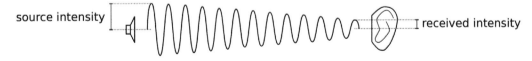

source intensity                                                                          received intensity

Figure 3.6: The received intensity of a sound wave is less than the source intensity.

### 3.4.2   Measuring Using Decibels

The intensity range within which stimuli can be detected by a receptor is often very wide. For example, the ear can register pressures from 0.0002 dynes/cm$^2$ to 240 dynes/cm$^2$—the lower end of the range being six orders of magnitude less than the high end.

If we wanted to specify how much more intense a sound at 20 dynes/cm$^2$ is than a sound at 0.0002 dynes/cm$^2$, we could say that it is 100,000 times more intense. An alternate scale, the **decibel** (dB), is often used to specify these ratios logarithmically, using smaller numbers. To get a value for the ratio between two numbers in decibels, we use the formula:

$$10 \cdot \log_{10}(I_1/I_2) = dB \tag{3.1}$$

where $I_1$ and $I_2$ are the intensities being considered. For example, the ratio between 100 and 50 (where the first number is twice as large as the second) in decibels is $10 \cdot \log_{10}(100/50) \approx 3$. If we flip the quantities to get the ratio between 50 and 100 in decibels, we get a negative value—indicating the first number is smaller than the second: $10 \cdot \log_{10}(50/100) \approx -3$. Note that decibels only give a relative difference between values—they are a scaled ratio, giving the intensity of one value ($I_1$) relative to another value ($I_2$) and do not place a value on any absolute scale. Also note that decibels can be used to give a relationship difference between any two values, not just audio intensities.

The decibel scale is useful for discussing stimulus intensity for two reasons in. The first reason is that it allows us to work with numbers that are a reasonable size—we can say a particular light is 70 dB brighter than another, which may be an easier number to work with and understand than saying the light is 1,000,000 times brighter than the other. Second, the decibel scale corresponds closely to the way we perceive differences in stimuli. Humans tend to perceive intensities, frequencies, and other quantities on logarithmic scales rather than linear scales.

## 3.5 PERCEPTIVE TASKS

What happens between the sensation of a stimuli and it being perceived? We've already mentioned that some conversion to a perceived intensity occurs within the mind, and that context can influence the perceived intensity value as well.

Whether you are aware of it or not, you're constantly performing a series of tasks whenever you receive stimuli. There are four basic tasks involved with perceiving—detection, identification, discrimination, and scaling. These tasks allow us to answer questions such as if there is a difference between two colours or how far away an object is. These problems are the domain of **psychophysics**—the field of study that determines the relation between the magnitude of a sensation and the magnitude of the corresponding perception.

### 3.5.1 Detection

**Detection** is the task of determining if a certain stimulus is present. In order for a person to *detect* a stimulus, its received intensity must be above a certain value. If the received intensity is below some value, we physically can't detect it. This minimum value is referred to as the **absolute threshold**—stimuli below this intensity will not be registered by the observer, while stimuli with magnitudes above this value will be sensed, shown on the graph on the right in Figure 3.7. In practice, however, this threshold changes user to user as well as with specific qualities and contexts of the stimuli. Because this is not a sharp cut-off, the actual detection curve is more like the curve shown in the graph on the left in Figure 3.7, where the probability of detection increases as the intensity of stimuli increase.

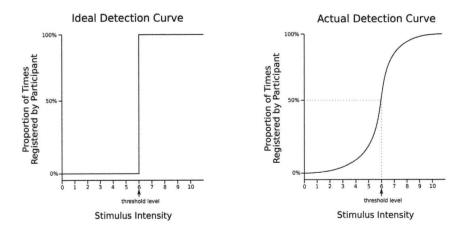

Figure 3.7: An ideal detection curve (right) and an actual detection curve (left).

A good example of how the detection threshold works in practice is in audio detection tests. In these tests, tones of varying intensities may be played. Around the "threshold value," tones barely lower in intensity are heard less often by participants than tones above—a participant may be able to hear the lower tone two out of ten times. Similarly, a tone just above the threshold value is heard more often, but not all the time—say, eight out of ten times. If we wanted to define a threshold value, it would make sense to do it based on the probability of a tone being heard. Practically, the threshold is defined as the magnitude value for which the probability of the stimulus being registered is 50%.

The presence of **background stimulus** can also affect the threshold at which we're able to detect a target stimulus. If there are other stimuli in the background, we're less likely to hear a target stimulus; alternatively, in order for us to hear it reliably, the intensity of the target stimulus should be increased. Not only are there background stimuli within most environments, but we constantly deal with general background "noise" caused by our own senses—even in a pitch black room, we see little flashes in our vision, and even in a silent area, we hear the sound of our own breathing or the random firings of neurons searching for a sound.

## 3.5.2 Identification

**Identification** is the task of distinguishing a chosen stimulus from other stimuli present. We identify when we try to make out a particular conversation at a loud party or distinguish a wild animal from a stand of trees. How hard it is to identify a particular stimulus depends on a few factors. The more stimuli there are in addition to the target stimuli, the more difficult the task becomes. Additionally, if the competing stimuli are very similar to the target stimuli, identifying the target becomes more difficult.

**Information transmission** is the process of getting information to the observer. If we have a certain stimulus, and the observer is able to identify it correctly, every time, the information is transmitted perfectly. If the observer isn't able to identify the stimuli but can determine several times it definitely is not, then only some information has been transmitted. In reality, people are modest transmitters of information.

To be able to quantify the amount of information transferred, we use **information theory**. Information theory is a qualitative system that is used to describe the number of alternative stimuli to identify between. In this sense, information transferred is greater when there are more stimuli possibilities to identify between.

Information is measured in **bits**, as it is when discussing information theory in an electrical transmission context. The amount of bits of information transmitted increases by one when the number of alternatives to choose between doubles. For instance,

- 2 alternatives to identify between = 1 bit

- 4 alternatives to identify between = 2 bits

- 8 alternatives to identify between = 3 bits...

This can be expressed by stating if there are n choices available to identify between, that a choice contains $log_2 n$ bits of information. If only a portion of the possible stimuli characteristics can be deciphered between, the information has not been transmitted perfectly, but some information has still been transmitted. For example, if a light has four colours it can flash (orange, red, blue, and green) and you see it, but can only determine it was not blue or green, you are still able to determine between half of the possible alternatives and have transmitted 1 bit of information.

**Channel capacity** refers to the amount of information that can be transmitted reliably over a given channel. Humans receive information across many different sensory channels, and based on the context and assumptions made by our brains as we see and hear things, a great deal of information can be absorbed from our environment. Different characteristics of a stimuli have different channel capacities: for example, people can differentiate between more frequencies of sounds than sound intensity levels.

Information theory is particularly important for usability design. If we want a user to remember a number of different states—for example, what various flashing lights represent—considering the channel capacity and transmission accuracy are important. For the user to even be able to distinguish between lights, we need to ensure that the number of different flash types matches the channel capacity. If we varied the flashes in, say, colour and intensity, the user would be able to identify more states than if we had just varied colour alone.

### Displaying Directly to the Brain

We've discussed how we can only ever provide sensation to a user through sensory inputs and cannot affect perception directly. As technology advances, we may be able to use **brain computer interfaces** (BCIs) to "write" directly to perception, bypassing sensation entirely. Experiences like dreams and hallucinations are proof that we don't need sensation to perceive something—in both cases, people are perceiving something that isn't presented as a stimulus, but it can be just as convincing as if it were. As perception merely "forms" images our senses receive, these experiences suggest that it may be possible to form complete images entirely in the brain. Many novelists and futurists see BCI as the future for VR and perhaps the only way to practically achieve a true first-order system. If BCI VR devices become common, they may be writing information to the same parts of the brain that dreams and hallucinogens activate. In this case, the developer will not have to worry about providing sensation or how it translates to perception—they can write to the perceived reality directly. Additionally, if we were able to directly simulate the brain experience of reality, what would be the limits of that reality? Could we directly stimulate the vestibular experience of weightlessness? Or 9 g of acceleration? Or a sound of 200 dB (beyond the threshold of pain)? What would happen to a brain which is provided with neural impulses representing impossible scenarios? Are the limits of sensation related to the physical characteristics of our sensing organs or to the conduit between those organs and the brain? The complexity of the human brain is immense, however, and many components of perception are unknown. Determining how to use neurons to simulate the perception of an environment may be *much* too complicated to ever consider doing with consumer electronics.

### 3.5.3 Discrimination

**Discrimination** is the task of determining if two stimuli are the same or not. Just like there is a minimum threshold for us to be able to detect an object, there is a **minimum difference** between two objects for us to be able to discriminate between them.

Of course, what we mean by "two objects being the same" can differ. Are we wanting to tell if two sounds are exactly the same or if they just have the same frequency? Technically, the first problem, trying to judge if two objects are the same in every regard, is a combination of many instances of the second—if we judge two objects to be the same in every dimension, they are the same in every regard. Due to this, we'll discuss only discriminating based on a single dimension—as discriminating in multiple dimensions is the same task, performed multiple times.

Much like detection, discrimination follows a threshold. Also, like detection, this threshold is not abrupt—there's an area where we may or may not be able to tell the difference between two stimuli. For example, assume we're asking a participant to determine if a sound is louder or quieter than a "reference value" we have given them. For sounds much louder than the reference, the participant is able to say confidently that the sound is louder. But when the difference between the reference and the sound is smaller, the participant isn't always able to tell if the sound is louder or quieter—maybe they think it's louder 80% of the time. The closer we get to the reference value, the closer the percentage of choices between louder and quieter gets to 50%. At this point, on average, the user perceives no difference. The point where the user perceives that the stimulus is louder 75% of the time represents a point at which the difference is noted half the time—at the 50% point, the difference, on average, is not perceived. Similarly, there's a point on the other side where the stimulus is perceived as quieter 75% of the time. Between these two points is the **interval of uncertainty**, shown in Figure 3.8—within this area, on average, a difference is perceived less than half of the time.

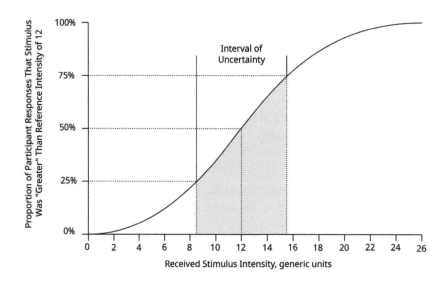

Figure 3.8: The interval of uncertainty for determining if stimuli are greater than a reference value.

If someone is good at discrimination, they're better at picking up smaller and smaller differences between stimuli. The smaller the size of the area of uncertainty, the higher a user's **sensitivity** to changes in the associated stimuli. The **difference threshold** represents how much more magnitude a stimulus must have for the difference to be perceived 50% of the time and is equal to half of the interval of uncertainty. The interval of uncertainty (and therefore the difference threshold) not only differs from person to person, but also on contextual factors. Of course, we're better at differentiating between certain types of stimuli than others. We're good at discerning the relative colour of an object—we're less adept at discriminating differences between light intensities. As well as differing from stimuli to stimuli, the difference threshold varies depending on the intensity of stimuli. As a stimulus's intensity increases, it becomes more difficult for us to discriminate between it and other stimuli, even if the difference between the two intensities is the same as it would be for a lower intensity level. For example, it's more difficult to differentiate between a pair of lights that give off 100 candelas and 102 candelas, respectively, than a pair that give off 2 and 4 candelas. The difference threshold increases linearly as the stimulus intensity increases. This relation is known as **Weber's law**, and it follows a simple formula:

$$\Delta I = k \times I$$

where $\Delta I$ is the size of the difference threshold, I is the stimulus intensity, and $k$ is a constant that varies depending on the type of stimuli, conditions, etc. Regardless of the stimulus, Weber's law illustrates a strictly linear relation. The constant, also known as the **Weber fraction**, indicates the proportion by which the stimulus must be changed from a reference I to be detected 50% of the time. Comparisons of Weber fractions across different sensory inputs can be used to determine that input's sensitivity. More sensitive inputs, able to detect smaller changes in the intensity of a stimulus, have a lower value for the Weber fraction.

### 3.5.3.1 Reaction Time

Even if two of the same type of stimuli are above the difference threshold, we're quicker at discriminating some values than others. It's easier, for example, to discriminate green from red than orange from red. We'll likely be able to discriminate both of them with 100% accuracy, but it may take a significantly shorter amount of time to do so in the first scenario. This difference is quantified through **reaction time**—a measurement of the time from the presentation of a stimulus to the user's response.

There are two types of reaction time. **Simple reaction time** measures the time it takes a participant to perform an action, like pressing a button, if a certain condition is met. For example, a user will be instructed to press a button whenever a light flashes blue. **Choice reaction time** is also a measurement of the time required to perform an action, but requires the user to perform different actions for different stimuli. The participant may have to press a blue button whenever a light flashes blue, and a different, red, button if the light flashes red. Making a decision is a different cognitive task than a simple reaction, and reaction times can differ for similar stimuli with these different tasks.

In terms of simple reaction times, a reaction time is faster when a stimulus is more intense. Figure 3.9 illustrates this relationship. As stimulus intensity (in this case an audio stimulus, measured in dB) increases, reaction time rapidly improves, before plateauing as the intensity gets higher.

The same relationship exists for choice reaction times, except that choice reaction times are slower than the corresponding simple reaction times. Additionally, as mentioned in Section 3.5.3, increasing the set of possible choices increases reaction time, as well as increasing the likelihood of errors. As we increase the number of reactions to a varying stimuli, we're also increasing the amount of information (in bits) encoded by the stimuli. If we have four choices, the stimuli encodes 2 bits.

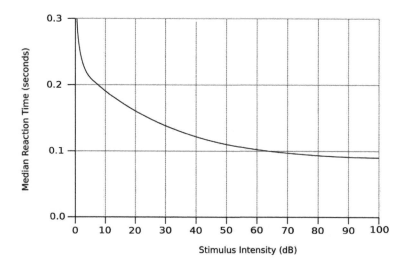

Figure 3.9: Reaction time improves as stimuli intensity increases.

One theory of why this happens is that humans are able to take in information at a constant rate. Under this assumption, reacting when we have several things to choose between takes longer, as it takes us longer to obtain the information needed to make the decision. Figure 3.10 shows that the relationship is roughly linear between the amount of information encoded and the time to make a decision. This relation is referred to as **Hick's law**[3], named after the psychologist William Edmund Hick, and is an important consideration for interface designers—we can roughly determine how much longer it would take a user to make a choice if we increase the number of options.

### 3.5.4 Scaling

**Scaling** is the task we perform to quantify differences between objects. Where scaling differs from discrimination is that you aren't trying to determine if two dimensions are different, but instead, you're trying to determine by "how much" they differ or how they are related. These differences can be in any dimension—determining how much larger an object is and how much brighter a light is are both scaling tasks. Humans evaluate the quantitative difference between two stimuli using an internal reference called the **prothetic continuum**. This continuum allows us to have a sense of "scale" between stimuli by making comparisons with recently encountered stimuli. On the prothetic continuum, changes in sensation come from adding or subtracting from the present stimuli. For example, if you are in a dark room and someone shines a flashlight at you, the sensation of brightness increases. If the present stimulus was a well-lit room, the flashlight would not seem as bright—even though the bulb has the same intensity in both cases. There are also non-prothetic continua—a continuum for qualities, not quantities. For example, our judgement of how red or green a light

---

[3]Hick's law is also used in the context of usability to encourage designers to reduce the number of choices a user must make in order to reduce cognitive load and increase decision efficiency.

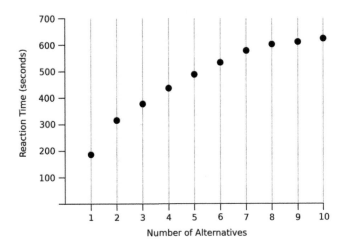

Figure 3.10: Hick's law. Reaction time increases with the number of alternatives in a choice task.

appears is on a non-prothetic continuum. Red is not "more than" or "less than" green; they're just different.

An important metric for scaling tasks is the **just noticeable difference**. According to Weber's law, the difference threshold—the minimum difference in magnitude between two stimuli for them to be noticeable by a person—increases with the intensity of the stimuli. This means that the higher the intensity of our first stimulus is, the bigger we'll have to make the difference in intensity before someone can notice the difference exists. As a quantity of perceived difference, the just-noticeable difference can be used as a unit to describe how far apart two stimuli seem to be—for example, two stimuli might be 5 or 50 JND apart. With this method, we're able to create graphs that match the difference in intensity to the difference in perceived intensity.

## 3.6 SUMMARY

Although VR has the potential to simulate a wide variety of realities, each of these simulations has a common point of reference: the human wearing the VR headset. We must ensure that the realities we construct take into account the ways in which humans sense and perceive the world. Our senses have evolved over thousands of years to support our interactions with the only world we know, and as we create new unimagined worlds, our senses will remain the same. Perhaps we may be able to simulate new senses or ways of perceiving the world around us, but until we are able to directly stimulate the brain, our connection to the realities within our mind will be restricted to the portals provided by our senses. In the next two chapters we will investigate the ways in which each of our individual senses can be used to simulate realities. First, we will consider the primary senses: sight and sound. In the following chapter we will consider the secondary, senses including taste and smell, touch and feeling, and the ways in which we perceive our own bodies and emotions.

# CHAPTER 4

# Supporting Primary Senses

## 4.1   VISUAL SENSORY INPUTS

Visual stimulus is often the primary sensory focus of a virtual reality (VR) system. Developers of VR hardware usually prioritize improvements to displays for the visual system over other those for other senses. This raises a question—why do VR users and developers value vision so much?

One explanation could be that people are used to consuming media in a visual form. With the notable exceptions of music and telephone communication, most of our interactions with media contain a visual component. From paintings to television and modern internet browsers, it's what we've become accustomed to.

Another reason visual simulation may be such a priority is that the visual sensory inputs are in constant use while we're awake. Other sensory inputs, such as those related to touch, only register when an action is taken, and thus we are only receiving input from them for a fraction of the time that we spend processing visual input. In this way, we can classify touch to be an **active sensory unit**. In contrast, the sensory units involved in vision are considered **passive sensory units**, as they are receiving stimulus even when a sensorimotor contingency is not being executed.

Several other sensory categories could also be considered passive—for example, hearing and smelling. However, whereas these senses are always open to sensory information from the outside environment, they are a conscious focus far less often than the visual senses. For example, although our ears are always open, we'll often only notice sounds when we're focusing on them as part of a task (like conversation) or a loud or abnormal sound captures our attention. Similarly, although there is constantly some background scent in the air, we'd consider ourselves to be smelling "nothing" the majority of the time. In contrast, it would feel very odd if you didn't see anything—we're constantly reacting to and consciously interpreting visual stimulus. A virtual world that you couldn't see would be a lot harder to overlook than a virtual world that is missing sound or scent.

A third possible explanation is that people are biologically predisposed to rely heavily on sight. Roughly half of the human brain is either directly or indirectly involved with processing or interpreting vision in some form. However, this cannot be the sole reason vision is so heavily emphasized in VR, as sensations related to touch have an even larger portion of the brain dedicated to their processing, yet

DOI: 10.1201/9781003261230-4

aren't nearly as prioritized for VR as vision is. This bias towards vision over other senses could be based on practicality—it's a lot easier and cheaper to simulate the visual sense, which relies on receiving light as its form of input, as opposed to other senses such as touch (which requires physical pressure as stimuli) or taste and smell (which both require chemical stimuli). The set of different inputs the visual sense can take is limited to a small band of the electromagnetic spectrum, which current technology is very capable of displaying.

The first section of this chapter describes the visual sensory inputs in detail, starting with a rough anatomy of the eye. Although we will present specific sensory inputs as simple input-receiving machines for the rest of this chapter, understanding what components make up the eye is important for a full appreciation of the eye's strengths and limitations.

**Visual VR Displays: The Chicken or the Egg?**

The fact that cheap, readily available visual displays exist is at least part of the reason VR systems prioritize visual input. Much of the technology required to simulate vision had already been developed before VR headsets became commonplace. Over history, we've developed a number of displays that are able to output images across most (but not all) of the visual spectrum. However, one can pose the question—did we develop these display technologies because we rely so heavily on the visual sense or do we use the visual sense for communication because these technologies were easy to make?

Another theory of why vision is so predominant in media and technology is that it is relatively easy to make permanent changes to the visual world. A person can mark the walls of a cave with a sketch of a bison, and those marks are there for centuries; a song or a poem vanishes into the air the moment it is created. Human communication first emerged as sounds that could be heard, but human history was first recorded as marks that could be seen.

With the development of better technology for copying written words, more people could read, and with the development of technology that could record spoken words, people could hear. If someone developed spatially accurate audio in the radio era, would this have been considered VR? Although this is a philosophically interesting thought experiment, its real purpose is to try and get you to let go of the notion of a "primary sense." It's important to consider the value of the senses in simulation outside of their current ubiquity, something that we'll touch on throughout the chapter.

### 4.1.1 Anatomy of the Eye

The human eye is mostly hollow. Not quite a sphere, the eye itself is just over 2 cm in diameter and can be broken down into four primary "optically active" components, meaning those that are involved with the focusing and processing of light.

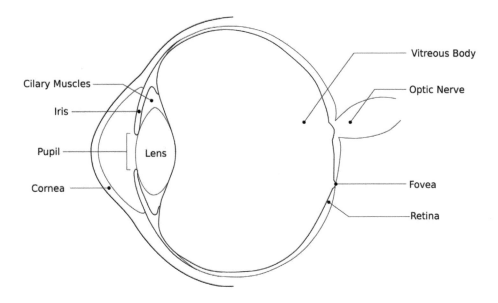

Figure 4.1: The anatomy of the eye.

These four elements are the cornea, iris, lens, and retina, shown along with other parts of the eye in Figure 4.1. At the front of the eye is the **cornea**, which acts as a lens to concentrate light into the chamber of the eye. While the rest of the eye is mostly spherical, the cornea bulges out a bit in front of the eye—this allows the cornea to focus light from slightly behind the head into the eye.

The next element, the **iris**, is located after the cornea and controls the amount of light entering the eye. The iris functions in a manner analogous to the aperture of a camera—it acts to change the size of an opening, called the **pupil**, in order to adjust to different levels of brightness. The pupil can range from as small as 2 mm in diameter in bright conditions to up to 8 mm in dark conditions. With a smaller pupil, not only does less light enter the eye, but there are fewer distortions in the image received, and the distance range in which objects appear to be in focus is greater. This range for which objects are in focus is referred to as the **depth of focus**.

**Pupil Responses**

Although its primary purpose is to adjust the level of light entering the eye, the pupil also may enlarge when someone is on drugs, sees an object (or person) of interest or affection, is dehydrated, and in several more situations that seemingly have nothing to do with brightness.

After light passes through the pupil, it is then focused further by the **lens**, aptly named, as it functions much like its glass counterpart. Unlike the cornea, which also acts as an optical "lens" in that it focuses light, the lens is able to vary its focal length by squashing and stretching. Several muscles attached to the eye, referred to as the **ciliary muscle group**, can cause the shape of the lens to distort in order to provide a clear image. How much the lens distorts is dependent on the distance of the object being viewed from the user. Near objects require a more spherical lens shape, while distant objects require a flatter lens. This process of focusing the lens is referred to as **accommodation**, shown in Figure 4.2.

In addition to visual information, the brain uses preoperative information from the tension of the ciliary muscle group to influence how far away it interprets objects in an image to be. As the tension of ciliary muscles depends on the actual distance of the light source from the eye, this can present a common sensory conflict when the actual distance of an object does not match the distance it appears to be, as is the case when using a head-mounted display (HMD). If the display is a pair of screens located 3 cm from the eyes, that is the distance the ciliary muscles will focus to—which may disagree with other depth cues, such as perspective and stereopsis (discussed later), that imply that an object is much further away. This problem is referred to as the **accommodation-vergence conflict** and can cause negative impacts to presence, eye strain, and even VR sickness in extreme cases.

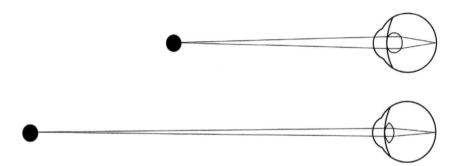

Figure 4.2: A diagram illustrating the process of accommodation for near and far objects.

The cornea, iris, and lens work together to focus an image onto the **retina**, a biological array of light sensors in the back of the eye chamber. Although the three optical components previously discussed are responsible for the focus of the image the eye receives, the retina deserves particular attention from VR developers, as the biological receptors it is composed of determine the range and fidelity of light that the eye can detect. The retina's process of converting light into a neural response that the brain can interpret is referred to as **transduction**, a term analogous to its use in signal processing—the analogue input of electromagnetic waves is being turned into an electrical signal in the nervous system.

Two types of cells in the retina are responsible for light reception—**rods** and **cones**. Approximately 120 million rods and 60 million cones exist in the retina, respectively—collectively, these cells are referred to as **photoreceptors**. Both types of photoreceptors detect the level of light by absorbing it via pigments and transmit a signal to other neural layers once a certain amount of light has been absorbed.

Two more layers of cells, the bipolar cells and the ganglion cells, further process neural signals coming from the photoreceptors, concentrating in a thick bundle of neurons called the **optic nerve**, which leads out of the back of the eye and to the brain.

## 4.1.2 Angular Measurements

When speaking about the area of light captured by the eye, the size of an object as seen by the eye, or the speed of eye movement, typical Cartesian distance or velocity measurements aren't ideal. For example, a small cube close to the observer and a larger one further away may take up the same amount of space on the retina. Although the Cartesian sizes of these cubes are useful in many circumstances, it is helpful to have a measure to specify the amount of space they occupy in the visual field. In this regard, we turn to angular measurements.

### 4.1.2.1 Degrees, Minutes, and Seconds

You are probably familiar with **degrees** as a measure of angular distance or length— a unit that represents an arc length of 1/360th of a circle. Objects on the eye, as well as the size of regions on the eye, are often specified in **degrees**—for example, that the size of a person's view of central vision is 5 degrees in the horizontal direction. When a smaller unit is required, the angular measurements of a minute (1/3600th of a circle) or a second (1/216000th of a circle) are used.

Figure 4.3 shows two cubes at a distance from the observer's eye. Notice that although the cubes are different sizes and distances away, they take up the same amount of space on the eye, which is reflected in their labelled angular sizes. To differentiate angular minutes and seconds from the similarly named units of time, they are often referred to as **minutes of arc** and **seconds of arc**. Other angular units such as radians are often used in other fields of study, but degrees of arc are most often used in optics.

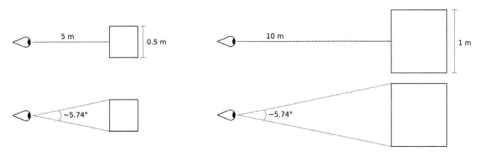

Figure 4.3: Cartesian distances with sizes (top) versus angular units (bottom).

## 4.1.3 Photoreceptors

While both rods and cones detect light by absorbing pigment, they differ in that they are specialized for functioning under different conditions and for absorbing different wavelengths of light. Cones are better suited to seeing in high light conditions (referred to as **scotopic vision**), such as direct sunlight or a well-lit room, while rods are responsible for vision in low light (referred to as **photopic vision**). Rods are not capable of colour vision, which is instead a function of the cones.

Cones and rods are distributed unevenly throughout the retina. Cones are particularly concentrated at the centre of the retina. A small pit in the very centre of the retina, referred to as the **fovea**, contains the most cones of any portion of the eye, of all colours (with the exception of a small region 25 minutes of arc in the central fovea that contains no blue cones). Thus, the light that hits the centre of the eye is received in a higher resolution than any other part of the eye, as the cones in the fovea are much closer together. While the human field of view encompasses a full 220 degrees in the horizontal direction and 135 in the vertical direction, the fovea only captures 2 degrees of that. The portion of the field of view captured by the fovea has an angular resolution of 60 pixels per degree, but at a point just 10 degrees away, this drops to 6 pixels per degree. Figure 4.4 depicts this dramatic difference, demonstrating the importance of our fovea in receiving a clear image.

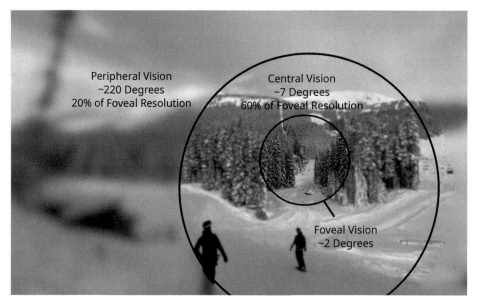

Figure 4.4: Image illustrating resolution of various areas of the visual field.

**Foveated Rendering**

Since the human eye is only capable of seeing a very small portion of the image in a high resolution (that which falls in the fovea), VR developers have realized significant computational efficiency by rendering the portion that falls outside the fovea in a much lower resolution. This technique is referred to as **foveated rendering** and, if implemented correctly, would be indistinguishable from an image rendered completely in high resolutions when viewed by the human eye.

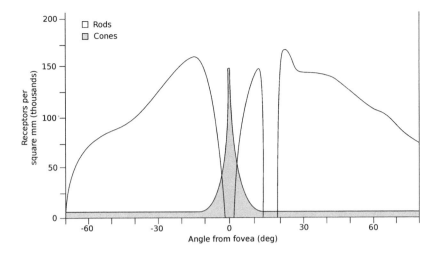

Figure 4.5: Retinal distribution of rods and cones, given as degrees from fovea.

However, in order to achieve foveated rendering in a real-time simulation, a device would have to track the position of the fovea, to keep track of what portion of the image should be rendered in full resolution. As such, foveated rendering is one of the major factors encouraging headset developers to incorporate eye tracking into their HMDs. As the fovea moves at over 180 degrees per second during saccadic eye movement, the tracking of fovea movement must be at least as fast for foveated rendering applications—if not, the image will appear to be blurry.

The reason we interpret the world as being in focus instead of a mostly blurry image (like the one in Figure 4.4) is due to quick involuntary movements of the eye called **saccades**, intended to capture many areas of a scene within the fovea. Just as we see video as a moving picture, and not a series of static images, our brain is able to stitch together the various high-resolution details captured during saccades into one clear image.

As mentioned previously, the fovea is entirely composed of cones. Since cones rely on high light conditions, the high resolution that the fovea allows for is only present in well-lit environments. As the concentration of cones in the eye decreases with distance from the fovea, the concentration of rods increases, as shown in Figure 4.5. Note the blind spot between 13° and 19°—this part of the retina is occupied by the optic nerve, so no photo receptors are present in this area. Rods are also better at greyscale vision, while cones are responsible for seeing vivid colours. Because of this, we rely relatively more on our peripheral vision at night or in dark rooms. Peripheral vision is also better suited for detecting fast motion and is less sensitive to slow motions than the fovea.

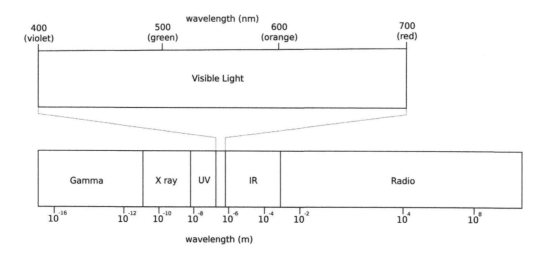

Figure 4.6: Diagram of the electromagnetic spectrum.

**Why is Yellow So "Bright"?**
The yellow portion of the spectrum contains the absolute sensitivity peaks for both the red and green cones of the eye. This means that yellow stimuli can result in a maximal response from all of the red cones in addition to a maximal response from all of the green cones. Because of our high sensitivity to yellow, this colour appears particularly bright and vibrant to us, catching our attention—at least part of the reason we use yellow for caution signs and construction equipment.

### 4.1.4 How Light Works

Light is a form of electromagnetic radiation, and it propagates in the same way as any other electromagnetic wave. The characteristics of this wave determine how the light appears to us. The primary characteristics that impact vision are the wavelength, frequency, and amplitude of the wave, as introduced in the previous chapter of sensation and perception.

The wavelength of a light wave (commonly denoted as $\lambda$) is defined as the distance between two successive peaks of the wave. This wavelength affects the colour and visibility of the wave—the only way any two colours of light appear different from each other is because of their differences in wavelengths. In fact, aside from differences in wavelength, visible light is the same as every other sort of electromagnetic radiation on the spectrum. People are only able to see light with wavelengths between 380 and 760 nanometres (nm). Electromagnetic radiation with wavelengths longer and shorter than range cannot be seen by humans, but functions in much the same way as visible light.

While the wavelength is defined as the distance between two successive peaks of a wave, the period (denoted as $T$) is defined as the time between two successive peaks of a wave. Frequency (denoted as $f$) is the inverse of period—it's a measurement of how many cycles the wave completes per unit of time (most often expressed in Hertz (Hz), cycles per second). The frequency of an electromagnetic wave doesn't change easily—unlike wavelength, which can be changed by passing the light through a medium which slows it down. Frequency and wavelength are related by the speed of the wave—wavelength is equal to the speed of the wave multiplied by the frequency: $\lambda = v \times f$. If the speed of the light is held constant (the light does not move from one medium into another), the frequency and wavelength are proportional. The final attribute of a light wave is the amplitude. The amplitude of a light wave determines how intense the light is. The larger the amplitude of a light wave, the more intense the light is and the brighter it tends to appear if all other factors are equal.

**Applications of Non-Visible Electromagnetic Radiation in VR**
The visual display is not the only component of a VR system that utilizes electromagnetic radiation—other non-visible wavelengths are used within the hardware for communications and tracking.

**Radio waves** are used within VR devices for internet connections or identifying wireless hardware. Common protocols such as Wi-Fi or Bluetooth utilize electromagnetic waves in the radio range in order to pass data between HMDs, computers, and controllers.

**Infrared waves** are used in some headsets for tracking controllers and HMDs. Although humans may not be able to see infrared light, many cameras can. Headsets that use infrared tracking systems will often embed infrared lights into hardware, allowing for a pattern of lights in a known configuration to be tracked by a computer without being visible to the user.

### 4.1.5 Colour

In the natural world, the perceived colour of an object is determined primarily by the wavelengths of visible light that object reflects or emits. Light is emitted by light sources, such as light bulbs, the sun, or digital displays, but non-source objects can also be seen due to light from sources reflecting off of them. Different objects reflect some wavelengths and absorb others—only the reflected wavelengths are received by the retina and perceived as colour. Different angles of viewing an object may result in different wavelengths being captured by the eye, explaining why the colour of water may look different when viewed from the shore than it does when looking down into it from a boat or why iridescent objects (like bubbles or oil slicks in parking lots) appear to change colour as you move.

When using a VR display, the vast majority of light seen by the user is being directly emitted by the display. As human sensory systems cannot differentiate between

Figure 4.7: These infrared lights on the Oculus Rift headset and controllers show up on tracking cameras, but are not visible to the user.

emitted and reflected light, the user of a VR HMD perceives the emitted light the same way they would perceive identical reflected light from a physical environment.

The wavelength of light received influences only one characteristic of the perceived colour—its **hue**. Hue is only one of the dimensions describing the psychological characteristics of colour, the other two being **brightness** and **saturation**.

The perceived **brightness** of a colour is strongly correlated with the intensity of the light. With all other variables held constant, brighter colours are perceived when the amplitude of the light wave is greater.

**Saturation** can be described from an observer's standpoint as how much "white" appears to be part of a colour—colours with high saturation are more vibrant, lacking white tones, while an unsaturated colour is closer to pure white. For example, red would be a more saturated colour than pink. From a physics perspective, a colour appears less saturated the more wavelengths it is made up of—multiple wavelengths combine to make whiter colours, while a single wavelength is as saturated as a colour can get.

As discussed in the section on eye anatomy, detecting colour is primarily the responsibility of the cones. Three different cone types detect light from three

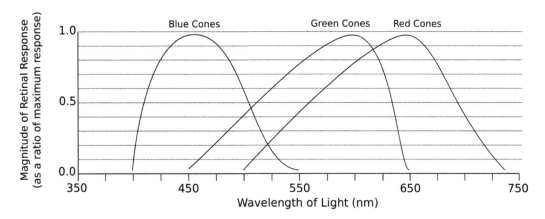

Figure 4.8: A graph showing the range and magnitude of response for each type of cone.

overlapping sections of the electromagnetic spectrum—previously, we have referred to these as red, blue, and green sensitive cones. These cone types are referred to as short-wavelength sensitive cones (also called S-Cones or blue sensitive cones), medium-wavelength sensitive cones (M-Cones or green sensitive cones), and long-wavelength sensitive cones (L-Cones or red sensitive cones). Each type of cone responds to a different range of electromagnetic radiation wavelengths with different magnitudes: the function describing this response is shown in Figure 4.8.

Despite having different peaks, the wavelengths able to activate the cones overlap significantly. Mutations in the genes responsible for cones can cause alterations of the distributions of light that each cone is able to detect, changing the range of light we consider to be one colour. Because of the similarity between the red and green light distributions, mutations that affect either of these cones can make it difficult to distinguish between these two colours in particular—this is why red–green colour blindness is so common.

Note that signals from cones only correspond to three ranges of wavelengths—as such, differences in any colours we perceive are due to different combinations of the strength of these three signals. Colours such as orange and purple are perceived when signals from cones responding to different portions of the spectrum respond simultaneously. The limitations of seeing colours as a combination of only three cone types are not shared by all organisms—many animals have more variety in cones than us (including a species of mantis shrimp that has 12 different types of photoreceptors).

### 4.1.5.1 Designing with Colour Vision Defects in Mind

The term "colour-blindness" is often colloquially used to refer to any number of conditions where a subset of a person's cones is non-functional, restricting their ability to discriminate between light of some or all wavelengths. Different forms of colour blindness are the result of different cones being affected.

Two forms of colour blindness make it impossible for users to discriminate between any colours. The first occurs when a person lacks any functioning cones—called **rod monochromacy** or **achromatopsia**; all vision is performed via the rods, which also makes it uncomfortable and difficult to see during high light conditions. The second form of total colour blindness occurs when only one type of cone is able to function. Referred to as **cone monochromacy**, a person with only one functioning type of cone is unable to distinguish between different colours. Unlike rod monochromacy, people who have cone monochromacy are able to see comfortably in both photopic and scotopic conditions. Both conditions are relatively uncommon—rod monochromacy affects less than 0.004% of the population. Individual cone monochromacies are even less common, with blue cone monochromacy occurring in only 1 in 100,000 people and only a handful of cases of red cone and green cone monochromacy ever having been identified.

**Dichromatic colour vision** occurs when only one form of cone is non-functioning: in this case, only a specific portion of the light spectrum cannot be perceived. **Tritanopia** occurs when blue cones are non-functioning, making it particularly difficult to discriminate between colours that differ by the amount of blue light present. This is often referred to as blue-yellow colour blindness, but this name doesn't refer to blue and yellow being easily confused. Those with tritanopia find it more difficult to discriminate between light blue and grey, dark purple and black, mid-greens with blues, and oranges with red.

The condition where red cones are non-functioning is called **protanopia**, and the condition where green cones are non-functioning is referred to as **deuteranopia**. Due to the overlap between the wavelengths perceived by red cones and the wavelengths perceived by green cones, both protanopes and deuteranopes have difficulty with discriminating between many of the same sets of colours. Both deuteranopia and protanopia are referred to as red/green colour blindness, which refers to the section (red/green) of the light spectrum that isn't perceived in both cases. Protanopes and deuteranopes both have difficulty discriminating between pale shades of colours, between browns, oranges, reds, and greens, as well as some blues with purples.

There are also many variations of the above conditions where a type of cone has a reduced or altered sensitivity to light as opposed to being completely non-functioning. This is referred to as **anomalous trichromacy** and, like dichromatic vision, can be categorized into three types based on the cone that detection is altered for: **tritanomaly**, **deuteranomaly**, and **protanomaly**. The effects of these anomalies on vision ranges from near-typical trichromatic colour vision to the associated form of dichromacy.

Worldwide, 8% of men and 0.5% of women suffer from colour vision deficiencies of some sort, with half of those having a mild anomalous deficiency (for colour blindness to manifest genetically, both x chromosomes must contain the gene for colour blindness—as men only have one x chromosome, it is much more common in men). Over half of men with abnormal colour vision are deuteranomalous, with the rest being almost evenly split among protanopes, deuteranopes, and protanomalous, respectively.

One of the best ways to avoid creating usability problems for the colour-blind subset of users is to avoid using colour cues for essential discrimination tasks. Using other cues, such as shape and size, allows for other methods of discrimination. However, colour is particularly good for discrimination tasks for small objects. It's faster to group objects by colour rather than shape if the objects are small and numerous; thus there are many cases where it may still be desired to use colour for discrimination tasks.

Another solution that allows developers to still leverage the usefulness of colour grouping and discrimination is to use colours that are unaffected by colour blindness. Greyscale hues can be discriminated between by all types of colour vision, and resources for many other palettes that work with all colour vision defects can be found elsewhere.

### 4.1.5.2 *Quantifying Colour*

There are many models that exist for numerically specifying colours. A common model, often used when working with monitors or digital displays, is the **RGB colour model**, which specifies a range of colours based on how much red, green, and blue they contain, respectively. This is an additive colour model—much like in nature, adding pure red, green, and blue tones together will create a colour perceived as white. Each of the three colours can range from 0% (no component of that colour) to 100% (the brightest saturated component of that colour).

This is the **CIE standardized RGB model**—CIE uses imaginary colours to mathematically define a triangular colour gamut. Because the cones respond to a range of light rather than a single pure tone, a triangle between three pure tones serves as an approximation of the full collection of colours we can see and a reflection of how colour is produced on computer monitors: as combinations of three pure colours. Because of this, there are colours we can see outside of the triangle that cannot be represented in this model and cannot be displayed by computer monitors using current technologies. Colour perception being relative, however, this does not serve as a significant problem for computer monitors and our use of them

We can specify any colour with a triplet of values, with the first number in the triplet giving the red value, the second the green, and the third the blue. For example, (100%, 0%, 0%) would give a pure red tone and (0%, 100%, 100%) would give a vibrant yellow—the mixture of green and blue. However, on a computer, the range of colours isn't continuous—they're discrete, based on the amount of colours the system allows. For example, most computers allow a value to be specified from 0 to 255 (the greatest integer that can be represented with a singe byte) for each colour. Each increase by 1 will increment the value of the colour—this allows for 16,581,375 separate colours to be displayed on the monitor, as a combination of three channels (red, green, and blue) will result in a unique colour ($256 \times 256 \times 256 = 16,581,375$). The range of colours allowed is often specified by the **bit depth** of an image, which gives the number of colours for each channel as a power of 2—in this case $2^8 = 255$, so

Figure 4.9: Two images with different bit depths.

the system specified above has an 8-bit colour depth. Figure 4.9 shows how a higher bit depth allows for colours that are closer to the continuous colour spectrum seen in the real world.

Objects in the physical world can reflect a continuous range of colour values, as opposed to the discrete values of colour displayed on a monitor. Despite the fact that there are technically infinite colour variations present in the real world, we aren't capable of perceiving an infinite amount of different colours.

If two colours are similar enough, we perceive them as identical. The **just noticeable difference** (JND), discussed near the end of Chapter 3, is a metric that defines how different two stimuli have to be for a person to be able to discriminate between them. For colours, the relationship between colour increments on an RGB scale and the JND between colours is non-linear. Figure 4.10 shows the non-linearity of JND in the RGB colour space. Colours we see as green are more similar for a given area on the gamut, compared to colours we might label as purple.

The **CIE L\*a\*b\* colour space** is an alternative colour model designed to have the distances between colours on the scale correspond to the "distance" humans perceive between two colours. Like the RGB model, L\*a\*b\* colours are specified by three values. The first value, lightness (L), ranges from a value of 0 for black to a value of 100 for white. The second value, (a), gives a value that specifies where the colour lies between red and green. If the "a" value is negative, it is more green, and if it is positive, it leans more towards red. The final component, the b value, specifies where the colour lies between blue and yellow. The negative b values give more blue tones, while the positive tones are more yellow. Often, computers will specify a and b ranges as being between $-128$ and $+127$.

The L\*a\*b\* colour scales are non-linear—the location of colours in the L\*a\*b\* space has larger or smaller distances between two colours depending on the area of the space than an RGB space would have. Figure 4.11 illustrates the difference in how colours are laid out in CIE RBG and L\*a\*b\* spaces.

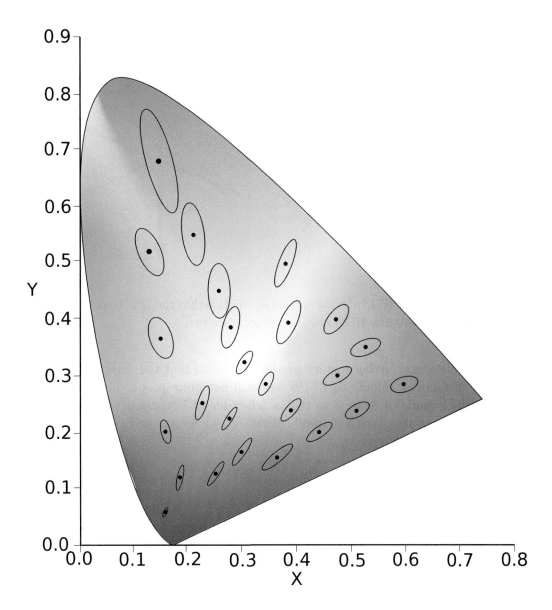

Figure 4.10: Equal JND colour ellipses. Notice the non-linearity of ellipses in space.

The non-linear way in which colours are laid out in the L\*a\*b\* space was chosen to be a rough analogue to the way people perceive colours. L\*a\*b\* space was defined with the goal that the distance between colours in the colour space would be proportional to the difference perceived between them. Initially, the distance between two colours in the 3D L\*a\*b\* space, denoted as $\Delta E$ (Delta E), was intended to be equal to 1 when two colours were separated by the JND.

$$\Delta E = \sqrt{(L_2 - L_1)^2 + (a_2 - a_1)^2 + (b_2 - b_1)^2} \qquad (4.1)$$

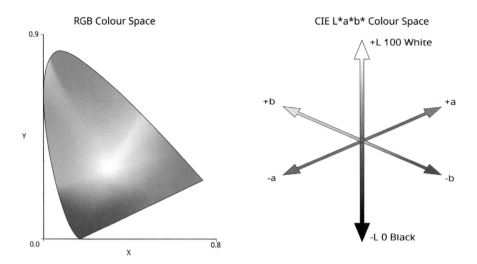

Figure 4.11: RGB and CIE L*a*b colour spaces—notice that the L*a*b space occupies three dimensions, while the RGB space only occupies two.

Despite this effort, further inquiry by the CIE found that the mapping from the perceptual distance of colours to L*a*b was still not quite proportional, and they updated their formula to make it so that a $\Delta E$ value of 1 represents the JND. The latest formula, known as **Delta E 2000** (dE2000), has become an industry standard for calculating colour differences.

### 4.1.5.3 Display Colour Capabilities

There are myriad colour display technologies available today, with varying specifics in terms of the rate at which the colours can refresh at, the amount of pixels present in the display, and the resolution. To describe a display's efficacy in terms of the sensory range for human colour vision, two parameters must be considered: the total *range* of the display and the *quantization* of that range. The quantization value of a colour display is given by its bit depth. As colour in the real world is continuous, many may first assume that for a display to match this, it must have infinite bit depth. However, the human perception of colour is not infinite—as discussed previously, a user will only see two colours as different if the difference between the two is greater than the JND. Thus, if the difference between each level of quantization is less than the JND, this will be perceived the same as the truly continuous colour would be.

Provided that the JND for various portions of the colour space is known, the colour depth required for a first-order colour display can be estimated. For the sake of brevity, this colour depth estimate used here is carried out using the RGB model (which is not ideal) and involves two false assumptions. The first assumption is that the discrete steps a colour will be divided by will be even, and the second assumption being that each channel, red, green, and blue, will be given the same bit depth. This is suitable for the sake of estimation, but a more accurate calculation of required colour depth would differ depending on what channel is being quantized, would have uneven quantization, and would have to use a colour model that more closely maps to how colours are perceived by people.

The smallest MacAdam's Ellipse for any colour is for deep bluish hues. Its semi-minor axis is 0.01 on the red scale, which implies that 100 levels are required on the red axis to recreate all colours noticeable to the human eye. This could be accomplished with a 7-bit colour depth ($2^7 = 128$), so existing displays with an 8-bit colour depth have more than enough quantization to simulate every perceivable colour, if it is assumed quantization is the same on the green and blue axes.

The other aspect of a display's range efficacy is the total range of display. This matter is a bit more complicated to simulate—although computer displays can generate light in many of the wavelengths people are capable of seeing, they aren't able to generate all of them. However, there is a standard measure for quantifying what colours a display can show: the colour gamut.

### 4.1.5.4   The Colour Gamut

The range of colours that a particular display is capable of emitting is referred to as that device's **gamut**. Although different devices support different gamuts, none of them support the full spectrum of colours visible to humans. This is also why a printed image may appear to be a different colour than when viewed on a screen—the pigments used by the printer absorb different wavelengths than the digital display emits; thus the display and the printer have different gamuts. Figure 4.12 shows the distribution of two different colour spectra able to be generated via displays, overlaid on the distribution humans are capable of seeing [1]. In order to ensure the colours being simulated are perceived to match their real counterparts appropriately, developers can take two approaches—limit an experience to the colours supported on a particular display or use clever tricks to make the mind perceive colours that aren't there.

### 4.1.5.5   Colour Constancy

While light may have absolute values in terms of its wavelengths and amplitude, the colour a person sees when that light hits their retina is a perceptual interpretation. Although colour is primarily influenced by the attributes of the light that produces it, other factors, such as competing stimuli, can change how it is perceived.

Several optical illusions demonstrate that the way colour perception functions is entirely separate from its sensation. For example, all five papers shown in both the images of Figure 4.13 are the same colour in both images, but appear to be different due to altered lighting conditions: the sheet that appears pink in the image on the left seems grey in the right image. This is due to a perceptual phenomenon known as **colour constancy**. Colour constancy results in the mind interpreting a colour as

---

[1]Note that, as this image is limited by the colour gamut of the printer this book was printed from, the full human vision colour space does not actually show all colours, but is merely scaled to show the proportion of colours these gamuts cannot produce.

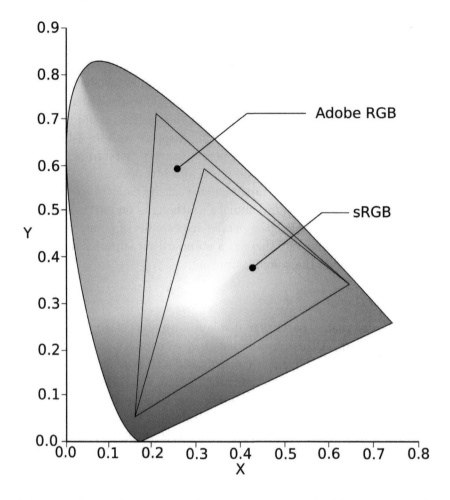

Figure 4.12: The image shows two colour gamuts supported by monitors, the sRGB and Adobe RGB gamuts, overlaid on the total colour space.

constant, regardless of the change in lighting around it—it's why a red pen is still perceived as "red" when in low lighting conditions. This means we adjust what we feel the colour of an object is based on the background, which is why the papers appear to be different colours.

Colour constancy is an important mechanism to help people identify objects regardless of lighting conditions, but can also be used to alter the perception of colours for simulation purposes.

For example, imagine a headset that is capable of displaying the full gamut of colours visible by humans, but only in the fovea of the user—the peripheral area of the headset has a reduced gamut. Of course, wherever the user is looking directly will appear to have the correct colour, but the peripheral vision will be slightly different, appearing, say, a bit darker. However, if the scene followed a pattern like the checker-board above, the brain would interpret colours in the fovea and peripheral the same as long as the difference between the fovea set of colours and the peripheral set of

Figure 4.13: Two images with papers altered to have identical RGB values, illustrating colour constancy. (*Mike Young, open source*)

colours can be explained by some lighting condition—say, that the portion of the checker board in the fovea is always lit by a spotlight. Although this scenario is unlikely to be encountered in an actual implementation, it does show how the mind can accept two different colours as being "the same" due to colour constancy effects.

One limitation of colour constancy is that it is only in effect if the user has seen the original colour at some point in time—someone won't interpret an object as another colour due to constancy if they haven't seen the desired colour first. However, the "correctly coloured" image doesn't necessarily need to be presented to the user if they know from experience what the correct colour should be.

The second requirement for colour constancy to take effect is that the source of luminance for the object must have several different wavelengths. Colour constancy occurs due to the brain discounting the wavelength of the source of illumination or shadow to try and correct the colour of the object, and a large range of wavelengths is required for this interpretation to result in the illusion.

### 4.1.5.6  Colour Context Effects

Another reason the mind misinterprets colour is due to the colours of surrounding objects. A colour is perceived as being lighter than it actually is when it is surrounded by darker colours. Likewise, the same colour is perceived to be darker if the objects around it are made lighter. Colour context will influence the perception of every colour in an image as long as there are other colours present. On a desktop computer, the same image may be perceived as having slightly different colouration by two different users, solely due to the colours of background stimuli in the room surrounding their computer monitors. In a VR HMD, background stimuli are blocked, but the combination of colours that make up a virtual environment will determine the context effects that influence how each is perceived. Even colours on a black or white background are perceived differently than pure colour would be due to context.

The case where the HMD is being used to display one pure colour may be the closest condition for a user to experience a colour free of any constancy effects, but even in this case, temporal context can affect the perceived colour. **Chromatic adaptation** is the process by which long-term exposure to a specific colour of stimuli affects the perception of other stimuli. If someone is constantly exposed to a colour, then after the removal of that stimulus, other colours will lack elements of that colour—for example, if a person was exposed to a green tint for a sufficient duration, upon removing the filter the world may seem less green, possibly due to the temporary bleaching of green pigment in cones. This bleaching also causes an inverse afterimage to be seen when the fatigue is localized

Intenisty will also affect the perceived hue of a colour. If red or yellow-green colours are increased in intensity, they appear to take on a more yellow hue. Similarly, blue-green and violet are perceived as more blue when intensity is increased. This phenomenon is known as the Bezold-Brucke effect.

### 4.1.5.7    *What Sensorimotor Contingencies Affect The Perception of Colour?*

Colours are much more likely to be affected by changes to the environment than by changes in the user's view of it. Choosing how objects react graphically to being in shadow or being viewed through a transparent object of another colour can affect how a user interprets their function. In traditional desktop games, objects that are part of the "game environment" are often shaded following the the laws of physics, while objects that are part of the interface are shaded in a flat tone, regardless of changes in the outside environment—a common feature of heads-up displays (HUDS). In VR, every object or interface component appears to be part of a spatial environment, but colour and shading can be a good way to specify what is part of the "game environment" and what is not. For example, text indicating where a user should go within an environment can be left unshaded in order to emphasize that it's an interface component and should not be considered part of the game environment—it won't appear to be in its proper "place" from the user's perspective.

Colour, as a sensory input, is very influential in making a scene appear realistic. Even though there's no sensorimotor contingency that breaks when users see a colour in the game environment that's clearly poorly shaded, this can influence how "real" they feel an environment is on a higher cognitive level. Further, visual inputs such as perspective do depend heavily on colour and shadow to properly respond to sensorimotor contingencies. The role of colour and shadow in providing a sense of 3D space is discussed further in Chapter 6.

Luminance of a scene affects the colour discrimination ability of the user. In conditions with low light (scotopic vision), users may have much more difficulty in colour discrimination tasks than if they were in photopic conditions. Although scotopic conditions may be due to lighting choices in the virtual environment, they can also be influenced by screen brightness, which can vary across platforms or across users on the same platform if the brightness is user adjustable. As such, it can be helpful to test applications where colour discrimination is essential on several different platforms, and provide metrics to allow users to calibrate their brightness to a uniform level if needed. One of the simplest ways to achieve this calibration is to ask a user to lower their brightness from the maximum level until a reference stimuli can no longer be seen. The opposite approach, increasing screen brightness until a stimulus can be seen, will also work.

---

**Colour Perception and Age**

Mutations in the genes responsible for the cone detection spectra can cause people to interpret colours differently, but other biological factors can impact how colours are perceived—like age. As people get older, they tend to see everything with more of a yellow tint. The lens always has a slight yellow tint, and this increases with age. The effect of this is that some of the blue light entering the pupil is filtered out, and so blue tones are less pronounced. This leads to a few interesting interaction considerations when choosing colours for older user bases. Keep in mind that an older and a younger person may consider different objects as blue (although the difference in blue light received is subtle, the distinction can manifest itself in colours that are "partially" blue, like teal). If you need to refer to specific interface elements by colour and know your population consists of users of a wide age range, lean towards red or green colours. You could also design applications specifically for older people, boosting a constant blue shift across the graphics in order to compensate for the filtering done by the lens. By doing this, colours can be displayed to older populations as intended by the developer, resulting in an image that appears to have the same colour balance as the user would have seen when they were much younger.

---

## 4.1.6 Light Intensity

The way that light intensity is measured is different for light coming from a source, light interacting with an object, and the light that reaches the retina.

The amount of light emitted by a light source is referred to as the **radiance**. The SI unit for radiance is lumens, which is actually a measurement of the amount of visible light being emitted per second. A typical light bulb may give off 450 lumens, while the sun gives off close to 36 octillion lumens. As the radiance of a light source is a function of a total amount of light given off per second, it doesn't specify the direction or impact of the light. Despite the sun having such a high radiance value, the amount of light that enters a room through a window doesn't make the room much "brighter" than a 450 lumen bulb. The amount of light that falls on an area is called the **illuminance**, and it is measured in $lumens/m^2$, called lux. Many factors impact the illuminance of a surface lit by a single source aside from the source's radiance: the amount of light from the source directed towards the surface, the distance of the surface from the source (energy is lost as light travels over a distance), and the material the light passes through all affect illuminance. A specific quantity of particular interest to VR developers is retinal illuminance, illuminance measured on the retina.

Similar to illuminance, the amount of light that is reflected from a surface is referred to as the **luminance** of that surface—luminance is also measured in lux. A quantity called reflectance is also sometimes used, which is a simple percentage of the luminance of a surface over the illuminance.

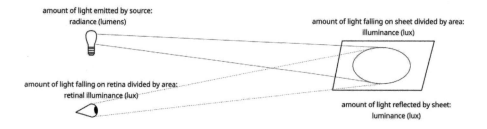

Figure 4.14: A diagram showing what quantities various intensity units measure.

### 4.1.7   Intensity and Brightness

Brightness was previously discussed as a synonym for perceived intensity. The word "brightness" was also used to refer to a quantity of colour describing how "white" a colour is, although this is a separate concept, and the term "lightness" will be used for this context going forward. Brightness is related to intensity—as the intensity (or amplitude) of a light wave increases, how bright someone considers it to be also tends to increase. However, many other factors affect how bright light appears to be. Brightness has been found to also be influenced by the wavelength of the light, the area of the retina the light hits, and if the user's vision is currently adapted to photopic or scotopic conditions.

Brightness perceived by the user is not directly proportional with the intensity of light. Brightness is given in terms of **brill**, a logarithmic measure above the light threshold, not unlike dB. One brill is 0.01 log units above the light threshold, in the same way that one dB is 0.01 log units above the audio threshold.

As shown in Figure 4.15, the relation between intensity and brightness is roughly logarithmic. This relationship can be approximated with the direct scaling technique, where apparent brightness is considered to grow as the cube root of physical intensity. In this case, for a light to seem twice as bright, its intensity must be increased to the square of the current intensity value. For a stage with eight lights to be made to seem twice as bright, 64 lights would be required.

Humans are capable of seeing a very wide range of intensity values. The highest intensity detectable by the eye is 10 billion times as intense as the lowest value that can be detected. However, like many sensations, the perception of the brightness of light is relative to the amount of light that the eye has adapted to. People are only capable of ascertaining differences between two intensities with a ratio of around 1/64, the threshold ratio. This minimum noticeable change increases with the intensity of the light being compared—the brighter the light is, the bigger the difference between the intensity has to be in order to be detectable (following Weber's law).

Figure 4.15: Curve depicting the roughly logarithmic relationship between apparent brightness and intensity.

However, for the VR developer, the fact that the level of intensity perceived is relative can allow a wider range of intensities to be perceived than a display may allow. To have a light interpreted as a specific intensity, the developer has to achieve the desired intensity ratio between the target stimulus and the adaptation (or prior) stimulus. Therefore, although it's possible to describe a display in terms of the maximum intensity it can output, this is a less useful metric for perceptual purposes than the intensity difference the display is capable of. Just as a person perceives a relatively sunny day as extremely bright after exiting a matinee in a dark theatre, a developer can slowly reduce the intensity of ambient light in a VR simulation to make a moderately bright light seem particularly intense.

Adapting to light takes longer than may be practical for constant readjustments of the user's "base" light level—adjusting to a very dark intensity after being exposed to a bright one can take over 20 minutes. It takes longer to adjust the threshold to the new light level the further away the initial light level is from the final light level. When separated by one order of magnitude, it could take as little as 5 minutes for the eye to adjust to around the threshold value, but for 5 orders of magnitude difference, it could take as much as 30 minutes for the threshold value to adjust.

The retinal locus also affects how bright objects appear to be. Due to the higher sensitivity of rods to brightness, objects in the periphery of the eye (where there is a higher concentration of rods) appear brighter than objects in the fovea. Certain wavelengths are also perceived as brighter than others. Light in the medium wavelengths, where receptors are more sensitive, will usually appear brighter than light in the low wavelengths and the high wavelengths. This is why blue light (low wavelength) is generally perceived as less bright than yellow light (medium wavelength) of the same intensity. Cones and rods have different sensitivity peaks, so what wavelengths appear brightest at a fixed intensity depends on whether conditions are photopic or scotopic. These two sensitivity distributions are shown in Figure 4.16.

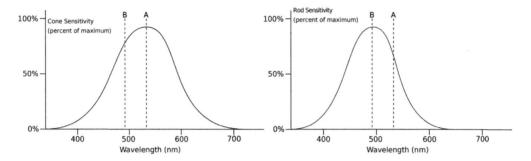

Figure 4.16: Two curves showing the sensitivity to wavelengths under both photopic and scotopic conditions. (diagram from sensation and perception).

### 4.1.7.1 Effects of Sensorimotor Contingencies on Perceived Intensity

There are several sensorimotor contingencies that can affect the intensity of light a person receives. However, since the intensity simulated by an electronic display is received in the same way that light from the outside environment is received, and because of the passive nature of visual sensory input, developers rarely have to accommodate for sensorimotor factors when determining intensity outputs.

There is one sensorimotor contingency that drops the user's received intensity to near zero—closing the eyes. Of course, with a HMD on, the user closing the eyes has the same result as closing their eyes in the physical world.

In a physical space, the intensity of a light source decreases with distance. In a computer simulation, rendering calculations use well-defined equations to determine the appropriate intensity fall-off.

When calculating the amount of intensity that a display needs to deliver to simulate a light source, both the user's virtual distance from the object and their physical distance from the display must be considered. Consider the simulation of a simple point source light. The fall-off of intensity with distance for a simple point source is given as $I_1/I_2 = d_1^2/d_2^2$ where $I_1$ is the intensity of the light source at distance $d_1$ from the observer and $I_2$ is the intensity of the light source at distance $d_2$.

To calculate the required intensity of a light at a distance, it is necessary to determine the radiance, or intensity, at the source. Radiance, measured in lumens, is the same regardless of distance from a source—it's related only to the energy the light emits—although it is directly proportional to intensity. Lumens quantify the amount of visible light available in a volume.

Illuminance is the measure of the amount of lumens that hit a unit of area. The measure of the amount of lumens per square metre is given in lux. Illuminance is the measure of intensity—it follows the inverse square law given above. As illuminance is a measure of flux per square metre, the value of illuminance three metres away from an object is lower than it is one metre away—the total flux is spread over a larger area. For a point source,

$$\text{lux} = \text{lumens}/(4 \times \pi \times d) \tag{4.2}$$

Below are listed the luminous flux values of several common light sources in Figure 4.17. When simulating one of these sources, the value of illuminance that the user should receive is determined. Following this, the luminous flux required from the display to result in the same imminence is calculated. Sources that are screen like have been given in lumens per square metre, which is actually lux, but multiplying by the surface area of the screen will result in a radiance value. For reference, a screen-like source has to have a value of 1000 lux to be readable in sunlight.

| Light Source | Luminous Flux |
|---|---|
| Movie Theatre Screen | 50 lumens per square metre |
| Cathode Ray TV | 100 lumens per square metre |
| Computer Monitor | 200–600 lumens per square metre |
| Light Bulb | 1700 lumens |
| Florescent Light | 1600–4000 lumens |
| Car Headlights | 2000–4000 lumens |

Figure 4.17: Typical radiance values for several common light sources.

For example, let's assume you want to simulate an open sign for a diner, and you know that this sign gives off a total of 500 lumens. If we assume the user of the headset is 5 metres away from the virtual sign, we can calculate the illuminance that the user would see. Assuming the sign can be approximated as a point source,

$$\frac{500 \text{ lumens}}{(4 \times \pi \times 5 \text{ metres})} \approx 8 \text{ lux} \tag{4.3}$$

In actuality, the only light the user is really seeing is that emitted from the HMD they are wearing. Assuming we can adjust the radiance for an area of the display, we would need to set the radiance so that it matches the illuminance value of 8 lumens. Assuming the display is a reasonable 3 cm from the user's face, we can calculate the required radiance as

$$8 \text{ lux} \times (4 \times \pi \times 0.03 \text{ metres}) \approx 3 \text{ lumens} \tag{4.4}$$

Notice that the value of radiance from the display is significantly lower than the value of radiance from the sign that we are simulating. Due to the inverse square law, any stimulated object will have a much lower illuminance as we get a moderate distance away from it. However, if the user gets closer to the light source, the illuminance increases—potentially to the point that the display may not be able to simulate the required illuminance. If we have a display with a low radiance value, we can still accurately support the simulation of sources with high radiance values, as long as the user does not get close to them.

### 4.1.8  Visual Detection of Movement

Movement, when discussed relative to the eyes, refers to the motion of any object in the visual field. This movement can come from one of two sources—an object is moving relative to the viewer (referred to as **object relative motion**), or the viewer's eye is moving relative to the object (**subject relative motion**). In fact, if no other cues were present to aid in the perception of motion (such as vestibular feelings of acceleration felt during subject relative motion), it is possible for the movement of a viewer relative to an object and an object relative to a viewer would look identical.

For example, imagine you are on a passenger train, waiting to leave the station, with another train directly blocking your view out the window. If the train you are in starts moving forwards, your view of the other train out the window would change, letting you see train cars closer to the front. However, if your train was standing still, but the train outside your window started moving backwards, the motion you would see out the window would be the exact same as when your train was moving forwards. This example shows that changes in the visual field due to the motion of the user as well as due to the motion of objects in the field can be treated in the same way. Users have higher object relative motion sensitivity than subject relative, for all but very short intervals. We may use examples in this section that apply to one or the other, but unless it is explicitly mentioned, the following principles apply to both types of motion.

Since motion of objects relative to the user and motion of the user relative to other objects can look identical, sometimes people get confused and assume the wrong object is moving. **Induced motion** is the perceptual error that occurs when the motion of one object is falsely perceived as the motion of a different object. For example, a chequered floor moving relative to a stationary chair may actually be interpreted by users as the chair moving instead for two reasons—in part due to the expectation that floors don't often move, and due to the expectation that smaller objects are more likely to move than larger surrounding stimuli.

The feeling of self-motion is referred to as **vection**. Vection can also occur via non-visual senses (like touching a moving wall can make you feel haptic vection or a moving sound can cause auditory vection). Vection occurs most often when people actually are moving, but can also mistakenly occur when the "background" is moving. The background, for the purposes of vection, consists of the visual stimuli that the subject is not consciously focused on. In particular, vection is more likely to occur when large stimuli are moving, and particularly within peripheral vision. Vection can be reduced by providing cues to signal to the user that it is the background environment, and not them, that is moving.

## Why Do VR Menus Scroll Horizontally?

When commercial VR started gaining more popularity in the 2010s, many early designers used existing web interface patterns for virtual interfaces. On the desktop, most websites are designed to scroll vertically. However, vertical scrolling had an unintended side effect when transferred to virtual reality—vection. While scrolling on the desktop, it's easy to see the background outside of the computer. In a virtual environment, however, the menu can be the entire background—thus, when a user scrolled down a page, they may have felt as if they were falling. This unwanted vection not only made users seem like they were moving whenever they'd scroll a menu, but it could also cause VR sickness.

To mitigate this, two features became commonplace in VR menus. First, menus were made to scroll horizontally, which reduced nausea. Vertical movement without accompanying sensations of acceleration tends to be more likely to induce nausea than horizontal movement without acceleration, so switching to horizontal scrolling alone did a lot to combat VR sickness.

Further, the scrolling of menus was changed from continuous to discrete. As most of the motion people experience is continuous, scrolling through a menu in a smooth, continuous, motion made it easy to interpret this as motion of the user, instead of from the menu. Discrete motion, having a menu suddenly "swipe" to the next page, was unlike what the brain typically interpreted as movement, while accomplishing the same task. Further, switching to discrete movement for menus was easier for those that used pointer-based systems, as continuous 2D control takes more effort from the user in VR. The combined strategy of horizontal menus with discrete scrolling to combine vection was a big part of establishing the standard for VR menus seen today.

### 4.1.8.1 Frame Rate

VR can be considered a form of *apparent motion*, the perception of visual movement when none actually occurs. The interpretation of film as a moving picture is a form of apparent motion—no actual movement is occurring; different pictures are simply being shown at different times.

Fundamentally, movies are really just a series of still images shown in quick succession—the speed at which the images are switched is the *frame rate*. 24 frames per second (fps) is the standard for film, and animations can often have frame rates as low as 12 fps. Humans perceive video at less than 12 fps as individual frames instead of fluid motion, and in general, a higher frame rate results in smoother perception of motion, until around 60 fps, past which humans typically don't see much improvement in the perception of smoothness. Smoothness is not the only criteria, however, and higher frame rates can produce improved feelings of responsiveness of a system. In VR, an additional factor is important to consider: VR devices using frame rates less than 90 FPS can result in nausea, disorientation, and headaches. Referred to as

VR *sickness*, the disorientation implies that for binocular vision, without any visual connection to the outside world, much higher frame rates are required to process surroundings as the real world. Although not the only reason, virtual reality sickness may have been partially responsible for the lack of interest in consumer VR in the early 1990s. Technology at the time didn't support the frame rates necessary to avoid VR sickness—for example, the Nintendo Virtual Boy was only capable of 50 fps.

A similar concept to frame rate is the **refresh rate**, which is a hardware-limited measure of how many times per second a monitor is able to refresh the display. Below certain frame and refresh rates, visible errors in the rendering of motion may be apparent. One such error occurs when the eye is trying to track a moving object in VR. As the eye is following the object as it moves, the object should appear stationary. However, due to frame rate being discrete, the object appears to "vibrate" or move choppily. This particular effect is known as **judder**.

Judder can be reduced by increasing the frame rate, as this makes the motion of the object closer to continuous. As the jumps in time between frames are smaller, the shaking of the object is reduced.

In order to avoid judder completely, the frame rate of the display must be sufficiently high to ensure that moving objects do not jump any pixels. As real motion is continuous, it is a discontinuous jump over pixels at low frame rates that causes judder and contributes to VR sickness.

For example, say our eyes are following a single-pixel wide object moving at 30 degrees per second. We can determine the number of pixels it will cross in a second given the angular pixel density of the display. If the display boasts 80 pixels per degree, the object will move 2400 pixels in a second. If we want the object to avoid any discontinuous jumps in pixels, we'd have to refresh the display at 2400 Hz for the motion to avoid skipping any pixels. Since sacaddes are even faster than this (up to 180 degrees per second), even faster refresh rates may be needed before simulated motion is indistinguishable from reality.

Notice that as the resolution of the display goes up, the required refresh rate to ensure no discontinuities goes up as well.

Another visual error in display motion perception occurs due to how the eye adapts to an image. After a frame leaves the display, the image persists on the retina for a short duration afterwards. If a new image is displayed while the previous image still persists, the user may perceive two copies of the same image—this phenomenon is referred to as **strobing**.

Strobing can be reduced by showing each image for a shorter amount of time. If the display is lit for only a portion of the frame, the image will not persist on the retina for as long. Screens that take this approach are referred to as **low-persistence displays**.

## 4.2 RESOLUTION

### 4.2.1 Using Angular Resolution

When determining what specifications are necessary for a visual display, a good starting point is to understand what the resolution specifications are for the human eye.

Many resolution measurements are given in pixels. For example, a video that is 720p is 1280 × 720 pixels. To get the spatial pixel density, in pixels per inch (PPI), we divide the pixel count by the area of the screen. Most often, "pixels per inch" is used as the spatial pixel density. For a $64^1/_2$ inch TV (note that this is the diagonal measurement—the TV is 57 in by $32^{11}/_{16}$ in) with a resolution of 720p, the pixel density is given as

$$\frac{1280\text{px} \times 720\text{px}}{57\text{in} \times 32.7\text{in}} \approx 48 \text{ pixels per inch}$$

Resolution isn't the only factor that determines the acuity of a screen. Our distance from a screen also influences how detailed an image looks on it. If we get closer to a screen, the pixels each take up a larger portion of our vision—similarly, the further we get from a screen, the more pixels there are in the same area of our vision. It's both absolute pixel size (which can be derived from pixel density, assuming all pixels are the same size) and our distance from the screen that determine how many pixels take up a portion of our visual field—a quantity we can measure as pixels per degree. Pixels per degree (PPD), the units of angular pixel density, can be determined by first finding the spatial pixel density in pixels per inch (PPI) and then adjusting for the observer's distance from the screen. Angular pixel density is given as

$$\text{PPD} = 2 \times d \times \text{PPI} \times \tan(0.5°)$$

where $d$ is the distance from the user's eyes.

For example, suppose an LED display has a spatial density of 80 pixels per inch. If we want to make a VR HMD with the display sitting an inch away from the user's eyes, we would have an angular pixel density of

$$2 \times 1 \text{ inch} \times 800 \text{ pixels per inch} \times \tan(0.5°) \approx 14 \text{ pixels per degree.}$$

Since the display is so close to the eye, the spatial pixel density of a VR display has to be much higher than that of a desktop or television to achieve the same resolution. Even a mobile device is held a foot or two away from the face. CAVE VR systems were more prevalent in research in the pioneering days of VR than they are now for a few reasons, but one reason for their early popularity was that the screens were a distance away from the user that allowed for a reasonable angular pixel density to be achieved. If we wanted to achieve the same angular pixel density as the theoretical HMD above, but instead were using a CAVE system, with the walls 10 feet away from the user, we'd only need a pixel density of

$$\frac{14 \text{ pixels per degree}}{2 \times 12 \text{ inches/foot} \times 10 \text{ feet} \times \tan(0.5°)} \approx 6.5 \text{ pixels per inch.}$$

### 4.2.2 Resolution of the Eye

People don't see everything in the same resolution. In addition to the differences in resolution between the fovea and the rest of the eye, we are able to make out smaller details on some objects than others. **Resolution acuity** is the ability to distinguish between closely placed lines and is one of the measures used to quantify human "resolution." The distance between the two lines determines the level of resolution acuity. Someone with 20/20 vision is able to distinguish between two lines as close as 1.75 mm at 20 feet away. When translated to a resolution specification for a display, this is close to 60 pixels per degree of vision. Considering many people with corrected vision can resolve closer lines than this, resolution acuities higher than this value are not unusual. **Detection acuity** is the measurement of the ability to make out a small dot in an image. Humans have better resolution in detection acuity tests than resolution acuity tasks. In fact, detection acuity has been shown to have an accuracy of 7200 pixels per degree—with participants being able to detect objects as small as 0.5 arc/seconds. Despite the ability to make out objects at such a high resolution, we're not able to differentiate between objects this small and ones that are significantly larger. In detection acuity, we see the average of nearby colours. We don't have enough resolution to actually make out the spot, but its effect on the average colour of the area is detectable. Only in the fovea is this full resolution reached. This maximal resolution covers the centre 50 degrees of the field of view—past that, it sharply drops off to about 25% of the foveal resolution.

### 4.2.3  Resolution / Visual Acuity

Visual acuity is the ability of the eye to resolve details. Visual acuity can be thought of as the reverse of angular pixel density. While angular pixel density determines the smallest detail that can be displayed, visual acuity determines the smallest detail that can be seen. Under ideal conditions, a person can see a line as thin as 0.5 arc seconds.

Acuity is not uniform across the eye—as mentioned before, due to a heightened density of rods and cones, the fovea is capable of a much higher acuity than peripheral vision.

Different tasks have different types of visual acuity. For example, the "ideal conditions" mentioned above determine the limit of detection acuity: the measurement of the smallest stimulus that one can detect in an otherwise empty visual field. As this situation is not encountered much in an actual environment, practical acuity limits are usually much lower. However, in an HMD, a situation where a dead pixel exists on an otherwise black display could be considered a near-perfect detection acuity scenario that actually occurs fairly often. Recognition acuity is another important measure, giving the distance at which we are able to perceive and recognize shapes or symbols. A common eye chart containing letters is used to measure recognition acuity. It's important from an interface perspective to understand differentiating between some symbols may be easier than others: for example, the distance required for an average person to be able to see the difference between an "O" and a "Q" is far less than the distance required to differentiate between the same "O" and an "I." The common measure of 20/20 vision refers to visual acuity—someone with 20/20 vision is able to identify letters at a distance of 20 ft that a typical observer can also read at 20 ft. A measurement like 20/30 means the observer is able to read letters at 20 ft that a typical observer can read at 30 ft.

**Visual angle** is a more general means of specifying visual acuity—this measures the size of the retinal image that an observer is able to see. A normal observer is capable of resolving details one minute of arc in distance across, but this changes based on the acuity task.

As the task of acuity is closely related to brightness discrimination, the same factors affect acuity. A user's visual acuity is less when they are transitioning between adaptation types.

In the same manner as brightness detection, the likelihood of a detail being detected increases as intensity or the amount of time displayed increases, with this increase levelling off after about 300 msec.

---

**Other Common Acuity Tests**

Separation acuity is the smallest angular separation able to be resolved. Grating acuity is the ability to distinguish elements of a fine grating vernier acuity: ability to perceive misalignment of two line segments—people are able to see acuities of 5 seconds of arc or less, which is why anti-aliasing is so important. Stereoscopic acuity is the ability to detect small differences in depth due to binocular disparity between eyes.

---

**The Blind Spot**

There's also one spot in our eye where the resolution is zero: our blind spot. Our optic nerve, about 15 degrees away from the fovea (left of the fovea on the left eye and right on the right eye), creates an area of our visual field where we are incapable of detecting stimuli. The density of rods and cones in the area from $\approx$ 12–19 degrees drops off abruptly around where the nerve is. Bioptic vision compensates for the blind spot—the image from the right eye is able to fill in the blind spot in the image from the left eye and vice versa. However, if you close one eye, the blind spot can be made apparent. There isn't a black hole near the middle of the visual field, as the brain is able to interpolate for what the missing part of the picture would be, but small objects can be lost in the blind spot. To find your blind spot, draw two dots, a few centimetres apart, on a piece of paper and hold the paper at arm's length. If you close your right eye and focus on the right dot, as you bring the paper closer to your eye, the left dot should disappear in the blind spot at one point and then reappear as the paper gets closer.

With a HMD, it is possible to change the images displayed to both eyes. If you were able to track the eye, you could put images in the blind spots of both (or just one) eyes that wouldn't be visible at all. As the eyes can't compensate for each other as they do in the physical world, whatever was placed in the blind spots would not be visible to the user—although practical applications for this may be limited.

## 4.3  AUDITORY SENSORY INPUTS

While the visual system is made of thousands of receptors (rods and cones) distributed spatially across the sensory field, the auditory system really only has access to information at two spatial locations: the left and right ears. Location information in the audio system is somewhat rudimentary compared to the visual system; however, the strength of the audio system is in temporal resolution. The inner ear contains structures which spread out the sound in frequency, much like a prism spreads out light into its constituent colours. It is this frequency separation and sensitivity that makes the human auditory system capable of receiving and decoding information about our surroundings.

The visual system is the focus of much VR technology development, but virtual reality audio has existed (in a manner of speaking) for years. We can put on a pair of headphones and hear sounds from some other place or time — some other reality and the processes for capturing or generating sound are well known and mature. The sound we hear through traditional headphones does not change as we move, so it would not be fair to call this form of audio reproduction interactive, but it is straightforward to add simple audio reproduction to any visually focussed VR system, just by adding headphones.

There is, however, a risk in assuming that audio is a solved problem. Because audio reproduction is such a mature field, VR hardware engineers or software developers may choose to make use of existing audio solutions in their VR systems rather than attempt to align the audio with the visual representation of the virtual world. For example, when you walk into a room that contains an object that makes noise, one approach would be to just play the sound of that object through the user's headphones. In the physical world, sound interacts with objects, bounces across flat surfaces, bends around walls, and its quality is changed as it proceeds through these interactions. The ear itself changes the sound as it is funnelled towards the eardrum, giving hints as to the direction the sound came from. Without representing these physical interactions, displaying a sound via headphones would be like displaying a flat image in VR. The user can perceive and interpret the content, but it lacks verisimilitude[2].

In this section we will review the anatomy of the ear, the physics of sound, characteristics of information-rich content like speech and music, and core interaction modes for sound, before describing how to simulate spatial sound and some examples of how sound is used well (and poorly) in VR.

### 4.3.1  The Human Auditory System

The ear can be divided into the outer ear and the inner ear (Fig. 4.18). The outer ear, also called the pinna, is the part we see off the side of our head, which collects and shapes sound waves. The inner ear, spreads the frequencies and converts them to electrical signals. As sound is concentrated by the folds of cartilage of the pinna,

---

[2] *Verisimilitude* is the appearance of being true or real. A photograph is a representation of a scene, but no one would mistake a photograph for the scene itself, because it is not believably true.

subtle shifts of frequency occur which act as indicators of the direction the sound originally came from. We also use time difference between the ears as a cue to direction, but these features will be discussed in the section on spatial audio reproduction. The sound waves travel down the ear canal and impinge on the eardrum (tympanic membrane), which vibrates in response. The eardrum separates an area of more constant pressure instead the ear (the middle ear) from the varying pressure outside, and the chamber of air in the middle ear is pressure regulated with a small tube (the eustachian tube) which connects the inner ear to the nasal sinus cavity. This tube can become blocked when you have a cold, making it harder to hear; additionally the chamber in the middle ear can be "re-set" with nasal pressure which is why you blow your nose on an airplane to make your ears pop.

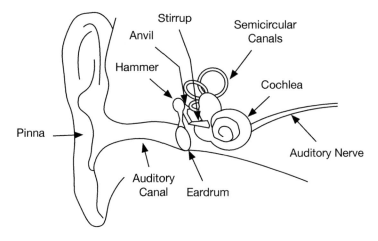

Figure 4.18: The anatomy of the human ear.

Three small bones transmit the sound pressure waves from the eardrum to the cochlea, a spiral-shaped organ containing fluid and nerve-connected hair cells. The bones vibrate an area on one side of the cochlea, and the sound waves travel around the spiral to the other side. As the sound waves travel, they interact with different areas of the cochlea that resonate at different frequencies. The result is that different hair cells will be stimulated by different frequency content in the sounds that we hear, and it is this spreading out of the frequency of the sound that allows to understand and interpret a wide variety of sounds corresponding to objects and people around us.

**Close your Ears**
Although it is possible to close your eyelids and actively prevent your eyes from seeing, it is not possible to close your ears. There is no mechanism by which you can choose not to hear a noise that is around you. People have invented artificial means to reduce the impact of sounds, from headphones to earplugs, but none of these completely prevent the perception of all sound, because sound

waves also vibrate the bones of your skull, which can also set up vibrations in the cochlea causing you to hear sounds through **bone conduction**. Designers must remember that users cannot turn off sounds around them from the real world and must actively choose to lower or mute the volume of the system they are using if they want to not hear the sounds. Because we cannot turn off our ears, sound is sometimes used to encourage or discourage certain activities. "Annoying" music is played outside of stores to reduce loitering, and storeowners can be specific about who they would like to drive away, because different populations find different types of music annoying. Music has also been used as a form of torture, playing the same music over and over again very loudly to cause emotional stress. Of course, we also choose to use sound to affect our own behaviour, with audio alerts on our phones and horns in our cars and even alarm clocks to draw us out of sleep. Individuals with atypical hearing sometimes are not woken up by alarm clock sound and must use another sense they can't ignore, like touch (via a vibrating alarm clock) to be roused from sleep.

### 4.3.1.1 Light Versus Sound

There is an analogy here with the eye, since the stricture of the eye collects and spreads out light, and different cells respond to different frequencies of light; however, it is worthwhile to be clear about the differences here. In the eye, the lens spreads out light *spatially* and does not alter the light in frequency - the cells of the eye respond to different frequencies that are inherent in the light as it arrives at the eye. Each red cone cell responds to the total amount of stimulating red light and by itself does not distinguish between colours—it is the relative response from different rods that allows us to see colour. The ear, on the other hand, spreads out sound in *frequency*, and each hair responds to a tiny range of frequencies. While there are only three types of rods, there are thousands of hairs that respond to different frequencies, but all of the hairs are "listening" to the same sound. It would be as if we could see a single speck of light, but be able to see the spectrum of the colour of that light with thousands of times more detail.

**The lake metaphor for hearing**

A famous metaphor for directional audio (and really how amazing hearing is in general) is to imagine being on a beach, on a lake. You dig two channels in from the water's edge, place two sticks across the channels, and hang a feather from each stick, just touching the water. Waves on the lake travel up the channels and disturb the feathers, causing them to move back and forth as the water shifts. Just looking at the feathers and how they move, it would seem impossible to determine anything about the source of the waves out on the lake, but human binaural hearing is a lot like this scenario. Waves travel towards sensitive membranes along directional channels and based on the motion of those membranes, we can hear things. It is as if you could tell how many boats are on the lake, how fast they are moving, and in what direction they are travelling, just by watching the movement of the feathers in the channels.

The other difference between our perception of light and our perception of sound is the speed at which changes in information can be perceived. The cones in our eyes respond to changes in light quality on the order of tens of milliseconds (faster for cones on the periphery, slower for rods), while the hair cells in our ears respond to changes in air pressure on the order of tens of microseconds, a thousand times faster. This is why 30 frames per second of light is enough, but to fully represent sound we need tens of thousands of cycles per second.

### 4.3.1.2 Limits of human hearing

The human auditory system is constrained in three specific dimensions that are relevant to the development of sound effects and environments in interactive systems. We can hear a specific range of frequencies, typically cited as between 20 Hz and 20,000 Hz, although this tends to fall off at the high end as we age; We can hear a range of loudness between 0dB and 140 dB, although this varies with the frequency of the sound being heard, and we can perceive a specific rate and ranges of sound events, beyond which individual sounds may be blocked by the perception of nearby sounds (in time or in frequency). The limits of human hearing in frequency and loudness are shown in Figure 4.19.

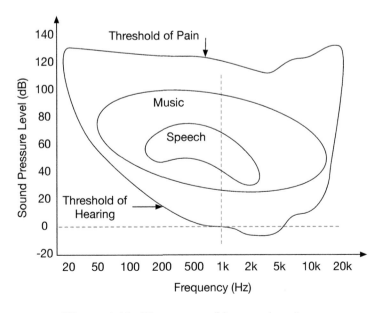

Figure 4.19: The range of human hearing.

Recall that decibel ranges are relative, and not absolute; the relative loudness against which sound pressure levels are measured is the perceived loudness of a somewhat arbitrary 1000 Hz signal just at the threshold of perception. This becomes the "zero" point for hearing, by definition, but note that we can hear sounds quieter than zero dB, depending on the frequency. We are most sensitive to sounds in the 2 kHz to 5 kHz range, in the upper bands of the sounds we produce when we speak. This corresponds well to a theory of co-evolution between our ability to produce language via sound and our ability to perceive sound and interpret it into language. The figure also shows why we tend to refer to humans as being able to hear between 20 Hz and 20 kHz. The range of sound pressure levels we can hear at these extremes is quite limited, and these also tend to be the sounds we lose first as we age, so the average human can hear well only up to around 15 kHz.

**Masking** occurs when a sound event happens near another sound, and the perception of this sound is blocked as a result. When a sound event is perceived, the human auditory system is deaf to similar sounds for a brief period of time, in a small frequency range. Sound events that happen in rapid succession can be masked, meaning that the first sound overshadows the second, and the second sound is not heard.

### 4.3.2 Sound as an Information Medium

Because the ear breaks up the sound into relationships between thousands of frequencies, we can interpret these frequency relationships into information about what we are listening to. The ability to hear and interpret language co-evolved with the ability of the vocal system to produce these sounds and the complexity of language to serve as an information communication system should not be underestimated. The ear is fine-tuned to detect subtleties of sound that we may not even be aware of. If you listen to someone speaking and focus on the sounds they are making rather than the words themselves, you will begin to understand the huge range of sounds we can make with our vocal system, which are subconsciously and automatically translated into language. You can get a better feel for this if you listen to someone speaking in a language you don't understand. For each sound you hear, try to explain or understand how different it is from the sounds made a fraction of a second ago. What is the difference between vowels and consonants? What is the difference between plosives (P, T), voiced fricatives (V, Z), and unvoiced fricatives (F, TH).

The power of the audio system to interpret information goes beyond speech. Based only on the sounds in the air, we can hear the difference between the songs of species of birds; the number of cylinders in a car engine (and if one of them is misfiring); walking on snow, gravel, or grass; the type of weapon being used (from firearms to lightsabers), and even the temperature of a liquid being poured into a mug. The power of audio to communicate is staggering, which is why it is all the more frustrating that software developers often leave sound as an afterthought.

## 4.4  THE PHYSICS OF SOUND

Sound consists of waves of pressure in the air (or another medium—we can hear sound when swimming in water, for example, but the quality of sound is significantly changed). These waves come from the physical interaction of objects, which cause the pressure waves to radiate outward from the event. Waves travel through the air in a spherically radiating wavefront, which means the intensity of the wave is reduced by the square of the distance from the sound-making event, as the wavefront on the surface of the sphere expands.

A discrete event (like two rocks banging together) creates an impulse wave—a spike of energy. This energy spike contains many frequencies and is perceived across a wide range of hair cells of the cochlea. Repeated discrete events are perceived as a chain of impulses, and we are highly sensitive to such rhythms. Perhaps we evolved this ability to be aware of subtle changes in the stride of a beast we were chasing (or being chased by), but we are hardwired to pay attention to rhythmic events, and this has lead to (or perhaps co-evolved with) the development of the rhythmic elements of music and dance in all cultures of the world.

In some cases when an object is struck, it creates *resonance*—when the energy from the collision will bounce around in the object and create repeating waves of air pressure radiating from the object. This also happens when the object is energized in different ways. The wind blowing through the trees rustles the leaves but sometimes can create a humming or a howling if the conditions are just right. This occurs when the direction of wind passes back and forth across a gap in the trees in just the right way. Our vocal chords do the same thing—we can control the shape and size of the opening of our larynx and how much air is passing through, and the result is a resonance of vibrations that causes a voiced vowel speech pattern. Hold your hand on your voice box and say "ooh," and you will feel these vibrations. As with the rhythm of regular discrete events, our brains and ears have evolved to pay specific attention to resonance, and, again, this has led to the development of the pitch-based elements of music in all cultures of the world.

In addition to generating resonance with our voice, we have developed the ability to build tools with the sole purpose of generating and amplifying resonance. Musical instruments work on the principle of making it easy to generate a resonance, manipulate its resonant frequency, and amplify and modulate the resulting sound. Musical instruments may manipulate vibrations in an object in one dimension, along a string or in a column of air in a pipe, or in two dimensions, across a drumhead or the surface of a block of wood, bell, or cymbal. In the case of 2D resonant objects, the control from the player usually comes from which object (or part of an object) to strike with which type of stick, but for one-dimensional objects, the player can control the length of the object and hence the pitch of the sound, by shortening or lengthening the string or the pipe. Shorter, smaller objects produce higher pitches, and longer, larger objects create lower pitches.

## 4.5   SOUND AND GAMES

The complete history of the use of sound in video games is a topic beyond the scope of this text, but there are many works in the area that the interested reader may investigate. It is worth noting, however, that many common approaches to sound have evolved from early constraints in video game technology. The earliest games had no sound, and even when sound chips were added, the amount of resources available for audio production was heavily constrained. Simple wavetable playback or FM synthesis was common practice, and clever use of playback speed allowed a single wavetable to be used for multiple sounds. Today, game sound consists of two approaches (soundfile playback and sound synthesis) to three main sound tasks: background ambience, event-based effects, and music.

### 4.5.1   Wavetables and synthesis

Soundfile playback is as simple as it sounds—regardless of the task, a soundfile is retrieved from memory and played; while sound synthesis is a wide area of research where individual sounds are created on the fly based on parameters of gameplay. The challenge with soundfile playback is that humans are well adapted to recognize repetition, so when a character's footfall sounds exactly the same one step to the next, it can become noticeable. The simple solution is to have a library of sound-files for each event that may occur: multiple footsteps, multiple weapon interactions, button interactions, object interactions, collisions, explosions, etc. Each event must be detected in-game and used to trigger the playback of a specific selection from the library of sounds appropriate for that event, and these sounds must each be recorded or synthesized (or purchased) and included in the asset package for the game. This approach has been used historically because it is simple and the alternative consumes resources thought to be better spent on graphics. That alternative is sound synthesis.

Sound synthesis is the process of designing algorithmic generation of sounds in real time, similar to the process of generating graphics in real time for display. While the graphics side of a game system must produce a complete render of the scene in time for the next frame (which should be at least 70 frames per second for virtual reality), sound production must generate a new audio value 44,000 times per second. Practically speaking, sound waves are generated by the audio system in frames, just like video, and these frames are played back in time rather than in space. Audio processing can be aligned to the sampling rate, the frame rate, or the physics rate of the system, depending on which characteristics need to be changed.

### 4.5.2   Audio use cases: background, events, music, and speech

The three components of sound typically found in game design serve separate purposes. Music is typically not diegetic and is used primarily for mood, feel, and background. In fact, music is so rarely part of the experience of the character, in games and in other media, that we call attention to it when it does happen, for example when a character listens to the radio. Music can be used to establish subconscious information for the player as well, for example when the player enters a more threatening environment, a change in the intensity of the music can help establish this.

Adaptive music is the practice of automatically generating musical content based on the current gamestate. This requires the music to be created in real time rather than being played back from a pre-recorded file and is a component of generative audio. Adaptive music can use the key, tempo, complexity, instrumentation, or other features of the music to communicate information to the player, but changes to the music should not happen too rapidly. Music features tend to change on the order of seconds, while the gamestate can change from one frame to the next.

If music is used to convey a sense of the conceptual gameplay context, background ambience is used to establish a sense of the virtual location the character is in. If a character is sitting in the cockpit of a spaceship, there may be a soft hum of machinery and the odd ping of some piece of equipment. Similarly, if the character is in a hospital, they may hear a hiss of oxygen and a machine that goes "ping." If the character is outside, they might hear the rustle of the wind in the trees or the chirping of birds. These sounds convey, often unconsciously, information about the world the player is in.

Sound effects are the most common use of audio in games—a game can be missing music or ambient effects, but if a player throws an object and it makes no noise when it hits the ground, that would be strange and require an explanation. Object interactions and events, especially those triggered by the player, are often sonified by simple wavetable playback selected from a library, as described above. The creation of these libraries is often performed using film techniques like foley, where sounds are generated and recorded in a controlled environment. Footsteps are the classic example, with a separate set of sound files required for each combination of character weight, gait, footwear, floor/ground surface, room acoustics, and other factors. As the number of separate files required adds up, the justification for writing a footstep engine becomes increasingly reasonable. Any time two objects interact, or the player interacts with another object, more files or adaptations to the sound engine may be required.

Speech is the primary way humans convey overt discrete information via sound, and speech is used in many ways in game design. Speech is often used to deliver narrative information to the player in the form of a dialogue tree, where each choice the player makes results in a pre-recorded speech event from the character they are interacting with.

Speech recognition is becoming more prevalent in game design, as a way to allow the player to interact more naturally with the world, but much like gesture recognition, the variability in speech patterns makes the recognition less reliable than a button press, and so speech remains a contrivance or a game-centric interaction mode in most cases today. As social games become more popular, real-time speech interaction between players becomes increasingly important, and although many developers choose to include voice channels in their games, many players choose to use third-party voice calling services while they play.

A subcategory between event sound effects and speech is interjections, where a character might utter a grunt, cry, sigh, or cough, or a filler word like wow, ok, hmm, or ouch. Interjectional phrases are also common in game design, especially in real-time strategy games where the player commands a set of minions. Each time a command is given, the minion may respond with an interjection phrase like "yes sir" or "it will be done." As with sound effects and dialogue trees, these phrases can become repetitive if heard often, so having a library of different responses is helpful.

## 4.6   SUMMARY

Most of the information we receive from the outside world is in sight and sound. High-fidelity audio replication has been available for many years via headphones, and current VR equipment is focussed on improving fidelity in the visual sense. Although vision can be completely occluded with a VR headset, some audio will inevitably leak through the system from the real world, even with high-quality noise-cancelation. Understanding the range and limitations of vision and hearing allow us as VR developers to create more realistic scenarios, but if all we can do is see and hear the virtual worlds we create, we are limited in what we can do there. The next chapter discusses the other senses that may be able to add depth to our worlds, but are currently much more difficult to block and simulate.

# CHAPTER 5

# Supporting Peripheral Senses

While modern virtual reality (VR) systems focus primarily on vision and, to a lesser extent, sound, the human body has many additional ways to gather information. The dream of many VR developers is to have a system that can perfectly replicate the complete set of sensations of the human experience, but it is clear that some senses are more appropriate, applicable, and practical to implement than others. In this chapter we discuss the senses that are less likely to be used in a VR system and why they may be more difficult to occlude and replace.

The senses can be classified as either **exteroceptive**, those that collect stimuli from outside of the body, or **interoceptive** senses, those that respond to stimuli inside the body. Although both senses discussed so far, vision and hearing, are exteroceptive, the senses discussed in this chapter include both exteroceptive senses (taste, touch, and scent) and interoceptive senses (motion and balance, hunger, time, and others).

The systems for taste (the gustatory system) and scent (the olfactory system) are closely related and will be discussed first. Both systems use receptors that respond to chemical stimuli (referred to as **chemoreceptors**), in the same way that photoreceptors respond to electromagnetic stimuli. The sensation of flavour is influenced by a combination of signals from both the gustatory and olfactory systems (as well as influences from tactile sensations of the food such as temperature and viscosity). These two systems, due to their similarities and interdependence, have been theorized to have evolved from some common sensory process.

## 5.1 THE GUSTATORY SYSTEM—TASTE

### 5.1.1 Taste Receptors

Receptors in the taste system respond to chemicals, transducing them into neural signals depending on their chemical composition and intensity or **concentration**. One major difference between gustatory and olfactory receptors is that gustatory receptors are only activated by chemicals that are water soluble—as such, a molecule must be dissolved in saliva in order to be detected by a taste receptor. As with other

DOI: 10.1201/9781003261230-5

types of stimuli discussed previously in this book, higher magnitudes of the chemical stimuli result in higher intensity neural activation from taste receptors.

The vast majority of taste receptors reside within the taste buds of the tongue (although there are a few notable exceptions—see box "Taste Receptors Outside of the Mouth"). Each of these taste buds holds up to one hundred receptors, of which four different types exist. Each receptor type differs in the molecules they can respond to, as well as the magnitude of their response to the various molecules in their ranges. Although much research has been conducted into the functioning of these specialized receptor cells, many aspects of their function are still unknown, and as such, intensity response curves such as those presented for the various types of photoreceptors have yet to be determined for taste receptors.

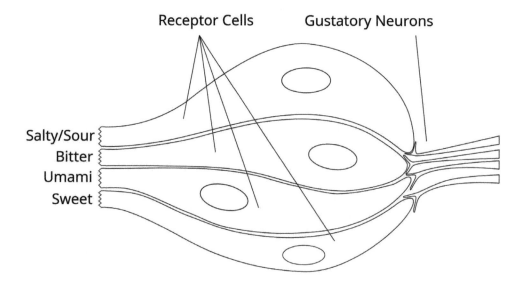

Figure 5.1: A tastebud containing multiple receptors.

**Taste Receptors Outside of the Mouth**
Although taste receptors exist primarily in the mouth, such receptors can also be found in the oesophagus, larynx, lungs, and several other unexpected locations in the body. It is not clear what evolutionary pressure would lead to the existence of taste receptors in such locations, or if there is simply little evolutionary pressure to remove them, people do not typically experience the sensation of taste through these receptors. Still, their existence suggests additional challenges for creating an "ultimate display," since to perfectly replicate the sensory experience of being human, we must perfectly replicate the sensory inputs of all sense organs and cells. Additionally, this fact may remind us that VR experiences need not be directly aligned with physical reality, unless realism is the goal. If a VR scenario calls for a character that tastes with

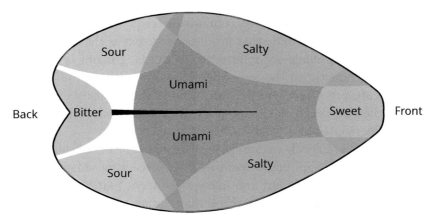

Figure 5.2: Regions of the tongue that are more sensitive to particular taste qualities.

their elbow, there may be a need to simulate such a sensation, as unusual as it seems.

As such, much discussion on the sensation of taste occurs a few levels of abstraction above the individual receptor level. For a long time, taste scientists have referred to a set of **primary taste qualities**, qualities of molecules that correspond to a specific neural response profile within the gustatory system. These are referred to as the *primary* taste qualities because every taste can be expressed as some combination of these five "fundamental tastes."

### 5.1.1.1  The Five Primary Taste Qualities

The five qualities considered primary are **sweet**, **salty**, **bitter**, **sour**, and **umami** (sometimes referred to as *savoury*). Taste receptors have some level of response to all of these qualities, but most receptors are more sensitive to one or two. Although taste buds usually contain multiple varieties of receptors, those that respond most strongly to specific primary tastes tend to have higher concentrations in certain regions of the tongue. Figure 5.2 labels regions of the tongue that are particularly sensitive to certain primary tastes. It's important to note that although these regions may be more sensitive to one particular taste category, individual receptors respond to multiple categories, so all tastes are received in all regions of the tongue.

Each of the taste qualities roughly corresponds to a group of molecules. Organic molecules (those composed of primarily carbon, hydrogen, and oxygen) usually result in sweeter tastes, in particular, those possessing a particular structure called the AB,H system. Bitter tastes also occur from organic molecules, and many of these also posses the AB,H system, but the configuration of the molecules that result in a bitter taste is spatially distinct from those that result in sweet tastes.

Salty tastes result from molecules that break into ions when dissolved into water. Substances with small **anions** (negatively charged ions) tend to taste saltier than substances with large anions. Similarly, sour tastes result from molecules breaking into ions, but more specifically those that produce hydrogen as the **cation** (positively charged ions). Such compounds are referred to as **acids**. Umami is a very specific taste, corresponding directly to the molecule glutamate, although other molecules, belonging to the category of nucleotides, can increase the intensity of activation for umami. Despite their influence on the intensity of umami, nucleotides are incapable of giving rise to the sensation of umami without glutamate.

The aforementioned molecule-taste relations are general rules of thumb, but there are many cases where they are not necessarily true (excepting umami). Some acids taste bitter or sweet instead of sour, and many substances that taste sweet in small amounts may taste bitter in larger quantities. Many other exceptions also exist, suggesting the process of taste may be very complex.

### 5.1.1.2  *Other Sensations Associated with Taste*

Not all sensations that arise from food are due to "taste," in the sense that they are not sensed by taste receptors. The perception of **flavour** includes information from other senses, in particular the olfactory system and the tactile sensations of the food being eaten. The fact that the same food takes on different flavours depending on its temperature, viscosity, or if your nose is congested demonstrates that taste and flavour are not identical processes—the taste, in terms of the specific pattern of taste receptors being activated by the molecules in the food, is the same even if these other variables are changed.

The sensation of spicy food comes from a molecule called capsaicin, which actually stimulates pain receptors as opposed to taste receptors. This is why foods high in capsaicin are referred to as being "hot"—despite this not referring to the temperature of the food, the same receptors are being activated that would be triggered by stimuli high in heat.

### 5.1.2  Taste Sensitivity

The threshold for detecting the presence of a taste chemical is influenced by many variables—not only is the amount of stimulus considered, but also aspects of the food that determine the amount of surface area available to the tongue, the viscosity of the food, and the temperature. As mentioned above, the sensitivity to particular taste qualities is also dependent on the region of the mouth in which the stimuli are located.

Taste sensitivities also differ across individuals, to a greater degree than other sensory modalities. Threshold values vary enough between individuals that taste sensitivity diagrams are even less accurate across individuals than sensitivity diagrams for other senses may be. As there is no pure stimulus for any of the taste qualities, sensitivity tests, such as those shown in Figure 5.3, are generally done on a per-compound basis.

Intensity of a particular taste stimulus is generally specified as a **molar** quantity—a measure of concentration. If two solutions have the same molar quantity, this means that the same number of molecules exist in the same volume of solution, and therefore

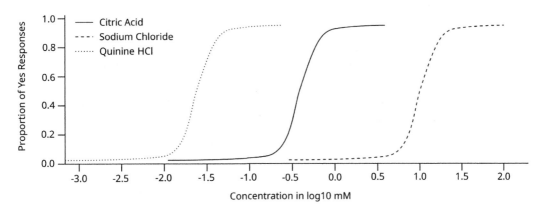

Figure 5.3: Taste threshold diagrams for several different chemical compounds.

the perception of that compound by the taste system would be similar for the same individual. As with other senses, it is possible that different individuals may have different mental experiences of the same concentration of a molecule.

### 5.1.2.1 Absolute Sensitivity to Taste

The limit for the taste threshold varies widely between chemicals, and to a lesser extent between individuals. Some rough averages for chemicals in each of the taste categories are shown in Figure 5.4. Notice that the most sensitive threshold listed (for quinine) and the least sensitive threshold (a tie between NaCl and sucrose) are over three orders of magnitude. Even chemicals that primarily excite the same taste quality differ greatly in their sensitivity threshold. For example, sucrose and 1-propyl-2-amino-4-nitrobenzene both taste sweet, but the threshold for the first is $10mM$, while the second can be detected at a concentration of $\mu M$—a difference of over four orders of magnitude. Bitter substances tend to have relatively low thresholds in particular.

| Taste Quality | Substance | Threshold for Tasting |
| --- | --- | --- |
| Salty | NaCl | 0.01 M |
| Sour | HCl | 0.0009 M |
| Sweet | Sucrose | 0.01 M |
| Bitter | Quinine | 0.000008 M |
| Umami | Glutamate | 0.0007 M |

Figure 5.4: Average taste thresholds for sample compounds.

Absolute thresholds across the population also differ on a per-chemical basis. The distribution of how the threshold differs among people also varies based on the chemical. While some chemicals may have the distribution of thresholds concentrated around a particular value, some are more evenly distributed, such as vanillin and phenylthiocarbamide. It is these chemicals with even threshold distributions that some portion of the population tends to be taste blind to.

**Taste Blindness and Supertasters**

Some individuals have reduced taste and flavour sensations, either because they have fewer tastebuds due to genetic differences or because of long-term exposure and familiarity with certain tastes. For example, individuals from cultures that eat particularly spicy food have a measurably lower reaction to the heat and temperature-simulating effects of capsaicin.

Similarly, there are individuals with a significantly heightened sense of taste, who are born with more tastbuds than typical. Such "supertasters" are particularly sensitive to bitter flavours and may be more inclined to overflavour their food to avoid the bitter flavours of vegetables or coffee.

By some measures, individuals with either fewer or more tastebuds than average might make up as much as 25% of the population, suggesting that variations in the sense of taste are broader and more common than analogous variations in the sense of vision, like colour blindness.

Different tastes also have different recorded reaction times. Reaction times are fairly similar for stimuli that have the same primary taste, but reaction times across taste quality categories are quite different. For taste reaction time measurements, it was required for participants to identify the primary taste of a stimuli—as these studies were performed in the late 1980s, umami, which was not considered a primary taste quality at the time, was excluded. Salty stimuli were found to have the quickest reaction times, followed by sourness and sweetness (which were roughly the same), and finally bitterness taking the longest to be identified.

### 5.1.2.2 Differential Sensitivity to Taste

Compared to our other sensory modalities, humans are relatively poor at discriminating between various intensities of taste stimuli. Across all various tastes, Weber fractions (see Section 3.5.3) range between 0.10 and 1.00, at the highest value meaning that the second taste must be twice as intense as the first to be gauged as different.

The relationship between taste sensation intensity and stimulus intensity is roughly linear. In a magnitude estimation function $ME = \alpha I^n$, where I is the intensity of the stimulus, $\alpha$ is a constant, and ME is the estimated (perceived) magnitude, n is roughly 1 for tastes—for table salt, n is 0.91, and for sucrose, $n$ is 0.93. Thus, a quantization of the sensory range for tastes would be roughly uniform. Note that the value for n for a particular chemical is dependent on the conditions in which stimuli are being tasted—in particular, tastes are strongly influenced by adaptation.

**Taste Sensitivity and Age**

It's a lot more common to hear a child complaining about having to eat their brussels sprouts and broccoli than to hear an adult object to the same foods.

Although this might be because the adult has learned to withhold their complaints in polite company, it may also have something to do with the changes in sensitivity to taste with age.

The Weber fraction for bitterness, a key influence in the flavour of brussels sprouts, has been found to increase with age. This means that it takes a larger difference in concentration for an older person to tell the difference between the intensity of two bitter stimuli. For example, for caffeine, young people are a lot more sensitive to differential intensity, with a Weber fraction of 0.40 compared to 2.30 for the elderly.

The sense of smell also begins to lose sensitivity around age 70—due to its close relationship with taste in determining flavour, a food may be perceived to taste very differently by a person who has lived 8 decades and a person who has lived 8 years.

### 5.1.2.3 Taste Adaptation

Taste adaptation occurs quickly relative to human adaptation to other sensory stimuli. For continued stimulation of the same type of taste, people adapt quite quickly, and this repeated stimulation also results in a raising of the absolute threshold of the taste. Figure 5.5 shows the adaptation curve for table salt—within nearly 7 seconds of constant stimulation, the threshold for detection increases by roughly 15%. The time to recover from adaption is nearly as fast—it takes roughly 5 seconds to drop back down to only 2% above the baseline threshold.

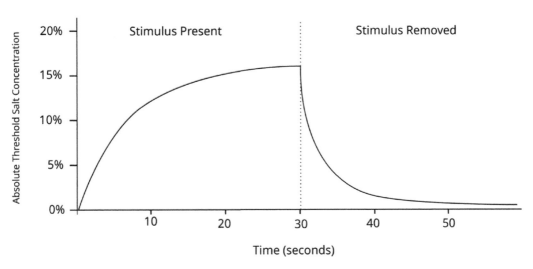

Figure 5.5: Adaptation and recovery process when exposed to NaCl (table salt).

However, this is only the time to recover back to the detection threshold—it takes a lot longer for perceived intensity to recover post-adaptation. It takes about

10 seconds for 50% recovery to the initial intensity level and up to two minutes for full recovery. These adaptive processes are true for all tastes with the same primary quality—adapting to one sour stimulus will result in adaptations to other sour stimuli. Conversely, exposure to stimuli of one primary taste may lower the threshold for tastes of other qualities. It's found that adaptations to some sour tastes can increase the sweetness of other tastes or bitterness can increase saltiness or vice versa.

## 5.2   THE OLFACTORY SYSTEM—SMELL

Many people underestimate the sensitivity of our sense of smell. Ask the average person how much smell factored into their day, and they'll likely reply "not much," unless they encountered an abnormally offensive smell or ate something particularly good.

Despite this common underestimation, humans in general have an impressive sense of smell, and some people are highly sensitive to smells. For example, an anecdote about the physicist Richard Feynman relates that he used his sense of smell to identify when individuals had touched an object. As a parlour trick, Feynman would ask five individuals to each grab a book at random from a bookshelf and then put them back. While they did this, Feynman would leave the room. Upon reentering, Feynman would smell the hands of all the individuals in the room and then smell the bookshelf, trying to ascertain who grabbed which book. After a minute or so, Feynman was able to determine all the individuals who had grabbed books and was able to correctly indicate which book they had picked up (for all but one pair of individuals, which he got reversed). This sense of smell is not unique to Feynman—many people have the ability to pick up on minute differences in scent, but we simply don't use it too often.

The olfactory sense is also more complex than many would believe, making it particularly tricky to simulate in VR. Sensory displays have changed little from when they were first introduced around the time of "Sensorama" (see Chapter 1), in that releasing pre-bottled scents is the extent of their abilities. This section, by investigating how the sense of smell works, hints at why smells are such a hard sensation to reproduce.

### 5.2.1   Olfactory Stimuli

Much like the gustatory system, the olfactory system transduces chemical stimuli into neural impulses. One aspect in which the sense of smell differs from taste is that we can smell things at a distance, while we can only taste substances when they are placed on the tongue. This is because the sense of smell detects molecules in a gaseous state—any object that has a detectable scent is a volatile substance, meaning that it has molecules in the gaseous state at ordinary temperatures.

The volatility of a substance does not correspond with how strong a substance smells—only how likely it is that molecules will reach the nose. A more volatile substance is more likely to have a higher amount of molecules in the air at a given time that can be carried over the air to land in the nose.

In the physical world, olfactory stimuli are usually mixtures of many components. For example, roughly 200 distinct types of molecules interact with olfactory receptors to result in the final perceived scent of coffee. Although it is likely that a small handful of these molecules are responsible for the majority of the perceived scent, in many cases a slightly different combination of molecules can result in a completely different smell—the complicated system of receptors located in the human nose is capable of distinguishing between trillions of different chemical combinations.

**Smelling and Memory**
The olfactory bulb has a very short and direct path to the brain. To be specific, it travels to one of the earliest parts of the brain to evolve, the limbic system. Aside from regions of the brain that process olfactory signals, the limbic system also contains the portions of the brain that are responsible for memory and emotion, the hippocampus and amygdala. Because of their proximity in the brain, memories are often triggered by olfactory stimuli compared to other sensory information. Due to this close link between memory and smell, olfactory stimuli have been experimentally used to aid memory recall in individuals with dementia.

## 5.2.2   Nasal Anatomy

Human scent receptors are located on the end of specialized neurons, attached in a clump called the **olfactory bulb**—the bulb and olfactory nerves are embedded in a tissue called the olfactory epithelium. The ends of these neurons contain hairlike structures, called **cilia**, which serve to increase their surface area. The olfactory cilia contain the actual receptor molecules that respond to stimuli compounds. The olfactory bulb and cilia reside in the nasal cavity, which scent molecules are able to reach through two separate paths.

The first path, through the nose, is referred to as the **orthonasal passage**—this is how stimuli from distant sources reach the olfactory system. The colloquial use of "smelling" as a verb is usually used to describe olfactory stimuli that are received through the orthonasal passage. The second pathway connects to the back of the throat and is called the **retronasal passage**. The retronasal passage allows the olfactory system to receive stimuli from items that are currently in the mouth, contributing to the sensation of flavour. The way the brain interprets stimuli coming from these two pathways is also distinct—when eating food, the way you perceive the olfactory sensation of flavour seems distinct from how you perceive the same molecules if you hold the food in front of your nose and smell it. Despite the transduction being identical in both cases, people perceive stimuli coming from the orthonasal passage and stimuli from the retronasal passage to be different mechanisms—in particular, people mentally group the gustatory and olfactory signals of flavour into a single perception.

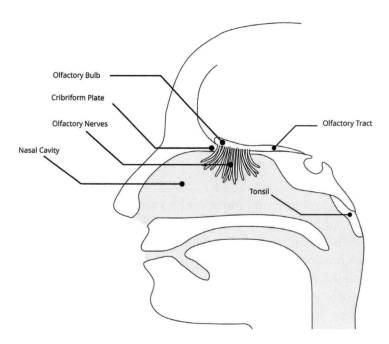

Figure 5.6: Components of the olfactory system.

### 5.2.2.1 Olfactory Receptors

The exact chemical mechanisms of olfactory reception are not fully understood. Only recently have scientists been able to examine individual receptors using modern equipment. The current understanding suggests that each unique receptor is able to bind with a set of chemical patterns in stimuli molecules. Humans have around 400 types of olfactory receptors, allowing us to respond to a very diverse set of chemical stimuli. Individual neurons carry a single type of receptor, and each type is encoded by a specific gene. Variations in these genes cause different individuals to perceive different olfactory stimuli with different intensities, or even completely different qualities. For example, the molecule androstenone is perceived by some as smelling similar to vanilla, while to others it smells more like urine. A more common example is the flavour of herb cilantro: some people find it appealing, while others report it tastes like soap. Similar to taste, there are many molecules that a small subset of the population cannot smell, including those responsible for the scents of vanilla and menthol.

**Smelling Disorders**
Due to the large number of genes determining the function of individual smell receptor varieties, it is fairly common for slight differences in this genetic code to lead to abnormalities in the way that people smell. Although it is estimated that there is around a 30% difference in the way that these genes are expressed between individuals, there are several named smelling disorders that cover several specific cases. Not all of these are genetic—certain smelling disorders

can be caused by injuries, illness, exposure to chemicals, smoking, or ageing. It's estimated that close to 20% of the population exhibits some variety of smelling disorder.

**Anosmia** is the loss of smell detection abilities, sometimes colloquially referred to as "smell blindness." Specific anosmia refers to being unable to detect specific smells, while total anosmia refers to the lack of any smell detection capabilities.

**Hyposmia** is the reduced sensitivity to smells. Like anosmia, it can be specific or total. Similarly, **parosmia** is the distorted perception of smells.

**Phantosmia** is the hallucination of odours, perceiving olfactory stimuli that are not present. The hallucination of unpleasant smells, particularly odours that could be categorized as "burnt" or "rotten," is more common—cases falling under this subset are referred to as **cacosmia**. Phantosmia can also be temporary and is often a symptom of other conditions—for example, the hallucination of a "burnt toast" scent that often precedes a stroke.

### 5.2.3  Smell Qualities and Intensity

Due to the complexity of the olfactory system, it is difficult to describe smells in any sort of categorical sense. Unlike sight and hearing, the stimuli that cause the perception of scents do not vary in a continuous manner—molecules differ in arrangement, shape, and combination in discrete ways, unlike the waves that act as stimuli for visual and auditory receptors. Compared to the sense to taste, the types of receptors are much more numerous—as opposed to the four taste receptor types that result in the perception of a combination of five qualities, the hundreds of different smell receptors that can be activated by airborne molecules create perceptions that cannot easily be categorized as a combination of primaries. While taste consists of amounts of each of the five primary tastes, smell consists of the presence or absence of hundreds of discrete smells, in combination.

This isn't to say that a set of primary scent qualities does not exist, only that they have yet to be discovered and may be too numerous for smells to be easily "factored" into these distinct qualities. Then again, it is entirely possible that we eventually discover that the principle components of smell primaries count in the trillions—an upper bound based on the rough estimate of how many smells humans can distinguish between. However, psychological studies have found that certain odours are perceived as being more similar to each other than others, and these self-similar clusters can be labelled with colloquial descriptors, as shown in Figure 5.7.

These self-similar smells were not defined by the names that they were given—testing conditions have participants quantify smells via comparison, resulting in these mathematically determined "distances" between smells. Note that although smells tend to cluster, this does not indicate that these dimensions are primaries and are simply categorizations. The molecular stimuli used in these trials were selected to be representative of compounds from many different permutations; therefore, it can be

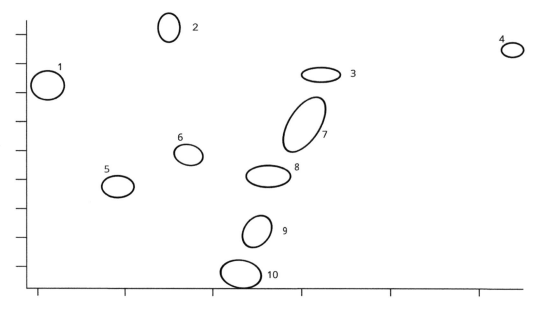

Figure 5.7: The ten distinct clusters of smells.

assumed that other smells would fall into one of these ten clusters. The ten smell categories with their descriptors and some examples are shown in Figure 5.8.

| Smell Cluster | Example Smells |
| --- | --- |
| 1 - Fruit | Most non-citrus fruits, acetone (nail polish remover) |
| Citrus | Lemons, limes |
| Fragrant | Roses, flowers |
| Woody/resinous | Cedar, turpentine |
| Pungent | Garlic, tobacco |
| Chemical | Copper, ammonia |
| Menthol/Mint | Camphor, peppermint |
| Sweet | Caramel, syrup |
| Toasted/Nutty | Popcorn, nuts |
| Decayed | Rotten flesh, refuse |

Figure 5.8: Smell clusters.

These categories only describe perceptual similarities of scents—the actual molecular qualities of the scents may differ greatly. Scents with the similar molecular structures are sometimes perceptually close, but may just as easily result in completely distinct perceptions. For example, many fruity scents are caused by molecules categorized as esters, but similar esters can also smell resinous (like glue) or citrus-like, differing from their fruity counterparts by only a couple of atoms.

## 5.2.4   Smell Discrimination

The number of smells that humans can discriminate between theoretically measures in the trillions. However, other specifications regarding what chemicals we can and can't smell are harder to define. Since the dimensions and boundaries of what stimuli the olfactory system can and can't sense are unknown, a range cannot be easily defined for the olfactory system the way it can be for some other senses. However, techniques like mixture discrimination testing, where two mixtures contain various amounts of the differing scent molecules, can be used to quantify discrimination abilities for the olfactory system.

One such study tested discrimination abilities using a combination of 128 different types of scent molecules. The molecules were selected to cover much of the perceptual dimensions of scent. Multiple types of molecules were combined in solutions, and participants were asked to discriminate between two identical solutions and one different one based on scent. Half of the participants were able to reliably discriminate between mixtures when the solutions shared less than 75% of the same molecules, suggesting that a 25% difference in two solutions may be the average just-noticeable difference (JND) for scents. None of the participants were able to discriminate between solutions that had more than 90% of the same substances in common.

## 5.2.5   Smell Sensitivity

### 5.2.5.1   Absolute Smell Sensitivity

The absolute individual human sensitivity for activation of a single smell receptor is quite small. Early modelling of the human olfactory system determined that it takes eight molecules at most for a human smell receptor to be activated, and it is possible for the receptor to be triggered by as few as a single molecule, dependent on the type of molecule and the receptor. It's also thought that individual smell receptors aren't any more sensitive in other animals as they are in humans—the increased ability to detect smells seen in animals such as dogs can be explained by those animals having a greater number of receptors than humans, as opposed to differences in the receptors themselves. Thus, it's more likely for stimuli to come in contact with at least one receptor in a dog's nose as opposed to a human's nose, but upon contacting the receptor, the sensitivity is the same in both. The firing of a receptor is heavily dependent on the stimuli molecules interacting with it. The threshold for stimuli to be perceived depends on several qualities of the molecules as well as other variables, such as if the molecules arrived via the orthonasal or retronasal pathways.

### 5.2.5.2   Relative Smell Sensitivity

The perceived intensity of odours can be described using the same magnitude estimation function that has been discussed with reference to other sensory processes. Much as the threshold for absolute sensitivity varies depending on the odorant molecules being discussed, the relative perceived intensity also varies from odour to odour. If the power function is given as

$$ME = \alpha I^n$$

then the exponent $n$ varies from 0.70 to 0.15 dependent on the odorant. In particular, higher exponents (those which are perceived as increasing in intensity more linearly with the actual intensity function) tend to correspond to stimuli molecules which are water soluble.

Much like the high degree to which smell discrimination can be performed between different solutions, humans are also adept at determining differences in smell intensity of the same solution. The Weber fraction for smell can be as low as 0.05 (yet again, dependent on the odorant molecule), making smell one of the most sensitive sensory systems in terms of intensity discrimination.

**Other Perceived Intensity Factors**
Aside from the actual intensity of the odour and adaptation effects, the perceived intensity of a smell can be influenced by other qualities. For example, if a scent is presented at the same time as an "appropriate," or associated, colour, the scent is perceived as more intense. Scents (such as strawberry) are perceived as more intense if an appropriate colour (like red, in the case of the strawberry scent) was simultaneously presented to the user. Flavour is influenced in large part both by scent and taste. The fact that flavour is also different when foods are different temperatures or textures suggests that there may be links between the olfactory system and the tactile and temperature senses.

## 5.2.6 Smell Adaptation

When compared to other senses, olfactory perception is particularly influenced by adaptation effects. Smells tend to fade very quickly as users are exposed to them for a long time—think about how your home seems to have no scent from day to day, but you can suddenly smell its unique aroma when you first open the door after a long vacation. The same adaptive process makes individuals blind to the smells of their body odours and perfumes. Both self-adaptation and cross-adaptation occur with scents—self adaptation leasing to the largest loss of stimuli. Depending on if smells are similar or different in perceptual dimensions, cross-adaptation can make an individual less or more sensitive to particular smells. All odours have some sort of cross-adaptive effect on the perception of other odours, however minor. Further, if a stimulus is above a certain level of intensity, adaptation to other scents has little effect on changing the perceived intensity.

## 5.3 SOMATOSENSORY SYSTEM

The sensory receptors within the skin provide information to several sensory categories. The senses of touch, temperature, and pain (nociception) all receive many of their signals from receptors in the skin (nociception also responds to receptors further within the body). These categories can be further broken down into several modalities—for example, touch encodes texture and pressure as separate modalities.

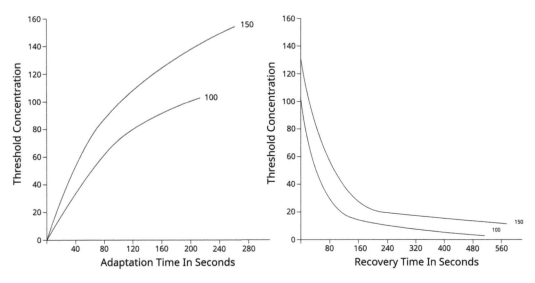

Figure 5.9: Time to adapt and recover to scent dependent on stimuli concentration.

The label **somatosensory system** is usually used to refer to the full set of all sensations registered by the skin.

As mentioned before, the somatosensory system is a set of **contact senses**, meaning that sensations arise from stimuli that are in direct contact with the skin. This makes it particularly well suited for tasks dealing with manipulation of objects by the body, such as moving a lever or tossing a ball. Tasks of this variety are common methods of interacting with a VR environment, but displays that provide somatosensory information have notably higher prices and lower resolutions when compared to displays for the auditory and visual senses. Due to this, VR applications often rely on cues from other senses more heavily than somatosensory information—users have to adapt to use other senses to compensate for a lack of accurate somatosensory feedback for these manipulation actions. Thus, studying the somatosensory system is useful even for VR developers who don't expect their application to be used with somatosensory displays—knowing how tasks rely on somatosensory information can help a developer determine how to provide the same information through other senses.

## 5.3.1 The Skin

The skin has many functions. It is often thought of as a barrier keeping the body separated from the exterior environment—the border between what is inside and what is out. Anything within the first layer of the skin is considered "the inside" of an organism, while everything beyond that is the outside. In addition to containing blood vessels and creating a barrier to keep the internal organs inside the body, the skin is host to a large variety of receptors with different functions. These receptors can be found under nearly every part of the skin, allowing contact to be felt on all parts of the body. When an object is pressed against the skin, the deformation of the skin also deforms receptors, causing the sensation of pressure or touch. The hairs on the skin each have receptors at their bases as well. Because of this, when an external object bends a hair, we also experience a sensation of touch.

Temperature, both of objects and the outside environment, is responded to by receptors in the skin and results in a sensation that is orthogonal to other skin senses. The degree to which temperature sensation is felt is influenced by both the temperature of the stimulus object and the temperature of the skin at the time.

In addition to pressure and temperature, receptors in the skin are also capable of responding to electrical stimuli. If a small electric shock is used as the stimulus, the sensation is felt as touch. If the electric shock is above a certain threshold, pain will be experienced instead.

### 5.3.1.1 Types of Skin

The skin covering the body can be categorized into two major types. Most of the body is covered in **hairy skin**, which is categorized by its ability to grow small hairs. The few areas that aren't covered by hairy skin, such as the palms, soles of the feet, and one side of the fingers and toes, consist of **glabrous skin**. The most obvious difference between the two is the lack of hairs on glabrous skin, but it is also different on the receptor level—glabrous skin contains many free nerve endings. This makes glabrous skin more sensitive and explains why it is found on many areas of the body used for holding and manipulating objects.

### 5.3.1.2 Layers of the Skin

The skin consists of two primary layers. The outermost layer of the skin is the **epidermis**. The epidermis is made up of many layers of dead skin cells on top of a single layer of living cells. The layer inside the epidermis is the **dermis**: it contains most of the nerve endings in the skin that act as sensory receptors, along with containing arteries and hair endings.

## 5.3.2 Somatosensory Receptors

Many different types of nerve endings exist in the skin. Although some endings correspond more strongly to some sensations than others, they aren't completely specialized—all endings respond to all types of skin stimuli, but how strongly they respond differs. Most of the "corpuscular" nerve endings—those that end in corpuscles, including the Pacianian corpuscles, the Meissner corpuscles, Merkel disks, and Ruffini endings—seem to be associated with touch stimuli, which they react strongest to. In contrast, the non-corpuscular and free nerve endings seem to respond most strongly to pain stimuli, and those that project into the epidermis may also act as cold fibres. It seems that specialization occurs further along the neural pathway, with the nerve fibres branching into common paths that react to specific categories of stimuli.

Sensory information is processed in the spinal cord, where it drives reflexive responses, as well as in the somatosensory cerebral cortex in the brain.

There are four primary mechanoreceptors that exist in the skin. Merkel cell nerve endings react to low vibrations—those between 5 and 15 Hz. They have a small receptive field compared to other endings, meaning that they have the potential for higher resolution. They also fade off slowly. They are found more densely in areas such as fingertips. They are found in the basal epidermis and hair follicles.

Tactile corpuscles, located in the dermal papillae, react to moderate vibration (10–50 Hz) and light touch. They respond quickly. It is these receptors that allow for tactile pattern perception.

Pacinian corpuscles handle the perception of coarser textures. They have quick action potentials. They have a large receptive field and, out of all the receptors, respond the strongest to vibrations (most sensitive to those around 250 Hz). Pacinian corpuscles react to sudden stimuli and adapt quickly

Bulbous corpuscles react slowly and respond to sustained skin stretch. They are responsible for detecting object slippage and play a major role in kinesthetic sense and in control of finger position.

Merkel and bulbous cells are myelinated and have a slow response as a result—the other sensors are not and thus have a quick response.

Among the various receptors, the pacinian corpuscle is the best understood, primarily because of its (relatively) large size. The Pacinian corpuscle has been found to react to mechanical input: deforming the membrane of the nerve via pressure allows ions to flow through holes that open in the membrane due to this deformation. This build-up of electrical potential causes an impulse to be sent by the ending, resulting in the eventual perception of a touch stimulus. It is theorized that temperature receptors use a chemical method to release ions in response to temperature changes, ending in a simmilar result. Electrical stimulation of the skin may be able to trigger spike potentials directly due to the potential created by the electricity across the skin.

### 5.3.2.1 Categorizing Somatosensory Receptors

The concept of **receptive field**, discussed previously, is particularly visible when used to discuss touch receptors. For a touch receptor, the receptive field is the area of skin that, when touched, triggers a response in that receptor. Receptors in glabrous skin can be roughly sorted into four categories, based on the size of their receptive fields as well as their time to adaptation:

- Receptors with small, well-defined receptive fields that adapt rapidly

- Receptors with small, well-defined receptive fields that adapt slowly

- Receptors with large, ill-defined receptive fields that adapt rapidly

- Receptors with large, ill-defined receptive fields that adapt slowly

The position of a nerve ending on the skin maps directly to where its information goes in the brain, regardless of receptor type. Thus, the spatial configuration of the brain that processes the area of human touch is a map of the touch receptor density in and of itself. This was actually determined experimentally, by electrically stimulating portions of the brain and asking the participant to identify where they felt a touch stimulus. This map is sometimes associated with the "sensory homunclulus," represented as a caricature of a human with their skin sized according to the amount of sensory dedicated information present. All touch information passes through the spinal cord, with the exception of those from the face and head, which travel via shorter cranial nerves. Eventually, these signals terminate in the somatosensory cortex of the brain. Thus, there is a regular and nearly universal "map" of the relationship between where a stimulus is applied to the skin and where neural activity occurs.

If we lose sensation in one part of the body, that area of the brain remaps to serve adjacent portions.

### 5.3.3 Touch

Touch differs from the other "four senses" in that it is made up of a collection of many different sensory channels measuring different aspects of our interactions with the physical world. Touch also works in combinations with movement senses (kinestesis) in order to help localize us in the world. Different nerve channels carry information for temperature, pain, pressure, shape, texture, and vibration. Often what people think of as the sense of touch is "active touch", which involves you moving your body to intentionally touch a stimulus, or a stimulus touching you. This is can also be referred to as haptic touch. Touch can be separated into two broad categories. Fine touch (sometimes referred to as discriminative touch) is a sensory modality that allows the subject to localize discrete details of an object, while crude (or coarse) touch provides wider contextual information, but does not allow for localization. Crude touch informs the subject that something has touched them without being able to localize where the touch has occurred. When the pathways for fine touch are disrupted in medical subjects, patients were able to feel that they were touched, just not where that touch occurred. Fine touch and crude touch work in parallel, but use separate pathways—fine touch information travels through the dorsal column, while coarse touch uses the spinothalamic tract.

#### 5.3.3.1 Touch Sensitivity

The skin's absolute sensitivity to touch varies widely across regions of the body. For example, the fingers are able to detect much smaller changes in skin tension than a given area on the back or chest can. In addition to locational differences in the absolute touch sensitivity threshold, there is significant variation in sensitivity within smaller areas. If you use a toothpick to touch several areas in a small 2 cm by 2 cm square on the arm, some points will result in an intense sensation, while others may result in little or none. Similarly, some points on your skin are more sensitive to temperature than other points.

If a stimulus vibrates, the absolute threshold for detection is lowered compared to a non-vibrating stimulus. Much like hearing, this absolute threshold varies as a function of the frequency of vibration. Humans can sense tactile vibrations between 40 and 2500 Hz under normal conditions, which is a noticeably smaller frequency range than for human hearing. The sensitivity to vibration also varies with temperature, as the higher the temperature of the skin, the lower the absolute threshold for vibration is. Vibration is often used in technology interactions, like cell phones, game controllers, and VR handheld controllers, to alert the user to an event. If they feel a vibration in their hand at the same time as making something happen or seeing something happen, it increases the sensation that the thing is happening to you, rather than you just watching the event.

Like other senses, we tend to adapt to constant touch stimulus over time—if you touch your skin and hold, eventually your perception of the sensation will fade. An example of this is wearing clothes—there is constant contact between the body and the clothes that you wear, but you may only notice this feeling when you first don clothes in the morning or when you consciously bring your mind to it. The heavier the stimulus, the longer it takes for the sensation to fade away. Conversely, the larger the area covered by the stimulus, the less time it takes for the sensation to adapt.

For touch, adaptation is very rapid for the first second, then gradually slows down. After 3 seconds, the intensity of touch perceived is at 1/4 of the original level. Several factors also affect stimuli adaptation: for example, vibratory stimuli generally take longer to adapt than static stimuli. Touch also adapts at different speeds for different body parts.

### 5.3.3.2 Touch Localization

Each touch sensation seems to be located (to the observer) at a particular position on the skin. The ability to localize accurately varies across different skin regions but seems to be directly related to the number of nerves in that area, and the amount of neural representation that area has in the touch cortex. The greater the representation of a particular area, the smaller the errors of localization generally are for that area.

The **Two point threshold** can be used to measure localization sensitivity: two touch stimuli will be felt as a single touch if they are close enough together spatially. The two point threshold thus measures the resolution with which the skin is able to perceive touch differences.

Compared to the rest of the body, the hands, feet, and face (particularly the lips) have very good localization. The two point threshold is also improved (i.e. is smaller) when the temperature of the stimulating object is further from temperature of the skin (in either direction).

### 5.3.3.3 Touch Intensity

Magnitude estimates of vibratory stimulus on the finger (at 60 Hz) follow the standard power function with an exponent of 0.95. Thus, for touch, the intensity experienced is very closely related to the actual intensity—much more so for touch than for other senses. The intensity power function exponent for glabourous skin is (0.70), and is (1.05) for hair skin.

Like sensitivity, perceived intensity of touch stimuli changes as frequency changes—there is a higher sensitivity for greater frequencies for a given amplitude. Vibrations around 300 Hz are perceived as the most intense (between 200 and 400 Hz) while vibrations around 30 Hz are perceived as the least intense. This is similar to the curve for hearing, which also relies on mechanical receptors.

Two distinct groups of receptors have different sensitivities to vibrations:

- The pacinian system (comprised of pacianian corpuscles and their nerves) is the most sensitive to higher frequency vibrations (250 Hz)

- The non-pacinian system (including meissner's disks and other corpuscular endings) is more sensitive to lower frequency vibrations (those under 200 Hz).

## 5.3.4 Touch Perception

### 5.3.4.1 Qualitative Haptic Exploration

Our sense of touch provides many ways to learn characteristics about the objects we handle or are in contact with. Information we gain on objects via the sense of touch is done through **Qualitative Haptic Exploration**, which describes the act of handling an object to collect correlated sensations and infer geometric features. Imagine walking on the beach; you pick up an interesting stone from the ground, you turn it over in your fingers to feel its weight and texture, and examine its shape, in order to determine whether it would make a good skipping stone. This qualitative haptic exploration leverages many different actions that each give different information about the object being handled.

- Lateral motion: move your fingers across the object to identify texture

- Pressure application: squeeze the object between your fingers to identify hardness

- Enclosure: wrap your fingers around the object to identify global shape and volume

- Static contact: touch the object briefly to identify temperature

- Unsupported holding: hold the object from one side, or from the top, or move it up and down a bit to explore the weight and mass distribution

- Contour following: move your fingers around the object to identify specific shape

Other specific actions are also possible, and different people perform these explorations differently. The combination of these actions helps build a better mental model of a given object, and although many of these qualities can be guessed using visual characteristics, they are only directly sensed through this qualitative haptic exploration, allowing you to determine the difference between a rock, and a piece of foam shaped like a rock.

### 5.3.4.2 Roughness

Tactile receptors allow us to perceive changes in pressure from textures on surfaces as we move them (or they are moved) relative to our skin surface. The greatest sensitivity to roughness exists on our lips, fingers, and forearms, while the heel, back, and thigh the are least sensitive.

Whether the skin moves relative to the object or vice versa has no effect on roughness perception—it is perceived relating to the relative motion between the skin and the object.

Vision and touch are close to equal in their ability to discriminate very coarse textures, but touch is far better for discriminating finer textures.

### 5.3.4.3 Tactile Pattern Perception

Tactile pattern perception is the task of recognizing and interpreting patterns of tactile stimulus—Braille, for example, is a system of writing that relies on tactile pattern perception in the same way that reading written words relies on visual pattern perception. Biological feature detectors exist for touch much as they do for vision and auditory pattern perception, and these are more highly developed in people who spend more time discerning patterns in each of these senses. Tactile pattern perception is also susceptible to masking in the same way that other senses are—forward masking occurs when an arbitrary tactile pattern is presented before a target pattern is presented, making it more difficult to distinguish the target stimuli. Backwards masking similarly occurs, except that the target stimulus is presented first.

The duplex theory of texture perception suggests that coarse and fine textures are perceived through different mechanisms: coarser textures are primarily perceived by spatial cues, while finer textures are primarily perceived via temporal cues.

Touch can be separated into two broad categories—fine touch (sometimes referred to as discriminative touch) is a sensory modality that allows the subject to localize touch finely. A second form of touch, crude (or coarse) touch, does not allow for localization. It allows the subject to feel that something has touched them without being able to localize where the touch has occurred. Fine touch and crude touch work in parallel, but use separate pathways—the dorsal column for fine touch vs. the spinothalamic tract for coarse touch. It is found that when the pathways for fine touch are disrupted, patients are able to feel that they were touched, just not where that touch occurred.

---

**Social Touch**

Affective touch, being touched in a social situation, many would assume would use the same pathways as other stimuli. However, this information is actually coded differently—intensity of affective touch is processed more similar to the emotional responses elicited by sight and sound.

It activates the anterior cingulate cortex more than the primary somatosensory cortex.

---

Passive tactile spatial acuity is the ability to resolve fine spatial details of a non-moving object pressed against stationary skin. A common method is the grating orientation task, where a subject is asked to identify the orientation of a grooved surface pressed against the skin in different orientations.

Studies have shown than passive tactile spatial acuity declines with age—one theory for this is that tactile receptors are lost during normal ageing.

**Inverse spatial acuity size**
Index finger passive spatial acuity is better among adults with smaller index fingertips. As women tend to have smaller fingers, women have better passive tactile spatial acuity on average than men. Similarly, the density of corpuscles is higher in smaller fingers. Thus children also have better passive tactile acuity. Passive tactile spatial acuity is also enhanced among blind individuals compared to sighted individuals of the same age.

### 5.3.5 Somatosensory Disorders

Many conditions may occur in which the sense of touch is altered. A very usual sensation is that of a limb "falling asleep." This is a subset of abnormal skin sensations referred to as **paresthesia**, coming from the Greek "para" meaning abnormal and "aisthesia," meaning sensation. The degree, frequency, and permanency to which individuals experience paresthesia are diverse—although in most cases paresthesia is painless. Paresthesias may be described as "tingling" of the skin or as numbness. Formication, the sensation of insects crawling on the skin—often associated with drug use—is another type of paresthesia.

Most people have experienced some form of transient paresthesia.

There are several causes of paresthesia, but most occur due to some restriction of nerves. One common paresthesic experience occurs with the banging of the "funny bone," a colloquial term for the ulnar nerve near the elbow. This manifests in what feels like an electric shock followed by fading numbness and tingling. Resting on a body part may restrict nerve impulses, as may applying sustained pressure over a nerve—both these cases can lead to the "pins and needles" feeling of a limb falling asleep.

Chronic paresthesia is common in those with poor circulation. Joint inflammation conditions such as rheumatoid arthritis and carpal tunnel syndrome can result in prolonged bouts of paresthesia, as can direct damage to the nerves themselves, for instance through injury or frostbite.

### 5.3.6 Tactile Illusions

Adaption-based tactile illusions—if you adapt to a certain position or level of stimulus, this affects stimuli afterwards. For example, if you put one hand in cold water, one in hot water, and then both hands in lukewarm water, the water will feel warm to the hand that was in the cold water and cool to the one previously in hot water. Showing that the touch maps to different areas spatially, if the index and middle finger are crossed, touching something between the two fingers feels like two objects. Similarly, it feels like you are still moving forward after you get off a moving treadmill.

Often what people think of as the sense of touch is "active touch," which involves you moving your body to touch stimulus or stimulus touching you. This is sometimes also referred to as haptic touch. The word "tangible" refers to objects currently able to be touched in the same way "visible" is used to refer to objects currently able to be seen.

Touch differs from the other "four senses" in that it is made up of many different sensory channels. Touch also works in combinations with movement senses (kinesthesis) in order to help localize. Different nerve channels carry information for temperature, pain, pressure, shape, and vibration (discriminative touch). As discussed before, touch consists of many different modalities.

Unlike vision and hearing, the field that touch can sense in external space is not three dimensional, instead being two dimensionally mapped to the skin.

With the exception of hot and cold, all sensations felt by touch are defined by the spatial properties of the object

## 5.4 THE PROPRIOCEPTIVE SYSTEM

Proprioception is the sense of knowing the pose and position of one's body. The primary responsibility of the proprioceptive system is to allow us to be aware of the position of our body parts without having to look for them. People without functioning proprioceptive receptors may be able to control the movement of their limbs perfectly fine while looking at them, but quickly become disoriented if they close their eyes or look away. Proprioception enables humans to know where their arms are relative to the body, as well as roughly at what speed and direction they are moving, and contributes information on forces on the body, along with the skin senses. The role of the proprioceptive system becomes immediately obvious in situations where it is impaired, such as when one is under the influence of alcohol. Without a properly functioning proprioceptive system, simple tasks such as walking in a straight line become difficult, making these movements a good test of sobriety.

### 5.4.1 Proprioceptive Stimuli

Unlike the other senses described so far, proprioceptive stimuli do not come from outside of the body. Instead, proprioceptive information is transduced by sensors within the skin, joints, and muscles, sensing the tension required to hold the body in a certain position. Receptors involved in the proprioceptive system are referred to as **proprioceptors**.

The proprioceptive system is an important part of the motor control and feedback system. Proprioceptive receptors integrate with other sensations such as vision and touch to provide accurate information, which is utilized as feedback during motion tasks.

The information gained from the proprioceptive system can be broken down into four categories. The first, **joint position sensing**, is the sense of where limbs are located in terms of absolute position. This information is what allows people to position their foot on a car pedal at a desired angle, set an airplane throttle to a desired position without looking, or other such tasks that require a sense of a limb's exact location in space. The joint position sensing ability can be tested by moving an individual's target limb to a specific position and then asking them to replicate that position themselves. Joint position is determined by the Ruffini endings as well as Pacinian corpuscles, receptors previously mentioned in regard to their somatosensory functions.

The proprioceptive system also allows for the sense of **kinesthesia**, the ability to perceive the motion of the human body. Moving around a room in the dark while avoiding furniture uses a combination of joint position sensing and kinesthesia to move the body to positions that avoid running into unseen objects. Kinesthesia is what allows us to sense all aspects of movements within the body that come from non-visual or somatosensory information — thanks to kinesthesia, the duration and direction as well as the timing of joint movement are known without having to see the limbs that are moving. Muscle spindles, receptors located within muscles that are stimulated by stretching, relay information regarding muscle length, and velocity that allows the brain to determine the movement of limbs in conjunction with simultaneous joint position information.

The third proprioceptive modality is that of **force matching**. While being able to feel how much force an object contacts us with falls under the domain of the somatosensory system, the reverse process, determining how much force one is exerting upon an object, is indicated by proprioceptive receptors. Both the Golgi tendon organs and muscle spindles exhibit a response proportional to the force exerted by a muscle, allowing us to gauge how hard we are pushing, hitting, or pulling an object. As voice modulation for speaking involves regulating tension in vocal chords, the ability to speak also relies upon proprioceptive force matching. Each Golgi tendon organ in a group will be activated at a different amount of muscle force, so what Golgi tendon organs are sending a response at a given time indicates how much force a given muscle is experiencing.

Finally, proprioceptive receptors also provide information about the velocity of vibrations on skin. Although this overlaps with some of the responsibilities of the somatosensory system, it has been found that vibrations are also detected and transduced by nerve fibres used for proprioceptive channels.

## 5.5 THE VESTIBULAR SYSTEM

In addition to housing auditory receptors, the ear contains a structure of bone and tissue that provides information for an important interoceptive system. This is the **vestibular system**, which provides the sense of balance and spatial orientation.

The vestibular system is comprised of two components that reside within a structure in the inner ear, called the **vestibular labyrinth**. These components include the **semicircular canals**, which are responsible for determining rotational orientation, and the **otoliths**, which detect linear acceleration.

### 5.5.1 Vestibular Receptors

The vestibular labyrinth is made of bone and has several cavities that comprise the three semicircular canals present in each ear. The labyrinth also holds the cochlea (used for auditory processing) and the otolithic organs.

Three semicircular canals exist in each ear, one for each possible dimension of rotation. The canals are orthogonal to each other and consist of the horizontal canal (which tracks rotation occurring about a vertical axis through the head), the anterior canal (corresponding to an axis through the ears), and the posterior canal (corresponding to an axis through the eyes to the back of the head). When rotation occurs about a given axis, the position of fluid within the bony canal indicates the current orientation of the head. Hair cells embedded within the cupula at the end of each canal transduce movement in the fluid to the neural signals used to discern rotation. Each canal only sends signals when rotational acceleration is present — if the head is stationary or rotating at a constant velocity, there will be no response from the canals.

The two otolithic organs, the **utricle** and the **saccule**, detect linear motion of the head. The utricle detects horizontal movement, while the saccule detects vertical movement, both through a similar fluid-hair interaction as occurs in the canals. In the same way as rotational acceleration is detected by the canals, linear acceleration is what is sensed by the otolithic organs. Therefore, the otolithic organs are unable to differentiate between no movement and movement at a constant linear velocity.

In addition to helping with bodily navigation, the vestibular system is important in helping prevent motion sickness in day to day life. The **vestibulo-ocular reflex** uses vestibular input, working in tandem with the visual system, to keep gaze steady under the course of movement. When you turn your head, the vestibulo-ocular reflex is how you are able to keep one point of your vision in focus. Without this reflex, it would be difficult to perform fine visual discrimination and identification tasks, such as reading, due to the constant vibrations of the body.

## 5.6  OTHER INTEROCEPTIVE SENSES

Besides the senses listed over the course of the last two chapters, there is plenty of other information that people are able to perceive about their bodies from various sensory receptors. Interoceptive senses refer to systems of sensations that collect stimuli from the body, as opposed to the exteroceptive senses that interpret stimuli from the external world. Proprioception is an example of an interoceptive sense—the receptors involved in the proprioceptive system give information about the joints of the body. Many interoceptive processes play a large role in our day to day lives. "Feelings" such as hunger or fatigue arise from interoceptive sensory processes, as are sensations like the feeling of running out of air while underwater or having a full bladder. Although this information is not coming from the outside world, it is vitally important to our survival. The interoceptive senses are some of the least understood sensory processes in the body, at least in terms of metrics like perceived intensity, quantization, or resolution. In fact, questions such as "what would even qualify as the resolution for the perception of hunger" have yet to be answered—these may be one dimensional processes, or they may be complex systems. In terms of VR, these may be some of the hardest sensations to simulate—not only due to our ignorance of their underlying function, but also from an implementation standpoint—it is a lot harder to immerse a sensory unit that is not external to the body. Being able to simulate sensations like thirst or exhaustion may have useful applications within VR, but the principles behind the technology required to do this may be fundamentally different from the immersion-based displays used for other senses today.

## 5.7 SUMMARY

The range of sensations available to a user is wider that usually simulated in current VR systems. Many developers and futurists imagine a day when VR will include "smell-o-vision," or be able to replicate the full-body sensation of swimming through a cool mountain lake, or feel the forces of a rocket launch and then to adapt to weightlessness. We can imagine technical solutions to simulating some of these secondary senses, but there will likely be sensations that simply cannot be reproduced while we live on a planet with gravity and atmosphere. Until we can find ways to isolate and reproduce every sensation we experience, VR will continue to be a copy of reality rather than being indistinguishable from reality.

# CHAPTER 6

# Perceiving Space and Scale

In Chapter 2, we discussed the importance of virtual reality (VR)'s ability to display stimuli that the mind interprets as a 3D space. When a user feels present in a virtual space, applications are easier to learn, training is more effective, and features from the physical world translate directly to interactions in the virtual world. These and other benefits allow users to interact in a space that shares many advantages of both the digital and physical realms. We've also talked about the body's mechanisms of registering stimuli, as well as the fields and ranges over which stimuli can be received. However, raw stimuli alone do not confer a physical space—it's the relation of stimuli to each other as well as the ways that stimuli change over time that makes a user's mind interpret digital input in the same way as the mind interprets more natural, "real-world" environments. This chapter seeks to illuminate this "missing link" between sensation and spatial perception.

The perception of space is an individual's understanding of the physical quantities of distance, velocity, and acceleration. Other qualities influence our interpretation of our relationship to spaces, such as the scale of objects, masses, and distances. Many senses contribute to our perception of distance—for example, vision and sound can allow us to estimate distances to objects; proprioceptive and vestibular input gives us a sense of the speed at which we are moving. Even time perception plays a role in the determination of how far a distance is—if you are bored and are walking slowly, you may assume a distance is further than if you had ran it. The novelty of an environment, maybe due to time perception, also impacts the sensation of distance— a walk through an area seems a lot longer the first time you go through it, but if you do it every day, eventually seems much shorter. The aggregate of information from these diverse sensations influences the brain's mental model of the space it inhabits.

We also use sound to determine information about the spaces we are in. When a sound bounces around a room, it reflects off of different surfaces, and the various reflections arrive at our ear at different times. The accumulation of these multiple reflections is known as **reverb**, and we are attuned to interpreting the feeling of a space based on the way the reverb sounds. Large concert halls have a long-duration echoic reverb, while a closet full of clothes (or an anechoic chamber) sound muffled and dense. Somewhat ironically, a wide open outdoor space also has no reflections,

DOI: 10.1201/9781003261230-6

but other sounds will contribute to the sense of space here, like the rustle of leaves on a tree or the chirping of birds.

We will first discuss a general overview of the biological mechanisms that are understood to have an impact on the interpretation of space and scale. Then, we will move into the more general missing link between sensation of stimuli and perception of space: depth cues.

Much as with our understanding of the mechanisms of general sensations across the senses, researchers have a much better understanding of how vision influences space perception than other senses. Although we will touch upon spatial cues coming from other sensory modalities within this chapter, the first portion will discuss the impact of the relatively well-understood visual depth cues. Following that, we will briefly summarize depth cues from the lesser understood senses, most specifically sound, before moving into a discussion on how spatial qualities are interpreted in the brain—what factors affect how we perceive distance, position, and movement. Finally, we close the chapter with a short discussion on digital spaces that act differently than the mathematical definitions that describe how space works in the natural world. These non-Euclidean spaces can have interesting applications and influences on users, be they unconsciously used to make a scene seem more realistic or a space seem larger or be a front-and-centre game mechanic.

## 6.1   INTERPRETATION OF SPACE AND DEPTH CUES

There are two different contexts in which position in a space can be determined. The first, determining the distance and direction of objects from yourself, is **egocentric** judgement of position. Egocentric localization allows us to know where our bodies are located compared to other objects and the environment. These judgements are useful in tasks such as navigation and interaction with physical objects. Words such as left or right, or forward or backward, reflect an egocentric frame of reference— these directions change based on our physical position. Egocentric judgements result in the perception of **absolute distances**, how far and in what direction objects are from us. Judgements of how objects related to each other, such as the **relative distance** between two objects, are **exocentric judgements**. Determining how far away an object is from another object and how much larger it is than another are both exocentric. Body-independent vectors, such as the cardinal directions (north, south, east, west), indicate an exocentric frame of reference.

Although we can interpret a continuous range of distances from ourselves, we mentally tend to categorize the space around us into several discrete categories. People mentally group sections of the external environment into three discrete chunks— personal space, action space, and vista space. In a flat plane, all three sections of space are roughly circular (although the limits of the environment may alter what we consider to be part of a particular space—i.e. walls) and are determined by the movement required to access items within that particular space.

**Personal space** is considered to be the space within the immediate reach of the arms. Proprioceptive depth cues are limited to within this space, and certain visual depth cues are also limited to personal space. In the physical world, we are limited to directly interacting via touch only with objects within our personal space.

**Action space** is the next circle out from personal space. This space can be considered to be limited to the range a person can locomote in the "immediate future"—a radius of 2 m to 20 m away from ourselves in a flat plane, but obviously limited by walls in an indoor environment. This is the space within which we carry out many "ranged" actions—comfortable conversation occurs within the range of the action space.

**Vista space** extends past the action space to nearly infinity. Many people might consider this to be the "background." Very few of our actions are capable of affecting objects within the vista space range.

Aside from these external ranges, there is also a psychological basis of what is considered part of our body's space that can change on a situational basis and is not always limited to the body itself.

The term **depth cue** is used to refer to patterns or relationships between stimuli that allow for perception of a third dimension in space. Although senses such as proprioception and the vesitbular sense may give us information in three dimensions, the sensory categories that provide the highest volume of information, the visual, auditory, and tactile senses, only map to a 2D plane of sensory inputs on the body, even though they may capture input from a three-dimensional portion of the environment. With such categories, the position of stimuli on our array of sensory units is not alone sufficient to determine the depth of objects in 3D space—instead, patterns in the stimuli received are used to determine the relative distance in the sagittal plane that we are from objects. Many sensory categories provide no depth information at all.

We can sort these two cases, where depth is sensed directly and where depth is inferred from stimuli patterns into cases of depth sensation and depth cues—these two combine to form our **depth perception**.

As mentioned previously, depth perception can be broken into depth information that is directly sensed, **depth sensation**, and depth that is implied by patterns recognized, referred to as **depth cues**. Depth sensations are rather rare—only one of our sensory processes, proprioceptive stimuli, provides direct information about depth, giving position in three-dimensional space. The rest of depth is inferred from patterns that arise from sensory stimuli—the depth cues. Depth cues are seen in sensory systems that map a 3D space to a two-dimensional sensor array. For example, the visual system maps photoreceptors within a 2D space on the back of the retina, but each of these photoreceptors can collect from a cone that projects into 3D space. The auditory system and olfactory system don't project into space, instead having their respective sensory organs within the head, but the fact that there are two ears allows sounds to be localized, and the existence of the two nostrils allows smell localization to occur to a lesser extent. However, being able to infer the third dimension is more coarse for both the auditory and olfactory systems—intensity is the primary

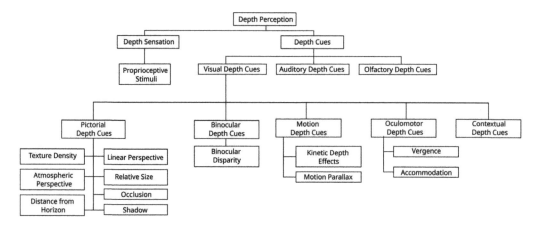

Figure 6.1: A diagram showing the categories that contribute to the sense of depth perception.

cue used to judge the distance of sounds and smells. The way that sounds refract off of objects can give a more accurate picture of where sound sources exist within a 3D space, however.

We rely primarily on the visual system for cues that allow for the inference of depth. The visual depth cues can themselves be sorted into five categories. We discuss the role each depth cue plays below.

### 6.1.1 Pictorial Depth Cues

Pictorial depth cues are those that arise from the way objects relate to each other in a single picture. VR isn't required for pictorial depth cues to be seen—the depth cues that are apparent in a movie or a still picture are all pictorial. Pictorial depth cues do not include cases where movement is required in order for depth to be perceived—these cases fall into the category of motion depth cues. When looking at a still photo, pictorial depth cues are the only way to tell the relative depth of the objects within the image—the information conveyed by what elements are in front of each other, the size of relative objects, where shadows fall, and so on.

#### 6.1.1.1 Occlusion

Occlusion occurs when one objects partially or fully obstructs one or more objects in the field of view. Occlusion provides strong information about the *relative* depth order of objects—an object in the physical world has to be in front of another in order to occlude it.

There are two important factors to note regarding occlusion in a still image. The first is that occlusion provides no absolute judgement of depth, only depth relative to other objects. One can use the cue of occlusion to infer if an object is in front of or behind another object, but not "how far" in front or behind the object is. In this regard, we can consider occlusion to be a **non-metrical depth cue**, meaning that it is able to provide information about the order of objects, but not specific magnitude

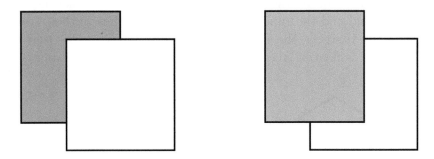

Figure 6.2: Two squares, showing that the one occluding the other is interpreted as "in front" when position held constant.

measurements of their depth. In contrast, **metrical depth cues** are those that are able to be used to quantitatively determine depth.

The second factor of note is that occlusion relies on us interpreting an object to be partially behind another object. It is entirely possible that we infer a shape to be occluded when it is not or that we infer a shape is not occluded when it is, as shown in Figure 6.3. The Gestalt principles play a large role in determining whether we interpret a figure as occluded or not.

Figure 6.3: The grey L shape depicted inaccurately appears to be a square occluded by the green object.

### 6.1.1.2 Shadow

Objects cast shadows based on the position of light sources, and where those shadows fall can give information on the position of objects. A subset of occlusion, the shadows of objects, can occlude or be occluded by other objects, even if the objects themselves don't occlude. Shadows also provide height information, which can change relative depth information. The cubes shown in Figure 6.4 are at the same position in both images, but in the first image, the shadows make the cubes look like they are both at rest on the ground and the cube higher in the image seems further away due to relative height cues. However, the shadow in the second image implies that the cube higher in the image is floating above the ground and is the same distance away as the first cube.

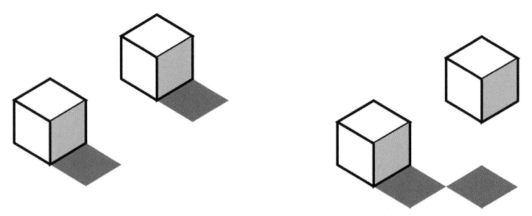

Figure 6.4: Cubes showing how shadow placement can influence relative depth.

### 6.1.1.3 Linear Perspective

In Euclidean geometry, lines that are parallel in three dimensions appear to converge in a two-dimensional image as they get further in the distance. On a set of lines that are parallel in the 3D space, the further away an orthogonal connecting line is, the shorter it will appear (despite being the same length within 3D space). Figure 6.5 illustrates this relationship with an object that would be a constant size in a 3D space, railroad ties. The ties that are further back take up as smaller amount of the visual field.

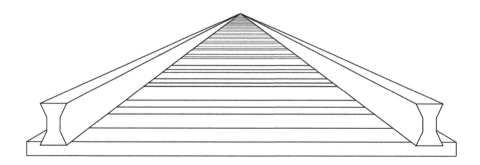

Figure 6.5: Diagram of a railroad track demonstrating linear perspective.

In Figure 6.5, all the lines parallel to the sagittal plane of the viewer appear to converge to an infinitely small point. This is referred to as the vanishing point. In a three-dimensional world, there is more than one vanishing point, and they are rarely visible—unless you happen to reside in a biome with flat topology, hills will block the view. There are as many vanishing points in a given scene as there are geometries that face different directions—the calculations for perceptive can become complex, but in all cases the further away a portion of an object is, the more the lines appear to converge. Multiple-point perspective is illustrated via the cubes in Figure 6.6.

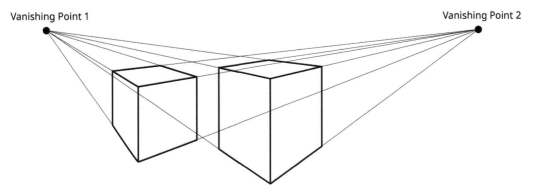

Figure 6.6: Cubes drawn in two-point perspective.

### 6.1.1.4 Relative Size

In Euclidean space, if a particular object is closer to us, it takes up a larger portion of our field of view than when it is further away. The depth cue of relative size utilizes this fact in using the general assumption that smaller objects tend to be further away from us than larger objects. Of course, various knowledge that we have about the size of objects comes into play when assuming the distance of objects given relative size—if a car and a house take up the same amount of our visual field, we tend to assume that the car is closer to us, as cars are usually smaller than houses. This additional depth cue is known as **familiar size** and is sometimes treated as a separate depth cue, but it often works in conjunction with the cue of relative size. Relative size and relative height both provide metrical information about the depth of objects—for example, by size we could assume that one object is twice as far away from us as another object. This is a relative metrical depth cue, as the information provided is given relative to one of the objects—the distance of one away from us is an observable fraction of the distance away from the other. With the addition of familiar size, we are able to infer absolute metrical information about the depth of the object—based on our knowledge of its size, we can judge the distance of the object away from us.

### 6.1.1.5 Relative Height

In Euclidean space, due to the phenomenon of linear perspective, the further away an object is from us, the closer it seems to be to the horizon. The depth cue of relative height relies on the assumption that objects closer to the horizon are further away. If an object is on the ground, those that are higher in the visual field tend to be further away, while objects in the air, such as an airplane, tend to be lower in the visual field (closer to the horizon) the further away they are.

### 6.1.1.6 *Texture Gradient*

How "fine" or "dense" textures get in certain areas of the scene is an important clue as to how far away they are. The further away an object is, the more densely packed and smoother its texture seems. This is partially due to visual acuity—the further away an object is, the smaller it is, and therefore the more difficult it becomes to resolve small details of its texture. Texture gradient is a combination of the cues of relative size and relative height—denser textures tend to be located closer to the horizon than coarser ones.

Very few real surfaces completely lack a texture, although this is somewhat more common in computer simulations. Giving textures to virtual surfaces and ensuring they scale appropriately with distance can go a long way to ensuring that objects seem a certain distance away.

Objects with coarser textures appear closer, but gradually the texture becomes less distinct and finer as it moves further from the observer. Different elements of textures can be visible and add to the depth cue at different distances—for example the fine grain of a wood floor is only visible at short distances, but the pattern made by the planks can be seen from much further away.

The texture gradient must follow enough other depth cues to be interpreted as a depth cue itself. When the picture of circles shown in Figure 6.7 has the texture gradient rotated upwards, they seem to be further away, but when rotated sideways, they do not. This does not mean that relative height and size always have to be obeyed in this manner for texture gradient to be interpreted as a depth cue, as shown by a brick wall in linear perspective which does have a horizontal gradient, but there must be several agreeing cues.

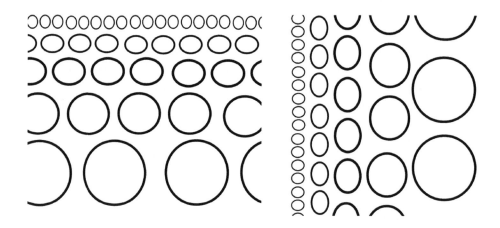

Figure 6.7: Depiction of the effect of rotation on the perception of texture depth.

### 6.1.1.7 Atmospheric Perspective

The atmosphere tends to scatter light as it moves through it. Thus, light received from objects that are really far away tends to be more scattered by the atmosphere—it appears fainter, bluer, and less distinct that if the light has to travel a longer distance. If you've ever driven up to mountains from a distance, you'll know that at first they are hardly distinguishable from the sky, appearing as a very washed-out blue, but getting darker and less blue the closer you get. This effect can be seen in Figure 6.8—although all the mountains in the picture are made of the same rock and would appear to be more or less the same colour if viewed up close, atmospheric perspective makes the ones in the background appear bluer and more washed out. Atmospheric perspective as a depth cue, also referred to as aerial perspective, relies on this assumption—all other things constant, we assume that fainter and bluer objects are further away that closer, more saturated ones.

Figure 6.8: A photograph of mountains that demonstrates atmospheric perspective.

## 6.1.2 Binocular Depth Cues

The phenomenon of binocular disparity is our binocular depth cue, meaning that it is a cue that uses the differences between the images viewed by each eye in order to interpret depth. The disparity is defined as the difference in locations within the retinal image of objects. How much disparity there is depends on how far the object in question is from the eye—the closer the object is to the eye, the bigger the disparity between the two images.

The disparity in an image also depends on the fixation distance—where the line from the two eyes cross. The fixation distance is often described with the concept of the **horopter**, an imaginary curved surface in the 3D space in front of the face with equal perceived distance from the person. The horopter includes the point where the two eyes are fixated (the point where the lines of action of the eyes cross) as well as a circle that includes the optical centres of the two eyes. A diagram of the horopter can be seen in Figure 6.9. Theoretically, the horopter forms a circle intersecting with the eyes, but empirically, perceived equal distance tends to enlarge with peripheral angle.

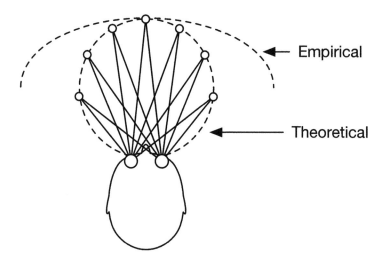

Figure 6.9: The horopter, showing objects of theoretical and empirical perceived equal distance.

The horopter acts as a boundary to define how disparities act—if an object is beyond the horopter, it has uncrossed disparities, meaning that the user would have to diverge their eyes to fixate on it. In the image received by the right eye, the object lies further to the right than it does from the left eye's view. If the object is between the user and the horopter, it has crossed disparities, meaning that the eyes would have to cross or converge, in order to focus on it. The effect of the disparity on the images received is the reverse—in the right eye's view, the object lies further to the left than it does in the left eye's view.

Binocular depth cues don't rely on pattern recognition to function, unlike monocular depth cues. As such, they are unaffected by other depth cues—while monocular depth cues appear stronger when additional monocular depth cues are present, binocular depth cues are just as strong without any other forms. Further, depth perception doesn't require a recognizable form or shape in order to see depth—random dot stereograms such as the one shown in Figure 6.10 don't have a form or any depth cue, but the disparity between the two images allows us to perceive it as having depth.

Stereoblindness occurs in about 10% of the population, meaning that they are unable to perceive disparities and therefore are unable to perceive stereopsis. The manner of stereoblindness can be partial or full—some people can't perceive any disparities, while others are only blind to crossed or uncrossed disparities, but not both. A discussion of stereoblindness, other visual disparities, and methods to support

Figure 6.10: A random-dot stereogram.

individuals who do not have typical vision is presented in Section 8.5. Although people with stereoblindness may not be able to perceive depth using binocular vision, the presence of many other depth cues makes it such that they are able to perceive depth fine in many cases in the physical world.

## 6.1.3 Motion Depth Cues

### 6.1.3.1 Motion Parallax

In motion parallax, the images of distal stimuli move across the retina at different rates dependent on the distance. Parallax occurs during any motion, but one of the most dramatic examples may be when you are looking out of the window of a moving vehicle. Objects closer to the road, such as telephone poles, may seem to move by very quickly, while further parts of the landscape, such as cows, move across the retina slower or objects like the mountains in the background seem to hardly move at all. The effects of motion parallax are illustrated in Figure 6.11.

Fixating on a single point changes how things appear to move—things on the near side of the horopter seem to move in the opposite direction as those on the far side of the horopter. Motion parallax, unlike binocular disparity, works in all directions.

### 6.1.3.2 Kinetic Depth Effects

The kinetic depth effect allows 3D structures to be perceived to have depth as they move—the perception of the depth of the object can be seen thanks to its movement even if the observer isn't moving.

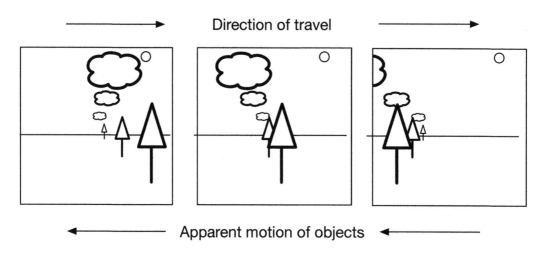

Figure 6.11: Motion parallax. Closer objects appear to move faster.

### 6.1.4 Oculomotor Depth Cues

#### 6.1.4.1 Vergence

Vergence is the motion of the eyes in opposite directions, the action that is taken to converge or diverge in order to result in comfortable binocular focus. Vergence is triggered by retinal disparity—we can feel in our muscles the movement of the eyes in the case of vergence, so it provides certain depth cues, but large differences in vergence muscle tension are limited to roughly 2 metres, so beyond this vergence does not play a huge role in depth perception.

#### 6.1.4.2 Accommodation

Accommodation is the muscular flexion that changes the focal length of the eye's lens. Accommodation allows you to focus on different objects—the accommodation muscles are held tight when focused on nearby objects and are held looser for further distances. Much like we can feel the muscles involved in vergence, we can also feel the tightening of the accommodation muscles, which can serve as a depth cue. Similar to vergence, this is only really a factor in depth perception of images up to 2 metres away. The blurriness of objects that are out of focus is also a depth cue, but cannot be used alone to determine if objects are closer or further from the focal point—they both appear blurred.

In VR, a phenomenon called the vergence-accommodation conflict can occur when lenses are used to allow the user to focus on a screen very close to their eyes, while displaying an image that appears to be far away from their eyes. In order for the virtual object to appear far away, the left and right versions of the object must be presented such that the direction each eye is looking is spread out (higher vergence); however, even with the help of the lens in the VR headset, the eyes are focussing on an image that is very close to the eye (lower accommodation). The eyes are accommodated to a much shorter distance than the vergence cues would suggest,

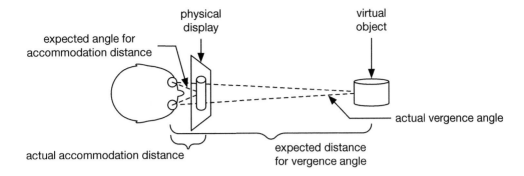

Figure 6.12: Vergence-accommodation conflict. The distance of the virtual object, as interpreted by vergence, does not agree with the distance of the physical screen, as interpreted by accommodation.

leading to a sensory conflict. A diagram illustrating this conflict can be seen in Figure 6.12.

### 6.1.5 Contextual Depth Cues

Some depth cues depend on the context in which a pattern is observed—for example, objects indoors are judged as closer than those outdoors, even at the same distance. Further, objects within reach are considered much closer than those out of reach, and hill slopes are estimated as much steeper as they actually are.

## 6.2 SPATIAL AUDIO REPRODUCTION

When applied to VR, a key adaptation of interactive sound is **spatial audio**, which is the simulation of sound coming from a specific direction. Spatial audio works best with headphones, because we can then control exactly what is presented to each ear. Like with vision, we are partially occluding the sounds of the physical world and replacing them with sounds from the virtual world, although it should be noted that completely occluding sound requires noise-cancelling headphones. Even with high-quality headphones, sounds from the physical world can bleed through into the virtual world, but noise-cancelling headphones create a cancellation wave that subtracts sounds from the physical world, more completely occluding them.

Given that we can control the sound that each ear hears, there are several possibilities of what to send to each ear to create given effects. As a starting point, what happens if we send the same sound to each ear? The result is that the listener perceives the sound coming from inside their head; this does not feel strange, however, and we are very used to monophonic audio in headphones, although stereophonic sound is usually preferred. Stereo sound is usually recorded with a pair of microphones, one for each ear, and the sensation of different sounds arriving at each ear makes the audio feel fuller, richer, and more dynamic, but it still sounds like a recording, in the same way that a photograph can look very rich, detailed, and well composed, even though it is still clearly a photograph.

To make believable spatial audio, we must reproduce not just the sounds, but the way the sounds are modified by the physical world before they arrive at our eardrum. Some large-scale techniques to make simulated audio feel more real include adding Doppler shift to sounds that are moving (which raises the pitch for approaching sounds and lowers the pitch for receding sounds) and make faraway sounds quieter and low-pass filtered, to simulate the dampening effect that long distance travel can have on sounds; but the most relevant change that happens to sound to give us clues to where it comes from is the changes that are made by our own body.

## 6.2.1 Head-Related Transfer Function

The head related transfer function (HRTF) is the modifications that happen to a sound as it travels around your head and into your ears. Sound waves approaching from the right will bounce off your right shoulder into your right ear and wrap around your head before they enter your left ear. As the sound arrives at each ear, the pinnae (folds of cartilage on the side of your head) change the sound in subtle ways depending on the direction it is coming from, and because the shape of those folds co-evolved with a brain designed to interpret them, those subtle frequency changes result in highly sensitive directional hearing. Additionally, the time difference of arrival of the sound wave between one ear and the other gives a strong indication of the direction the sound came from. Other animals have evolved more active sound modification techniques, with dogs and cats able to move their pinnae to focus the sound in different ways.

When sound is recorded with a regular microphone, the sound is not modified by the pinnae or the shape of the head, and so when that sound is played back on headphones, it does not sound present or spatial. There are relatively simple techniques available to record spatialized sound—all we need to do is record the sound after it has been modified by the HRTF. HRTF dummy heads, like the one shown in Figure 6.13, can be 3D printed or purchased, and as long as there are a pair of microphones where the eardrums would be, the sound recorded has the HRTF baked in, as it were. If you want to hear what HRTF sound sounds like, samples are available online. The classic example is the "virtual barbershop," where a person walks around an HRTF dummy chatting and snipping scissors. Listening to this recording on speakers sounds like a regular recording, but with headphones on, the listener can accurately identify the location of the barber as they walk around the listener—not just the direction but the distance as well.

## 6.2.2 Impulse Response

Generating synthesized spatial audio is somewhat more challenging, since it requires a recording of the transfer function itself, which can be convoluted with the sound that you wish to spatialize to produce the desired effect. This transfer function recording is called an **impulse response** and can be produced by recording a very short spike of sound, like a balloon pop or a gunshot. This spike of sound is called an impulse, and the way that impulse is changed by travelling to the microphone is the impulse response for that scenario. When convoluting, each sample of the sound you want to

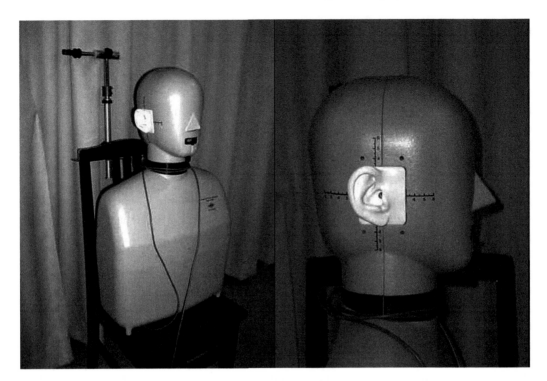

Figure 6.13: Head-related transfer function (HRTF) dummy head, also called HATS (head and torso simulator). *2014AIST, CCBY3.0*

change is treated as if it was an impulse and is multiplied by the impulse response. All these individual impulse responses are added together to create the sound as if it had happened in that scenario.

Impulse responses can be used to record the resonance of different rooms, or the way sound bounces off of walls or passes through doors. The only drawback to the impulse response technique is that it can only be used to simulate a sound happening exactly where the impulse occurred, perceived by a person standing where the HRTF dummy was placed. For interactive audio, where sounds and listeners move, more complicated techniques may be necessary, which can include audio-based ray tracing techniques or using an array of recorded or simulated impulse responses.

### 6.2.3 Using Spatial Audio in VR

The process of simulating spatialized audio in VR is similar to the process of simulating three-dimensional visual representations of a virtual world, in that the best way to accomplish this is to create a simplified representation of the virtual world you wish to represent, and render sensations out of that virtual world. In the early days of the development of computer games, shortcuts were invented which would allow a computer to generate the illusion of a three-dimensional world without actually having to create the full representation.

### 6.2.3.1 *Stereo, Panning, and VBAP*

Although visual illusions that give the feeling of three dimensions were common (as described above), audio illusions to indicate direction were initially primarily simple stereo effects. Playing the sound in one speaker and not another is a simple technique that will give the impression that the sound is coming from the left or the right, but does not give much more information than that. Taking the sound source and panning it back and forth between the speakers can give the illusion that the sound is moving from one side of the screen to the other. Although straightforward, this technique required separate positioning of different sounds, which was not available in early game systems. Only when the sound engine was moved back in the pipeline, allowing specific effects to be applied to individual sound sources rather than the complete produced audio, could individual sounds be moved through space.

The naive approach to panning is to reduce the volume of the sound in one speaker as you increase the volume of the same sound in the other speaker. This will produce the illusion of motion, but because humans hear sound pressure level on a logarithmic scale, this linear panning produces a drop in the perceived loudness of the sound as the source passes between the speakers. To compensate for this, **constant power panning** is used, as shown in Figure 6.14. If the crossfade between the two speakers is maintained such that the overall power is held constant, the result is the perception that the sound source maintains the same distance away as it pans from one speaker to another.

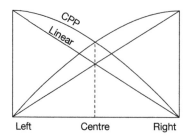
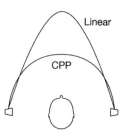

Figure 6.14: Constant power panning (CPP). Left: power to each speaker as a function of angle. Right: perceived distance to the source.

Although these techniques were initially developed for stereo sound, multispeaker environments with more than two speakers have become more common. In a 5.1 theatre configuration, or an eight-channel octophonic ring, panning between the speakers can be extended to three dimensions using a technique called vector-based amplitude panning or VBAP. In this case, the amplitude of the sound source in any nearby speaker is based on the direction of the virtual sound source and its angular deviation from the nearby speakers. A generalization of this technique, called Ambisonics, has been used to allow the recording of real-world spatial audio on an array of microphones and the playback on different configuration speakers.

Because VR is generated relative to the user and not the space, VBAP and Ambisonics are rarely used, although there is an ambisonic mapping that produces reasonably convincing effects for headphones. In practice, adaptive HRTF models are the most effective for VR simulations.

### 6.2.3.2  Spatial Audio Cues

Audio can be made to sound as though the source is closer or farther away using a variety of spectral techniques. By modifying the spectrum of the audio signal, one can simulate the effect of the sound passing through a significant distance of atmosphere. In a thunderstorm, we hear a direct result of this effect. When lightning strikes close to us, it sounds like a crack, while the same lightning strike occurring very far away would sound more like a rumble. As sound passes through the air, high-frequency components are attenuated and low-frequency components become dominant. In addition, the sound may echo among hills or buildings, causing the sound to spread out over time. Sounds which are quieter, lower frequency, and temporally spread have the illusion of being farther away than sounds which are high frequency, louder, and sharper. This is analogous to the atmospheric perspective that happens with pictorial depth cues (Section 6.1.1.7)

Sound sources which move can have an additional effect if the motion of the sound source is an appreciable fraction of the speed of sound. When an ambulance passes by, we hear the effect of the pitch of the ambulance's siren changing as it passes. As the ambulance approaches, the pitch is shifted up as the sound waves originating from the source are compressed in front of it, and as the ambulance recedes, the pitch is shifted down as the waves spread out behind the source. This effect is called the Doppler effect and is analogous to red-shifted or blue-shifted light from stars or galaxies that may be travelling away from us or towards us adding an appreciable fraction of the speed of light.

Another key cue in the spatial perception of sound is the effect of the physical space on the sound itself. When you hear footsteps in a large empty hall, the sound of each step bounces off of the walls of the hall and arrives at your ear with a slight delay. The combination of all of these reflections is the reverberation (or reverb) of the room, and every sound made in the same space reverberates in the same way. You can infer information about size and shape of the room you are in by the reverberation, as well as where you are in the room and how far away the sound source is. If the listener is close to the sound source, most of the acoustic energy that they hear will be in a direct line from the sound source, and the relative intensity of the reverberation will be small. If the sound is far away, the listener will hear more reverberation and less direct sound. In the audio industry, these situations are called "wet" and "dry" mixes, with a wet mix having more of the reverberation (or whatever effect is being applied) and a dry mix having more of the original sound.

When simulating these effects, it is tempting to apply a generic reverberation, Doppler shift, or distance filter to the sound effects within your VR experience. In flat-screen experiences like games, this technique is reasonably convincing, because the perspective of the viewer does not change. The user is always looking at the world through this frame of the screen, and therefore what they hear is mediated by the viewpoint they are using. Spatialized audio is less critical, especially when the user is not wearing headphones. In VR, however, the audio produced for the experience must always be relative to the head position of the user. As the user looks around, their ears change position, and what they hear should also change. As a result, audio should routinely be synthesized rather than reproduced. Playing the same sound effect for a football regardless of the direction to user is looking will not lead to a realistic simulation. A simple solution implemented by many frameworks is to use sound file playback that is panned between the headphones based on the direction of the sound to the user. The result of this is that more sound will come from the headphone closer to the sound source, but the directionality, resonance, spacialization, and presence of the sound will not add to the possibility of the simulation.

## 6.3  BIOLOGICAL MAPPING OF SPACE

As far as scientists are aware, spatial cognition is not handled in one concentrated area of the brain—several representations of space exist within the mind. A lot of the tasks we undertake require a knowledge of the space around us and the relationships between objects within it—not just navigation, the manipulation and rotation of objects require spatial thinking, and actions like throwing require an understanding of concepts like distance.

### 6.3.1  Space in the Mind

It is easy to objectively measure physical space—we can all agree that this space is three dimensional and can quantify distances with well-documented physical metrics. Physical space can be described as an *Euclidean Space*— essentially meaning that the geometry of the space adheres to a set of axioms defined by mathematicians over 2000 years ago. Many of these axioms seem like common sense when thinking about physical space, as we take for granted that these hold for all the geometry we physically interact with—as we interact and grow up in a Euclidean space, it's difficult to imagine that any other sort of geometry could exist. Several basic axioms of a plane Euclidean geometry (in two dimensions) include the following:

- Any two points in the space can be joined by a straight line.

- Any terminated straight line can be extended indefinitely.

- A circle may be drawn with any point as the centre and any radius.

- For any given point and any given line that does not include that point, there is exactly one line that can be drawn through the given point that does not meet the given line (a parallel line).

When extended to a three-dimensional geometry, there are some additional axioms that apply:

- There is a plane passing through any three points.

- If three points are non-collinear, there is no more than one plane that passes through them.

- If two points lie in a plane, then the line through those points lies in the plane, and every other point on the line therefore lies in the plane.

- If two planes have a point in common, they must have at least another point in common.

Although the physical space may abide by a set of well-established laws, the psychological storage of this space is markedly different in many aspects. Although psychological space is not well understood, a large body of investigation suggests that psychological space is distorted and tends to be interpreted in a heretical manner. The following information will try to establish an overview of several of the differences between physical space and spatial cognition.

It has been argued that vision and spatial cognition are very closely related, but in the end serve different computational goals—while vision collapses spatial dimensions, spatial cognition emphasizes this relation. Spatial cognition seems to be primarily done via the bilateral posterior parietal lobe. The dorsal pathway describes "where" an object is (spatial cognition), while the ventral pathway describes "what."

Three such centres collaborate to handle spatial cognition within the brain. The first of these centres is the parietal cortex (particularly the posterior parietal cortex), which receives projections from many sensory modalities—visual, somatosensory, and auditory information. Additional inputs are received from the subcortical collicular pathway, which is thought to control eye movement and spatial orienting. This pattern of inputs makes the posterior parietal cortex ideal for integrating spatial information across modalities. Studies show that the spatial representations in the parietal cortex are generally *egocentric*, meaning that the frames of reference (FORs) used to represent space are centred on body parts. An egocentric FOR is well suited for fact actions—they give information in a context that makes it quick for the eyes to fixate on a desired section of the environment, turning the head, or translating the body. It is also important to note that there are multiple egocentric FOR representations in the parietal cortex. It quickly takes information from multiple modalities and then segments it into different FORs suited for the different body parts it is telling to react—this segmentation is what allows such rapid reactions.

The hippocampus is also related to spatial cognition—the hippocampus receives inputs from various cortical areas, and as the final step in the cortical hierarchy, the hippocampus derives the representation of the entire cortical state. *Place cells* were discovered in the hippocampus of rats—these cells fire when the rat is located in a specific portion of the environment, regardless of view or orientation. This suggests that spatial memory is, to some degree, performed in the hippocampus, but exactly the functioning of this is unknown.

One theory to describe the role of the hippocampus is the cognitive map theory, which suggests that the hippocampus functions to construct a cognitive map that holds the environment in an *allocentric* or exocentric manner. Studies show that if this map does exist, it maintains a two-dimensional, Cartesian representation of the environment. The activation of a specific place cell neutron within the rat's brain corresponds to the specific physical location of the rat in the world.

In addition to the hippocampus and the parietal cortex, it is likely that other areas of the brain are involved with spatial processing—such as the frontal lobe. However, the exact function of these areas is even less understood.

### 6.3.2 What does a psychological space look like

If a physical space can be stored as a three-dimensional continuous field, a psychological space has a very different representation—unlike a physical space, it is not continuous—its amount of locations is not uncountable, nor does it allow unlimited spatial resolutions.

Studies seem to suggest that the psychological map of salience in the mind that prioritizes information is salient—neurons have been seen to fire when an object abruptly enters the field in an unanticipated manner vs. when a saccade occurs. When this happens, a visual location becomes salient. This suggests that a psychological map may be one of salience instead of a copy of the physical space—only the most salient points in a location are present. There have been suggestions that a spatial just-noticeable difference (JND) may exist that requires salience as an input, but this is speculation.

## 6.4 NON-EUCLIDEAN GEOMETRY

The physical world is described by Euclidean geometry, and this is the geometry of our lived experience in the physical world. It might similarly be simply named "geometery" as it reflects our understanding of the physical interactions of objects. In the context of the construction of VR worlds, Euclidean geometry is usually used to refer to a virtual world that obeys the laws of physics and matches our understanding of the physical world. Since virtual worlds are entirely constructed, however, there is no strict requirement that the virtual world must follow the physics and geometry of the real world. Any of Euclid's postulates, axioms, or constructions can be negated in VR, and the consequences of these changes to how the world works can be explored through the resulting virtual world. In much the same way that speculative fiction will take a feature of the world we know, modify it slightly, and explore the ramifications, VR experiences that incorporate non-Euclidean geometry do so for the physical world.

A distinction should be made here: in mathematics, non-Euclidean geometries refer to two very specific instances of modifications to Euclid's original postulates, specifically the fact that two lines separated by a distance and forming angles less than right angles will eventually meet. We can imagine a surface geometry, specifically on a sphere, where two lines at right angles to a third line do meet—lines of longitude on the surface of the earth have this property. In the context of VR, however, non-Euclidean geometry is a broad term used to refer to any VR scenario where laws of physics or reality are bent. In most cases, modifying these geometries leads to scenarios that are difficult or impossible to interact with, but if the developer is careful, the result will be a mind-bending but still understandable experience that is impossible in the physical world. Mathematicians suggest possibilities and develop theories, and if they find contradictions, the theories must be incorrect. VR can enable us to see what might happen if these contradictions were allowed to coexist.

A common non-Euclidean technique in games in general, and VR specifically, is to imagine what would happen if doorways worked differently in different directions or provided access to different locations in the world or could change characteristics of objects or characters as they pass through them. As is often the case, television, movies, games, and novels have explored some of these ideas already. Imagine a character walking through a maze and having the maze shifting behind and around them—it would be difficult or impossible to find their way traditionally, and they would have to use other methods to navigate besides their intuition of their location within the maze. A non-Euclidean maze is not a shifting maze, however. The arrangement of the walls does not change, but it is also not self-consistent, and a map of the maze cannot be drawn on a piece of paper. Figure 6.15 shows an example of how this might work. The user walks along the maze, and as they turn a corner, the wall they thought was there is now a passageway. If they return to the previous intersection, they see that the first wall is still there, but when they look around the corner they can walk through where the first wall would have been. This violates the principle that two things that are each equal to a third thing are equal to each other. The physical location of the path in front of the user and the path behind the user are the same, but the user can only be on one path or the other.

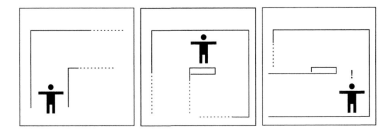

Figure 6.15: A non-Euclidean maze.

Another way that doorways or passageways can be used to implement non-Euclidean geometries is by changing features or characteristics of objects or characters when they pass through the doorway. The simplest implementation of this is the teleportation portal, where one side of the doorway is in one space and the other side of the doorway is in another space. Because this idea is not new and has been used in games and media, it is easier for us to understand the way this impossible physics works. The portal is simply a connection between two spaces, and as you pass through the portal, you instantly transition from one space to another. A doorway can change other characteristics of an object or person as well. One could imagine a doorway or passageway that would cause the character to grow or shrink. If you pass through the door in one direction, you emerge in the same place but you are larger than before, and doing so in reverse would cause you to become smaller. A game mechanic could be constructed around modifying objects to be the correct size to solve them by progressively shrinking or enlarging them, or modifying the size of the player in order to be aligned to the scale of the task at hand. Perhaps multiple players would be required to play at different scales, where a huge player would lift a tiny player to the top of the castle where they would have to crawl through a maze and then become large again to reach the key on the top of the shelf. Perhaps the huge player could even lift the castle and turn it on its side to allow the tiny player to reach an otherwise inaccessible area. When every rule of the world is question, opportunities for creative play emerge.

MC Escher-inspired spaces could be constructed and explored. Gravity can be different on different sides of a staircase. A circular staircase can shrink and grow around you so that you are always climbing up. Optical illusions, infinitely self-similar fractal spaces, and topologically impossible structures can be constructed in VR and explored.

In the physical world, objects that are far away appear to be smaller. This feature of reality could be altered such that close objects appear small and distant objects appear large. Instead of seeing a receding horizon line, the user would see all of the distant objects in the world piled upon each other, and as you approached an object, it would shrink until it was too small to see. In the physical world, distant objects appear to move more slowly as we pass by, due to parallax as discussed above. What if objects moved horizontally when they were close by and vertically when they were farther away? What if objects appeared to move only when the character wasn't moving? What if the motion of objects contained more randomness the closer they are to the character?

Developers can use these ideas to attempt to visualize or illuminate difficult or challenging topics in physics. The astronomical distances between stars could be visualized by warping the space around them, or the interactions of gravity could be displayed by showing the curvature of space-time in three dimensions. Relativity tells us that as speed increases, time slows down and light travels in curved paths. These features of relativity are difficult to understand and visualize, but if the effects could be simulated at non-relativistic speeds, like when a user was walking or driving a car, it might be possible to allow users to better understand the effects of these known physical properties of the universe. Similarly, effects on quantum scales are difficult to understand, but brought to the macroscale in a VR simulation they could be demonstrated more cogently.

VR can also be used to simulate and visualize dimensionalities of space different from our physical reality. In "flatland," Edwin Abbott imagines a two-dimensional world in which individuals cannot imagine what three-dimensional reality would be like, and the characters are amazed and terrified when a sphere passes through their world, starting as a point in space and growing to a circle before receding to a point again. Not only could VR be used to simulate the experience of a flatlander in 3-space, it can also be used to represent the experience of a three-dimensional person existing in 4-space. As a four-dimensional object passed through our three-dimensional space, what would we see? How could we interact with such objects? Projections of alternatively mathematical realities would be possible, although how a user would experience these worlds would be up to the developer— and care must be taken to ensure the user is able to psychologically conceptualize what is presented.

Being in VR is often enough to trigger nausea or anxiety, and being in a VR world that does not obey the laws of physics could be very disturbing.

Non-Euclidean spaces are not only useful for exploring the possibilities of worlds different from our physical world, they can also be used to remove limitations of our physical reality as well. When a user dons a VR headset and enters an expansive virtual space, they typically do so from within a physical room, and the walls of that room present a physical limit to what the user can do in virtual space. If the user wants to walk forward in a straight line, soon the reality of their physical location will come into conflict with the desires of their virtual self. **Redirected walking** is an attempt to use non-Euclidean principles to allow a user to think they are walking in a straight line, while staying within the confines of their physical playspace. Redirected walking and other non-linear gait-based locomotion techniques, as described in Section 10.4.1, provide methods for manipulating a VR user's space in a non-Euclidean way.

The use of non-Euclidean spaces can extend beyond the concept of space and scale, into almost any aspect of interaction within a virtual world. Mathematicians, philosophers, and computer scientists have often speculated about the true nature of reality and constructed proofs and simulations to imagine, in some small way, what reality would be like if some rules were bent or broken. With the advent of VR, users can experience these bent worlds first hand and explore the results of alternative realities, thereby learning more about our own actual reality.

## SUMMARY

The visual component of any VR experience can be projected into a 2-dimensional representation and rendered for a regular computer screen. The models, graphics, interactions and animations would remain the same, but the experience would be significantly reduced. What separates a flat-screen experience from a VR experience is the sense of space, the idea that the user can walk around within the world rather than simply watching the world through a window. Although the VR hardware provides many of these sensations of distance for free, it is the responsibility of the VR developer to engage with space, to consider the scale of objects or environments, and by extension, the scale of the user's avatar within that virtual space.

# CHAPTER 7

# Further Psychological Effects of Inhabiting a Virtual Environment

## 7.1 EFFECTS OF INTERACTIVITY

Interactivity is an inherent part of virtual reality (VR). As VR mimics "reality" from a sensory perspective by definition, the ability for a user to use movement to select what part of the environment to view (sensorimotor contingencies) is a fundamental choice present in all VR environments.

Interactivity is loosely understood by many to mean having "choice" or "control" over aspects of a particular piece of media. Breaking down the word further, we can see it is composed of two parts—"inter," meaning "between," and "active." The "inter" in interactive reflects that the course of an interactive experience is determined through a collaboration between the application and the user. The experience provides an environment for the user to see, and the user has the ability to influence what parts of the environment they see, as well as impact the environment itself. In this way, the "choice" in interactivity is the choice made by the user of what to see or do within the experience, and they may be able to "control" aspects of the environment, their avatar, or other elements of the application.

An interactive experience can be thought of as a conversation between the user and the application. As with any piece of media, the user is able to view and react to stimuli from the experience. However, interactivity means that the media can also interpret and react to input from the user. If it is interactive, content can demand you to respond to it and you can demand content to respond to you.

To qualify as interactive, it is not necessary that an experience offers both choice and control—for example, a movie on DVD could be considered interactive as the scene selection menu allows the user to choose what portion of the movie to start at, although this is at the lower end of what could count as interactivity.

Although interactive experiences have existed for a long time, in forms such as table games, digital systems have made it easier to create complex interactive media.

DOI: 10.1201/9781003261230-7

The ability of computers to change what stimuli they display based on real-time calculations has allowed for many new forms of interactive applications and experiences.

## 7.1.1 Simulation vs. Representation

Another lens through which we can consider the interactivity of experiences is through the comparison of simulation and representation.

An experience that is *representation* is the display of information from an actual recorded source. For example, a photograph would be a representation—the photograph displays a subject that actually existed in that form elsewhere. Similarly, live action film is a representation that displays what was in front of the camera. Representations are deterministic—if the representation contains a temporal component, it will exhibit the same behaviour at the same times whenever it is played back.

In contrast, an experience that is *simulation* displays content that was not recorded elsewhere prior—it calculates the output based on the variable input from the user or another outside source. Thus, a simulation is stochastic in that the path it takes is not predetermined and is instead influenced by outside input. In a simulation, users can have goals other than passive observation, as they are able to influence the simulation.

It is conceivable that a simulation and a representation may result in similar output—the output from a flight simulator between Fairbanks and Seattle may look very similar to a recording of a flight along the same path in real life. However, if the user wanted to, they could steer the plane elsewhere in the simulation, while the video is locked into a certain predetermined course. In this sense, simulations have the potential to be highly interactive (in the cases where the user is providing the input to the simulation), while representations tend to be either minimally interactive (for example being able to pause a video, which doesn't change the content itself) or not interactive at all.

Although simulations typically accept outside input, the points at which input is entered as well as their frequency differ. Input may be given before the simulation is started, such as in a finite element analysis simulation used to see how a structural design reacts to specified loads. Input could also be provided throughout the simulation, like in a computer chess game, where the user inputs a move every turn. In a VR system, tracking data is used as near continuous input in order to update the virtual viewpoint to match the user's spatial position.

Who or what provides simulation inputs can also vary. We often think of simulations that accept data from a user, but this may or may not be entered at the time of simulation—a researcher may compile a file containing data to run different simulations for and then set the simulation to run many times without supervision. Input may not come from a user as well—random number generators can also be used to provide inputs for portions of a simulation. Many games will use both user input and random number generators as inputs in order to result in a unique experience every time.

## 7.1.2 Frameworks of Interactivity

As it is with many characteristics of a simulation, we may have situations where we want to talk about interactivity in objective terms. While the term "interactive" is too abstract to meaningfully compare experiences without being subjective, there are several sub-traits that contribute to interactivity that can be discussed concretely.

Simulations, which could be considered a very large subset of interactive experiences, lend themselves to being quantified. The discussion of simulation as being defined by user input allows us to describe the level of interactivity of a simulated experience by describing it in terms of how it reacts to input. Below, three metrics for simulations are discussed.

### 7.1.2.1 Three Factors of Simulation

A simulation can be viewed as a series of reactions to inputs, possibly interleaved with prompts for inputs. One important factor of a simulation is its *speed*, defined as the rate at which the inputs are reacted to by the simulation. The speed in a modern VR system would likely be described with the delay in response. This is the time between an input being received and the point at which the simulation responds, which is often limited by software as well as hardware. Simulation speed for a VR experience can be increased by optimizing performance metrics in software, although there is a hardware limit on speed due to the propagation delay present in the components that make up VR equipment. A simulation that is faster is generally perceived as being more interactive, all else equal.

Another important characteristic is the *range* of the simulation, which describes how many different reactions are possible in the simulation at a given time. In the real world, an infinite variety of things could happen at any moment, but only a small, finite subset of those events are likely. Simulations that provide reactions to many different situations of user input are more interactive and act closer to the real world than those which severely limit what parts of the environment may react to the user.

A third factor is the *mapping* of the simulation, which describes the ability of the simulation to map inputs to outputs in the environment predictably. When people take actions, they use a model of cause and effect—they undertake a certain action with the intention of causing a certain effect. In order to complete a goal, users require that the way the environment reacts must conform with their expectations of cause and effect, be it the real-world or a VR simulation. Simulations for which most user actions result in the predicted effect are high in mapping and are therefore more interactive in this regard than simulations that have unpredictable reactions or no reaction to user input.

It is important to note that the factors of speed, range, and mapping are non-exhaustive—there are many more factors and metrics that could be used to characterize a simulation beyond these, such as input frequency or fidelity. However, the three aforementioned characteristics have been found to be particularly useful when comparing the interactivity of different VR experiences.

### 7.1.2.2 Verb Sets

Another way to describe the ways in which a VR experience is interactive is to categorize its possible interactions through *verb sets*. A verb set is a list of all the interactions a user can undertake, organized as a set of action words. The term "verb sets" was first used in the context of interactive systems, when describing early text adventure games—players would interact with the game by typing in verbs, which dictated what sort of interaction would take place (related to range, as described above), and then a noun which identified the portion of the environment the interaction would be carried out upon. For example, a player might add a key to their inventory by typing "grab key," or fight an enemy by entering "attack ogre"—in this case, "grab" and "attack" would be members of the game's verb set.

In modern experiences, we don't type in verbs to conduct actions, but interactions in a VR game or experience are often programmed into the back-end to be applicable at different points of the environment. Usually, these interactions are finite and are often written and added separately by game programmers—as such, a verb set is well suited to describing software, as it reflects the way interactions are typically programmed.

To try to name all the possible verbs that could be used in a VR experience here would be impossible. However, most interaction verbs (and therefore most interactions) fall into six broad categories, discussing their relation to the environment. These categories, as well as some example verbs for each that might be relevant for a VR experience, are listed as follows:

**Stimulus and Response:** view, look

**Navigation:** walk, teleport

**Control over Object:** select, rotate

**Communication:** speak, gesture

**Exchange of Information:** type, read

**Acquisition/Collecting:** grab, store

**Verb-based programming languages**
Using single-word commands as points of interaction is a common framework for the earliest computer programming languages. Each instruction to the computer consisted of an operation to be performed (also called an "opcode") like add, load, shift, and branch. Each of these command words had a very specific set of information associated with it that told the computer which piece of information to modify in what way. As programming became more complex and programs increased in size, developers built higher level programming languages with more nuanced grammatical structure. The verb-based interaction

persisted in some contexts, however, such as in the case of the Apollo 11 guidance computer. Astronauts controlled the computer by issuing verb-noun pairs, indicating what to do and what piece of information to act on. The computer only had a numeric keypad, though, which means the operator had to memorize or reference a numbered code for each verb and noun. Verb 06, Noun 84, for example, would be used to assign a change in velocity. Verb-noun pairs were also a common interaction technique in text-based interactive adventures, where a character might "go north" and then "look tree" and then "attack goblin." Organizing interactive options as verb lists can help to categorize and enumerate the different options available to users.

## 7.1.3 Effects on Presence

Interactivity has a significant effect on the degree to which a user feels a sense of presence in a VR scenario. In Chapter 2, we showed that a feeling of presence in a virtual world consists of two illusions: place illusion and plausibility illusion. If we look at what causes these illusions, we can see that certain kinds of interactivity are related to both.

Place illusion is what occurs when the brain interprets the virtual environment as a physical space, and it relies primarily on sensorimotor contingencies being supported. A sensorimotor action is an interactive relationship between the user and the system—the user performs an action, and the system must respond to support the expected sensory outcomes of that action. The act of a display updating sensory information to match what would happen from the point of view of the user in a physical space is an interaction, as the application is responding to an input given by the user. These responses must happen below the temporal just-noticeable difference (JND) of the particular sense being supported, so that the responses appear constant and consistent.

Plausibility illusion, which occurs when the brain interprets the virtual world as having real consequence for the user, is reinforced by having the supported interactions functioning as valid actions. Thus, ensuring a high degree of interactivity is almost always required in order for plausibility illusion to exist.

### 7.1.3.1 Effects on Place Illusion

The possible sensorimotor contingencies that a user could undertake within an experience form a verb set of actions. If an application supports this verb set accurately, a high degree of place illusion can be experienced by the user. In terms of the factors of simulation, the speed, range, and mapping of the simulation must appear to the user to match or exceed the corresponding factors within the physical world. We use the word "appear" in the previous sentence as actually matching these factors is likely impossible within a VR simulation—the real world is continuous in both speed and range, which a digital computer is unable to replicate. However, as the human threshold for detecting small values in speed and variations (range) of output is limited, it is only this threshold that the simulation factors must meet in order to seem to match the real world to a human user—this threshold could be considered the upper bound for place illusion increases due to increases in these factors. If these factors are below this threshold, some degree of place illusion is likely experienced by the user, but it will be lower than in the aforementioned ideal case.

Just as interactions that support sensorimotor contingencies reinforce place illusion, interactions resulting in failed sensorimotor contingencies can diminish place illusion. The most obvious case is when sensorimotor contingencies are not part of the available verb set of the experience. Creating an application that contains all possible sensorimotor contingencies that a user could take within its verb set would be an incredibly complex feat, but a far more practical approach is to determine and support the verbs that relate to the sensorimotor contingencies the user is most likely to undertake and to hide, dissuade, or prevent the user from undertaking unsupported contingencies.

Another common case of interactions resulting in failed sensorimotor contingencies occurs when interactions draw attention to stimuli outside of the VR world—for example requiring the user to enter text via a keyboard that exists in the physical world. Similarly, some interactions may not break sensorimotor contingencies in all cases, but may do so when considering many users' specific VR set-ups—an example would be requiring the user to physically walk a far distance in the virtual world, which could result in many users running into (and therefore being reminded of) objects in the physical world where their VR headset is located.

### 7.1.3.2 *Effects on Plausibility Illusion*

Plausibility illusion is entirely dependent on the user's actions being valid actions—as such, every interaction that the user undertakes must both be part of the verb set of the of the experience and result in the necessary updates to the display (valid sensorimotor action) and to the environment (valid effectual action) in order to increase plausibility illusion. Equally important to which actions are supported, the way in which the simulation responds to them, the mapping, has a great deal of influence in supporting plausibility illusion within a VR experience.

For a specific mapping to have a positive effect on plausibility illusion, it must be *predictable*. In the real world, actions are taken with a definite goal or expectation, which we have mentioned earlier as a relation of cause and effect. Any action which is responded to by the VR simulation counts as being interactive, but to build plausibility illusion, the effects of these interactions must make sense to the user. Making sense doesn't always mean that an event has to be completely predictable—in the real world, there are many occasions where we are not sure of the consequences of an action until after it has been done. In this sense, predictability should be relative to the situation—when you pick up a pencil, you can be reasonably sure that it will stay in your hand, but when you throw a ball, although you may have a rough idea of its trajectory, you likely don't know exactly how far it will travel until you throw it.

Being unable to interact with portions of the environment that seem like they should be accessible is one of the more common ways that plausibility illusion is reduced by choices surrounding interactivity. In many flat computer games, only certain objects are selectable or able to be interacted with by the character, while other similar items may be part of the background. Pressing a button on a controller may result in the player's avatar picking up a key that is needed to unlock a door later in the level, but pressing the same button will have no response if the avatar is in front of a similarly sized pencil. This may be a reasonable mapping when controlling an avatar in a flatscreen game, but if the same game were played in VR, the player may reach out for the pencil and be frustrated that they cannot grab it, when they can grab the key just by reaching out for it. When things don't happen the way the user expects, plausibility illusion can be broken.

In a flat-screen experience, the actions of the user are like commands to the user's avatar, but in VR, the actions of the user are directly mapped to the actions of the avatar —thus, the world needs to act less like a game and more like an environment, if plausibility illusion is to be maintained. If the user shouldn't be able to pick something up, they need to be able to predict why that object is not physically able to be picked up from cues in the environment.

## 7.1.4 Interactivity and User Experience

In addition to influencing the illusions of presence, the amount and type of interactivity allowed by a VR environment can have a significant impact on the perceived usability of the application.

One of the biggest consequences that interactivity has on usability is that it allows the user to make choices regarding what content to see, and changes regarding the environment, letting the experience better suit a user's tastes and preferences. An experience where the user is able to spend time viewing and interacting with things they enjoy is generally viewed as more usable than one where they have no choice but to suffer through content they may not find as fun.

Another advantage of interactivity is that it can lead to high levels of user *satisfaction*. It is satisfying for users to be able to make a choice through input that is reflected through meaningful changes in the environment, as this makes users feel that their choices matter. What constitutes meaningful is highly subjective, but can be loosely defined as having a large impact on the course that the experience follows for a particular user. For example, an avatar customization process could be very meaningful if the avatar's appearance can be seen throughout the game (such as through reflections and mirrors in a first-person VR game or by other players in a multiplayer experience), or if choices regarding avatar stats like strength and speed have gameplay effects, but the choices could be meaningless if the avatar is never seen throughout the rest of the game. Thus, user satisfaction relating to choices is a function of both what choices are offered to the user and how they impact the subsequent experience.

Most of the usability advantages conferred by increased interactivity can be attributed to its ability to provide users with *agency* over the simulation. The implementation of interactions has a multitude of other usability concerns, but these are very case specific and will be the primary focus of the second half of this book.

### 7.1.4.1 Agency

Agency is synonymous with giving a user control over aspects of an experience. If a user has agency over travel, this implies they have a degree of control over where they want to go within an experience. The developer of an application decides both where a user has agency within a VR application and how much agency to give the user in those areas.

Agency can have a significant impact on user attention, also referred to as *engagement*. In a passive experience, where the user is simply viewing content, it is easy for the user to not pay attention to the experience and have it finish regardless. When users have agency, they have to make choices regarding that aspect of the simulation, forcing them to provide attention to making those choices—because of this, users are more likely to be engaged (although not always to a large degree) with portions of a VR experience that they are given agency over. In this sense, interactivity and the agency it provides allow developers to direct engagement within a VR experience.

A problem that often impacts VR applications is **agency conflict**, points when the user's agency in the real world conflicts with the agency they have or should have in the virtual world. Avatar movement is a good illustration of agency conflict—avatars are often represented as matching the movement of the real-world user controlling them. The user's movement in the physical world is bounded by agency—a human user cannot pass their arms through solid objects in the physical world, even in the case where no object is present in the corresponding VR space. In this case, the user's agency in the physical world is limited where their agency in the virtual world is not—an agency conflict. The opposite case is also common—a wall in the virtual world may intend to block their avatar from moving forward, but there is nothing to stop them from moving forward in real-world space. Solutions to these problems will be discussed further in Chapter 7, fiction of physics, but it is important to notice that these situations arise due to conflicts in agency.

**Exploits and Agency Breaking**

Although developers are the ones who define where and how much agency users of their applications have, they may not be conscious of some of the possibilities for the agency that they have granted. An **exploit** is an interaction available in an interactive system that is not intended by the developer to be accessible to the user. Exploits are often related to bugs or accidents during the development process and may range from allowing a user to pass through a wall or enter an area that should be restricted, to the ability to execute arbitrary code on the underlying system. Many exploits within VR experiences result in some additional agency that the developers did not consciously intend for users to have—for example glitches that allow users to bypass a barrier to travel into a zone they were not supposed to enter, or a bug that allows them to duplicate virtual items.

Sometimes, developers view these exploits as detracting from the VR experience—for example, they may result in the player of a game having an easier time defeating an enemy than the developer intended. However, if users make the choice to take advantage of exploits, they are likely doing it for their own enjoyment and can allow for completely different (and often more efficient or fun) ways of experiencing VR content—for example, the practice of speed-running games often requires players to use exploits in precise ways to complete a game as quickly as possible, resulting in satisfaction from development and execution of skill.

### 7.1.4.2 Perceived Interactivity

How interactive an application is perceived to be may be disjoint from the actual factors regarding simulation and activity. The biggest influence on how interactive a user perceives a VR experience to be is their actions and expectations. If a user only undertakes actions that are within the verb set of the VR experience in areas where appropriate, the simulation will seem more interactive to them than if they attempt to interact with objects that do not react to the verb set. If the user expects an item to be interactive or expects an action to be able to be performed, and it is not, then they will perceive the application as less interactive than they did before.

Several other aspects influence how interactive a user considers an experience to be. The first is how meaningful their choices are—not only does the impact of choices affect user satisfaction, but simulations that respond meaningfully to user actions are assumed by users to be more interactive. With regard to the perceived interactivity, responses to user choices influence a running tally—if a user makes a choice and they judge the response to be trivial, their assessment of the level of interactivity decreases, while if their choices result in a visible, meaningful result, the assessment of interactivity goes up.

The controls available for interacting with the VR environment may also bias the user's perception of interactivity. If a user finds controls easy to understand and use, they will find it easier to perform the actions that they want and may spend more time interacting with the environment, which could increase perceived interactivity. Systems which are easier to learn, understand, and use may be perceived as more interactive even if the overall functionality is more limited. For example, computer-generated images can be created with a simple pixel art program, where the user draws directly with a mouse, or they can be generated with a complicated and low-level graphics programming library. Although the low-level library may be more powerful and may offer more range in the types of commands that can be issued to draw graphics at any given time (also meaning it has a larger verb set), many users would consider the simple pixel art program more interactive, partially because it is easier for them to understand and start using to draw and partially because responses to their actions are immediate rather than requiring scripting, programming, compiling and rendering to access. Further, programs where the user can input actions at any time during the simulation and see results are often perceived as more interactive than those where commands are entered first and then the simulation is executed.

## 7.2  EMBODIMENT ILLUSION

In the physical world, we are contained within our physical bodies. When we look at our hands, we see *our* hands. When we look in the mirror, we consider the face that looks back to be *our* face, because of course it is—it's the face we always have. In a VR experience, we are of course still within our physical body, wearing a headset, but when we look down, we see a different pair of hands, and a virtual mirror might show a face we aren't used to.

The concept of *embodiment* has been long discussed in the field of philosophy. Philosophers considered the study of embodiment to encompass questions about how people defined and experienced "the self," including how our concept of self-related to the body we inhabited. The modern cognitive science field of embodiment occupies a more concrete subset of the philosophical study. Modern embodiment researchers in cognitive science study how the brain represents the body, as well as how various neurological conditions can lead to changes in this representation. One of these conditions of particular importance to VR developers is the *embodiment illusion*, where a VR user's brain interprets portions of a virtual avatar to be part of the user's body.

## 7.3  COMPONENTS OF EMBODIMENT ILLUSION

Just as embodiment is not a single concept in the brain, but instead refers to many components of the brain's internal representation of the body, embodiment illusion in VR is comprised of several sensations that occur as a result of seeing and controlling a virtual body, or avatar. The representation of an embodiment in the mind includes a model of what our body looks like, what we perceive its volume of occupation to be, and other characteristics relating to the morphology, size, or structure of the body in addition to self-attribution. As with all representations within the human mind, a person's representation of their own body is derived from sensory information originating from the world around them. Visual, haptic, vestibular, and proprioceptive sensations all give us information about our bodies. As VR systems may be capable of displaying stimuli in these categories, this information may also contribute to the mental representation of the body, resulting in embodiment illusions where our representation of the body includes virtual components.

**Sense, illusion, or representation**

Embodiment illusion is sometimes referred to as the *sense of embodiment*, where "sense" refers to an internal representation in the same way it is used when discussing a "sense of direction," and is not to be confused with the meaning of the term "sense" as it is used to describe sensory processes. Further, there is a slight difference in connotation between the two terms—embodiment illusion refers to the specific case where one or more portions of an internal representation of embodiment are false, or illusory, as is the case when a virtual body becomes part of a representation, while the "sense of embodiment" refers to the representation as a whole. It may be more accurate to say that the "sense of embodiment" is a synonym for the "representation of embodiment." To avoid this confusion, we will mostly use the terms "embodiment illusion" and "representation of embodiment."

As mentioned above, the representation of one's body in the mind includes many different components. When discussing embodiment illusion, there are three aspects of this representation that are of particular interest—where a person believes their body to be located, the degree of control a person feels to have over their body, and if that body is "their body." These three aspects are able to be modified through interactions with a virtual body and are often referred to as the "components of embodiment illusion." Formally, these three components are known as the representations of *self-location*, *bodily agency*, and *body ownership*.

## 7.3.1   Representation of Self-Location

One's *self-location* refers to the volume of space that a person believes their "self" occupies. Space in the brain is generally categorized into three distinct volumes in terms of its relation to the body, also shown in Figure 7.1:

**Personal space** is defined as the space the body occupies. Its boundary is usually defined by the user's skin, with the volume inside being personal space[1].

**Peripersonal space** is the next volume out—starting at the outer boundary of personal space, it extends to the area adjacent to the body within arm's reach. If you are sitting on a chair, the volume of space underneath the seat of the chair is usually encoded as peripersonal space. If you are holding a tool or implement (like a sword or tennis racket), in many cases the area that you represent mentally as peripersonal space extends to encompass the range of the tool (a phenomena referred to as *tool embodiment*.) The personal space is also referred to as the person's "sphere of influence."

**Extrapersonal space** is all space that cannot be immediately reached by any part of the person's body (or tool they are holding). In relation to the other two volumes, extrapersonal space consists of all space outside the outer bound of peripersonal space. In Section 11.4 we discuss VR techniques for extending the

---

[1]In colloquial terms, "personal space" sometimes refers to the area immediately surrounding a person. Also referred to as the "personal bubble," in this text we refer to this as the peripersonal space.

peripersonal space, which in turn reduces the extrapersonal space, although with extended selection techniques the boundaries between these spaces can become indistinct. If a user can influence an object at a distance using a remote-controlled tool, does that interaction occur in the user's peripersonal space or their extrapersonal space?

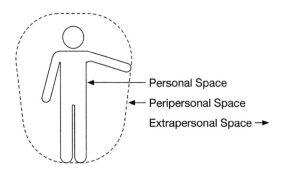

Figure 7.1: Three categories of self-location.

Self-location defines a relationship between the "self" and a "body"—it is concerned with the spatial experience of occupying a body. In many ways, self-location is analogous to place illusion—place illusion is the spatial experience of feeling like the self is located in other world, while self-location is the spatial experience of feeling like the self is located in another body. There is a dichotomy between the two—together, the body and the external environment constitute one's spatial representation. Self-location and place illusion could be considered to be parts of the same representation, with the only difference being what volumes of space are considered in each.

### 7.3.1.1 *Influences on self-location*

Considering the similarities between self-location and place illusion, it should be unsurprising that they share many of the same influences. Self-location is determined primarily through sensorimotor contingencies. More specifically, one's self-location is highly determined by visuospatial information—the point of view that one sees from is strongly assumed to be the location on one's head, which makes sense given that in the physical world we typically see from a first-person, or egocentric, perspective.

VR allows for non-first-person views of one's avatar—in this case, many users still assume that their "self" is located at the camera, although some self-location may be attributed to the avatar. In cases where a threat was posed to an artificial body within VR, users have been found to have stronger physiological responses, such as heart rate increases and sweating, when the players viewed their artificial bodies from an egocentric (first person) perspective rather than an exocentric (third person) perspective. This implies that a stronger sense of self-location is felt with the avatar in first-person views, but also that it is not impossible to have some degree of self-location at a space that does not match the typical visuospatial location of the head.

Vestibular signals also have a large degree of influence over a user's representation of self-location. As these signals provide information with respect to the translation and rotation of the body, they contribute to a user tracking the change in what part of the environment the body takes up as they move. These are third-order signals, as they give sensations for linear and rotational acceleration that the brain integrates into a positional representation. The vestibular system also provides first-order information on the body's orientation relative to gravity. As vestibular simulation is more difficult to provide with VR, a VR developer usually considers vestibular information as something that needs to be suppressed or that the simulation needs to line up with the expected vestibular experiences of the physical world in order to avoid conflicting sensorimotor information, when wanting to enhance the feeling of self-location within a virtual avatar. VR treadmills and motion simulators can allow different physics from the physical world.

## Using third-person view to enhance place

It may be counterintuitive to consider that a user in third-person view may have an enhanced sense of place compared to a user in first-person view. If you are looking through your avatar's eyes, the assumption goes, you will feel more embodied and more connected to the virtual world. The problem is that we do not sense the world only with our eyes. As VR technology advances and begins to engage more of our senses, we may find the sense of place that the first-person view provides to also improve. In the physical world, people instinctively develop a model of their surroundings based on sensations other than vision. You can hear when someone is sneaking up behind you; you can feel subtle changes in temperature and air pressure when someone opens the door behind you. You can feel the tree branches all around you as you walk through the forest. In a first-person view, none of the senses are available, and you can feel a sense of isolation; in a third-person view, however, you can see the peripersonal space around you and build a mental model of your surroundings without those additional sensations. When you drive a car in first-person view, it is difficult to judge how close you are to the cars around you. When you drive a car in third-person view, however, tight manoeuvring is easier to accomplish.

An interesting consequence of the fact that there is little first order positional information provided by the vestibular system is that it does not have the same bias towards egocentric perspectives that the visual system does. The proprioceptive system, which encodes second order spatial information as well as first order spatial information (but only with reference to the body as opposed to the environment), is much the same in this regard. If a user was truly receiving vestibular sensation from a body displaced translationally from their current body, it would feel the same as their current location (the same could not be said orientationally in the case where the second body is rotated such that its relation to the gravity vector is altered).

The tactile senses also contribute to the sense of self-location. As the skin is the border between the body and the environment, if a sensation is felt on the skin, the origin of that stimulus heavily influences the perceived location of the self. The rubber hand illusion discussed in Section 2.4.3 is able to achieve such a high degree of self-location in the false hand due to tactile stimulation agreeing with simulated visuospatial information. Tactile information is biased heavily in determining self-location—the position of seen objects touching a body can override the visual perspective when accompanied by physical tactile stimulus.

## 7.3.2 Representation of Body Agency

We've just discussed agency in the context of control or influence over a simulation, and in being a trait of interactivity. Agency also can increase a user's feeling that their virtual body is their real one, when it allows the user to have control over the movement of their body. We will refer to this subset of agency with relation to the body as *body agency* in order to distinguish it from the more general way we have discussed agency with relation to overall interactivity.

A user feels like they have body agency over an avatar when they are able to have motor control over the avatar—being able to initiate motion of body parts, and motion of the body itself through the environment as reasonable. Body agency does not require that the motions of the user and the motions of the avatar line up, although this is one of the most common control schemes for avatar movements in tracked VR systems.

In real life, we generally have body agency, feeling like we are able to control the movements of our body. However, some exceptions do occur—paralysis prevents agency over portions of the body. The more common case of temporary sleep paralysis causes many people to panic over a sudden loss of agency, as people consciously try to move their unresponsive body and are distressed when their body does not move as a result of their attempted agency. A much rarer example is the case of anarchic hand syndrome, where patients feel they have a lack of control over movements that their hand (or another limb) undertakes.

One theory of virtual body agency is that it is determined by the comparison between expected sensory consequences of user actions, and the actual sensory consequences. In this model, if the user thinks the result of raising their real hand will be to see the avatar's hand be raised as well, and this occurs, the user will feel agency over the virtual body. If the virtual hand stayed still while the user's hand was up, the feeling of agency over the avatar would be small or non-existent. When you can predict the effect of your inputs on the actions of an avatar, you consider yourself to be the agent of those actions. The movement of the avatar's hand need not be identical, and small differences between the intended action and the actual result can provide additional information to the user—perhaps the object the user is holding is particularly heavy. More discussion on the mapping between what a user expects and what happens is found in Section 11.3.

In VR, feelings of a lack of body agency can be generally sorted into two categories: cases where the avatar does not move when the user would want it to and cases where the avatar is moving but the user cannot control its motion. In both cases, the user's actions in the physical world do not affect the avatar in the way the user wants, and thus body agency may not be felt. Further, when the responses of the avatar have a significant delay from user actions, less agency is also felt; however, when used carefully and consistently, a delay in motion can indicate weight or inertia of an object being held. Temporal differences of more than 150 ms between a user's action and corresponding avatar movement can result in reported lack of agency, unless there is a conceptual justification for this delay.

### 7.3.3 Representation of Body Ownership

Just as place illusion (the feeling of being in a real environment) is distinct from plausibility illusion (the feeling that it is "you" in that environment), the feeling of being located within a body (sense of self-location) is distinct from the representation of whether the body you are in belongs to you. This second representation, which deals with the self-attribution of a body, is referred to as the representation of **body ownership**.

Body ownership can be considered to be influenced by information belonging to two internal models—bottom-up and top-down understandings of the body. When a person uses the bottom-up model, they define the body that belongs to the self as the one that they receive sensory information from. The "self" experiences sensations, and thus the body that is the source of these experienced sensations must therefore belong to the self. The mechanisms that support a bottom-up representation of body ownership (a lack of conflict in sensorimotor contingencies) are primarily the same mechanisms that lead to one's representation of self-location, in the same way that place illusion and plausibility illusion also both rely on accurate sensorimotor contingencies. The rubber hand illusion also demonstrates body ownership, as the participants only recoiled when the knife struck the false hand because they had interpreted it as "their hand." The rubber hand and follow-up experiments showed that body ownership in this case only emerged when seen and felt stimulation both followed the same pattern—when the false hand was seen to be touched at the same time that the real hand was touched, participants believed the hand was theirs. Conversely, when this stimulation was not synchronized, participants did not consider the hand part of their own body or did so but not as strongly. Synchronous visuoproprioceptive correlations were also shown to have the same effect—if the rubber hand was moved in the same pattern that the user moved their unseen real hand, body ownership was attributed to the false hand.

The top-down model of body ownership consists of higher level beliefs and understandings of what one's body should be like. For example, most people have an innate notion that their body should be humanoid, or their memory may encode certain identifying characteristics, such as their height or the way their joints tend to move, as ways to identify if a body is "theirs." Other characteristics such as skin, colour, or gender similarities can lead to increased ownership over an avatar as well, although they have a lesser effect than characteristics that affect the way sensory information is gathered, and over time a person can develop a sense of ownership of an otherwise alien-feeling body if they live into it and have sensorimotor contingencies confirmed by it.

The morphology of a body has significant effects on the strength of body ownership—the more closely a virtual body's morphology reflects the user's physical body, the stronger the sense of body ownership is, all else equal. A user with non-typical morphology, for example a user missing a finger, would feel a stronger sense of body ownership if their virtual avatar was missing the same finger. The similarity of spatial configurations between the user's real body and the avatar also increases ownership. For example, if a user's resting position is to have both arms at their sides, and the virtual arms of their avatar are in a different position, perhaps with the arms out to the sides or pointing forward, the user will feel less ownership than if the arm orientations matched.

To refer back to the rubber hand illusion yet again, various follow-up experiments tested if body ownership could be induced if other objects were used in place of the fake hand. Objects that looked closer to a real hand resulted in higher feelings of body ownership—for example, the original rubber hand would solicit higher responses from users than an unpainted wood hand, which in turn would result in a higher response than a mechanical grabber. However, as all of these objects had some morphological similarity to a real hand, some degree of ownership was able to be induced for each—objects with no similarity to a human hand (e.g. an apple) did not result in ownership responses under the same conditions.

### 7.3.4  Degree of Embodiment

Much as a user can feel different degrees of presence in a virtual environment, we can also describe the degree to which the illusion of embodiment exists for a particular user controlling a particular avatar. Considering embodiment illusion is comprised of three main components, the sum of the degree to which each is experienced could be taken to be the overall "degree of embodiment." However, it may make more sense to consider each of the components separately in order to define an overall view of how embodiment is represented for the case of that specific user. For example, in real life, feelings of self-location, body agency, and body ownership are typically maximized in our real body. For a virtual body, we can consider these three components to fall somewhere along a continuum for each depending on the specifics of the user, avatar, and environment.

**The Three Bodies Experiment**

In his discussions on embodiment illusion, Mel Slater describes a theoretical experiment by which a single user's representations of self-location, body agency, and body ownership could be each assigned to different virtual bodies. The experiment uses three bodies (A, B, and C) within the same virtual environment. Sensory evidence is presented as if from the location of body A—the user sees from eyes that are in the same location in the virtual environment as body A and hears sounds from the environment as if their ears were located in body A. In this way, the user's self-localization should be within body A. At the same time, the user's physical movements are not mirrored by body A, but instead by body B. When the user lifts their arm, only the arm of body B, and not those of body A or C, responds appropriately. This attributes the user's body agency to body B. Finally, the user's sense of body ownership is attributed to body C, which looks the most human out of the three bodies. In addition to this top-down reinforcement, bottom-up visuotactile stimuli are used—when the user sees body C touched, they feel a touch in the same spot on their physical body. These three different influences on embodiment are shown in Figure 7.2

The experiment not only demonstrates that the three component representations can be independent in the mind, but is also useful for getting a grasp of what is strongest at inducing each component.

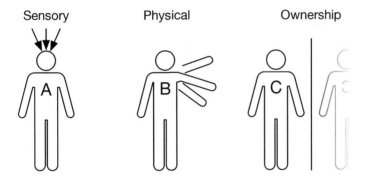

Figure 7.2: The three bodies experiment.

Although one's representations of self-location, body agency, and body ownership have been discussed as separate components and can in theory be induced independently, many of the factors that contribute one may also contribute to another. For example, both self-location and bottom-up views of body ownership are influenced by receiving sensorimotor contingencies in a spatial configuration that matches a virtual body. Experiments also suggest that inducing one of these sensations for a virtual body may lead to the user attributing degrees of the other components to that body through inference. For example, while the rubber hand experiments were designed to directly induce self-location and body ownership in the hand, participants reported perceiving agency over the hand, despite never moving it. These inferences may result from our experience in the real world, where our representations of self-location, body agency, and body ownership typically point to the same body.

## 7.4   EMOTION AND EMPATHY

It may sometimes seem as if we have little control over our emotions. For every time where we can mentally change our outlook and attitude or calm ourselves down, it may seem that there are just as many instances where our emotions are involuntary—an uncontrollable fear in response to a spider in the bathroom, anger that arises as a result of being stuck in traffic, or sudden laughter that we attempt to suppress when our boss makes a gaffe at a meeting. Emotions often (but not always) arise in response to external circumstances, and the goal of many pieces of media throughout time has been to elicit emotion (specific or otherwise) in their viewers—be they modern Hollywood movies, a Renaissance painting, or one of Shakespeare's plays. Many VR games fit into this category, where the objective is to elicit a feeling of excitement, amusement, fear, or accomplishment in the user. VR experiences that include narratives, including some VR games and most VR films, have the goal of making the user feel a certain way in response to the events they are observing unfold. Even the most utilitarian applications, like spreadsheet software or an engineering simulation, have an implicit emotional goal—to *not* make the user feel a sense of frustration with the software and interface.

When VR started to make a resurgence, many people assumed that it could lead to more emotional and more moving experiences or solicit emotions in new ways. Documentary companies and charities were some of the first parties to produce VR films for the new commercial headsets, perhaps hoping to leverage the new media's supposed power to move people emotionally and generate empathy. Considering the main psychological difference of VR from other digital media at the time was its ability to produce an illusion of presence, the generally accepted hypothesis seemed to be that higher levels of presence would lead to higher levels of emotion in users.

Researchers studying the emotional effects of VR since before this commercial wave found that this hypothesis didn't hold water—in most cases, emotions as a response to content or narrative were no stronger in VR than in other media, such as novels and television. Exceptions were cases where the goal was not to induce emotions through narrative but instead through mimicking real-life scenarios—responses of fear and anxiety were found to be higher in VR horror games than in horror movies, and on the other extreme, sitting in a serene VR garden would be more relaxing than looking at a picture of that garden. In cases where emotion was induced by replicating real-world scenarios, it was found that VR was less effective than real life in soliciting emotions (although many of the scenarios VR is capable of generating are not practical to experience in real life), but VR was more effective than less immersive media, in line with the "response as if real" reaction discussed in Chapter 2.

VR has the unique capacity among media to make a user react similarly to how they may react if they were in a physical environment, and thus has unique emotional consequences in this regard. Further, VR has the same potential to elicit emotion through narrative that many other media have. Because of this, it is important to understand how VR may impact a user emotionally and how this relates to user experience goals—questions that belong to the domain of *affective computing*.

### 7.4.1 Affective Computing

**Affective computing** is the study of the relationship between digital interfaces and emotions. This includes looking at how digital systems affect the emotional state of a user, but also encompasses relationships going the other way: utilizing user emotion as a potential input for a digital system and making a computer appear to have emotions both fall under the domain of affective computing.

Affective computing reflects a view that emotions are constructed or at least influenced by interactions. These interactions can be between people, between people and their surroundings, or between people and machines, such as a VR system.

In the sense that it is used here, the term "affective" refers to the ability to produce an emotional response. For example, affective behaviours in humans are those that can produce an emotional response—the behaviour of smiling at another person can make them happy as well, and the behaviour of yelling at a person can lead to feelings of shame. The *affective aspects* of a VR experience are the components able to cause certain emotional responses from users—they are the artificial analogue of human affective behaviours.

In order to understand the impact that affective aspects of a VR simulation have, it is necessary to be able to have a basic understanding of how emotions work, and ways in which they can be classified. There are many different models of emotion, and like any model, the quality of a model is related to how useful it is in the context for which it is intended. The somewhat simplistic description of emotions presented here is not intended to fully describe the inner workings of our emotional selves, rather it is a functional model, useful for working with affective aspects of VR. Because VR has the potential for deeply affective reactions and interactions, developers intending to built VR applications that centre around eliciting emotion should consult a variety of emotional models to understand the effect their scenarios can have on the emotional state of their users.

#### 7.4.1.1 Emotion and the Body

Emotions have both a psychological and a physiological component. Although many of our emotions are the result of cognitive interpretations of external events, they often are either influenced by or caused by internal physiological mechanisms such as hormones. In addition, emotions often cause involuntary or automatic physical reactions: the tensing of muscles with fear or veins dilating in the cheeks in order to make someone blush are both unconscious and automatic physical reactions that accompany emotions. These reactions are governed by the sympathetic nervous system, which is the system responsible for activating the fight-or-flight response, among other things. The system is responsible for involuntary actions, and physiological reactions that accompany fear and embarrassment occur *before* they are consciously registered in the mind. Many of these involuntary physiological reactions are a result of the hormone adrenaline, which is released in response to stress, including external stimuli that the mind interprets as threatening.

The other set of emotions, although not involuntary and hormone activated, may still be accompanied by unconscious physiological behaviours—for example, emotional states can influence an individual's posture and facial expressions. Although we have a degree of conscious control over our facial expressions, research suggests that some short-lived facial cues, referred to as *microexpressions*, are subconscious responses to emotions that cannot be consciously suppressed. Although they last less than 0.5, microexpressions have been able to be picked up and categorized by computers. Facial reflections of emotion, be they microexpressions or the longer lasting macroexpressions, seem to be innate to the human species—the same expressions occur for joy, anger, sadness, and many other emotions regardless of culture.

The fact that emotions result in external responses in the body is what gives VR systems or other computers the capacity to respond to the emotional state of the user. Without using a brain-computer interface or monitoring the levels of hormones in the bloodstream of a user, a VR system can still use sensors and tracking data from a user to infer emotions, such as computer vision analysis on video feeds of a user's face, or pose data that records a user's posture. Other external features that indicate a user's emotional or stress response include heart rate, galvanic skin response (a measure of if and how much the user is sweating), blood flow, and skin temperature, all of which can be measured using inexpensive sensors connected to the VR system. Such measures may be considered invasive and should be used with consent.

**Emotion and the Body**
Although emotional state affects the body in physiological ways, the physiology of the body can effect our emotional state as well. Forcing a smile when you are feeling sad can result in increased feelings of happiness, and self-help gurus have long harnessed the fact that adopting a more confident pose can lead to feelings of self-assurance. Exercise can have a positive influence on a person's mental state, reducing stress and encouraging feelings of euphoria. More direct physiological changes are also co-mingled—a person under stress produces more adrenaline, but a person injected with adrenaline will feel additional stress. Major depressive disorder and generalized anxiety disorder are two conditions that result in the body producing too much or not enough of certain hormones, resulting in feelings of anxiety or depression without an external cause; the treatment for these disorders is, among other things, to medically rebalance the neurotransmitters that result in these emotions. Although VR cannot be used to inject neurotransmitters, it might be useful for encouraging certain body functions, activities, or movements that can have an influence on a user's emotional state.

### 7.4.1.2 Categorizing Emotions

Many models within psychology exist for comparing or categorizing different emotions, but most are beyond what would be useful in the course of VR development. Although we will avoid describing a comprehensive continuum of all emotions, we will introduce two characteristics that can be used to describe emotions: *emotional valence* and *arousal*.

An emotion's *valence* describes that emotion's "direction." One may consider valence to be a continuum that describes if an emotion is "positive" or "negative"—although these are subjective value judgements, it can be understood objectively that delight and sorrow are opposite in valence, as they result in very different responses. If someone's emotions change, they could be moving along the valence axis—going from feeling neutral to feeling happy includes a change in valence. Valence is also sometimes described as "pleasure" in emotional models.

The level of *arousal* of an emotional response describes the magnitude to which the emotion is felt. The aforementioned change in going from feeling neutral to feeling happy likely has also changed in regard to the amount of arousal—feeling neutral is a low arousal, but happiness is higher arousal. Because of how subjective the words we use to describe emotions are, just saying something like "happiness" could refer to a range of arousal levels for the same emotional valence, and even the valence could have a slight range. The fact that we have so many names for similar emotions but that few are concretely defined makes them even more nebulous—thus, using metrics such as changes in arousal and valence is more useful in situations when a change in emotion is observed. Although in theory absolute measurements of valence and arousal could be used, deciding the base level and how to scale between different emotions, which are subjective experiences, would be very difficult. It's important to note that the combination of arousal and valence does not universally distinguish between emotions, unlike some other models—only that they are tools that can be used to describe emotions in more useful ways than without.

In some models of emotion, additional axes may be to the valence-arousal continuum. *Dominance* relates to whether the person has control over the emotion or not, or alternatively whether the emotion encourages action or not. Both anger and fear are negative-valence, high-arousal emotions, but anger may spur a person to action, while fear may encourage a person to retreat or even cause a person to freeze in terror. Another axis sometimes added to emotional models is *complexity*, recognizing that some emotions like fear or joy are simple and fundamental, while other emotions like melancholy or regret are more complex and situational. Complex emotions can often be described in terms of simpler emotions with specifiers; for example, loneliness is sadness related to a lack of human connection, and grief is sadness related to loss. Grief and disappointment are different emotions both involving sadness related to loss, and although they may be considered similar valence with differing arousal, it is not simply a degree of scale that separates them. Emotional models that attempt to categorize human experience are necessarily reductive, but may be useful if they help us understand the breadth of human experience and design scenarios that evoke or avoid emotions as may be reasonable.

## 7.4.2 The Effects of VR on Emotion

As mentioned in the introductory discussion on emotion, VR is not unique among media in its ability to elicit emotion through content and narrative, but is unique in that it allows for a "response-as-if-real" in situations where the user experiences a high degree of presence. Thus, while reactions to other media have significant range, VR can be more reliable in eliciting certain emotional states—environments that would relax a person in the real world are likely to relax them when presented in a virtual scenario. It should be noted that although emotional responses show commonalities across cultures and experiences, the specific stimuli which may cause a person to relax, make them happy, or cause anger is likely to differ significantly from person to person, and thus the effect of an intentional emotional trigger may be unpredictable. People feel emotions when listening to music, but the emotions they feel is highly dependent on their personal familiarity with, and experience of, that music. Some more fundamental emotions may be more predictable. The fear response when presented with disturbing or threatening imagery is predictable; however, people who have played zombie games regularly are less likely to be afraid of zombies. Lower level stimuli like surprise are more consistent, and games that intend to create a sense of terror often make use of jump scares to more reliably cause fear in their players. VR is particularly reliable in inducing fear—and to a higher level of arousal than traditional media.

VR's capacity to induce fear and to allow users to safely be exposed and become familiar with frightening scenarios has led to its use in a variety of related situations—besides horror games, fear in VR is also useful for training simulations in cases where participants would be put in nerve-wracking environments, something that made the military interested in VR in the very early days of the technology. Just as training in VR can help lead to lessened fear when faced with a similar scenario in practice, VR has also found use in exposure therapy for treating phobias. In exposure therapy, the subject is gradually exposed to the source of their fears, in situations with progressively increasing arousal, in a safe and controlled environment, with the understanding that becoming used to experiences that include their fears may help alleviate these fears. VR is useful for providing an environment that is as controllable as a therapist needs it to be for a particular patient, and can allow the therapist to scale the amount or type of feared stimulus according to the needs of their patient. Further, VR provides a way to expose a patient to fears that may be expensive or dangerous to obtain in the real world—for example, VR could be used to simulate many short flights to treat a person with a fear of flying in planes, while purchasing an equivalent number of plane tickets may not be financially prudent.

Two pathways exist by which emotions can be elicited, both of which can be stimulated by VR environments. First, emotions can be induced through the *perceptual emotion pathway*—immediate emotional reactions to stimuli in the environment. Reactions prompted through the perceptual pathway are often instinctive—an immediate fear response to a jump scare would be an example of a reaction induced through the perceptual emotional pathway. The more perceptual stimuli there are relating to a specific emotional outcome, the stronger the magnitude of the reaction.

Emotions can also be activated through the *conceptual emotion pathway*. In this pathway, reactions are induced by receiving information. Whereas claustrophobia could be induced through the perceptual pathway when a person sees they are in a small box, it could similarly be induced by informing a blindfolded participant that they are located within a small, enclosed space. In general, reactions through this pathway are more subjective than those induced through the perceptual pathway, but generally produce weaker physiological signs of activation.

### 7.4.3 VR as a Tool for Empathy

One of the ways fiction is able to generate emotional reactions from participants is through empathy—users feel for the characters within the story due to their circumstances. Empathy is defined as the capacity to which someone is able to understand (and to some degree, feel) what another person experiences. Empathy can be separated into *affective empathy*, which consists of responding to the emotions of another by feeling an appropriate emotional reaction, as well as *cognitive empathy*, which is the capacity to understand the mental state or perspective of the other party.

In addition to the narrative devices used to produce empathy, VR offers a unique way to induce empathy in users—due to its ability to invoke presence, VR offers a way to literally allow users to "walk in another's shoes." Through avatars, VR allows users to inhabit other bodies—whether humanoid or other. Some claim that placing a user in a specific avatar can make it easier for them to empathize with that avatar, but as true empathy is difficult to measure, the conclusion that "VR generates empathy" is difficult to reliably claim.

One effect of being within an avatar that has been identified and is often used to argue that VR is able to establish empathy is the **Proteus effect**: the ability of an avatar to influence users' attitudes and behaviours. For example, putting a user in an avatar resembling a historic figure leads the user to, at least temporarily, attribute some traits associated with that figure to themselves—one such study showed that users who used an avatar resembling Albert Einstein performed better on cognitive tests, which could be the result of an increased measure of confidence in that area.

## 7.5  SUMMARY

The first time a person puts on on a VR headset and looks around a virtual world, the experience is engaging and exciting. The first time a person moves in a virtual world, the effect can be disorienting and challenging. When a person spends any significant amount of time in a virtual world, the differences between the real world and the virtual world begin to assert themselves more aggressively, especially if the developer does not take care to compensate for these differences. We must remind ourselves regularly that these VR worlds are simulations, and by necessity these simulations are imperfect. Different people with different experiences will experience these psychological effects differently, and we must take care to provide options within our experiences that take these effects into account, otherwise we significantly reduce the player base that may be available to experience the worlds we create. In subsequent chapters throughout Part 2 of this book, we explore the design principles that enable us to take advantage of the opportunities that VR provides.

# II

Designing Virtual Interactions

# CHAPTER 8

# Experience Usability

## 8.1 INTRODUCTION

Information flows between a user and a system in two directions. The system presents information to the user, which the user must interpret. The user then decides on an action based on the information and activities presented by the system. Finally, the system must interpret the users' intent based on the actions they perform. In both cases, poor usability design can lead to errors: in the interpretation of the state of the computer by the user and of the intentions of the user by the computer. Donald Norman identified the sources of these errors as "gulfs," as shown in Figure 8.1.

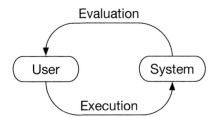

Figure 8.1: The gulfs of execution and evaluation.

When a user attempts to extract information about a system, this is called evaluation. The **gulf of evaluation** corresponds to the ways in which it is possible for the user to misinterpret the state of the system. This gulf can be closed by improving the display of information from the system to the user. After the user has collected information about the state of the system, the user then chooses an activity to pursue. The **gulf of execution** refers to the difference between the activity the user wants to pursue and the activities available, as well as the ways in which the system misinterprets the intention of the user. This gulf can be closed by improving the design of the activities available to the user.

When a system is not designed for usability, these gulfs can compound on each other: the user may misinterpret the state of the system, choosing an inappropriate activity based on that misinformation; the system then misinterprets the intent of the user and displays incorrect information, and the cycle repeats.

DOI: 10.1201/9781003261230-8

This chapter presents a summary of the foundation theories of usability as applied to interactions and activity design, the goal of which is to reduce the gulf of execution. We want to make the user's options obvious and clear to them, and we want to make the result of each activity predictable, so that the user knows how the system is likely to respond to a specific activity. Chapter 12 will cover the design of coherent and complete information display systems, the goal of which is to reduce the gulf of interpretation. We want to correctly represent the state of the system to the user and as much as possible avoid ambiguity and misinterpretation by the user.

### 8.1.1 Diegesis

When a game or other interactive experience attempts to tell a story, it creates a narrative structure for the character and, by extension, the player to experience. In these contexts, the developer can design interactions for either the player or the character, and the separation between these two is important to consider. Interactions that the player performs in order to control the character happen out-of-universe, in the "real world" where the player lives. When the game says "press X to not die" it is clear that the communication is between the game system (and by extension the developer) and the user playing the game. The character walking around the artificial universe is not holding a game controller and has no "X" button to press. As players learn the game, they learn the connection between the real-world actions they take (on a game controller or keyboard) and the activities that the character will perform. The separation between the action the player takes and the activities performed by the character is an example of the gulf of execution. The player hopes that by pressing a button, the system will interpret their command to the character, and the character will carry out the action. There is a separation between the user's interaction with the system, the user's interaction with the character, and the character's interaction with the game world.

In narrative structure, **diegesis** describes the character's ability to perceive certain aspects of the world. The term is used in movies and shows to describe whether or not a character can hear the soundtrack of the narrative. Often, music is playing that the audience can hear but the characters within the narrative cannot hear. This happens when a soundtrack is used to build emotion within the context of the show. Such music is referred to as non-diegetic, meaning that it exists for the benefit of the audience but is beyond the perception of the characters. Non-diegetic features are part of the *style* of the story, whereas dietetic features are part of the content of the story. Musical theatre contains good examples of diegetic and non-diegetic features—when the emotion of a scene becomes so intense that words are not enough, the characters begin to sing, and when that cannot convey the emotion sufficiently, they begin to dance. The singing and dancing are understood to be stylistic elements of the story, and the characters themselves do not know they are singing or dancing. Postmodern musicals will sometimes draw attention to the absurdity of randomly breaking into a well-constructed chorus or a choreographed dance routine, which reminds the audience that they are watching a show, momentarily breaking the difference between diegetic and non-diegetic elements, a technique also known as "breaking the fourth wall."

In interactive software design, then, we can make use of the framework of diegesis to consider an extension to the original conceptualization of the gulfs of evaluation and execution. If a player is controlling a character, and the character is interacting with the world, there are two possible modes of interaction. In diegetic interaction, the character perceives and interacts with the world, and the player experiences the world by proxy. The player only knows what the character knows and can only interact with the world via the character. In these scenarios, diegesis can be used both in evaluation and execution—the world may present imperfect information to the character, and the character may make imperfect actions within the world. In non-diegetic interaction, the player has additional (possibly imperfect) information that the character does not have and can interact with the world through other means besides the character.

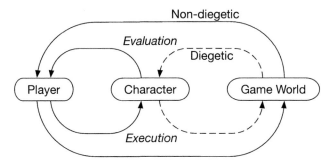

Figure 8.2: Diegetic and non-diegetic gulfs.

The metaphor of the game is relevant here but the same can be said for any situation where a user interacts with a system through a proxy. If I ask you to perform a task using a system and report the result, there may be a gulf of execution between me and you, and there may be a second gulf between you and the system. Once you have interacted with the system and performed an action, there may be a gulf of evaluation between the system and you, and a second one between you and me before I receive the result. Gulfs exist wherever miscommunication is possible, and there are multiple ways within a single system where miscommunication can happen.

Within the context of virtual reality (VR), these gaps in understanding are important to consider for several reasons. First, when your senses are occluded and replaced by sensations generated from a virtual world, there are fewer opportunities to verify information or be reminded of the correct steps for execution. It is problematic to have to remove your VR headset every time you have to look up a process in a manual to remember how to do a thing on the system, and second, it is more difficult to present non-diegetic information to the user. VR experiences are usually set in the first person, where the user inhabits an avatar which interacts with the world. Most information must therefore be communicated to the user diegetically, although there are methods for non-diegetic information presentation which will be discussed in Chapter 12. Presenting information in a diegetic way can improve plausibility, but can also widen the gulf of evaluation. Overlays, pop-up windows, and text display itself can be more difficult to perceive, and showing what information is important within a virtual world can be challenging. On a flat screen in the physical world, if the developer places information for the user based on good usability theory, it is reasonable to assume that the user will understand most of it. Although a virtual world seems to open the floodgates of possibility for presenting information and performing actions, the opportunity for mistakes is greater, and different processes must be followed to ensure that users know what to do and how to do it.

Often in VR, the perspective of the user and the perspective of the character are the same. The user dons a VR headset and can see through the character's eyes, hear through their ears, and experience the world the way the character would experience it. Because this first-person experience is so common as to be a default in VR system design, diegetic experiences are also predominant. The user sees only what the character sees. In flat-screen experiences, the user often has access to an informational overlay, showing the score, the tasks to be accomplished, resources available, or a map of the area—in VR, this type of overlay is usually not present, and these sources of information must be presented to the user diegetically, on a display that makes sense within the context of the world. The diegetic display of information will be discussed further in Chapter 12.

## 8.2 USABILITY THEORY

People use tools every day, and the best tools are the ones best aligned with the task they are intended to support. A "good" hammer has a comfortable grip and a heavy, flat head orthogonal to the direction in which it is swung. If the head was not flat, or if the grip was not comfortable, it would make the task of hammering much more difficult. Tool design evolves as the tasks change, but most simple tools for simple tasks tend to converge on a small set of optimal designs. The challenge inherent in designing computer systems or whole virtual worlds for "good" usability is twofold: first, the tasks are significantly more complex, making simple interfaces difficult to do well, and second, the tasks change regularly, making converging on an optimal design difficult. As a result, usability theory must be considered directly when designing computer systems or virtual worlds, because it is not practical to iterate usability on failures; rather, it must be successful when first released.

### 8.2.1 Human action cycle

The study of usability requires analysis of the tasks people perform and the way they make decisions about which actions to perform and when. A common model to formulate decision-making around activities is the **human action cycle** which lists three stages: goal formation, execution, and evaluation, also sometimes described as "plan, do, review." Depending on the model formulation, these three stages may have have sub-stages; for example, sometimes execution involves breaking a problem up into smaller tasks that then must be accomplished in a specific order, and evaluation often involves first observing the results of the task (which may or may not be accurate based on the gulf of evaluation) and comparing the outcome to what the user expected.

Each part of the "plan, do, review" cycle must be considered when designing and evaluating an interface, and these can be framed as reactive (was the user able to accomplish tasks) or proactive (what will the user do to accomplish tasks).

Although the specific display of information will be covered in Chapter 11, aspects of the design of the interface itself are key to enabling the human action cycle. Seeing the results of an action in the change in the state of the world is often sufficient for the evaluation phase, without the need for a display of data related to the activity; however, there are also circumstances where the user needs information about the state of the world *before* they attempt an action. Collecting information is part of the planning stage, and users must know where to look and what to look for in order to have the best information for the goals they set.

### 8.2.2   Interfaces and Mediation

An interface is, at core, a conduit through which information and intention pass back and forth. Interfaces therefore serve to *mediate* the relationship between a user and the system they are using. When a user establishes an intent and makes a plan, this plan is directly shaped by the interface the user knows they will be using. If the interface is unfamiliar, the user may need to first perform a learning task or they may rely on expectations of familiarity. Regardless, the tasks that a user can perform with a system form the set of possible goals, and therefore the first stage of the human action cycle is fundamentally shaped by the design decisions made by the developer of the interface. This mediation is critical to understanding the experience of the users of the system. The designer may ask why a user isn't following a particular workflow, but the choices a user makes are heavily influenced by the interface available to them. Developers often blame problems on "user error[1]," but since the user's interactions with the system is defined by the interface available to them, the developer must take some responsibility for the errors the users may make and choose to use good user interface design principles from the beginning of the project.

### 8.2.3   The Five "E"s of Usability

A common framework for evaluating the success of interface design is the five "E"s:

**Effective:** Does the system enable the task to be accomplished?

**Efficient:** Can the task be accomplished quickly? Can you quickly change between tasks?

**Engaging:** Does the system encourage the user to interact with it? Is it satisfying to use? Does the user get fatigued or bored using it?

---

[1]User errors are sometimes labelled as "PEBKAC" errors (problem exists between keyboard and chair) or "ID-10-T" (idiot) errors. It is a common trope among developers that users are the cause of most errors, but user error can be reduced by a good interface.

**Error Tolerant:** Is the system designed to avoid errors? Does the system prevent incorrect use? Does the system recover from errors when they do occur? Does the system adapt to common errors?

**Easy to Learn:** Can a user walk up and use it? Can a user learn it quickly? Can a user improve their skills as they use it?

### 8.2.4 Usability and Game Design

Games are a foundational component of what makes us human. Games allow us to test our abilities against one another, allow us a framework to learn new skills, and provide us with a structure to experience the satisfaction of solving problems. Our brains have evolved to reward us with a hit of pleasure whenever we gain new knowledge or accomplish a goal, and games are a way to reliably and safely deliver these experiences. Game design is a large and complex topic, beyond the scope of this book, but it encompasses many factors including the aesthetics of the game, the rules, the way players interact with each other or the game system, the balance that makes the game feel fair, the rewards that encourage users to play the game more often, and the progression that allows the game to continue to deliver new experiences and opportunities for problem-solving.

In many ways, game design is in direct contradiction to the application of the theory of usability design. Each of the five "E"s that makes a user interface better may actually serve to reduce what makes a game satisfying to play. Good interfaces allow tasks to be accomplished, but good games contain tasks that are inherently difficult to accomplish. The *interface* to the puzzle may be effective, in that the player can make a move, choose a piece, pick a number, or otherwise activate the goal of progressing in the solve, but the solve itself is designed to be difficult. A jigsaw puzzle with four pieces is unsatisfying to an accomplished puzzler, but a puzzle of 1000 pieces will take some time to put together. If the pieces do not fit well, if the pieces break and jam together, or if the puzzle is made out of paper, it will be more difficult to accomplish each individual subgoal of solving the puzzle, which will be unsatisfying. The *process* of solving the puzzle or playing the game should not be effective, but each individual interaction within the game play should be effective.

Similarly, the efficiency of a game or puzzle must be very carefully considered. It is satisfying to solve a puzzle quickly or win a game with few moves, but only if that feels like a great accomplishment. Speedrunning a video game is a kind of meta-game, where the player must first play the game as intended and then find exploits and tricks that allow them to complete the game as fast as possible, competing against other speedrunners who post their times and criteria online. Ironically, cheating in speedrunning is taken very seriously by the community, implying that although the goal is to find ways to bypass significant portions of the game, it must still be done within a set of strict rules. Competition is meaningless unless the rules apply equally to everyone and the challenge requires training and skill—although the world championship of rock-paper-scissors is a competition that would seem to go against this statement. Of course, some games involve completing tasks quickly and some don't—although champion-level chess involves a clock, the decisions made are slow and methodical, and a very different game than speed chess, where decision-making time is significantly reduced. Efficiency should be considered at all levels of game design—individual actions should be efficient once decisions are made, like the movement of a piece or the playing of a card. Placing a card improperly should not grant a disadvantage unless that is a component of the gameplay, in which case it may be considered a **minigame**—a game within a game, added to provide a short burst of solving satisfaction or to draw out the time spent playing the game. Game designers must be cautious when considering the efficiency of gameplay components or minigames especially in the context of progression. If a certain number of successful gameplay moments are required before the next stage of the game is available, this can allow the developer to ensure that the player is "ready" for the next level and that the next level will be satisfying; however, too much progression gating can turn the game into a "grind," where users gain no satisfaction from completing tasks, rather they do so only to open the next level of progression. Particularly egregious examples of this will move the player from progression gate to progression gate, never providing satisfying gameplay (after the first initial "hit") but only providing the next boring task to accomplish.

Engagement in games is almost an unspoken assumption. Games should be fun, and being fun is why we play games in the first place. Playing sports with friends is fun because we are interacting with our friends, but the sport itself must also be entertaining, with sufficient opportunities for display of skill—which allows us to show off to our friends, and randomness and balance—which allows each player or team to have a reasonable chance at success even if there is a mismatch between the skill of the players. Card collection games are engaging because there are a large variety of cards available and each player has a hidden deck, so there is an element of surprise when your opponent plays an interesting card from their deck, as well as a challenge to attempt to determine the strategy that this card may foreshadow. Engagement can come from good game design—the strategy and structure of the game can lead to moments of surprise and satisfaction that make the game engaging to play. Engagement can also come from good interface design—the way in which the elements or activities of the game are put together make them satisfying to accomplish. Unlike efficiency or effectiveness, game design and usability design are not typically in competition when it comes to engagement—colourful, interesting, active tasks make good games just like they make good interfaces; when a game becomes disengaging, and players become bored, it's not a good game anymore and players begin to complain about the "grind" as discussed above. In games where the purpose is to collaboratively create patterns, the engagement itself can be the primary purpose of the activity; on the other hand, casinos and pay-to-play mobile games often disguise simple and predatory gameplay behind exaggerated engagement—each time you complete a level, bells and whistles and fireworks and applause all drive engagement, and the player then seeks that affirmation rather than exploring the game for the sake of the gameplay. In a puzzle, the engagement comes from the feeling of satisfaction when the puzzle is solved. In predatory engagement, the bells and whistles emulate that feeling without providing any satisfaction. See the box labelled "gambling and pathology" for further discussion of predatory gameplay.

Error tolerance is a component of good usability design, but good game design instead allows *error recovery*. If the advent of gameplay in early human evolution came about as a way to learn and train with reduced risk, then making mistakes would be a critical component of this type of activity. We learn best by doing, and by understanding what we have done wrong, we understand how to avoid that mistake in the future. Games provide vast opportunities for making mistakes in a controlled and safe environment, and well-designed games, rather than avoiding errors, encourage them and provide ways to recover from them. If two people are fighting with swords, the first one to make a mistake loses the fight and probably dies. Fencing and other swordplay games build mechanisms to allow a person to lose a swordfight and not lose their life, in order to become a better sword fighter. Weapons are dulled, protective equipment is worn, rules are established, and points are awarded to determine a winner. A single bout of fencing contains dozens of individual swordfights which would otherwise be fatal. Most competitive games involve many interactions between players, so that a single error by a player does not normally end the game—however, at very high levels of competition (like grandmaster chess) or with very simple games (like rock-paper-scissors) a single error by one player is enough to give the win to the other. In these cases, losing a single game has little long-term consequence, and a player will lose many games before they become proficient enough to begin winning.

Being easy to learn is the usability characteristic that applies in the most variety of ways to game design. Some of the most challenging and long-lasting games, like chess and go, have a straightforward and easy-to-understand rule set and can be learned very quickly. Collectible deck-building card games like Magic and Pokemon are significantly more complex, with rules and conditions that evolve over time as new cards are added to the game. This allows the game to continue to be interesting, but may become frustrating if the new cards or rules are not balanced with the existing rules and cards. There is pressure on game designers to introduce new rules or cards that are "better" than the existing rule set, not only to add interest and complexity to the game but also to encourage long-time players to spend money on the new cards. The balance here is very difficult and can lead to *power creep* where players who do not buy the new cards will be at a disadvantage. New players attempting to learn the game may also be frustrated at the large diversity of rules and options in the game, which is at once a benefit to the enjoyment for long-time players, and a detriment to accessibility for a wide player base. If the complexity of the rules of the game is a component of what makes the game enjoyable and engaging, then a hard-to-learn game can be a well-designed game, but designers should carefully consider if the difficulty to learn the game is a feature of the game or if it becomes exclusionary. Designing ways to learn a difficult game is a usability problem in itself—game instructions and tutorials are usually built by the designers of the game or long-time players, and the challenge of developer familiarity occurs here as well—it is difficult to remember what it is like to not know something, and it is easy to make assumptions about what people learning your game should know.

**Gambling and pathology**

Each of the gameplay elements described here can also be designed pathologically—casinos and pay-to-play games are designed specifically to provide small doses of satisfaction and lure the player into spending more and more real money to achieve the next "hit" of success. The result is, in effect, the exploitation of a brain system to steal money from people who are particularly susceptible to gambling addiction. Many jurisdictions around the world have made gambling and other incremental paid pseudo-chance games illegal.

There are multiple levels of trade-offs in game design, between easy to use (in the context of the five "E"s) and fun to play. Lower level mechanics of a game should be usable, otherwise mundane aspects of the game would become annoying; while higher level mechanics of a game should be challenging, in order to give a sense of pride and accomplishment when tasks are completed successfully.

## 8.3 HUMAN FACTORS IN USABILITY

Humans create machines to help us accomplish tasks that are boring, tedious, difficult, or dangerous; we create machines to augment our skills, by improving our accuracy, consistency, and repeatability, and we create machines to amplify our senses, allow us to see farther, hear more, and understand the world. Designing an interface for a machine to be used by a human can be seen from one of two different perspectives. Either we see the machine as accomplishing a task, and the human directing the machine, or we see the human and the machine working together to accomplish a task. In the former case, the interface between the two can easily be considered an afterthought—the machine is designed to do the job, and the human must adapt to the way the machine works if they are to interact with the machine. In the latter case, however, we recognize the strengths and weaknesses of both machine and human and design the interaction between them to compensate for weakness and to build upon strength.

While machines (and computers) bring competencies in precision, repeatability, speed, memory, tirelessness, objectivity, patience, and physical robustness, people bring competencies in holistic pattern matching, creativity, initiative, exception handling, learning from experience, judgement, ethics, social context, flexibility, and adaptability. We build things to do the things we are not good at, so it makes sense that the intersection between the "skills" of systems and the skills of people is small. Machines need people to direct their operation, and people need machines to augment our weaknesses. Because of this, the interaction between the machine and the person is critical to the success of the person-machine system. Understanding the limitations of the way humans can interact with machines will allow us to craft interfaces that are, as Raskin said, "responsive to human needs and considerate of human frailties."

### 8.3.1 Memory

Computers can remember, with perfect recall, as many pieces of information as they are given and as their storage will allow. Humans, on the other hand, remember small amounts of information, imperfectly. Human memory has been studied for decades, but many facets are still not well understood. Human memory is generally classified based on how long ago you experienced something (sensory memory, short-term memory, and long-term memory), what is being stored or recalled (episodic versus semantic memory), and how the memory is recalled (by trying to remember a fact, by demonstrating a skill, or by being reminded of a memory by a sensation or context). If we expect a user to perfectly remember everything in a training document in order to use a system, that user will be frustrated and the system (the user and the machine together) will not be able to accomplish the goals set out to it. Rather the system should, as much as possible, present information in such a way that the user does not have to actively remember how to use it; the activities should be familiar, obvious, intuitive, and supportive. Supporting the memory of the user should be a key factor in the development of any interface. Early computer interfaces were nothing more than a command prompt, which required the user to remember or look up all interactions and commands. (See Section 13.1.1 for a further discussion of command-line interfaces.) Modern general-purpose computer interfaces make common commands readily available in menus and provide access to additional functionality through apps. The challenge with supporting human memory is that human memory changes over time as people learn things. If a user can't remember a command, it is supportive to provide that command in a menu or a manual. Once the user has learned the command, it is supportive to allow the user to invoke the command quickly and easily. Menu systems often include hotkey combinations (which also must be learned) that allow rapid access to the command without navigating to the menu.

### 8.3.2 Locus of attention

Computer systems can see wherever we put sensors for them, but humans can only collect information through the senses that evolution provided. Our eyes are in front of our face, and we cannot see behind us. More importantly, but less overt, our brains can only focus on a few things at a time. The **locus of attention** is the name given to the thing we are currently paying attention to. This concept is critical in usability design, because it is easy for a human to not notice a thing that happens outside of their locus of attention. When a person looks in one direction, they obviously cannot see things that are happening in another direction, but this effect is much more focused than people often understand. The visual locus of attention encompasses the foveated portions of the visual field. Although we can notice things outside of the fovea, and our attention can be drawn away from the fovea to a new thing, that new thing must be moving or changing sufficiently to draw attention, and in that case we move our fovea away from what we were looking at, to the new interesting thing. If small subtle things happen in our peripheral vision, we may very well miss them. When a developer wants to communicate something to a user, this communication should happen within the locus of attention, where the user is focused, or it should be sufficiently dramatic in order to draw the user's locus of attention to the communication. Warning messages and pop-up windows are designed in this way to interrupt a user's attention when the system needs specific user input. If the message appears slowly and quietly in the corner of the screen, the user may not see it at all.

Feedback to the user should also occur within the locus of attention. If a user is looking at an object when they activate a command (and the object is the target of the command), that object should produce some indication that the command was successful. If the user does not see that anything happened, they may believe that the command was unsuccessful and may try again.

Although the locus of attention is primarily visual, other senses can be used to help draw the users' attention when necessary. For example, when the system must produce an alert, a sound can also be played in order to draw the users' attention towards the alert. Yes a sound event and a visual event happen at the same time; the user will interpret that these are artefacts of the same underlying event.

Sound has a locus of attention as well; however, it is involuntary. People can choose to look where they want to look and can ignore (for the most part) visual distractions in order to concentrate on a task. Audio, on the other hand, is much more difficult to ignore, especially audio that contains speech or audio that is particularly loud. This is why we use sound in our alarm clocks and why particular music can be used as torture or to drive teenagers away from loitering in front of the shop. Developers should be cautious when using audio as an alert indicator, because in addition to being difficult or impossible to ignore, it cannot be guaranteed to happen at all. Many users mute the sound of their computers or listen to music when interacting with a computer and therefore you cannot assume that a sound event will be heard.

The concept of the locus of attention also extends to our ability to focus on and understand multiple things at once. When focusing on language, we can hear and understand only one stream at a time. When two people are talking over each other, it is very difficult to understand what either of them are saying. Indeed, it is difficult for us to understand what we ourselves are saying if there is too much sound happening, and in situations where we are hearing ourselves, if there is even a slight delay, it will be almost impossible to form sentences. Our conscious brain operates in these streams in most tasks, and while it is possible to become hyperfocused on a single activity, doing more than one cognitive thing at a time is very difficult. Multitasking, which is the ability to do more than one thing at a time, requires either a distribution of attention (where you may be listening to one thing and doing another) or rapid task switching (where you are fully focused on one task and switch to another and back quickly). True multitasking, where you could talk to two people simultaneously or do two similar tasks at the same time, is difficult or impossible for humans.

## Split Brain and Attention

The brain consists of two halves connected by a bundle of nerves called the corpus callosum. Usually, the two halves of the brain communicate with each other through this bundle of nerves and act as a whole. Although spoken language occurs primarily in the dominant brain (left brain for right-handed people), both sides of the brain can read language and each side controls one hand. In people who have had this connection split for some reason, by trauma or accident, we discover that the two brain halves are much more separate than we normally understand. Each side can have its own locus of attention, can focus on separate things, and can operate independently of the other. The understanding is beginning to emerge that each side of the brain may be a separate consciousness, but that because only the left brain speaks, we identify our "selves" with the left brain.

### 8.3.3  Mental Models

*All models are wrong, but some are useful (aphorism, attributed to George Box).*

A **mental model** is a collection of assumptions, reasonings, and understandings that a person uses to make decisions about the world. When I reach out to pick up an object, I am using a collection of past experiences, physical assumptions, memory, and guesswork to determine the likely outcome of wrapping my fingers around the object and attempting to lift it. Many of these assumptions will be incorrect, but if the result is that I can predict what will happen, the model is useful. If the object is much heavier than I expect, if it is glued to the table, or if I am in VR and the object doesn't actually exist, my mental model will be incorrect and I will have a mismatch between my expectation and reality.

Mental models are much like scientific theories in that they predict the world and attempt to explain the world that is not necessarily a reflection of the actual truth of the world. Newton's laws of motion describe how objects behave when in motion. Before Newton, the common explanation of how things move related to the inherent energy in the object, and when that energy runs out, the object would stop moving or fall to the ground. This model is inaccurate in that there is no essential energy within the object that causes it to continue to move until that energy runs out, but it is useful; it explains what happens to objects when you throw them; eventually they fall to the ground. His laws are more accurate in that they explain why an object runs out of momentum—something acts upon it to strip away its kinetic energy and make it slow down. Today, we know that Einstein's theories of motion are more accurate than Newton's: they allow us to understand that when objects move very fast, the way those objects experience time and space changes. Most of the time, we do not have direct experience with objects moving close to the speed of light, so Newton's laws of motion are sufficient to predict the future with a reasonable degree of accuracy. They are not "correct," but they are good enough.

When a user experiences your system, they will build internal mental models of what will happen when they do something. If I press *this* button, the system makes *this* noise and my character moves in *this* way. The design of your system can help your users develop these mental models. This can happen explicitly, with direct training, explanation, and reference, so that the user is told what will happen in any given circumstance, and it can happen implicitly, where the user may experiment with certain activities and build their own model that explains the system to the best of their understanding. There is no guarantee that the model a user builds will be the same or even similar to the model the developer intends, and developer models and user models are usually fundamentally different.

Although "all models are wrong," models that are *inaccurate* can be problematic. A mental model may encode information about the world incorrectly, but as long as the predictions they make end up being correct, the model is useful. If the model results in incorrect predictions, we say the model is inaccurate.

If a user expects one thing to happen and a different thing happens, or if a user finds it difficult to predict what will happen, the mental model is not as useful as it could be. Again, designers have some agency here. A commonly cited example of a user interface design technique that leads to inaccurate or non-predictive mental modelling is the idea of a **modal interface**, one in which the same control may do different things depending on the mode of the device. Model interfaces are used when a designer wants to limit the size or complexity of an interface that they are building and so implements several different layers of functionality onto a single set of controls. The classic example of a problematic modal interface is the multifunction universal television remote control. This device, examples of which are pictured in Figure 8.3, is exemplified by a row of mode buttons across the top that allows a single remote to control many devices, like a TV, DVD, cable box, digital video recorder, stereo system, or other devices typically found within a home's media set-up. The first problem with these devices is that the type of devices changes regularly, so while early universal remotes had a button for VCR, most homes do not have a VCR in them anymore. To build some future functionality, designers often add generic selectors, like "aux" for auxiliary—of course the user must then remember what "aux" refers to. Additionally, before the remote can be used, a complicated and difficult process of programming must be employed, allowing the remote from one manufacturer to control a device from a different manufacturer. This programming process can be lost if the remote runs out of batteries, requiring the process to be repeated.

The modal challenge with remote controls, and the one that informs our discussion on mental modelling, is that while the remote can be used to control many devices, it is difficult to tell, just by looking at the remote, which device it is currently set to control. When you press the "TV" button, the remote will set itself to the "TV" *mode*, and each button will do something specific to the TV. The arrows might change the volume or change the channel, the gear button might activate settings, and the number buttons would let you select a channel. The media control buttons (play, pause, stop, etc.) may not do anything in TV mode, because the TV cannot play or pause anything. Alternatively, in DVD mode, the media controls would play and pause the playback and the arrows may select chapters of the DVD, but the numbers may not do anything. Not only does each button do a different thing depending on the mode, some may not do anything. The user must build a complicated mental model of the functionality of the unit in order to plan an action and accomplish the

Figure 8.3: Universal remote control.

action. The universal remote makes all functions accessible, but most of the time all the user wants to do is adjust the volume or change the channel.

The primary problem with model interfaces is that it is difficult or impossible to build a mental model of the outcome of each interaction. In order to adjust the volume, I must first either ensure that the remote is in TV mode, by invoking an additional action of pressing the TV button, effectively doubling the number of actions for that activity, or I must add the additional cognitive burden of remembering that the remote is in TV mode or not. The alternative is to greatly increase the number of errors made in the interactions, because when the user attempts to change the volume, they instead make an adjustment on a different device. If this adjustment is obvious (and within the user's locus of attention), then they will notice it, undo it, press the mode button, and finally engage in the activity they were planning in the first place. If, however, the result of the incorrect activity is not in the user's locus of attention or is otherwise hidden, or if there is no result of their activity, the user may press the same button over and over again without effect.

Incorrect mental models can also emerge from situations where the user does not understand the physics or mechanics underlying a process, even though they may well understand the interface between themselves and these processes. The climate system in a car has two main points of control—the user can adjust the temperature or the fan speed. If you get into a cold car and would like to quickly warm the car to the desired temperature, what settings do you select? Many users will set both the temperature and the fan speed to maximum, and then later in the car ride they find themselves too hot and must turn the temperature down. The reason for this is that the heating element will warm up at the same rate no matter the final target temperature, even though most users imagine that if they set the heat higher it will heat up faster. This is an incorrect mental model, and the result is an increased gulf of execution. The desired outcome is a comfortable temperature—the actual outcome is a car which is too hot and the need for a further interaction. Indeed, even when the car is at a reasonable temperature midway through a drive, some users will adjust the temperature when they feel cold, even though the temperature is already set to a comfortable temperature. The user should be adjusting the fan if they want to change the rate of heating. This example is a bit different if the goal is to cool a hot car—most users will initially roll down the windows. Although this will not cool the car below the ambient temperature of the air around it, a parked car in the sun is likely to be hotter than the air around it, so venting the windows will result in an initial reduction in temperature. If, however, the user would like the car to be cooler, they must first close the windows and then engage the air conditioning.

### 8.3.3.1 Uncanny Valley

An example of a situation where an unconscious mental model can change quickly is the concept known as the **uncanny valley**. This scenario arises from the desire to create human-looking models in animation, robotics, and interactive systems and the challenges with producing convincing simulations of human faces and actions. Humans have evolved to quickly recognize and attend to faces they see, such that people see faces in abstract collections of shapes, and collections of punctuation can be used to exemplify simple emotions such as happiness :), sadness :(, playfulness :P, and anger >:|. There is a striking difference, however, between an abstract drawing representing a face and a realistic human face. Drawings, cartoons, animation, and video games have historically relied on affective abstractions to allow a character to represent a human. Such abstractions tend to emphasize the facial features most salient, such as the size and shape of the eyes or the movement of the mouth. The exaggeration of these features allows us to see something engaging and expressive when it is objectively not human. Our mental model ascribes personality and connection to these animated characters, and the more human-like or *anthropomorphic* the character, the more engaged we become. Abstract objects can elicit an emotional response if it behaves somewhat like a person, and we even attribute human motivations and behaviours to inanimate objects (a pet rock) or abstract concepts (the weather) as a form of mental modelling.

When developers first tried to create realistic human simulations, in robotics and animation, an unusual pattern emerged. Our emotional response tends to increase as objects become more anthropomorphic, but only to a point. Animations or robots that approach human simulation can, surprisingly, elicit a very negative emotional response if the simulation is "too good." It seems that at a certain point, our mental model will shift from interpreting a non-human object as having human characteristics to that object being interpreted as a human object with non-human characteristics. It's no longer an emotionally resonant non-human; now it is an emotionally dissonant human. There is something not quite right about it, and it is difficult to put your finger on it. The effect was recognized in early computer-generated movies and early robotics research, when more human-looking robots were more appealing but only to a point. It is called the uncanny valley because there appears to be an affective gap between human-like objects and actual humans, and designers should make their human-like creations somewhat *less* human-like to avoid this gap.

## 8.3.4 Decision-Making

When presented with multiple scenarios, multiple mental models, or multiple options, a user must make a decision about how to proceed. This may be as simple as which mission to choose to play next, or as complicated as which high-level tactic to use to accomplish a particular goal. Users make decisions on many different levels, from micro-decisions that happen at a semi-conscious level thousands of times a day to life-changing decisions that take years of preparation and hinge on a single moment. Decisions that need to be made within the context of a computer system are supported by the designer by providing access to the information and procedures the user needs to make these decisions. **Decision support systems** are interactive systems built specifically to enable users to make complicated decisions more easily. Many business processes can be augmented by implementing a decision support system, including scheduling, inventory, marketing, and investments, and many games (particularly strategy games) can be framed as decision support systems. These systems usually operate by collecting information and presenting it in such a way that the user can make a decision. Sometimes, these systems will advocate for a particular course of action, and the user can accept, reject, or modify the proposed decision. Decision support systems usually contain a framework or model that tries to encapsulate the problem domain about which decisions are being made. If that internal model is inaccurate, the decisions will be untrustworthy.

Humans make use of many tools for decision support, one of the most obvious and fundamental is taking notes while collecting information. In the early days of video games, before the internet, players did not have access to walk-throughs, hints, speed runs, or other meta-information about the game. Instead, players would often have a notebook near their computer to write down the solutions to puzzles or make strategy notes as they proceed. This process of notation is not practical in VR because although it is possible to have a notebook with you, it breaks the feeling of presence to have to remove your headset every time you want to make a note. Games and experiences should be designed in such a way that users can either take their own notes internally within the structure of the game or are not required to take notes in order to complete the game.

Making decisions can be mentally challenging. If several possible solutions exist, the user will spend time and effort to collect enough information to decide which solution is best, even (especially) if the solutions are similar. If one route across the map takes you through a dangerous valley and another route requires you to cross a treacherous mountain, the choice of which route to take may have implications for risk, resource usage, and the likelihood of success. Some choices will lock out other options once they are made, increasing the importance of the selection and increasing the stress of making a wrong decision. As these features compound, decision-making can become more difficult and take more time. **Hick's law** (Section 3.5.3) states that the time it takes to make a decision increases with the number and complexity of choices. When selecting a product to purchase, more choice is often seen as a virtue, but when the competing products are mostly similar, people can be frustrated spending significant time deciding which package of noodles to buy. In such circumstances, where the decision is between mostly identical options (in some cases actually identical, where the product is manufactured in the same factory), users instead turn to less salient metrics like branding, packaging, or a difference in price of a few pennies.

Mental modelling can assist users with decision-making, but when mental models are inaccurate, an incorrect decision may be made. If a user has multiple competing mental models for a single situation, they may have difficulty making a decision. In the same way that many options can make decision-making difficult, many different ways of thinking about the options can also be problematic. Mental models can be created based on a variety of levels of information—a conceptual model is built around abstract reasoning, while a locational model is built around physical structures. What my remote control does might be dictated by the location of the buttons, or it might be dictated by the mode which it is in. How I get from one place to another in a city depends on whether I am travelling by car, by bicycle, by transit, or walking. The path I will plan to take is different, of course, but the conceptual model of the travel is different as well. If I travel by subway, I don't really care about the twists and curves that the subway track may take—instead, I enter the subway in one location and I exit in another. It is more like teleportation than travel, and this is why subway maps can be more useful when they are drawn in an abstract or conceptual style, rather than when they are more accurate or locational (see Figure 8.4.) If the subway were to break down and I had to walk up an emergency exit onto the street level, I would have no idea where I was or how to get home. I would have to *reorient* myself, revising or rebuilding the mental model of my travel, in order to figure out which direction I should walk. Alternatively, I could call a ride, which would again be a more conceptual solution—I request a ride, I wait till the ride appears, I get in, and I get out when I am home.

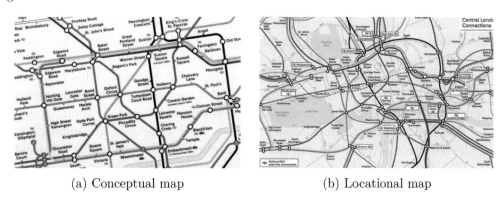

(a) Conceptual map                    (b) Locational map

Figure 8.4: The London tube underground system.

## 8.4   MULTIUSER CONSIDERATIONS

Much of the theory of usability revolves around a single individual interacting with a single system. As we have seen with the extension of the gulfs of evaluation and execution to include proxy actors, interactive experiences often extend our understanding of the initial theories involved in usability. As networking bandwidth and computer processing power have increased, more and more interactive experiences have become multiuser interactive experiences. Early multiuser scenarios were typically asynchronous, with the ability for multiple individuals to interact with the system individually, one at a time, and the system integrating these interactions into a shared narrative and shared world. Synchronous interactions were added as technology allowed, ranging from turn-based pseudosynchronous interactions to fully synchronous shared-world scenarios.

Because these multiuser scenarios are often exemplified in gaming situations, the terms "player" and "user" will be used here interchangeably. The reader should consider situations where the lessons taken from multiplayer games can be extended to other multiuser scenarios, especially in remote, distributed, or asynchronous contexts. Individuals can collaborate to solve problems together, teachers can work with students across distances, doctors can diagnose patients in remote areas, and families can stay connected through a global pandemic. Communication tools have existed that allow individuals to communicate across large distances, but the defying factor of multiuser interactions is that collections of people can interact with each other beyond simple communication. Users can work together for a common goal even when they are not in the same place.

## 8.4.1 Turn taking

The simplest form of multiuser interactions is inherited from multiplayer tabletop games where the state of the world must be decided either by the rules of the game or the interpretation of one of the players. In rules-based multiplayer scenarios, each player must know, trust, and abide by the rules of the world, so that the activity is fair and fun. Differential rulesets, where each player has a different set of rules, can make strategy and interactions more complex and interesting, but are typically difficult to balance. Tabletop role-playing games allow higher levels of complexity but usually require one of the players to take on the role of the world, reacting to player actions and interpreting the rules to make decisions about what happens. This role, called the **game master** (GM) or dungeon master (DM), requires significant preparation and world building and is often rewarded with status as a result. Depending on the group, the GM may rotate from session to session, or campaign to campaign, and while the narrative of the world and the actions of non-player characters are decided by the GM, the rules of the game are usually externally published and agreed upon by all players and the GM, with the understanding that the GM has the final say on the interpretation of the rules in order to remove a point of conflict between players.

Turn taking typically requires an agreed-upon order image to take turns, so that each person knows when it is their responsibility to act and can be prepared accordingly. In tabletop games, turns may pass around the table, and clockwise or anticlockwise order or a more complicated turn-based order can be developed using a mechanic of initiative. Each player may have certain features that give an advantage to initiative, and then randomness may be introduced, such as the role of a dice, in order to ensure that the same person doesn't always go first. Once the turn order is set, each individual user performs actions based on the current state of the world and all other users in it, and once they had completed their actions, the next person in the list would perform their actions based on the new state of the world. This turn-taking procedure was used in early online multiplayer games, such as multiuser dungeons (MUDs), and many aspects of the gameplay beyond the game mechanics were also inherited from tabletop role-playing games involving dungeons and possibly dragons.

Turn taking continues to be popular in certain scenarios where each individual player should have complete control of the results of their actions outside of the influence of other players. In modern gaming, this is often referred to as **asynchronous multiplayer**. While initially developed in order to avoid the strenuous network requirements of synchronized play, the interactive benefits are sometimes retained in scenarios or circumstances where asynchronous play may be desirable.

### 8.4.2 Synchronous Multiplayer

In contrast to asynchronous multiplayer, or turn taking, synchronous multiplayer refers to the situation where individual users can interact with the same world at the same time as other users. Although most card games are asynchronous, with individuals taking turns to pull or play cards, a small collection of card games allows individuals to make actions at the same time: Double Solitaire two-player version of solitaire where both players can build onto any of the eight suit stacks whenever a play is available. The first person to play all of their cards is the winner. The game is fast paced and interactive, requiring quick thinking and decision-making, since a move that a player plans may not be available once the user attempts to execute that move and a move by one player may open up options for the other player. Pig, Snap, and Slap are historical card games with some or all of the gameplay requiring quick reflexes when a certain table condition is met. Most team and competitive sports are synchronous, with each player reacting to the changing world state of the game in real time. Not all synchronous games are fast paced requiring reflexes and quick decision-making. Rock-paper-scissors requires both players to choose a course of action without knowledge of what the other will do, but the actual gameplay is simultaneous—the winner is not determined by speed.

### 8.4.3 Co-presence

Playing the same game at the same time has historically meant being in the same place at the same time. Early multiplayer video games required players to be together, in the same room, looking at the same screen. The screen would either limit the view to the scenario where both players could see what they were doing or would provide **split screen** gameplay, where each player would see their character on their half of the screen and (by unspoken agreement) would not look at the other half of the screen where their opponent (in competitive games) or their partner (in cooperative games) was working. If you did look at the other player's screen, this was called *screen peeking* and was considered not in the spirit of fair play.

Players would sometimes bring their computers together to be able to play with each other. Such events were called "LAN parties" (LAN short for local area network), and before the internet connected users together across the globe, LAN parties were a popular way for players to interact with each other in a shared virtual space. LAN parties were physically difficult to organize as well, since computers were large, bulky, heavy, and consisted of many pieces that needed to be connected together. The network was connected computer-to-computer, and each person would then be able to interact with the shared word that the computers collaborated to created.

### 8.4.4 Telepresence

As networks became faster, individuals would be able to join these networks remotely. First, via telephone connections, and later, across internet connections. As these experiences were mostly related to the playing of games, most players interacted with each other through their characters or avatars. In some circumstances, however, the ability to interact with other people far away as yourself became more salient and desirable. **Telepresence** is the attempt to digitally project yourself into another space and be able to interact with that space. Like VR the more ways in which a user can feel present, the better the experience of telepresence. Arguably, the first forms of telepresence were technologies like the telephone which allowed a user to hear and be heard at a distance. Video calling is an augmented form of telepresence, where a user can demonstrate their emotions and show their surroundings to others far away. Today, telepresence usually refers to abilities to interact directly with the world at the other end of the connection. A user might reach out their arm, and a physical arm at the other end would lift in response. The user could grab something and feel the texture of that object back through the connection. In these ways, the similarity between VR and telepresence is clear—while VR is projecting your agency into a virtual world, telepresence is projecting your agency into another location in the physical world. Telepresence usually involves interaction with the world through a remote proxy physical avatar of some kind. In a "perfect" telepresence implementation, this avatar would have all of the same senses and abilities as the person using it—a fully humanoid robotic interface. In practice, however, telepresence is usually limited to the specific activity being enabled. A doctor may use a telepresence robot to perform surgery on a patient in a different location, for example. As multiplayer interactive systems advance, telepresence will become more important, as it allows individuals to interact with each other through these remote proxies as well.

### 8.4.5 Latency

Synchronous interactions in the context of computer systems require the communication of activity intentions and results across distances almost instantly. The user presses a button on their local machine, and that event is sent to the game world, which updates the game state accordingly and sends the result back to the user's local machine, which renders the new state of the world for the user. In general, as long as the delay between the user's input and the result in the game world is below the frame rate of the system or the just-noticeable difference of the user, the effect will be preserved. **Latency** is the time differential between the moment the user makes a control change and the moment the system displays the result of that change, and is a combination of the time for each of the subtasks involved in that activity. When playing with multiple people, the latency is compounded. Each player's activities are transmitted to the central server which is hosting the game, and the server then distributes the new game state to each player in the game. If any component of a user's connection to the game server is slowed down or interrupted, the user may receive a delayed version of the game state and make different decisions that they would if they received an up-to-date version of the game state.

Latency can be controlled to some degree by limiting the number of players interacting in the game world at any one time. A smaller number of players reduces the load on the server and the outgoing bandwidth from that server—each player's computer requires a single connection to the server, but the server must connect to every player simultaneously and update the game state for everyone at the same time. **Instancing** refers to the separation of a large set of players into individual but separate game worlds. Players sometimes join a game lobby first, where they wait for enough users to run an instance, at which time the game event itself will spawn the players in. Each instance of the world is controlled by a separate server and accepts a limited number of players. If the world persists across time, each instance must also update the central game state, but these centralization updates are usually less frequent and may happen only after the conclusion of the action within a specific instance. For instancing to result in a satisfying game event, players should be matched with others of similar abilities, which requires the game to maintain a method for measuring player skill. Friends who wish to play together may need a method to supersede the randomized instancing system, which may come in direct conflict with the player balancing system, since friends may be at different skill levels.

### 8.4.6 Asymmetric Multiplayer

In most contexts where multiple people participate in a shared experience, one of the goals is to ensure that the experience maintains equity between the individuals involved. Players play by the same rules, even if their experiences and contexts may be slightly different. An alternative take on multiplayer experiences is to specifically set players with very different goals and rulesets. Asymmetric multiplayer has the potential to broaden the user experience, giving players multiple ways to engage with the scenarios in the game, as well as providing an opportunity for players to replace traditionally developer-driven aspects of a scenario. Returning to the example of tabletop role-playing games, different character classes are not typically considered asymmetric since although they have different abilities, they typically play by mostly the same rules and fill mostly the same high-level role in the game context—while a fighter and a magic user approach problems differently, they still are fighting monsters and exploring dungeons. The game master is asymmetric to the players, however, since they play by a completely different set of rules and fill a completely different role—the game master *is* the dungeon, the monsters, and the world.

Asymmetric multiplayer experiences can arise from the understanding that there are already significantly different roles in the shared experience. Although the player roles are usually filled in the same way, the shared experience often contains other roles typically filled by an algorithm or an artificial intelligence, such as enemies, puzzles, or world mechanics. Asymmetric multiplayer experiences can allow different players to fill these different roles within the game world, but care must be taken when transitioning a traditionally algorithmic role to player agency. Algorithmic components of game worlds are often simplistic and predictable, and enemies are often weaker than playable characters, since it is expected that playable characters will defeat many enemies over the course of the game. It would not be a satisfying experience to simply turn control of a parade of weak and incapable minions over to a player, unless a new mechanic was formulated that turned the procedure into something challenging and interesting. In this way it is important to recognize that when creating an asymmetric multiplayer experience, it is more accurate to consider that developers are creating two different games that share a common world, rather than creating a single game with different points of entry.

Shared user experiences can also be asymmetric in how they are controlled or accessed. A user in VR may access the same world as a user with a flat-screen computer, and by the nature of their modes of access to the world, their experiences and rulesets will be different enough to be considered asymmetric in most contexts, even if they are filling more or less the same roles. An example of this from traditional media is the role of "operator" in the Matrix movies. The characters experience the virtual world of the Matrix directly, but the operator exists outside of the simulation, can view the simulation from a different perspective, and can give the characters different information than they are able to perceive directly.

## 8.5 DESIGNING FOR ACCESSIBILITY

As mentioned throughout this book, it is critically important while designing interactive experiences to keep in mind that humans are different. In a large population, it is reasonable to consider statistical averages, but individual humans are not statistical averages. Each person experiencing your software will approach it with a unique and individual context and history, a unique set of motivations and goals, and critically, possibly unique set of senses and abilities. Although it is easier to design a single experience for all users, doing so *will* exclude some users.

**Terminology and Diversity**

It is tempting to refer to the typical collection of senses and perceptions as "normal." It may even be technically correct, since many characteristics of diversity follow a normal, or Gaussian, distribution, with a "norm" of the experience that the majority of humans share. In this way, you might be tempted to refer to trichromacy (seeing in three colours) as "normal," and you wouldn't be wrong; but we must always consider the impact of our language as well as whether it is correct or incorrect. Referring to a trait as "normal" implies, even if unspoken, that those who diverge from this trait are "abnormal," which is also technically correct, but has a flavour of negativity which can be problematic. If a dichromate (someone who is colour-blind) is abnormal in one way, perhaps they are abnormal in other ways. Indeed, people who are left-handed were historically discriminated against for being different, somehow lesser than their right-handed colleagues, to the point where the Latin for "left" (sinistra) has come to mean "evil." In this text, we will use "typical" to refer to the qualities of a trait shared by the majority of humans and "atypical" or "diverse" to refer to the qualities of a trait that differ from typical, since there are often a variety of ways in which the traits may be different. Others have used the term "divergent" to refer to traits that differ from typical, but this term has also taken negative connotations. It should also be noted that terminology is fluid and what is seen as acceptable in one time-period may be unacceptable in a different time period. Doctors used to refer to children with learning disabilities as "retarded," meaning that their intellectual or social development was slower than typical; in French, "retard" means "late" or "delay" and is not generally pejorative—delayed flights are "en retard." Over time, the word was used in a derogatory way against people with intellectual or developmental disabilities, and as it took on a pejorative sense, doctors chose to use it less until it was removed from general practice, although it remained on some US federal law and paperwork as "mental retardation" until 2010.

Throughout the book, when a human skill, sense, or behaviour is discussed, we try to remind the reader that these are general metrics and that individuals may differ. In general, humans see three colours of light, but some humans only see in two colours of light; in general, humans can taste a specific range of flavours, but some humans can taste a much larger range of flavours; in general, humans can hear up to 20,000 Hz, but as people age their ability to hear higher frequencies is reduced. Across wide sectors of the population, low-level human perception is very similar, but even if we have the same sensations, our higher level interpretation of these sensations can differ depending on culture, history, or shared experience—all components of "context" as discussed in Chapter 3. A classic error in the design of user experiences is to assume that all humans will have the same experience as you, the developer. Not only is this generally incorrect, but the developer's experience with their own software as they build it makes them unique to the point where *no users* share the familiarity the developer has with their own creation. A developer may decry the fact that their users don't know that shift-alt-F7 is used to activate the green cube, but while that may be obvious to the developer, it is only because they have been using that key combination for the last 6 months as they build out the green cube part of their code.

Designing for accessibility does not mean building a separate copy of your software for every human on the planet. It does, however, mean taking into account the differences between humans and the different ways humans perceive and interact with the world, and making *informed* decisions about the inclusion or exclusion of specific perceptions and abilities. The term **accessibility** means "easy to access," in the same way that usability means "easy to use"; but just as usability has the many factors, so does accessibility. For something to be accessible, it must be approachable, obtainable, and understandable, as much as possible, for all users.

**Accessibility and VR**

VR has the potential to make some computing experiences more accessible. It should be more approachable and understandable, since mediation is reduced by allowing users to interact directly with objects rather than interacting through a screen and keyboard combination, and, depending on the experience, users should be able to inherit real-world understanding. On the other hand, VR is expensive and requires significant physical space to use, which means that it will be less obtainable to people who don't have the resources to buy one, or who don't have access to a living space with a significantly tall, open, and empty room to use it in. VR is awkward to use and can trigger anxiety, stress, and VR sickness, which means that some users will never feel comfortable using VR. VR headsets are manufactured by large corporations with competing motivations including enriching shareholders and controlling virtual spaces, which means that some users will choose not to participate for economic or justice-related reasons.

Although often associated specifically with disability, accessibility also considers social and economic factors such as culture, education, gender, and race, as well as the systemic ways in which individuals are treated differently due to these factors. VR itself is not fully accessible, since it is often expensive to obtain and may be difficult to use for people susceptible to VR sickness. Additionally, since VR is primarily a visual medium (although other senses will be more fully supported as technology advances), people without a typical sense of vision may not be able to approach the medium in the same way that typically sighted people can. It can be very difficult for a typical human to remember or imagine all the ways in which humans can be atypical. Section REF will discuss common ways in which humans are uncommon, but first we will discuss the options for implementing support for diverse populations in VR experiences.

## 8.5.1 Supporting Diversity

There are four main approaches to acknowledging and supporting typical and atypical populations within a VR experience, or any experience for that matter. These approaches differ primarily on how an experience acknowledges and provides access to populations who may differ from the expected average human who will access the system. Systems choose between a single version or multiple versions, and between separate or interacting populations Figure 8.5 shows a visual metaphor for these four categories:

**Exclusion.** There is one system, and only typical users can access the system. Atypical users are prevented from participating.

**Inclusion.** There is one system, and all users can access the system equally. There are no barriers to participation, and all users can interact.

**Segregation.** There are multiple versions of the system, which are not connected. Atypical users can access a different version of the system, separate from the main experience. All users can participate, but typical and atypical users do not interact.

**Integration.** There are multiple versions of the system. Atypical users can access a different version of the system within the main experience. Typical and atypical users can interact, but their experiences may be different.

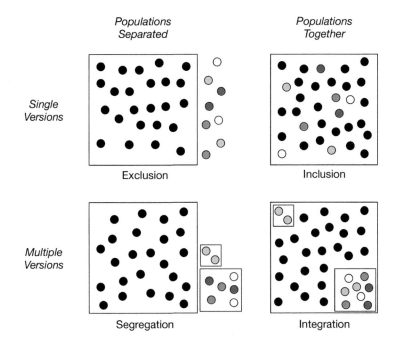

Figure 8.5: Four options for supporting diversity.

As a simple example, left-handed people have trouble with scissors designed for right-handed people. **Exclusion** would be to design scissors for right-handed people and ignore the needs of left-handed people. As a result, left-handed people would not be able to use scissors at all or would have to adapt to right-handed scissors. **Segregation** would be to design both left-handed and right-handed scissors, but left-handed people would have difficulty using right-handed scissors and vice versa. **Integration** would be to design a pair of scissors that could be converted from left-handed to right-handed, so a single pair could support either population. **Inclusion** would be to design an ambidextrous pair of scissors that could be used by either population without modification. Each of these approaches has advantages and drawbacks. A manufacturer making right-handed scissors serves 90% of the population, and developing a production line for left-handed scissors might be too expensive or have too small a market to be worthwhile. Left-handed and right-handed scissors would work best for everyone, but may be difficult to tell them apart, and a household may need to buy multiple pairs of scissors. A household would only need one pair of convertible scissors, but they may be complicated and expensive to manufacture. Ambidextrous scissors may be manufactured to address the entire population, but may not be "perfect" for either handedness. Although it may seem like exclusion is always morally wrong, and full inclusion is always to be preferred, in practice any of these approaches may be preferred, depending on the specific feature or problem being addressed.

Taking an example more specific to VR, people who are blind may be excluded from experiencing VR, since it is a primarily visual medium, but VR experiences could be developed that present a black screen and only use sound as an interaction medium (inclusion), offer sound as an alternative medium to experience the same world alongside vision (integration), or build a separate experience that retains the same audio but replaces visual information with braille that sighted people who do not know braille would not be able to use (segregation). This example is extreme, but shows that any population can be considered using this framework.

## 8.5.2   Case Study: Locomotion Options in VR

As will be discussed in detail in Chapter 10, movement in VR is a complicated and dynamic topic, partly because different people experience motion in VR differently. Some people respond well to using drifting about a virtual world, and others become quite ill. As a result, teleportation is often provided as a discrete option for moving around a large virtual space, alongside other continuous motion options. People's tolerance for VR sickness as a result of motion also changes over time, as some people get used to it, and others never do. If both options are available to all players, this might seem like full inclusion, but in fact this is closer to integration. Within the VR world are two separate experiences, and although both players using discrete motion and players using continuous motion can interact together, their experiences are not, strictly speaking, the same. In competitive gaming environments, it could be that one locomotion option is more tactically advantageous than another, and so people who are able to tolerate continuous motion may perform better than people who can't. In fact, most competitive video games are integrated in this way, since individual players have different computer hardware, different size screens, different controllers, and different internet access. A player who can afford "the best" equipment may have an advantage. In this way we can see that accessibility is not just related to who you are but also what you have access to.

Imagine a specific VR scenario where continuous motion provides a known advantage over discrete motion for some reason, but some players cannot tolerate continuous motion due to VR sickness. With regard to this scenario, we can again consider the four options for supporting this diversity in the player base:

**Exclusion.** The game only uses continuous motion, because it is better. If continuous motion makes you sick, you shouldn't play.

**Inclusion.** The game only uses discrete motion, so that all can play. The strategic possibilities of continuous motion are not included.

**Segregation.** The game uses both continuous motion and discrete motion, but on separate servers. If you are a continuous motion user, you will only play against other continuous motion users, and discrete motion users will only play against other discrete motion users. The game developers must develop and support two separate products off of the same codebase[2].

**Integration.** The game uses both continuous motion and discrete motion, and players can interact together. Players using continuous motion may have an advantage.

Each approach has advantages and disadvantages, and the developers will need to make an informed decision. If continuous locomotion is fundamental to the gameplay of the experience, it may be the preferred option, but the developers may need to be prepared for frustrated backlash from the portion of the gaming community that is being excluded.

### 8.5.3 Common atypical experiences

The ways in which humans use senses to perceive and interact with the world are described in detail in the first half of the book. What follows here is a summary of the most common ways in which our senses and experiences may be atypical. It is somewhat counterintuitive to be considering the "typical atypical" cases, but studying the different ways in which people are diverse can help us understand the typical experience, as well as remind us that there is no "typical human" and everyone has experiences which diverge from typical in one way or another.

In addition to being aware of these atypical experiences in order to accommodate them, VR developers may choose to build experiences specifically focussed on these atypical experiences, in one of two ways. First, a developer may choose to build a VR scenario that somehow replicates the experience of someone with atypical sensation or perception. For example, a developer may build a game around the theme of blindness, where visual aspects are reduced or even eliminated in favour of a primarily acoustic experience. People who have impaired vision may even find that they have an advantage in playing a game where sound is the main way in which users interact. The second way a developer might employ the theme of atypical sensation or perception is to build an environment which attempts to replicate a particular sensory divergence in order to educate the majority of the population that has not experienced this sensory divergence. For example, a developer may build a VR scenario that replicates the experience of being colour-blind, in order to help trichromatic people understand what it means to see the world with only two cones.

#### 8.5.3.1 *Vision*

Although vision is the primary sense that we associate with VR, vision is also the sense which has the most, and most common, ways in which the experience can be

---

[2]This happens regularly in cross-platform games, although cross-platform tools make this easier than supporting different locomotion modalities.

diverse from "typical." Perfect eyesight is somewhat uncommon, and some estimates say myopia (nearsightedness) occurs in almost half of the North American population. Myopia has increased significantly over the last 100 years, and although direct causes are unknown, theories include increased time spent indoors, with less natural light during development, as well as most recently increased time looking at screens. Regardless of the cars, it is reasonable to say that most people who use your VR experience will be nearsighted. Contact lenses can allow nearsighted users to wear a VR headset comfortably, but some users will need to wear glasses while wearing a VR headset. Although nearsightedness is the most common vision problem, many other vision problems exist which will affect a user's ability to experience VR at all and may affect a specific experience within VR. Making adaptations for common vision problems will allow a wider audience of users to take part in your experience, but as with all atypical experiences, some users will not be able to participate. In situations where decisions are critical, some people with atypical vision may be prevented from participating, for example, in the case of airplane pilots being required to have good vision. Common differences from typical vision are listed below. Visual impairment comes in many forms, since vision is a multifaceted sense. People can have problems with visual acuity, visual field, colour vision, motion vision and depth perception. Visual acuity is a well-known indicator of the quality of vision and is measured using a Snellen eye chart. 20/20 vision means that at 20 feet away, the person can see as well as a person who needs no correction would be able to see at 20 feet. The metric version of the measure uses a distance of 6 metres, so someone with 6/6 vision can see what a person would see at 6 metres if they didn't need glasses. The metric is constructed so that the fraction represents, in some way, the quality of vision. A person with 5/6 vision can see at 5 metres what an uncorrected person can see at 6 metres, which is not as good. A person with 7/6 vision can see better than a person with 6/6 vision. 20/20 or 6/6 vision is not "perfect," but it is considered typical and what glasses are intended to correct to.

## Glasses in VR

Wearing glasses in VR is possible, but can be uncomfortable and may lead to damaging both the lenses of the VR headset and the lenses of the glasses, since the glasses may come in contact with the lenses in the VR headset. Some users are able to wear contact lenses, and custom lens sets can be purchased as headset inserts to correct the focus of the scene on the user's retina. Custom lenses are expensive and restrict the VR headset to a single user, unless the lens sets are interchangeable. As VR headsets become less expensive, it may become more common for each individual to have their own headset rather than sharing between users, and in this case, custom hardware adapted to a user's specific sensory needs may become common. Not only would these headsets adapt to vision correction, but they could also be customized to address colour blindness, asymmetry, auditory differences, and even motion-related adaptations. This level of personalization will require VR developers to build adaptive features into their experiences that can be implemented by the headset, in much the same way as developers make use of localization to allow a user to interact with their experience in different languages. Are these individual customizations considered exclusion, inclusion, segregation, or integration?

**Vision Loss.** Persons with no sense of sight. This can happen from birth or due to accident or progressive development. Complete loss of sight is somewhat uncommon, and blindness is defined by a visual acuity of less than 20/500 and a visual field less than 10 degrees.

**Low Vision.** Persons with severely reduced sense of sight. Often defined as unable to read at arm's length, even with corrective lenses. There are many causes (the more common of which are described below), and adaptations such as large type, high contrast, and high brightness can allow them to interact with text and other detail elements. VR may benefit by being able to directly present elements with increased brightness, size, and contrast without the need for the user to manually apply these adaptations. Blindness and low vision are most often caused by **cataracts**, when the lens in the eye becomes opaque and cloudy over time, although other conditions such as macular degeneration and diabetes can lead to low vision or blindness in one or both eyes.

**Myopia.** Also called nearsightedness or shortsightedness. The person is able to focus well on objects that are near, but objects in the distance are fuzzy and out of focus. Myopia is prevalent in more than 50% of North American and European populations, and increasing. Persons with nearsightedness can correct this using glasses, contact lenses, or laser surgery. Wearing glasses may affect the fit and comfort of using a VR headset.

**Hyperopia.** Also called farsightedness. Less common than myopia, but becomes more common with age—most people need reading glasses as they get older. People with myopia who develop hyperopia may need multifocal lenses (bifocals or progressives) to correct, and although multifocal contact lenses are available, the correction is not as successful as multifocal glasses. Laser surgery is also an option, and some people choose to correct one eye to distance vision and one eye to near vision. The brain would prefer the eye that is clear at the distance being perceived. Although this gives sharp vision at a range of distances, depth perception can suffer as a result.

**Astigmatism.** An uneven shape to the eye means different parts of the visual field have different acuity. Specialized glasses or weighted contact lenses can help to correct astigmatism. Since it often occurs in conjunction with myopia or hyperopia, persons with astigmatism may need specialized corrective lenses.

**Ambliopia.** One eye is dominant to the point where signals from the other eye are ignored by the brain. Also called "lazy eye," this condition can occur as a result of misaligned eyes (strabismus), or differing vision between the eyes, to the point where one is favoured over the other. All people have a dominant eye—you can determine your dominant eye by making a circle with your fingers and looking at a point on the wall through the circle. Close one eye; if the point on the wall is still within the circle, that eye is your dominant eye. Ambliopia occurs when the dominant eye takes over the sense of vision and the secondary eye stops contributing to the sense of vision and is ignored. The result is a deficiency in stereoscopic vision, which infers depth by making use of the differences between the visual field of both eyes looking at the same object. Depending on the cause, ambliopia can be treated by encouraging the secondary eye to strengthen, either physically, by blocking the primary eye or redirecting the secondary eye, or medically with eye drops. VR has the potential to address challenges with certain types of ambliopia, since a different image could be presented to each eye. Strabismus could be addressed by adjusting the direction of the image presented to each eye, allowing further personalization and adaptation, as well as possible therapeutic treatment by slowly adjusting the direction of the image presented to the secondary eye, thus encouraging it to realign over time. Although uncorrected ambliopia usually implies the stereoscopic component of depth perception is unavailable to the user, other depth cues such as motion parallax, occlusion, and distance fading will still function, and the key advantage of VR (that the field of view changes when you move your head) will still be effective.

### 8.5.3.2 Hearing

Hearing loss is usually measured depending on the frequency of hearing. While the standard description of typical hearing ranges from 20 Hz to 20,000 Hz, most people cannot hear frequencies near 20,000 Hz and high frequency hearing loss over time is very common, and most adults can only hear up to 15,000 Hz. The most important fundamental frequencies for hearing speech and music are between 300 and 10,000 Hz, and frequencies between 10,000 Hz and 15,000 Hz exist primarily as resonances and overtones of other sounds we hear, so even with significant reduction in the perceptions high frequency sounds, typical adults do not have trouble understanding speech or music. Audiologists test the perception of different frequencies via sound waves and via bone conduction and can identify progressive hearing loss over time in order to prevent or treat these conditions. Hearing loss due to exposure to loud environments can be mitigated by wearing ear protection, but once the individual sensing hairs within the cochlea are damaged, they cannot be repaired.

Hearing loss is treated using hearing aids, which usually consist of a microphone and amplifier connected to a small actuator placed in the ear canal. Sounds from the outside world are amplified and presented to the eardrum, but because the actuator is small, the sounds it is able to produce are typically high frequency. This can help compensate for hearing loss in high frequencies, but hearing aids change the overall spectrum of sound that people hear, accentuating high frequencies, which also serves to amplify noise. Hearing aids are customized to the specific frequencies of hearing loss in the individual, which can compensate for this frequency shift. Bone conduction hearing aids are surgically implated and directly resonate the skull, bypassing the ear canal. This technique can provide hearing for individuals with hearing loss resulting from damage to the outer or inner ear.

Some hearing aids can be connected to external sources of sound, like a FM transmitter or external microphone. There is the potential to adapt VR hardware to be able to directly signal an existing hearing aid, which can then personalize the frequency response of the sounds presented to the user. Hearing loss and associated correction with hearing aids are usually different between the left ear and the right ear; however, it is unusual for a person to have complete hearing loss in one ear and not in the other, unless the source of the hearing loss is also not bilateral. Because higher frequencies are key in determining the location or direction of the sound, both hearing loss and the frequency modifications brought about by hearing aids can negatively impact a person's ability to localize sound.

People who are deaf or hard of hearing from birth may have challenges acquiring language and speech in the way that a typical hearing person would. Our first experiences developing language are primarily verbal and result from auditory interactions between a child and the adults around them. Children develop categorical perception of speech sounds based on the language spoken around them as they develop language, leading to native speakers of different languages being able to perceive or not perceive different speech sounds. Children who are born with hearing problems or who develop them early in life can have challenges understanding spoken language later in life even after hearing aids are made available, and so early childhood intervention to provide treatment for hearing loss is critical.

Another common hearing issue is **tinnitus**, or a ringing in the ears. Tinnitus is common, negatively affecting about one in five adults in Europe and North America. Tinnitus is sometimes described as a buzzing, roaring, ringing, whooshing, hissing or humming and affects different people at different frequencies and intensities. In a perfectly quiet situation, most people will perceive some "sound that isn't there," but tinnitus is categorized by hearing such a sound in otherwise normally noisy environments. Tinnitus may be *subjective*—perceived by the person but not by others around them, or *objective*—able to be detected by instruments or other people. Objective tinnitus is thought to be the result of sounds generated psychologically within the body, either in the inner ear itself or due to some other effect. The ability to hear your own heartbeat would be classified as a form of objective tinnitus within this definition.

Some potential treatments for subjective tinnitus exist, but in general it is a condition that people learn to live with. Some people can ignore their tinnitus, while others can be distracted by it to varying degrees. Tinnitus can get worse when you pay attention to it, so advice from audiologists is often to try to ignore it, but this advice is somewhat self-defeating.

Sound in interactive experiences is often considered secondary, and as a result some users choose to turn the sound of a game off completely. Developers sometimes attempt to counter this by indicating to the user that the experience is "best with headphones;" however, developers should be considerate of users who have different experiences with hearing.

Immersive experiences in VR often emerge from a combination of senses, and while being considerate of differences in hearing is important, audio cues are often fundamental to a VR experience. A user may only know to look behind them if they hear something happening behind them. Sound localization, both directional and environmental, is a key component in establishing presence, but providing information *only* via sound may have an impact on users with hearing loss.

### 8.5.3.3 Neurodiversity

In the same way that humans are broadly similar but specifically diverse in the abilities that allow us to sense the world, we are also broadly similar but specifically diverse in the abilities to analyse, interpret, and make decisions about the world and our roles in it. **Neurodiversity** is the term given to variations in brain and behaviour that manifest in differences in how (and how fast) people can learn, how people are able to dedicate attention to a specific task, how we are able to regulate our moods, and how we can understand and interact with the brains within the humans around us. Neurodiverse individuals are often categorized as such in comparison with someone who is **neurotypical**, and as with other considerations of accessibility, it should be reinforced that "normal" is a problematic word in this context because it reinforces the idea that neurodiversity is abnormal, and negative. People with neurodiverse characteristics often have challenges navigating the world or experiences that developers create, but is this challenge because these people are disabled in some way or is it because the world expects them to behave in a certain way that they find difficult to do? In fact, simple accommodations made broadly available allow neurodiverse individuals to participate fully in society, and the challenges that come with some neurodiverse contexts also grant some benefit, with individuals who may have challenges in one are actually excelling above typical performance in other areas. The most common and well-known ways in which people are neurodiverse include autism spectrum disorder (ASD), attention-deficit hyperactivity disorder (ADHD), and dyslexia, although some definitions also include anxiety, depression, bipolar disorder, schizophrenia, and other mood disorders. Note particularly that the names of some of these conditions contain the word "disorder," inherently suggesting a difference from "order" or normalcy. Framing these conditions as "different ways of thinking" rather than "diseases of thinking" has been advocated by neurodiverse individuals and supporters, in order to allow people with neurodiverse brains to be more accepted in society; this framing can be controversial, however, especially when the divergence is particularly troubling and can be treated.

Treatment exists for some forms of neurodiversity, including antidepressants for the treatment of anxiety and depression, stimulant medication for the treatment of ADHD, and antipsychotic medication for the treatment of schizophrenia. Medical interventions do not exist for ASD and dyslexia (at the moment); however, cognitive and therapeutic treatment courses are often prescribed to allow neurodiverse individuals to modify their thinking and behaviour away from that which may be undesirable for the individual, towards more typical ways of being in the world. The framing of neurodiversity as "not a disease" or "different, not disordered" can prevent some individuals from seeking treatment that may be helpful, and it is important to recognize that neurotypical people participate in voluntary behaviour modification as well—if I decide to lose some weight, I will need to modify my behaviour to eat less and exercise more. If I want to be successful in school, I will need to modify my behaviour to play video games less and study more. If I want to be successful in business, I need to be confident and competent, and if I want to be a musician, I need to practise my instrument. The difference with neurodiverse individuals is that the behaviour changes and required activities to affect these modifications are often suggested externally, and these changes are intended to bring these individuals back to "normal." It is this framing that neurodiversity advocates are attempting to change.

Most neurodiverse conditions exist on a scale or spectrum, with some individuals mildly affected by it, while others are strongly affected. Some individuals develop coping mechanisms to allow them to behave as if they were more neurotypical, and stress and other confounding factors can exacerbate the effect of these situations.

### Designing to Support Difference

Several resources exist which describe specific things that can be done to make it easier or more comfortable for users with non-neurotypical traits to interact with a system. A small collection is presented here. Note, particularly, that some support mechanisms may be in conflict. Supporting the diversity of human experience is challenging, and if your users are more likely to fall into one category than another, tradeo-ffs may be required.

- Users with autism can be better supported by making instructions simple and clear, avoiding the use of metaphor and symbolism, keeping designs consistent, and arranging information in organized frameworks.

- Users with vision challenges can be supported by adding optional descriptive text for images and videos, providing high-contrast interfaces, and making extensive use of colour.

- Users with dyslexia can be supported by keeping text formatting simple, using more diagrams, and offering audio or video alternatives to large chunks of written text.

- Users with motor challenges can be supported by making interactable targets larger and adding more space between them, by providing keyboard or button options for interaction.

- Users with hearing challenges can be supported by adding subtitles to otherwise non-textual interactions and by reducing the requirement for relying on audio cues.

- Users with anxiety can be supported by reducing time-based tasks or removing timers, clearly explaining requirements or assumptions, reminding users of the consequences of each action, and allowing users to go back if a mistake is made.

A **neurological disorder** is a deficiency or disease of the brain or nervous system that leads to specific, generally negative, symptoms. Some conditions, like generalized anxiety disorder, may be considered more of a neurological disorder rather than a neurodiversity, since the symptoms of generalized anxiety disorder are negative and sometimes debilitating, and treatment exists to mitigate these symptoms. The classification of conditions as neurological disorder or neurodiversity is controversial primarily because these conditions are typically invisible. You can see when a person has a broken leg, but you cannot see when they have an overactive or misfiring amygdala. The brain is highly complex with multiple interacting processes, and as such, neurological disorders vary widely in their severity and presentation. One way we learn about the functioning of the brain is by studying individuals who have had brain injuries in specific areas—this is how we know that different aspects of language are processed in different parts of the brain. A person with damage to *Broca's area* can understand the meaning of words but cannot form or understand larger or more complicated grammatical structure, while a person with damage to *Wernicke's area* does not understand the meaning of individual words but can parse and form sentences with natural-sounding cadence and grammar, even though they contain nonsense.

**Epilepsy and VR**
Many VR experiences begin with a warning that flashing lights could induce a seizure in photosensitive people. There are two main concerns with photosensitivity in VR—flashing lights caused by visual effects created by the developer, and the perception of flashing caused by low frame rate and rapid head movements. In the former, the risk is similar to flashing lights in other media and should be addressed in a similar way. The latter could be more of a problem for photosensitive individuals; however, this is a problem that can be better mitigated by improved hardware technologies. The number of individuals with epilepsy who are susceptible to seizures triggered by rapid flashing is very small; however, brightly flashing lights can cause general discomfort to a much wider contingent of the population, and for this reason, settings to reduce or disable flashing visual effects should be made available to the user.

Because the intent of VR is to "get closer to the brain," so to speak, brain differences between individuals may be more relevant than with traditional computing interfaces like flat screens or phones. Individuals who are susceptible to anxiety may find themselves more anxious in a VR scenario, since the brain is being drawn towards responding as if real. If the mind thinks it is real, it can produce the same responses, and if those responses are detrimental, the user will have a detrimental experience. Users with ADHD may find themselves far more engaged in an experience than typical, especially if it is something they are enjoying or passionate about and may spend more time in VR as a result, becoming more susceptible to long-term physiological effects like fatigue or VR sickness. Users with dyslexia may find it more difficult to read text in VR, especially if it is small or far away (subject to increased vergence accommodation conflict) or the resolution on their headset makes it more difficult to read. Users with autism may find it more challenging to interpret facial expressions intended to communicate emotion, especially if the animation models used fall into the uncanny valley (see Section 8.3.3.1).

VR might also be usable as a way to deliver more effective therapies intended to help mitigate the effects of neurodiversity or neurological disorders. Although some neurological conditions can be treated medically, others are treated with techniques like cognitive behavioural therapy and attention-bias modification, and VR has the potential to improve the effectiveness of these therapies. Because of the illusions that develop presence, and the fact that experiences can seem more real, exposure therapy can be more effective, and safer, than similar therapies in the physical world. Because the physical world can be more completely excluded, attention can be focused and attention modification techniques may be more effective. Individuals who experience specific anxieties (such as a fear of heights or a fear of spiders) can participate in incremental exposures which can help to desensitize them to these triggers, and effective therapies for occupational stress injuries such as post-traumatic stress disorder may be more effective within the presence of an immersive VR experience.

**Temporary Non-Typical Perception**
Although the classifications of non-typical perception that have been discussed above are usually representative of ongoing characteristics of individuals, there exists a collection of non-typical perceptions which may impact a person's experience on a temporary level. These may come about due to active or passive effects and can impact individuals to varying degrees. The most common and relevant example of these temporary effects is fatigue—as people get tired, they become less able to notice things and make decisions, and performance on mental tasks can suffer. Psychoactive drugs and alcohol can also have a significant effect on perception, and especially on adaptation to virtual environments. Because mismatches can occur between senses in VR, the changes in balance and decision-making brought about by being drunk can be exacerbated. In general, users should be disencouraged from partaking in mind-altering substances when experiencing VR.

### 8.5.4 Localization

Accessibility is usually associated with conceptually negative differences—a user is visually impaired, so we must make an accommodation to allow them to participate fully in what we are doing. It is important to remember that although some differences are negative, identified primarily by their deficiency from the typical human experience, the primary way in which humans differ is based on common variation of human experience—what languages we speak and what culture we participate in and understand. This difference is no less significant when it comes to support in the development of a VR experience, and it is equally easy to forget. Everyone around me looks like me and speaks like me, so everyone around me will be able to use the system that requires them to speak and understand my language. Everyone around me can see, hear, and smell like me, so I should be able to assume these abilities in my VR experience. This is the same fallacy as developer familiarity. People tend to assume that their experience is typical and therefore that others will have the same interaction with what they are building. When the software you develop will be shared around the world, most people are likely to approach your software with a different experience than you, and users like you are likely to, in fact, be atypical.

**Localization** is the process of modifying your software so that it fits the language and culture of the person using it. Modern development practices allow features of software that may change based on language and culture to be tagged, and a collection of local data be inserted based on the new location. This can be quite straightforward if the way language is used is straightforward, but if language is a key component of narrative or procedural aspects of your system, the localization process can be challenging.

Movies and shows provide examples of how localization can be performed at a few different levels, and many of these techniques apply directly or indirectly to VR. The simplest way to localize a show is with subtitles—the show remains in its original form, and an accessibility feature is added for people who do not speak the language. Subtitles can also be used in the original language (usually called captions rather than subtitles) to aid comprehension for people with limited literacy. Children learning their first language, people learning an additional language, and people who have challenges with hearing can all benefit from the use of captions (see Section 8.5.6). Audio description can also help with language and localization, although the primary intention with audio description tracks is to make the show more accessible for people with visual challenges.

The language in a show can be removed and replaced via overdubbing, where the same visuals are used but a new audio track is recorded separately. This results in mismatched movement between the actor and the sound, as well as the requirement to re-record background audio and sound effects. Each language has its own particular cadence, rhythm, prosody, and idiomatic structure, and it is very obvious when a person is moving their mouth in one language but you are hearing a different language. Overdubbing teams often attempt to modify the translations of the text to better fit the motion of the actor's mouth, which can sometimes result in better alignment but more awkward or unnatural text. If the show is animated, overdubbing can be somewhat more effective, since the animated mouth movements are often generic and abstract rather than directly following the text being spoken.

If the show is produced with the intention of localizing the language, the sound effects and background audio can be recorded separately, and only the language would need to be replaced. Additionally, actors may be able to record multiple takes in different languages, to allow certain scenes to be localized more effectively. This is only effective if the actor can naturally speak the additional languages, and if there are not too many languages to localize into.

The restriction of localization languages, of course, leads to a larger problem—that popular media is primarily localized to popular languages, and speakers of less common languages must learn the more common languages in order to watch shows and participate in culture, which has a homogenizing effect on both language and culture. If diversity of thought and expression of ideas is an inherent good, reduction of the number of spoken languages should be avoided. There is a trade-off here, of course—translating a show into other languages increases the number of people who might be interested in watching the show, but restricts their experience of the original language of that show. Ideally, more people would learn more languages and experience more cultures, but increasing accessibility by developing linguistic bridges is a step in that direction.

Localization is not just modification of spoken language, either. Written language should, where possible, be localized as well. In movies and shows, written language is often used to advance the plot—text on signs, text messages on phones, content of letters, and material that the characters are meant to be reading are often presented to the audience in such a way as to imply that the audience should be reading this material. Here, localization can be done by adding subtitles that indicate the meaning of the text on screen, or replacing the text elements in the shot with similar elements in the target language. In live-action shows, these replacements require a re-shoot for each target language, which can be expensive, but in computer-animated shows, these replacements can be straightforward. A simple asset replacement can provide text on a book cover or signpost to be rendered in any language.

Attempts to localize should always employ individuals familiar with both the original development context and the development context in which the system will be used. In the province of Quebec, Canada, cultural regulations require that signs be presented in both official languages of English and French. Stop signs in Quebec often have either "stop" or "arrêt" or often both. Using both words is intended to support bilingualism; however, there is some debate over the requirement for both words since "stop" is a valid French word. If a developer is building a driving experience that includes road signs, which word should be used on signs if the experience is used in Quebec? What if the experience is intended to replicate a road in Europe? Most countries in Europe today use the text "stop;" however before this standardization was in place, local language prevailed. Local street signs should, of course, reflect the local information, but whether to translate this information to the language of the user is a question of a trade-off between usability and authenticity.

Localization can extend beyond language as well. Idioms, cultural artefacts, and connotative assumptions all provide narrative shortcuts that allow an author, producer, or developer to establish features of their characters or their world without requiring explanation, as long as the audience understand the shorthand being used. When a character in a show makes a gesture with their hand, that gesture is understood by the audience only inasmuch as they are familiar with the cultural significance of that gesture. A "thumb's up" gesture in one culture may be positive, but may be negative in another culture. In Western culture, nodding one's head indicates positive acknowledgement or asset and shaking one's head back and forth indicates a negative reaction or dissent. In some Eastern cultures, these head gestures are reversed. The importance of physical objects can also have different meaning depending on the culture, and certain specific colours have different meanings as well. A computer-generated movie had a scene of a child disliking pizza with vegetables on it, and in the American version, the offending vegetable was broccoli. In the Chinese-language version, the pizza had green pepper instead, since culturally, the trope of children hating vegetables applies more to green peppers than it does to broccoli. Because the movie was computer generated, swapping out the digital artefact and a couple of lines of dialogue (which would all be re-recorded for localization anyway) was a simple change to align a culturally relevant scene to more locally relatable content.

Recognizing and attempting to account for such a wide collection of possible differences is intimidating. Localizing to this degree is an enormous amount of work, and the pay-off depends on the interest in your product in a wider market, as well as an assumption that, without such localization, your product would not have access to this market. The trade-off of additional implementation versus reduced market must be considered carefully. Constructing your world with the option of localizing it is good practice—if your experience becomes popular, it is worthwhile to be able to go back and retroactively localize the experience if the need arises. Some changes, like asset replacement or language modification, may be straightforward, but other changes, like which side of the street you drive on, may be significantly challenging to implement.

### 8.5.5 Personalization

While localization requires the production of different versions of your software for different contexts or locations, including language and culture, **personalization** is the process of allowing the individual user to make selections about the way they interact with their copy of your experience. Localization is dependent on the developer making assumptions about the way in which a person in a location will respond to an experience, while personalization is dependent on the user making selections about their experience. If an experience is available in multiple languages, the selection of which language to use, by the user, would be personalization, while the creation of those different linguistic versions would be localization. To some degree, personalization requires implementing accessibility. If a user is left handed, and your VR experience requires the right hand to do most of the work, the user will be unsatisfied. If, however, your experience allows them to swap right and left hands, that would be a feature of personalization.

The degree to which personalization is available depends entirely on the variety of selections the developer makes available to the user. In a fighting game, many weapons might be available, and a user can select the weapon they would most like to use. If a particular scenario encourages the use of a specific weapon, this may be more driven by the plot or context of the experience. If the choice of weapon does not particularly preclude an advantage in a scenario, but the user can still choose it, it becomes a personal choice. Skins and other cosmetic selections allow personalization with no impact on gameplay, but may be important for distinguishing individuals in a multiplayer environment.

In VR, especially in contexts where a user's presence is represented by an avatar, it is important to allow a user to modify that avatar based on personal features that may be cosmetic or may be functional. Each player in VR will be a slightly different height, and interactions you develop may change based on the height of the user. Blocks that fly at a user to be sliced in half by a sword may be easy to see if the user's eyes are above the line of blocks, but may be much more challenging if the blocks approach at eye level. If a user is expected to reach to the floor to pick something up, this may be more or less difficult depending on personal features of the user—Are they in a wheelchair? Are they using a VR treadmill? Do they have a back injury or a cast on their ankle? Even the choice of locomotion pattern (see Chapter10) can impact different people differently, and the design of your world should take this into account. Users should be able to personalize important interactive aspects of the experience, as long as such features are available and do not lead to advantages or disadvantages in competitive gameplay.

### 8.5.6  Accessibility benefits all

Understanding the differences in the way people collect and understand information, and making an effort to increase the usability of your system taking into account atypical experiences, will, in general, improve the experience of all the users of the system. Accessibility features that are designed to benefit a very specific category of users will often end up improving the overall experience. Mobility-compromised individuals argued for years to improve the accessibility of sidewalks in busy cities. As a result, curb cuts became common and improved the experience of everyone on wheels, including parents with strollers, travellers with rolling suitcases, and bicyclers. Vision-impaired individuals successfully argued for auditory cues at stoplights as well as tactile paving, and these features have also served to benefit the increasing number of pedestrians with their attention fixed on their phones as they walk through the city, as well as aiding in wayfinding and navigation for many people. Tactile paving in metro stations adds a level of safety that would not be there without it.

Considering accessibility also serves to make the typical population more aware of the many prevalent but often invisible ways in which the design of the world around us and our virtual experiences make assumptions about how humans work. Most things in the world are built with typical human abilities and experiences in mind, and it can be easy to forget that few individuals are typical in every way.

Seeing multiple languages on signs reminds us that not everyone speaks our language. Hearing stoplight pedestrian audio signals reminds us that not everyone can see as well as we can.

When developing VR experiences, we can go a step further. More than simply accommodating difference, we can build experiences that give advantages to those who have typically been disadvantaged, or focus stylistically or narratively on the experience of people who may be atypical in some way. Several VR games have been developed which attempt to provide a snapshot of what it is like to be blind— temporarily or permanently blocking the visual component of an experience and forcing the user to rely entirely on their sense of hearing. Because people who may have an impairment in one sense sometimes develop heightened abilities in another sense (the brain may re-task typically visual areas into audio processing), providing examples of what this experience might feel like to users with typical vision may provide narrative or experiential benefits. We can build VR experiences that show what it is like to slowly lose your vision, or your hearing, or to slowly lose your memory or your ability to process language. These experiences can build empathy for people experiencing dementia and may result in doctors who are more able to understand what their patients are going through.

Additionally, as mentioned previously, we can use VR to experiment with augmenting our senses. What would it be like to see with the eyes of an eagle, who can make out movement hundreds of metres away? Or to navigate magnetically as migrating birds do? Or to experience a wide range of smells, like a dog does, or feel electricity or to smell colour or to hear gravity? **Synaesthesia** is the experience of sensation of one type of information, interpreted by a sense system typically associated with another sensation. Individuals who experience synaesthesia report associating specific colours with letters of the alphabet, or specific spatial locations of numbers, specific tactile feeling of sounds, or words that have a specific smell. VR has the potential to stimulate these sensations, because the presentation of sensations can be coupled together, and typical presentation can be occluded. We can remove the user's vision and then present bright colours every time a sound is heard. These experiences, again, suggest a potential for significant expansion of the human experience beyond the typical. VR is effective in replicating the experience of the physical world, but can also take us beyond these experiences into a realm of possibilities never previously conceived. VR is still experienced by humans, of course, and so the human experience must be taken into account, but this means not just the common and typical experience, but also the diversity of experiences.

## 8.6 SUMMARY

Many developers learn how to write code and to build systems that enable functionality, but do not consider how these systems interact with the humans that use them. Human factors, as a computing discipline, is an attempt to remind developers that the complete system includes the human as well, and that the software systems we build are of no use unless the humans that use them can do so effectively. In the first half of the book we spent time understanding how humans receive and process information, and in this and the following chapters, we explore how humans make decisions and have an impact on the world. The impact we can have on virtual worlds must be similar to the impact we can have on the real world, otherwise we revert to being merely observers within the context of the simulation.

# CHAPTER 9

# Fictions of Physics

## 9.1 THE RULES OF A SIMULATION

In the real world, a consistent set of physical principles affect the objects around us at all times. The laws of physics and the properties of matter ensure that we cannot move our bodies through solid surfaces (like a table), but can easily move through matter in other states (like air or, with a little more difficulty, water). When we toss an object, we expect it to continue moving with the momentum our hand imparted to it, slowly changing direction due to the effects of air resistance and gravity.

It's easy to forget how we rely on these consistent laws for everything we do, even tasks that aren't generally thought of as physical. For example, reading a book would quickly become frustrating if the pages interacted inconsistently with our fingers. If page five was solid and heavy to turn, while turning page six felt like slapping jello, or if our fingers passed through page seven like it wasn't there, or if page eight was as heavy as a brick, it would be hard to focus on whatever material we were trying to read.

It's difficult to fathom what a world would be like where these laws didn't apply consistently or were missing entirely. However, in a virtual reality (VR) experience, rules for physical interaction are not inherent—it is the developer's responsibility to determine what parts of the virtual environment conform to physical rules, as well as what behaviours those rules allow. In a poor or unfinished virtual environment, scenarios similar to the inconsistent book described above can easily take place—without a consistent or reliable set of physical principles, even basic tasks can become frustrating or distracting for the user.

Many computer games and simulations perform physics calculations for the objects in their environments—to the degree that most modern game engines include a robust physics engine for simulating all manner of real-world physical forces and constraints. As such, applying these models to objects within a VR virtual environment is not difficult. Where VR environments differ from these software applications is that two sets of physical rules influence a virtual environment: the rules of the real world in addition to the rules of the virtual world.

Since the raw input to a VR program comes from tracking the user in the physical world, we can be confident that this input will conform to the physics of the real world. We may also want to enforce a particular set of physics rules within the virtual

DOI: 10.1201/9781003261230-9

world—the avatar's hand should not pass through solid objects, heavy objects should require more effort to drag around than light ones, and so on.

For the most part, the rules governing physical interaction in the real and virtual environments may line up—it's only where the physical rules of the two environments disagree that a difficult decision must be made. For example, if a virtual table exists in a space that, in the corresponding physical environment, contains only air, how would we handle the case where the user moves a hand through the virtual space occupied by the table? Could we stop the user's hand, the avatar's hand, or a combination of both? Could we divert the avatar's hand around the table or move the table out of the way? When should we do so?

This chapter seeks to answer these questions by exploring the considerations related to the physics of a VR simulation. As computer-simulated physics is an established field, and general physics calculations are built into most engines, we focus on the unique considerations and boundary-case rules that must be considered for VR systems. We discuss if and how the user's avatar should affect physics objects within the environment, as well as the effects these objects exert on avatars. We discuss what to do when the physical constraints of the physical and virtual environments don't line up, as well as the most common cases where this occurs. We introduce several interaction patterns for handling these disconnects, simulating the effects of physics on the avatar, and other physical concerns. Finally, we discuss where physics simulations should be used and when they should be abandoned for other methods.

## 9.2   ADVANTAGES OF A CONSISTENT SET OF PHYSICS

When we are performing tasks in the real world, the laws of matter and physics are rarely our conscious focus. Despite this, these laws are always exerting an effect on any work or play we may do. People have evolved in an environment where a consistent set of laws of physics governs the objects around us, the environments we interact with, and even the movement of our bodies.

Having a similar set of rules in a virtual world borrows from our real environment in this regard. However, in a virtual world, the laws of physics can be as malleable (or non-existent) as the developer wishes. Digital simulations have the advantage of letting us define physics that better fits the virtual environment or the goals of the application. Different VR experiences may have different rules for how gravity works, how objects collide (or which ones don't collide at all), how (and if) momentum of objects is conserved, if objects are movable or not, or any number of other possible rules that govern how objects interact with each other and the player.

Although the "laws of physics" across VR applications may differ from each other, it's rare for a set of physical rules to be applied inconsistently within a single application, unless there is a compelling reason to do so (such as the environment or location changing to a space where alternative physics rules apply). Having a consistent set of physics applied to the interactions and objects of an application confers advantages for both the usability of an application and the ease of development.

### 9.2.1 Advantage 1: Physics Consistency Increases Learnability

Having all objects in an application follow a consistent set of physical rules makes it easier for users to determine how to interact with new or unfamiliar objects. If each object or circumstance in a VR experience followed a different set of physical laws, the user would have to learn and internalize a new set of rules for every object they encounter.

### 9.2.2 Advantage 2: Physical Rules Add Constraints

Adding physics and collision detection to objects allows their position and motion to be constrained within 3D space. A simulation that doesn't detect collisions between objects may make it easy for the user to move objects freely, but can also make it difficult for users to intuit how objects should interact with each other.

To illustrate this, we'll use the example of using a virtual key to unlock a virtual door. In the first case, we'll assume no collisions are simulated between the door and the key. In this first case, the user may be able to move the key to intersect with the keyhole, but there is no visible or spatial difference between when the key is in the hole and when the key is simply clipping through the door. It is still possible to see when the key and hole may line up, but as both objects are treated as non-solid, the user has to determine entirely from visual shape if the key and hole are aligned, and they may not know what actions they have to take in order to unlock the "door." Simply touching the key to the hole could be enough, but a specific key depth may be required, or turning the key may need to occur before the door will unlock. Regardless of which case is correct, all three will seem roughly the same to the user: different positions of the key clipped through the door object.

Now, consider the case where the key and the hole possess collision physics: if the user pushes the key through any part of the door except the keyhole, the key will collide against the door and its motion will be limited. However, the user is able to push the key into the hole! By constraining the set of locations of the key to conform to physics, the action the user must take to unlock the door becomes clear.

At this point, it may still be ambiguous whether the key needs to simply be inserted, or if it has to be turned afterwards—but the reaction of the door at this point would narrow down the correct option. It's clear that the key is inserted correctly: the constraints of the physics system ensure that there is only one way this can be done. If the door still doesn't open, turning must be the only option left. In this way, adding physics constraints to objects makes it easier for the user to determine the range of actions they are able to perform on or with objects, as well as where to perform these actions.

### 9.2.3 Advantage 3: Universal Physics Makes Development Choices Easier

For a small VR experience, with a few objects, it may be possible for a developer to program separate behaviour for how the user should be able to interact with each object. However, as the amount of objects increases, it quickly becomes tedious to define separate rules for each object. Further, as discussed above, even if a developer wanted to define separate rules for each object, this approach could have a negative impact on the usability of the experience.

Additionally, defining a cohesive set of physics that includes how objects and avatars should behave at the boundaries of the game eliminates the need to check and fix boundaries after the environment has been developed. It is rarely a desired feature for the user to be able to clip through walls or see the unrendered surfaces of an environment, but conditions that allow this to happen are often created unintentionally during development and have to be discovered and resolved in a testing phase. Defining boundary physics that handles how objects and avatars interact with the boundaries of the environment can reduce the amount of unwanted boundary-breaking conditions that exist in the application. Instead of worrying about patching the gaps in the simulation manually, these exceptions can be handled by the physics conditions. Although consistent physics systems are handy for quickly adding or altering objects without having to re-decide how they function, one of their most important contributions to an environment is that they help ensure that these cases where the user experiences unwanted behaviour due to exceeding the environment's boundaries are handled. Such cases are referred to as **world inconsistent boundaries**.

## 9.3 WORLD INCONSISTENCY BOUNDARIES

Due to the tracking of the user's motion and position, VR simulations are bounded by two sets of physical rules, the relation between which is illustrated in Figure 9.1. The first set of physical rules, **computed physics**, consist of the calculated physics that is handled by the computer. These rules apply forces and determine collisions in the virtual world, either between two or more virtual objects, between virtual objects and the user's avatar, or between avatars. Different sets of physical rules may apply to different parts or objects within the virtual world—for example, some objects may be purely part of the environment and may be immovable and only interact by having other objects collide with them, while others may be physics objects that can be moved and thrown by the user's avatar. As computed physics is simulated by a computer, they are discrete computations and often only approximate the physics of the real world. Perfectly simulating the real-world physics is technically an impossible task for a computer, but many modern physics engines are more than accurate enough for all practical purposes.

The second set of physics rules that influence virtual environments, **real physics**, consist of the physical forces in the world of the user. The motion of the user, the reactions of objects within the room they are using the VR system in, and the actual motion of the VR hardware all obey the laws of real physics. The data that results from user tracking is often used to influence the movement of the avatar to varying degrees, creating a relation between user and avatar. Note that the proportion of influence of tracking data on avatar motion is not necessarily proportional to the proportion of user motion tracked.

In a VR experience, the user's motion often exerts some degree of control over the avatar: thus, the avatar is indirectly influenced by real physics. Experiences tend to differ in the degree to which the avatar is controlled directly by user motion.

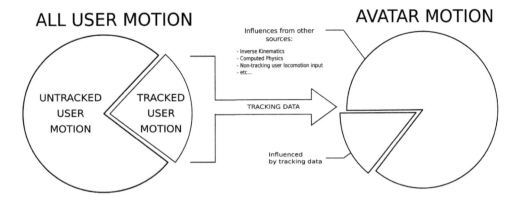

Figure 9.1: The user-avatar relation for physics influence.

Experiences could range in this way from a fixed HMD camera angle which doesn't respond at all to user motion, to an avatar programmed to exactly reflect a fully tracked user. In between these two extremes lie systems where the user is only partially tracked, or the avatar is only partially influenced by user's tracked motion.

Although avatars will be discussed in more depth in the following chapters, the higher the degree of user-avatar alignment, the higher the degree that the avatar is influenced by real physics.

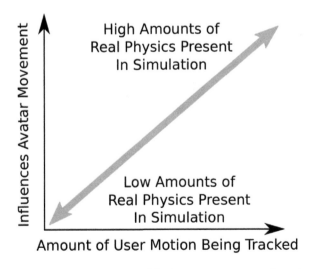

Figure 9.2: Influence of real-world physics on a simulated environment.

Many situations exist where these two sets of physics (computed and real world), may conflict. For example, consider the common case where the user of a VR system hasn't cleared out enough physical space around them. As they go to reach for an item in the virtual world, their hand runs into a chair in the physical world. From the point of view of computed physics, nothing is in the way, so the chair from the real world getting in the way conflicts with the physics of the computed world.

The inverse problem is also quite common, where an object exists in the virtual world that is not reflected in the physical world. For example, a wall might block the user's progress in the virtual world, but as it doesn't exist in the physical world, there's nothing stopping the user from putting their head right through where the virtual wall is. An easy way to understand the interplay between systems of physics in two worlds is to envision the virtual world as being overlaid on the physical world, as shown in Figure 9.3.

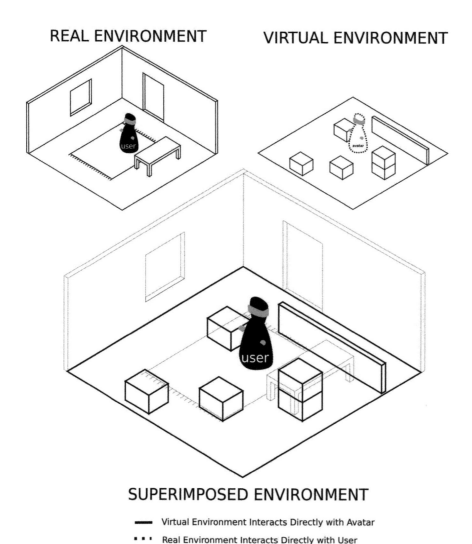

Figure 9.3: An illustration of how the physical and virtual environment overlap within one superimposed environment.

Any place within the overlaid map where inconsistencies between the two worlds may result in conflicting physics can be considered a **world inconsistency boundary**. World inconsistency boundaries also apply to inconsistencies that we may not consider to be "physics issues," like when the tactile textures of the floors between the two worlds aren't the same (an example discussed in the chapter on presence). Although these non-physics inconsistencies can also impact the usability of an experience or the degree of presence felt by the user, they are often less extreme in these impacts as major physics inconsistencies.

### 9.3.1   Classification of World Inconsistency Boundaries

To list every conceivable world inconsistency boundary would require an exhaustive list of every sensation possible—any two sensations can conflict, resulting in an inconsistency. However, any inconsistency can be classified into one of the three following categories.

**Real-Simulated Inconsistencies**: This category includes situations where two active stimuli, one from the real world and one from the simulated world, give the user conflicting information. For example, the case where the user sees a carpeted floor in the virtual world, but feels the tile floor of the physical world, would be a real-simulated inconsistency. For an inconsistency to be classifiable as a real-simulated inconsistency, two active and contrasting stimuli must be received by the user's senses. In the case where one stimulus is received that contrasts with a *lack* of sensation (null stimuli), the inconsistency is not a real-simulated inconsistency and instead falls into one of the following two categories.

**Real-Null Inconsistencies**: Inconsistencies where a sensation from the real world is met with no associated stimulus from the virtual world. For example, running into a wall that exists in the real world but is not shown within the virtual world would be a real-null inconsistency. A real-null stimulus consists of stimuli from the real world that have no accompanying stimuli in the simulated world.

**Null-Simulated Inconsistencies**: The reverse of real-null inconsistencies, a null-simulated inconsistency, is when active stimuli from the virtual (simulated) world have no accompanying stimuli in the real world in a sense that would anticipate it. For example, seeing a wall in the virtual world that the user cannot touch in the real world would be an example of a null-simulated inconsistency.

## 9.4   IMPACTS OF WORLD INCONSISTENCY BOUNDARIES

Often, the purpose of a VR program is to generate a digital world that is isolated from the physical world that the user is actually in. As such, world inconsistencies are counterproductive to this fundamental goal of VR—they are the instances when the physics of the actual world interferes with, or "seep into," the simulated world. Because of this, world inconsistencies can lead to quite a few different negative impacts for a VR user.

## 9.4.1 World Inconsistency Boundaries Reduce Immersion

In Section 2.3, we introduced the concept of *unsupported sensorimotor contingencies*, which describe when the user carries out an action that would result in a change in sensory input if it were performed in the real world, but the expected change does not occur in the virtual environment. We could define a world inconsistency in terms of sensorimotor contingencies—*worlds are inconsistent in areas where sensorimotor contingencies are unsupported.*

If a sensory input is fully immersed, in theory it is possible to support all of that sense's sensorimotor contingencies. Thus, a world inconsistency can only occur for unimmersed or partially immersed sensory inputs. As presence is a function of the sensorimotor contingencies successfully reinforced by the VR application, the user who interacts with areas where world inconsistencies exist will experience a decrease in presence. As such, if we want to encourage the highest degree of presence within a particular VR application, it is important to mitigate world inconsistencies.

## 9.4.2 World Inconsistency Boundaries Impact User Safety

Wearing a headset allows the user to view a virtual world, but restricts the view of the real environment. This lack of visibility makes it easy to bump into obstacles in the real world—a problem that is exacerbated by high degrees of presence taking the user's mind off of the placement of objects in the real environment. Conversely, high degrees of presence can make it easy for users to forget that virtual objects may not have certain physical qualities that would exist in the real world. Users may attempt to set their controllers down on a virtual table or lean against a virtual wall, only to find that these virtual objects are incapable of providing support.

Removing world inconsistency boundaries is one way to resolve this issue, but adding indicators that display where objects (or areas without objects) exist within the real-world space can solve some of the safety concerns discussed above. More strategies are discussed in further detail later in the chapter.

## 9.4.3 World Inconsistency Boundaries Lower Usability

The virtual world and the available segment of the real world are not always the same size. One common usability issue related to discontinuity between these two worlds occurs when the real-world space available to the player is too small to allow access to all of the virtual world. In such a scenario, the inconsistency between the virtual world and the real world makes it hard for the user to interact with parts of the VR interface that exist beyond the boundaries of the usable real-world area. World inconsistencies also include when the expectations of simulated physics clash with the real-world physics associated with the avatar. If objects behave differently with the avatar than with the rest of the world, it can make it difficult for the user to determine what rules of physics apply where. Further, active stimuli from the real world can interfere with the usability of the simulated world. Imagine trying to accomplish an audio-related task in a simulated world (perhaps listening to discern between two musical notes) while a loud sound from the real world can be heard, like a lawnmower or leaf blower just outside your window. These sorts of world inconsistencies can be detrimental to usability if the real-world stimuli cannot be occluded by the VR system. Such interference makes it hard to interpret the intended simulated stimuli.

### 9.4.4 World Inconsistency Boundaries Can Create Exploits

A virtual drawer is locked, requiring a key to open. As well programmed as the key and lock are, they hold little purpose if the user is able to pass their hand through the drawer as if it were not a solid object. Although the key and lock in this example conform to the simulated physics of the world, the avatar's hand is only bound to the physics of the real world—as no drawer exists in the real world, the avatar's hand meets no resistance. There are many such instances where real world physics may be used to bypass the rules of the simulated world. Passing your hands through virtual objects to gain restricted entry, passing your head through a virtual wall to see the other side, and other such exploits are difficult to prevent unless the user is properly immersed, or unless the system properly identifies and restricts these activities. If the system knows that the user's head is beyond the wall, the system can restrict or alter the user's vision, display a message indicating the user is out of bounds, or simply adjust the location of the user to be back where they are supposed to be. Although it is difficult to completely remove these world inconsistencies, they are fairly easy to compensate for using simulation-side rules.

## 9.5 RESOLVING WORLD INCONSISTENCY ISSUES

In most cases, the effects of world inconsistencies are undesirable. There are several ways to resolve these negative effects, with varying degrees of separation from the original root problem, shown in Figure 9.4.

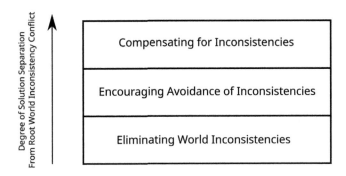

Figure 9.4: Solutions for resolving world inconsistency conflicts.

The layers nearest to the bottom avoid all negative effects of world inconsistency boundaries by making both worlds consistent. The layers at the top treat single "symptoms" of world inconsistencies—they resolve some of the problems world inconsistency introduces, but often avoid addressing other issues the inconsistency introduces. In between is a spectrum of approaches that solve the problem by mimicking or simulating world consistency that cannot be actually implemented.

This diagram is not necessarily arranged from the "best" to the "worst"—implementations closer to the bottom often resolve the root issues at the expense of significant trade-offs: they may compromise or limit the scope of an application, be costly or technologically impossible with current devices, or be impractical to use or develop. In many cases, the methods higher up on the diagram will better suit an application.

### 9.5.1 Method 1—Eliminating Inconsistencies

Occupying the bottom of the diagram is the "ideal" method of resolving inconsistency-related issues. The ideal way to remove these negative effects is to eliminate world inconsistency boundaries by making the two realities consistent. As there are two realities that are inconsistent in any conflict, there are two paths to create consistency for any particular world inconsistency boundary. We can either make the physical world's physics match the virtual physics or vice versa.

Depending on what the inconsistency we want to resolve is, changing the physical world's physics can be very simple or very difficult. Real-to-null inconsistencies are generally simpler to eliminate than null-to-simulated, but can often still be difficult. For example, if the inconsistency is that the user is running into a chair in the area where they have their VR rig set up, removing the chair will make the real world match the virtual world. However, if the inconsistency is that the user is running into a wall in the real world, the wall would be a lot more difficult to move. The VR rig could potentially be moved to an area with more space, but in theory there will always be a VR application that requires more space. However, the null-to-simulated inverse of trying to make the real world reflect a virtual wall could require significant expense. Augmented virtuality (below) is another option to resolve null-to-simulated or real-to-null inconsistencies.

There are two possible methods to remove inconsistencies completely: world conforming and augmented virtuality. Both can be done from the simulation or real world side and may be more appropriate to approach in one way as opposed to the other.

#### 9.5.1.1 World Conforming

World conforming is the removing of elements from a world (either virtual or physical) to conform to the other. World conforming can be done with reference to either the real environment or the virtual environment. In the first case, world conforming with reference to the real environment removes elements from the virtual environment to match the *reference environment*, in this case the real environment. Likewise, when world conforming is done with reference to the virtual environment, elements are removed from the real environment to match the virtual.

Removing a table in the real world that does not show up in the virtual environment would be an example of world conforming with reference to the virtual environment, while removing a virtual table that has no real environment counterpart is conforming with reference to the real environment.

### 9.5.1.2 Augmented Virtuality

Whereas world conforming removes elements from the non-reference world to match the reference world, augmented virtuality consists of adding elements to bring the two environments into agreement. Just like world conforming, augmented virtuality can be real or virtually referenced. In the virtual-referenced case, objects are added in the real world to reflect the virtual environment. For example, using a real-world controller with a gun-like grip while partaking in a combat training simulator that has the avatar holding a gun would be virtual-referenced augmented virtuality.

Real-referenced augmented virtuality involves adding information to the virtual world that reflects objects in the real world. This can be done by hard-coding aspects of the real environment into the virtual environment, but would also include cases where the environment changes dynamically based on information about the real space the user has their VR equipment in. For example, VR experiences that resize the virtual environment to fit within the space available to the player in the real world are using real-referenced augmented virtuality—the virtual environment has been altered to make its size consistent with the real space.

Null-to-simulated inconsistencies involving smaller objects can be resolved by asking the user to align a real-world object with a virtual object. For example, in a scenario where the user is walking on a balancing beam, adding a real balancing beam to their physical environment, and ensuring it is aligned with the virtual balance beam, can greatly increase the sense of presence for the user. Such inconsistencies can also be resolved by allowing the user to add a virtual-world object that is then aligned with a real-world object. For example, if the user's physical space has a chair in it and the user is able to add a virtual chair that is aligned with the physical chair, the user can stand and sit whenever they want to without leaving VR.

### 9.5.2 Method 2—Encouraging Avoidance of Inconsistencies

While removing an inconsistency will ensure that it will not be encountered by the player, in many cases it is either impossible, infeasible, or defeats the purpose of the simulation to remove a world inconsistency entirely. In many cases, however, the user can be encouraged to avoid inconsistencies at a more conceptual or diegetic level. For example, if the user specifies an area of their physical space that is free from obstacles, a developer can design an experience such that the tasks the user has to perform within the virtual world occur in the physical-world space that is free from obstacles. In this case, this is an indirect form of encouraging the user to avoid the world inconsistency boundaries—the developer isn't necessarily addressing the boundary itself, but instead encourages the user to direct their attention elsewhere. The user can always ignore this content and encounter the boundary, but this strategy decreases the effect the boundary has on presence and usability by reducing the amount of time the average user spends interacting with the boundary.

A scenario discussed before in reference to plausibility illusion is the case where the user doesn't touch a virtual sawblade because they unconsciously fear physical consequences due to plausibility illusion, or because touching the sawblade will deduct points or cause other in game consequences. This is a direct form of encouraging avoidance of an inconsistency boundary—gameplay or presence actively discourages the user from "touching" the virtual sawblade and feeling the inconsistent lack of physical feedback. These strategies are similarly effective. The weakness in this approach when contrasted with the indirect approach to encouraging boundary avoidance is that there are many boundaries that it is difficult to diagetically justify discouraging—not every virtual wall should be presented as a dangerous electric wall to prevent users from touching it. However, the indirect approach usually prevents boundaries from being encountered by having users engage with some other portion of the environment, likely the focus of the application—unless this focus also involves boundary inconsistencies, this method usually minimizes the time spent in boundary conflict in a non-intrusive way.

The other side of this technique is that developers must be careful when designing interaction activities to not encourage the user to move *into* the boundaries. If the character in the virtual world is put into a situation where they are encouraged to take a step backward, for example if they are attacked by a monster and decide to retreat, or if an object approaches them quickly and they decide to duck, it is possible that the user will take a step back into the boundary, invoking the visual barrier and interfering with presence. Locomotion methods that allow the user to move virtually but not physically should be encouraged in these instances, but immediate interactions often encourage specific motions that could cause the user to invoke the boundary. Care should be taken not only to encourage avoidance but also to discourage disavoidance.

### 9.5.3 Method 3—Compensating for Inconsistencies

In the cases where a boundary inconsistency cannot be avoided or removed, the inconsistency can often be compensated for in some way that reduces the effects of the inconsistency on player safety, usability, or presence. For example, if the user is grabbing a virtual ball, the inconsistency in not being able to feel the physical ball may lead to usability issues in that there is uncertainty over if the ball is held or not, as well as a negative impact to presence by not receiving any feedback aside from a visual update that the ball is held. Although it might be difficult to make the user feel the sensation of holding a ball, haptic vibrations while the ball is held or an audio cue when the ball is picked up can compensate for usability impact by providing another channel for the user to identify when the ball is held. As for the effects of presence, although the sensation may not be as strong as if the proper SCs were reinforced, having some feedback for the user's action, even if it is **surrogate feedback**, that is feedback that comes from a sense or in a form that would not be present in the physical world, leads to a greater sense of presence than when there is no feedback at all. There are many ways to compensate for an inconsistency, but what specific actions will work are best determined by investigating what the impacts of the inconsistency are. If an inconsistency provides a null or false affordance, for example, the usability impact could be compensated for by providing signifiers in its place.

One particularly important category of world inconsistencies are those that create safety issues for the user. As using a VR system isolates the user from some physical stimuli in exchange for virtual stimuli, this can cause issues when these senses cannot be used to avoid physical harm. Thus, the next section gives special attention to the ways that these particular inconsistencies can be removed, avoided, or compensated for.

## 9.6 CREATING BOUNDARIES FOR PLAYER SAFETY

Until VR can replicate avatar actions based strictly on the user's conscious thoughts, real-world body movement will be required for virtual-world interactions, and there will always be a risk of interacting with the occluded physical world while in VR. As spatial displays get closer to the virtual end of the continuum, the amount of the user's sensory field that is isolated from the real world increases. Despite immersion in a virtual world, the user is still very much at the mercy of real-world physics. Without being able to see or sense the physical world, users may be unable to avoid running into physical objects within their playspace. If the user is unable to hear outside sounds, they may miss some important stimuli (such as a fire alarm). In these cases, the definitions of the boundaries of a simulation can potentially mitigate these safety concerns. As such, it's important to consider what measures can be taken to prevent the user from injuring themselves while simultaneously inhabiting real and virtual environments.

### 9.6.1 Method 1: Keeping the Action Inside the Boundaries

One of the best ways to prevent the user from running into physical obstacles while engaged in a VR experience is to limit the superimposed space according to the real space that is free of obstacles. This can be done in a few ways—for example, the application could specify to the user a minimum amount of space that must be clear around the VR system for the user to be able to safely use the software. Another solution is the opposite case, where the user indicates the available physical volume of space to the application, and the application adjusts accordingly.

This method ensures that the user is able to safely move around a virtual space without running into objects in the real space, although it does introduce some limitations. First, this method limits the scope of one-to-one environment mapping that can be done, since interactable virtual environments cannot be larger than the available physical space. Although the conceptual virtual space can be as large as needed, at any given time the portion of the virtual environment that the user can move about through tracking is limited to the size of the safe area within the real environment. Although an application could request that users have a larger area available in order to safely use the virtual environment, increasing the size requirements for this environment may limit the number of users able to make effective use of such software. Indirect locomotion strategies can be used to infinitely increase the size of a virtual environment beyond that of the real tracked area, but this limitation on suitable locomotion strategies may not suit all applications.

Another limitation of this method is that application or user-defined boundaries are necessarily static—obstacles (or other people) moving into the real tracked area will not be indicated to the user unless another method is used. However, use cases where moving obstacles are common are limited, so static boundaries are appropriate for a wide range of applications.

### 9.6.2 Method 2: Indicating Obstacles Within the Virtual Scenario

An alternative to limiting the size of the experience to remain within the safe play area is to provide an indicator or representation of the boundaries of available physical space within the experience. One of the more common ways that this is implemented is by having a transparent element or overlay within the virtual environment that shows the area that the player should not move beyond. Sometimes, this transparent wall is always visible, but in other cases may not appear unless the user approaches a boundary. This outline is typically non-diagetic, as most diagetic boundaries would fit into Method 1 as discussed above.

The dimensions of the boundary used may be generated automatically to maximize the available space based on the user's available area or maybe set as a constant (e.g. specifying that the user of a VR system must make a 2m × 2m space available). Some VR systems allow the player to define what the boundaries of their space are, by requiring the user to highlight what space is safe within an augmented reality view of their surroundings. Implementations that show the safe area within the VR application also may display obstacles within the area in addition to the boundary, if the VR system knows about these objects or is capable of detecting such objects in real time.

One potential drawback of using an overlay boundary to indicate a safe area (as compared to resizing the VR environment) is that the non-diagetic elements may break plausibility illusion and could lead to lower levels of presence than otherwise. However, in cases where the boundary indicator only appears when the user approaches the boundary and is in danger of hitting something in the physical world, such boundaries may only be visible for a small fraction of the experience, as a player learns to stay within the boundary. Further, as users gain familiarity with this feature, they may be able to maintain plausibility even when the boundary appears.

One strength of this method is that it allows the user to trust that they are within the safe area. When the environment uses an indicator and the user does not see the indicator, they know they are in the middle of their playspace and can ignore the physical world and concentrate on the virtual world. If no indicator is used, it is easy for the user to "get lost" and forget exactly where they are in the physical environment, since the virtual environment is typically very different. The user in this situation may feel a sense of anxiety, similar to someone who walks around with their eyes closed—they are never sure if they are about to run into some unseen object. A boundary removes these anxieties—the user knows that an indicator will appear before they run into an object, so they feel more free to move around when the indicator isn't present.

### 9.6.3 Method 3: Using Mixed Reality in Hazardous Areas

A very similar approach to the proximity boundary method discussed above is to instead transition to a mixed-reality view of the user's environment when boundaries are approached. In the same way as above, this method would allow high levels of presence when the user is not near a boundary, but would also allow the additional functionality of allowing the user to move beyond their boundary while keeping the headset on, perhaps to set down or grab a controller or otherwise interact with the outside environment. In theory, if the headset is able to detect obstacles instead of requiring them to be tagged by the user, this method could allow for unlimited playspace—the user would be able to move through the outdoors or a public space, with the headset allowing them to see the physical world when a hazard is approached. In terms of presence, it could be argued that the more jarring transition of seeing the virtual world suddenly replaced by the real one would have a bigger impact on plausibility illusion than seeing a boundary overlaid. Depending on the VR environment and context, the user could even become confused over which objects are part of the real world and which are part of the virtual. Although what method of the three works best differs depending on the application, all three can be used to allow the user to safely avoid obstacles in the physical world while they focus on a virtual one.

## 9.7   INTERACTION PATTERNS FOR BOUNDARY HANDLING

We've discussed ways to show the user physical boundaries within the virtual world, but another common problem is how to enforce virtual boundaries when there is no physical component to stop the user from moving through them. In the physical world, a wall is solid, and thus a person cannot easily move their hand or head through the wall to grab or see objects on the other side. However, the user can easily move their physical body to a portion of a virtual environment that should be inaccessible, as there are no inherent limiting factors preventing this motion. The following subsections discuss methods to enforce virtual boundaries in cases where restricting access is crucial to the application.

### 9.7.1   Head Movement Boundaries

When using a 6dof HMD in a virtual reality environment, viewing one's surroundings is quite similar to how it works in a physical environment, with translational and rotational movement resulting in appropriate updates to the view displayed. However, in the virtual world, if the avatar (and therefore the camera) is not limited by physics, it may be possible for the user to view areas that shouldn't be accessible. Unless rules are put in place in the virtual world, the user could in theory move anywhere within the real-world space they have available to them, allowing them to access portions of the virtual environment that should be limited. For example, the user could look through walls and drawers or go through a virtual door without having to open it first—without any programmed handling for such cases, the user's avatar is in function non-corporeal. In many cases, a non-corporeal avatar presents little issue. If allowing the user to clip through physical objects does not affect the function or intended experience of the application, it doesn't need to be addressed. However, clipping can lower presence—unless justified within the application, it breaks plausibility illusion due to its impossibility within an actual physical environment. Additionally, clipping can make environments seem unpolished or unfinished and, in some application types, allow the user to exploit the application. If areas of the environment should be inaccessible at certain times, having the user's view clip through objects may allow them to circumvent core parts of the experience. In effect there are two ways to resolve the problems related with a lack of head movement boundaries: visibility alteration and camera limiting.

### 9.7.1.1 Visibility Alteration

The first method of addressing view clipping, **visibility alteration**, visibly masks portions of the environment that the avatar shouldn't be "physically accesing."

Visibility alteration methods are in effect "censoring" portions of the environment that shouldn't be accessed or are accessed illegitimately. Such methods could include blurring the screen, blacking it out, or replacing the virtual world with pass-through mixed reality. One thing to be cognizant of when choosing a visibility alteration method is to ensure that the user can still find their way back to the accessible area of the VR environment after the view has been altered. For example, although fading the screen to black may effectively censor areas, the user may not know how to return to the initial area that they inadvertently departed. Shaders can provide many effects that can indicate inaccessible areas while allowing the user to see geometry. Visibility alteration can be incorporated diagetically into an experience—however, visibility alteration of any type (even non-diagetic) affects presence in different ways than traditional clipping and is often a better solution presencewise. Although there is no real world analogue for much of visibility alteration, it's more plausible than being able to see inside solid walls or objects.

### 9.7.1.2 Camera Limiting

While visibility alteration relies on changing the elements of the scene that can be viewed when the in-application "camera" intersects a prohibited area, another way to prevent these areas from being viewed is by restricting the motion of the camera. **Camera limiting** is the method of not letting the camera pass through walls to begin with. For example, collision detection could be used to disconnect the avatar camera from the user's actual head position, having the camera stop at the wall while the user continues past it. This method is very effective in replicating the limitations of what we can view in the physical world, but in a room scale or tracked camera environment where the user has no limits on where they can move their physical head, the discrepancy between head and camera movement can be very disorienting and potentially cause VR sickness. However, in VR environments where the head is not tracked, this becomes a lot more viable option. With regard to presence, removing the ability for the virtual head to clip through walls is more plausible in many scenarios, but divorcing camera movement from user head movement breaks several sensorimotor contingencies, so preventing camera movement can have a significant impact on plausibility illusion if user is expecting the camera to update.

### 9.7.2 Hand Movement Boundaries

Just as there is nothing to stop the user from moving their head through the space occupied by virtual objects, the user's hands (or for that matter, any tracked body part) can similarly be moved in the physical world with no regard to the contents of the virtual environment. Like the head, hands can also cause plausibility and gameplay issues, should they be allowed to clip through objects. Similarly, several different methods of addressing the problems created by allowing free hand clipping exist. However, object clipping with reference to hands presents some major differences from the head clipping problems. For one, the action of the hands is not always visible. The user can be reaching for an object they feel should be accessible while looking somewhere else, and won't realize that they have been prevented from grabbing it. As such, methods for dealing with hand movement boundaries should incorporate some sort of non-visual feedback (or present feedback in the user's locus of attention) to ensure the player is aware of the state of the hands, even if not looking at them.

There are two fundamental ways to handle how hands should interact with physics objects in the environment. Either the hands will be non-corporeal (also known as "ghost hands") and will interact with the objects of the game world only when pressing buttons or other inputs, or the hands will interact with physics objects. These methods don't have to be applied to the hands universally—hands can be non-corporeal or physics responsive only for certain objects in the environment, at certain times, or two representations of the hands can exist at once within the environment of different types. Quite often, a combination of the two approaches can be beneficial.

#### 9.7.2.1 Non-Corporeal Hands

As introduced above, non-corporeal or **ghost hands** refer to when the hands of the avatar are allowed to clip through objects when not in an interaction mode. Ghost hands are useful when the purpose of the hands in the environment is similar to that of a mouse cursor—environments where the hands are used for selecting objects or accessing UI elements, but not actually exerting changes on the objects in the scene. Generally, the lack of response of non-corporeal hands to the virtual environment reduces plausibility illusion unless it can be explained diegetically. Additionally, seeing the hand pass through an object and not feeling anything can break the sensorimotor contingency of force feedback, again, unless it is explained and expected. Due to the direct spatial mapping to the user's physical hands, non-corporeal hands are often the most intuitively manoeuvrable and can serve to reinforce proprioceptive sensorimotor contingencies.

### 9.7.3 Physics-Responsive Hands

Avatar hands that are physics responsive are able to have an effect on objects in the virtual world. How the objects are affected depends on the choice of the developer: colliding an avatar hand with an object may move the object, restrict the avatar hand's movement, activate a function of the object (like pressing a button), or any other appropriate reaction. In cases where the avatar hand's motion is affected by an object, the avatar hand may become unaligned from the position of the user's physical hand.

Implementing physics-responsive hands allows interactions with objects to be consistent: if the interactions with objects are simulated based on physics calculations rather than conceptual or logical (i.e. hard-coded) interactions, the same set of rules can be applied to determine the outcome of any hand-object interaction, even as new objects are added to the virtual environment.

The de-synchronization between avatar and user hands, much like de-synchronization between the head of the user and the avatar, can break sensorimotor contingencies—in this case, the virtual visual input contrasts with proprioceptive information from the physical world. A disconnect between virtual and physical hand positions can also lower usability, making it harder for the user to move their hand into a desired position due to conflicting sensory feedback. These usability concerns become increasingly severe as the displacement between the physical and virtual hand position increases. Trying to control an avatar with appendages in different positions from the user's hands may cause the user to feel separate from the avatar, as if the user is puppeting the avatar instead of it being a mirror of their body.

Further, making a virtual hand be constrained by the physical environment without having accompanying hand sensation can make it frustrating to execute difficult motor tasks within the VR environment. For this reason, the usefulness of physics-responsive hands in performing virtual motor tasks increases when accompanied by some level of appropriate haptic feedback.

### 9.7.4 Building Hybrid Hand Models

In many cases, it is appropriate to have hands be non-corporeal for some instances of a simulation, while being physics responsive in other instances within the same simulation. Generally, physics-responsive hands are best to use for diegetic objects, allowing the user to affect the diegetic object. The same expectations of being able to affect objects through traditional touch interactions may not be present for non-diegetic UI elements, and thus non-corporeal hands may be better suited. If an object can't be interacted with directly, it might be better to have interaction with it be non-corporeal. An important usability consideration when implementing context-dependent hybrid hand frameworks is that there should be some signifier of which objects or elements of the environment are interactable via physics-responsive interactions, which are responsive to non-corporeal interactions, and which are not interactive.

Another hybrid approach is to have hands be physics responsive until the user's hand motion desyncs from the avatar's hands, at which point a non-corporeal representation of the hands appears. This approach addresses one of the major issues with physical hands, the positional feedback conflict when the physics-responsive hands are seen in a position that does not match up with the proprioceptive feedback corresponding to the user's physical hands.

It is acceptable and often advantageous to mix and match which hand approach is being used depending on context within the application, as long as the current mode of the system is well conveyed from a usability perspective. Different hands suit different tasks, and until proprioceptive and haptic display technologies evolve further, the chosen avatar hand approach must balance what is more important for a given scenario: visual or proprioceptive accuracy.

### 9.7.5  Hand-Object Boundaries

Hands can interact with or phase through objects in a virtual environment, but one of the primary tasks of avatar hands is allowing the user to grab or move virtual objects. There are many different ways in which a virtual object and a virtual hand grabbing that object can interact with each other. For example, if the object should move separately from the hand and if the hand behaviour should be modified while holding the object are both questions that have seen a variety of different implementations across applications.

First, we will discuss three ways to handle collisions with other objects while the hand is holding an object of its own. Then, we will discuss if and why physics behaviour should change with an object in hand. Later in the book, in the section on physical interactions, we discuss how the actual action of grabbing an object should be implemented.

#### 9.7.5.1  Hand-Object Protocol 1: Object Stops, Hand Continues

One solution to the situation where a hand holding an object collides within another object is to have physics collisions affect the object, but treat the hand as non-corporeal. This implementation is appropriate when the physical behaviour of the held object with other objects is important, but user coordination is prized above visually appropriate behaviour. However, having different interactions for the hand and the held object decreases plausibility—as a consistent choice is not held on if objects are non-corporeal or physics response, it may also be confusing to users. From a usability perspective, however, this approach can be useful as it allows for physics-responsive interactions between objects without causing a disconnect between visual and proprioceptive hand position information.

#### 9.7.5.2  Hand-Object Protocol 2: Object and Hand Stop

A second approach in the held-object/object collision problem is to have both the held object and the avatar hand be physics responsive, either stopping at the collision or moving the other object. In terms of plausibility and usability, this approach has the same disadvantages as the solid hand pattern discussed outside the context of holding objects. This approach allows for continuity in the way the hand reacts with objects if the hand is solid when not held, which both boosts plausibility and also confers the usability advantage of making it easy for the user to predict how the hand will react. A hybrid approach that is also common is to pair this implementation with a hand that is otherwise non-corporeal when not holding an object—if physics-responsive behaviour only occurs when an object is held, it will similarly be easy to predict what behaviour will occur in a given case.

### 9.7.5.3 Hand-Object Protocol 3: Ghost Object and Hand

Like the example where the hand is non-corporeal, in this implementation, once an object is grabbed by the hand, it becomes non-corporeal as well for the duration it is held. This implementation maintains the same advantages as ghost hands—it makes it easy for the user to move the virtual object as well as the avatar hand to whatever position they desire. The ghost object and hand implementation also has the same disadvantages as the ghost hand method, but it also has an added limitation in that objects held in the hand cannot physically react with other objects. This limits the amount of applications for which this is a practical solution—if objects don't need to physically interact with each other (for example if they are simply for appearance and have no physics simulation), this method may work well, but any desire for physical reactions while the object is held would make this implementation ill-suited.

### 9.7.5.4 Deciding How Hands and Objects Should Interact

Although allowing high levels of presence is often a goal of VR applications, in most cases, ensuring functionality should come first. Thus, one of the major factors in determining which approach to take to hand-object physics is what functionality is required from the held object. If we want objects to be able to interact with other objects, we should use one of either paradigm 1 or 2.

Consistency with the hand physics implementation that occurs when an object is not held is another factor that may be important. For example, if non-corporeal hands are used while an object is not held, implementation 1 (where the hands are non-corporeal but the object is physics responsive) may be better from a usability perspective—it retains consistency in the way the hands behave, while allowing held objects to act upon other objects.

Similarly, implementation 2, where both the hand and object are physically reactive, is consistent with the hand-only physics-responsive implementation. As stated briefly before, implementation 3 works best of applications where objects don't need to interact with each other in a physical manner.

Just as with hand-only patterns, it is possible to mix and match which implementation is used during what context as appropriate. For example, small objects could be treated as non-corporeal while held, while larger ones could be responsive to physics. It's also possible to do something similar to the "two sets of hands" approach described in the hand physics section, conferring the same advantage of the user being able to have a visual of their actual hand position.

The main hazard of splitting into many different hand-object behaviours based on context is that the number of different interactions could confuse the user. A system with many different context-dependent hand-object behaviours could be made usable by employing well-signified or afforded objects, but without usability adaptations in other areas, increasing the number of potential options can have a negative impact on usability. Conversely, having a small number of consistent hand interaction methods will make it obvious to the user how to interact with any given object, once they are familiar with the interactions implemented in the system.

## 9.8 PHYSICS-BASED INTERACTIONS

### 9.8.1 Translating Physics Across Boundaries

We have previously discussed how two sets of physics influence a VR simulation: the physics of the real environment and the physics of the simulated environment (computed physics). The motion of the user's body, used to influence the movement of the avatar, is bound by real physics. In this way, the user's avatar is a one-way vessel for physics across the two realities. We refer to this influence as one way since physics is typically not translated from the computed world which is able to constrain the user, although haptic systems can sometimes modify available actions in the physical world. Only in the direction from the real environment to the virtual one does physics exert influence on the virtual avatar.

User avatars can, of course, exert physics on the virtual environment, as well as be affected by the virtual environment to varying degrees. This discussion can be abstracted further to consider how an avatar can be influenced by physics of both worlds in varying amounts.

#### 9.8.1.1 *Physicality of the Avatar in a Virtual World*

An avatar can be represented physically within the world with varying degrees of fidelity. On the low end of the spectrum, we have a "ghost avatar"; much like ghost hands (Section 9.7.2.1), a non-corporeal avatar cannot interact with objects in a scene. A ghost avatar is passive with regard to the environment and as such may not need to be fully simulated, as the avatar cannot collide with the environment. Sometimes all avatar a ghost consists of is the camera and hands—in such a case, ghost avatar would consist simply of the previously discussed design patterns for a clipping head and non-corporeal hands.

The second level is what could be described as a "selective avatar," capable of interacting with a limited set of objects within the environment. The interactions with these objects may not be done via physics simulation either, instead acting more like pointing and pressing a button to "activate" the object, or they may "snap" to the hand upon pickup. The scripting governing object behaviour when interacting with a selective avatar can avoid physics calculations, and use of the hands may involve many pre-rendered animations. Manually specifying hand poses may be more efficient for the developer if the number of interactions is small, but as these cases grow, procedural determination of hand-object interactions through physics-based interactions becomes more practical.

An avatar that utilizes physics colliders would be the third level of interactions— most or all objects in the virtual environment are affected by being touched by the avatar, and these interactions are determined in part through physics calculations. The avatar is not limited to interacting with a subset of the environment or in preset ways. The fidelity of the colliders used for avatar interactions can also vary from a single oval-shaped collider for physics purposes, to a dynamic and detailed set of colliders programmed to follow the contours of the body and update with avatar motion. It is worth noting that physics calculations must be performed in real time when evaluating collisions and that these calculations tend to be very computationally expensive—thus, the more "accurate" a collider is, the more computational resources it tends to require. After rendering, physics calculations tend to be the largest draw on hardware resources, so a simulation requiring extensive collision evaluation can have significant performance impacts.

More physics-accurate interactions aren't inherently better, either from a usability or a presence standpoint—VR gives the freedom to interact in ways that aren't identical to the physical world, and abstractions of physical interactions may be better than more "realistic" simulations.

Having an avatar that can only interact in limited ways creates constraints which can help the user understand which actions should be taken. Avatars that have a higher degree of physics interactions can be frustrating if the VR system does not have enough tracking for full articulation, making manipulating the avatar difficult. However, as mentioned before in the context of real-time physics, physics-based avatars save time for the developer in ways—instead of having to program how the avatar is to interact with different types of objects, this is handled by the physics engine instead.

### 9.8.1.2 Physicality of the Virtual World on the Avatar

The inverse direction from the influence an avatar has over the world is how much effect the world has on the avatar's motion. At the lowest end is a "ghost world"—objects and the environment of the world have no physics effect on the avatar. If an object is thrown at the avatar, it will pass right through. At the highest end of the spectrum, the avatar is controlled fully by the physics of the virtual world—a rag-doll avatar with fully physics-based movement. This extreme case was seen in fixed-camera 3-DOF VR, but is generally not useful due to the lack of control the user has on their avatar.

In between are situations similar to the in-between cases for avatar on world—only parts of the world are able to exert forces on the avatar, or pre-programmed physical consequences may occur to the avatar following certain events. As exerting physics upon the avatar results in involuntary changes to the user's senses, exerting physics upon an avatar may result in involuntary motion or feelings of a loss of avatar control. In both cases, these actions can cause sickness and negative impacts to presence—as such, having the world affect the avatar is usually done to a lesser degree than having the avatar affect the world and must be considered carefully.

It should be clarified that both directions of world-avatar effect are independent. If a ball is thrown at the avatar, and it is stopped by the avatar (impacted by the avatar), this means the avatar is physically present on the first spectrum. Conversely, if the ball is thrown and the avatar is moved partially by the ball (avatar impacted by the ball), the avatar exists somewhere on the second spectrum as well. It's possible to have the avatar affect objects but not be affected by them, and vice versa. A fully physically realized avatar would be maximized on both spectra, as bodies are in the real world, but this is not always the ideal usability choice.

## 9.9  SUMMARY

The difference between observing a virtual world and inhabiting that world comes down to the way the world replicates physicality, and the way the user's body maps to the virtual world. We can replicate the senses that the user experiences, but until we recognize that the virtual world must also include physical objects that the user's avatar can interact with, we are limited in the realism that such a world can provide. The world needs to feel real before we can move through it (as discussed in the next chapter) and interact with it (as discussed in the chapters after that).

# CHAPTER 10

# Locomotion and Navigation

## 10.1 INTRODUCTION

When we use traditional interactive systems, like computers and games, our physical bodies are typically not moving. We sit on a couch or at a desk, watching a screen and manipulating interactable objects to effect change in the system we are observing. When we use computers for much of the day, first to work and then to play, we end up sitting for hours at a time, which is not healthy. Some computer and game systems, like the Wii, PlayStation Move, and Microsoft Kinect, have been developed to encourage users to move more when using computer systems, mostly by converting body movements into control events. Even if the avatar of ourselves in the game we are playing is instructed to move around the simulated world we are observing, we ourselves are not moving (or are only moving a proxy amount), and there is a separation between our commands to move our avatar and the motion we see in the simulation. In some situations, we may choose to walk while we are playing a hand-held game or using our phone, but this is generally considered dangerous and could increase the chance of tripping or bumping in to things. Augmented reality software—systems that add a layer of information to the physical world through a device like a smartphone—can make a connection between our motion in the physical world and what is shown to us through our screens, although the location and direction of the phone or AR device is the primary way in which the user's motion is understood by such system.

As may be familiar to the reader by now, virtual reality (VR) is different. In much the same way that reaching out to pick up an object feels different than pressing a button to cause an avatar to pick up an object, walking around a room feels fundamentally different than moving a joystick to move an avatar around the room. Our sensorimotor contingencies reinforce our perception of the virtual world as if it were real, and a deeply natural, intuitive mode of interaction becomes available to us—we can walk over to something interesting and interact with it.

The challenge, of course, is that the physical spaces we are in when we use VR are usually not the same shape and size as the virtual world we are in, so walking about very quickly causes us to break presence by bumping into walls or tables, or by allowing us to walk through a virtual wall that should stop us. Because of

DOI: 10.1201/9781003261230-10

these mismatches, developing methods to move about in virtual worlds has become a significant source of innovation and frustration.

The ability to perform **locomotion**, or to move around an environment, is necessary not just to accomplish tasks that may be out of reach but also to increase the extent to which environments can be perceived—we can look around corners and walk into rooms to see what we couldn't see before we moved. Well-implemented movement in a virtual environment, when combined with good practices for immersing sensory units, can enhance the user's sensation of presence within the environment. Conversely, poorly implemented or unsuitable movement can be detrimental to the user's overall experience. As such, it is important for VR developers to understand several aspects of locomotion, including the following:

- The physical and psychological mechanism by which locomotion occurs

- The purpose(s) of locomotion in a VR scenario

- The different categories of locomotion strategies that can be used

- Design principles and considerations for selecting and implementing locomotion strategies

- Techniques for analysing the effectiveness of locomotion strategies across different types of virtual environments

- The benefits, drawbacks, and overall implications of locomotion strategies

The psychological component of locomotion, which is comprised of identifying a path between one's origin and a destination, as well as orienting themselves within a physical space, is known as **wayfinding**. In order to effectively wayfind, a user must be able to spatially analyse an environment, understand their current location relative to their goal, and plan how to move from here to there. The process of moving towards a destination along a desired route is the physical component of locomotion, which is known as **travel**. Travel can also be described as the observable output of a locomotion or navigation system. Often, wayfinding and travel happen together, or in cycles (check the map, walk to the next waypoint).

Historically, in the physical world, wayfinding has been a challenging task requiring accurate timekeeping, direction finding, surveying, and map making. Improvements in each of these tasks have led to technologies (the chronograph and the compass) that have improved these and other aspects of our lives, but the development and launch of satellite-based location systems like GPS and GLONASS, and the subsequent removal of dithering, has meant that it is essentially impossible for anyone on the planet who owns a smartphone to be lost. GPS signals do not function well indoors, but technology such as Bluetooth beacons mean that indoor automated wayfinding is also available.

In the physical world, locomotion is usually intuitive and subconscious. Once a destination and route have been identified, ambulatory individuals[1] can simply walk along this route if the destination is nearby. If the destination is sufficiently distant that walking would be impractical, then a bicycle or motor vehicle might be used instead. These vehicles, despite eliminating much of the physical exertion in walking (or walking-adjacent motion), still contain hardware that translates a user's physical movement into travel (via mechanical or control assistance). Additionally, travel in the real world is only ever restricted by external factors, which can either be temporary (e.g. passers-by and construction zones) or permanent (e.g. buildings, bodies of water, and cliffs).

In contrast, the extent to which walking can be performed in a virtual environment is constrained by the size of the user's physical play area. As a result, unless the virtual environment's size is also limited, walking on its own is usually insufficient for exploring the bounds of the virtual environment and can rapidly lead to the user interacting with the boundary of their playspace. Such a discrepancy can negatively affect the user's experience, especially if an environment's inaccessible areas contain stimuli with which the user expects to be able to interact. As such, the vast majority of VR experiences contain alternative strategies for moving about in the virtual world. These strategies generally provide greater locomotive range than walking, but often at the cost of performance in other areas, including ease of use, appeasement of the vestibular system, reduction of plausibility illusion, and overall effect on the sensation of presence. Thus, it is necessary to understand the benefits, limitations, design considerations, and overall ramifications of each particular locomotion strategy.

**The Suitability of the Term "Walking" in VR**
We often make a general assumption that the majority of VR users are ambulatory, while also acknowledging that this is not universally the case, and that designers may need to take this into account when planning locomotive methods. Non-ambulatory users may be able to move themselves by way of surrogate devices, such as wheelchairs or electric scooters, but many "walking" locomotive experiences in VR assume that users can walk and therefore may be exclusionary if the user is unable to do so. Throughout this chapter, "walking" will be shorthand for one-to-one movement in reality and VR. The accessibility implications of locomotion strategies that require such one-to-one movement are discussed in Section 8.5

This chapter begins with a discussion of the concept of travel, including its most common tasks, its overall purposes, and its ability to be separated into subtasks and subsystems. Next, the most prevalent locomotion strategies in modern VR experiences are categorized. The chapter then contains a discussion on various techniques

---

[1]In much the same way that vision is typically prioritized in VR hardware development, walking is often prioritized in VR locomotion systems. Not everyone can walk, and developers should keep human diversity and difference in mind when designing locomotion systems.

for quantifying the efficacy of locomotion strategies, with proposed metrics including outright performance, utility, effect on presence, and synthesis with other strategies. Following this section, design principles for maximizing the ease of use and contextual justification of locomotion strategies are explored, as is the concept of movement being a mechanic in and of itself. Additionally, a framework for the environment-influenced suitability of locomotion strategies is proposed, which includes environments designed specifically to accommodate particular strategies. Finally, prevalent adverse effects of locomotion strategies are discussed from a holistic perspective, including vection and VR sickness, ergonomic concerns, and accessibility issues.

### 10.1.1  Locomotion terminology

Because locomotion is such a fundamental aspect of VR experiences and remains difficult to address, there are many approaches to any given locomotion problem, and a few terms have emerged in common practice that may be confusing for the new developer. Further, some of these terms, although seemingly generic, have been used to describe specific implementations of specific techniques.

**Continuous motion** is sometimes used to mean an artificial motion that is not discrete, for example when a user uses a thumbstick to indicate a direction and the view drifts in that direction. This type of motion is called "continuous" to separate it from discrete motion such as teleportation or angular rotation. We will use the term "continuous" to refer to any motion or rotation that is not discrete, whether caused by the thumbstick, some other control, or involuntarily. "Voluntary continuous motion" (VCM) is the term we will use to describe manipulating a control, like a thumbstick, to drift through the environment.

**Natural locomotion** is sometimes used to refer to a specific implementation of a technique of swinging your arms or walking in place to move. The rate and direction in which you swing your arms translates to the direction in which the view drifts. We refer to this technique as "arm cycling" or "walking in place."

## 10.2  PURPOSES OF LOCOMOTION

At its core, the goal of locomotion is to get the user from one place in a virtual world to another. The scope of this general task is broad, ranging from walking across the room to pick up an object to travelling around the world or across space to visit another location. The core aspect in all of these tasks is the movement of a user's agency from one context to another, that is allowing the user to affect change in another virtual location. Some tasks that appear to require locomotion (like reaching an object on the far side of a room) may be implemented instead by *action at a distance* as discussed in Section 11.4. The developer should consider whether locomotion itself is required or whether moving objects or contexts may also be possible.

### 10.2.1 Travel Tasks

There isn't one correct way to implement locomotion in VR. Many different VR locomotion strategies exist because suitability is dependent on the task for which they are used. As such, it is important to understand both the different types of travel tasks, the reasons for which each task is performed, and the implementation options available.

Besides simply seeking a destination, travel tasks can also be classified as *exploration, search*, or *manoeuvring*, as shown in Figure 10.1. Exploration means you are learning about the environment, searching means you are looking for something specific in the environment, and manoeuvring means you are accomplishing some specific task within the environment.

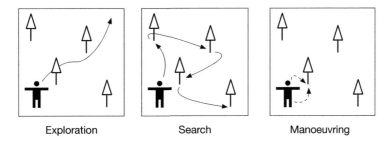

Exploration      Search      Manoeuvring

Figure 10.1: Common locomotion tasks.

**Exploration tasks** are characterized by the user lacking an explicit goal for their locomotion. Instead, the primary purpose of the user's movement is to obtain information about the environment such that any explicit goals may be more easily accomplished. Exploration tasks are primarily performed when the user first encounters an environment; however, they may be performed again in latter stages of an experience if new goals or stimuli appear, or if the environment changes.

Sometimes, exploration is initiated by unexpected stimuli—a user may abruptly deviate from their current path if they encounter something interesting in the environment. This control should enable users to alter their destination and orientation at any point throughout the travel process and carry minimal cognitive load. Exploration tasks are necessary for VR experiences with large open-world environments and a non-linear progression of gameplay, but for experiences where the user must perform tasks in a smaller or well-known environment, searching may be a preferred method.

**Search tasks**, in contrast to exploration tasks, are goal directed; they involve travel to a specific location or locations (possibly unknown) within the environment. Prior to initiating travel, the user consciously chooses a desired destination which may or may not contain the goal state; thus, search tasks involve both travel and wayfinding. There are two subcategories of search tasks:

- **Primed search tasks** are tasks in which the user knows the location of their target destination, as well as a path by which to reach it.

- **Naive search tasks** are tasks in which the user lacks knowledge of either the destination's precise location or a path by which to reach it.

Naive search tasks are different from exploration tasks because the user does, at the very least, have a destination in mind for their travel; thus, the path of locomotion observed in a naive search task will usually be linear. Primed search tasks may also contain elements of exploration if the user wants to explore an alternate route, but the final destination is fully explicit, and the user still possesses knowledge of at least one method of access. In contrast, exploration tasks are entirely unstructured, and the path of travel may be linear or cyclical.

Despite these differences, exploration and search share several common aspects. Both types of tasks involve user-directed movement for the purpose of obtaining or corroborating environmental information; the user's findings are reinforced by sensorimotor information at each step in the locomotion process. As such, locomotion strategies with wayfinding techniques and feedback systems may be better suited for search tasks than those with purely general mechanics.

Finally, **manoeuvring tasks** are performed whenever the user must precisely position their avatar in order to perform a specific action in the virtual environment. For example, if the user is playing a VR basketball game and wants to shoot a three-point shot from the corner, they must first navigate to the approximate location, which is a primed search task. However, the process of carefully positioning their avatar such that it is behind the three-point line, and turning to face the net in order to maximize their chances of making the shot, is a manoeuvring task. Manoeuvering tasks are perhaps the most difficult of the three travel task types to implement effectively, as many locomotion strategies enable a wide range of motion in exchange for low fidelity and poor precision, while others are advantaged with respect to precision but suffer in the areas of speed and range. In order to accommodate manoeuvering tasks, locomotion strategies should feature a balance between speed and precision.

## 10.2.2 Movement Subtasks

Beyond simply identifying a destination and establishing a route to it, there are numerous characteristics of travel tasks and the overall process of locomotion. These characteristics may influence the duration of wayfinding and exploration or be directly tied to the exact locomotion strategy that the user invokes if several locomotion modalities are present in the same experience. Because most physical playspaces are small relative to the virtual worlds they represent, many locomotion strategies are invoked artificially (i.e. by some mechanism other than physical motion). When multiple locomotion options are available, the user must both plan a path to a destination and choose which technique to use to follow that path. Some examples of these deductions are listed below.

### 10.2.2.1 Determining an ideal range of locomotion

The suitability of a locomotion strategy for travel in a VR environment is influenced not only by accessibility and usability but also by the properties of the environment itself. If the virtual environment's area is comparable to the user's playspace, then direct locomotion may be sufficient. In environments with larger (but still limited) dimensions, a strategy that either is invoked artificially or enforces a difference between real-world and virtual-world displacement is likely necessary. In open environments with primarily long-ranged travel tasks, locomotion strategies with velocity control may be more efficient.

Note that for manoeuvering tasks specifically, the size of the virtual environment doesn't matter since these tasks may always be accomplished by short-ranged physical motion. However, if a manoeuvring task is associated with other travel tasks, it may be more appropriate to align or combine manoeuvring with another strategy or remove the requirement for manoeuvring by having the local alignment of final destination be "right" with respect to whatever task may be needed at that location. If a user is running from place to place and taking cover at each location, the system could automatically put the user in a crouched position at each new location.

### 10.2.2.2   Explicit selection of a destination

An important factor in the transition between wayfinding and travel in virtual environments is whether the destination can be explicitly selected or not. In locomotion strategies such as teleportation, wherein the user points their controller at a location in the environment and is discretely transported to it, explicit destination selection could be argued to alleviate the user's cognitive load, as it makes the process of travel passive. In contrast, most locomotion strategies with continuous transitions force the user to actively facilitate each stage of their travel. The range of teleportation here is a critical design strategy, since short-range teleportation may still require wayfinding, while long-range teleportation may allow the user to select a destination and involve a cutscene rather than motion through the environment.

The primary caveat of locomotion strategies with explicit destination selection and passive travel is that the discrete nature of the motion may cause errors in movement precision. Teleportation that requires direct selection of a destination has the same challenges as object selection techniques (see Section 11.4.1) and can therefore have challenges with accuracy and control, when compared to continuous motion. If locomotive accuracy is an integral feature of a VR experience, then it is necessary to consider whether the physical and cognitive advantages of explicit destination selection outweigh its higher propensity for errors.

### 10.2.2.3   Reorientation and recalibration

The ability to view a virtual environment at different orientations is just as important for wayfinding, exploration, and manoeuvring as the ability to view at different positions. In the physical world, both repositioning and reorientation are accomplished via physical motion. The former two metaphors are likely still suitable in environments with comparable size to the user's designated play space, but in larger environments, long-distanced travel is generally invoked by artificial means, while walking is best suited for manoeuvring tasks.

In an open virtual environment which affords primarily artificial locomotion, the question of how reorientation should be performed gains several layers of complexity. On its own, physical rotation of the head-mounted display is advantaged with respect to simplicity and cognitive load. People are used to performing head rotations in the real world; a one-to-one head rotation requires no user translation of a physical action to a virtual interface, and the ocular system's sensorimotor feedback matches feedback received by the vestibular system. However, if physical head rotation is combined with an artificial locomotion strategy for translation, then cognitive load may actually increase due to the presence of multiple interaction metaphors—especially if the artificial translation occurs in a non-continuous manner, such as in teleportation.

If you push a thumbstick forward to begin to drift, the direction of drift may be specified by the direction of the thumbstick, or the direction you are looking. It may be more natural to walk in one direction and look in another, but controlling drift direction with a thumbstick may require an alignment to a world coordinate system that the user might not be able to perform.

In contrast, artificial rotation's primary weakness is its tendency to cause VR sickness if its transitions are continuous, as the changes observed by the ocular system do not stimulate the vestibular system. If the rotation occurs in discrete segments, then this problem is largely mitigated, as the task of rotation becomes passive. It is worth noting that, in a similar vein to explicit destination selection, some teleportation systems (see Section 10.3.3) additionally enable the user to preemptively choose an orientation for their avatar post-teleport. In addition to relegating reorientation to a passive task, this strategy enables amalgamation of search tasks with manoeuvring tasks, which saves time and reduces cognitive load. However, any significant change to orientation will prevent the user from immediately analysing the accuracy of the change in position, and vice versa. Consequently, error recovery increases in difficulty.

Other advantages of artificial rotation include timeliness, as the user need not consciously navigate between multiple interaction metaphors, and ergonomics, as the lack of physical motion mitigates prolonged strain on the user's cervical spine.

### 10.2.2.4 *Travel as a subtask*

There exists a subset of search tasks in which the user is not consciously aware of the fact that they are selecting a destination and travelling to it. In these scenarios, travel is a necessary subtask of some overarching supertask—in other words, it is a means to an end. For example, in a VR experience designed to teach the principles of recycling, the user may intuitively develop an awareness of the recycle bin's location, as well as the simplest path by which to access it. However, the user's objective is not to simply arrive at the recycle bin—what they really want to do is dispose of the plastic water bottle in their hand. In situations where travel is a subtask, it is important that the selected locomotion strategy does not distract from or interfere with the user's focus on the supertask. For example, if the controls for holding the bottle and for activating locomotion are on the same hand, the user may not be able to do both at the same time.

## 10.2.3 Wayfinding Aids

In its simplest form, wayfinding is a combination of *perception* (identifying clues along a route and recalling their significance), *attention* (interpreting new stimuli and building a mental model), and *memory* (comparing current stimuli to recalled information from previous exposure to the environment).

Just as wayfinding in the physical world is difficult without the aid of compass, chronograph, GPS, or signposts, well-constructed virtual environments may also be too complex for the user to independently identify what sources of information will best guide their travel. Furthermore, complex virtual environments are prone to causing disorientation and inaccurate perceptions of depth, especially if the available locomotion strategies cause a mismatch between the ocular and vestibular systems. As a result, virtual environments benefit from the inclusion of *wayfinding aids*, which assist users in forming mental models and maintaining a sense of bearing. There are two primary types of wayfinding aids:

**Environmental wayfinding aids** are sources of navigational information that are diegetically (see Section 8.1.1) present in the virtual environment, and whose existence is justified in the context of the overall experience. Examples include road signs, buildings, trees, terrain changes, and other unique signifiers. Environmental wayfinding aids are often visual, but other wayfinding aids exist, such as auditory (the sound of traffic indicating the presence of a nearby road), tactile (bumps on a sidewalk indicating a curb), or olfactory (following the smell of a bakery).

**Personal wayfinding aids** are sources of navigational information carried with the user, like a map or a compass. These may be diegetically present in the virtual environment, or they may be part of an overlay or heads-up display (HUD), like a mini-map, goal indicator, or route marker.

**Mini-maps and game mechanics**

A mini-map is a small representation of the game world that the user can see. Traditional gaming scenarios usually situate the mini-map on the user's HUD or makes the map diegetically available on a tool (like a handheld screen or GPS) available to the avatar, and subsequently seen by the user. Mini-maps are usually top-down and usually two dimensional, appearing much like a traditional map or GPS display in the physical world. Topographical features may be indicated by lines or shading, but the location of the avatar and objects or enemies in the world is represented in two dimensions. As such, players may not have complete information, such as which floor of a building an enemy is on. VR provides the opportunity for three-dimensional mini-maps, which can be used not just for information display but also for interaction. The "world-within-world" design pattern offers the user the chance to interact with the mini-map and in some cases even interact with the game world directly through the mini-map. "A fisherman's tale" (Innerspace VR/Vertigo Games, 2019) provides a compelling example of this design pattern. A fisherman is in a shack, and on the table is a model of the shack he has been working on. When he lifts the roof of the model, the roof of the shack he is in lifts, and he gazes up to see an enormous version of himself holding the roof. Likewise, down in the model, he sees a tiny version of himself interacting with an even smaller model of the same shack. The game allows clever gameplay events where one version of the fisherman can pass objects to a smaller or larger version, similarly acquiring a smaller or larger version of the item.

If an environment lacks wayfinding aids, or the structural model of its wayfinding aids conflicts with the user's interpretation of previous environments, then it may be necessary to alleviate the process of mental mapping and simply display the information directly. In such circumstances, personal wayfinding aids are ideal. A map system on a HUD that updates in real time and displays the user's position, for example, ensures that the user can easily identify their location regardless of the degree to which their mental model of the environment has developed. A compass is another alternative, which provides a sense of direction without being tied to environmental stimuli. Due to the relative ease of operating a compass, especially while in motion, a compass can be implemented as a physical object within the environment. Depending on the context, this may be a more favourable design choice than a non-diegetic HUD element with respect to inducing the sensation of presence.

### 10.2.3.1 Markers

A *marker* is an object or interface element which helps a user remember or navigate to a location. Markers may be added by the user themselves, or by an agent or task within the experience. Markers straddle the line between environmental and personal wayfinding aids, because they can appear on local maps or out in the world, or both. An object becomes a marker when it is used to navigate—thus a building can be a marker if the navigation task includes "turn right at the bakery." Markers can exist non-diegetically in the form of pushpins or coloured shapes on a HUD map, or diegetically in the form of flags and territory markings. Markers can also take on the form of trails, which suggest a path to take rather than a location to find. If trails are marked by directional cues, such as footprints or arrows, then they can provide even more information.

Markers enhance the user's ability to develop a mental model of the virtual environment. Providing users with numerous markup options with respect to form, colour, and size provides the opportunity for a "legend" to be established, which can improve spatial comprehension. As well, providing a variety of marker types enables users to use different types of markers for different purposes, either defined by the application or by the user themselves. For instance, users may decide to use yellow markers to indicate areas that have already been visited, while cyan markers indicate areas that look interesting and need to be visited later. Experiences which afford such a degree of interactive analysis can accelerate wayfinding and ensure that minimal time is lost due to travel-related confusion.

## 10.3 ARTIFICIAL LOCOMOTION STRATEGIES

In the physical world, locomotion is simple. We walk, run, roll, or ride to get from one place to another. Sometimes, we are in control of where we are going, and sometimes, someone (or something) else makes those decisions for us. In the virtual world, we are not constrained to these methods, and therefore there are a large variety of possibilities when it comes to transitioning our agency from one place to another.

One of the primary factors for choosing a locomotion technique is its tendency to cause VR sickness. Any kind of situation where the user's eyes see one thing, and their vestibular system feels another, can lead to feelings of nausea and dizziness, as described in more detail in Section 10.6. For this reason, many developers choose locomotion techniques that are less prone to causing VR sickness. Because some users have developed "VR legs" and are less susceptible to VR sickness, developers often add several locomotion techniques for the user to choose from, which can also lead to confusion and differential accessibility (see Section 8.5).

We begin by considering the locomotion methods that are inherited from traditional flat-screen games and experiences and are very different from walking in the real world. We refer to these techniques as **artificial locomotion**, where the user themselves remains largely stationary, in the physical world, and travel in the virtual world is invoked by some type of gesture or control interaction. These are in contrast to **physical locomotion (described later in this chapter**, where the user must move in some way in the physical world, for their avatar to move in the virtual world).

The advantages of artificial locomotion are that the user can stay in one place in the physical world, meaning the technique is more useful for small playspaces, and more generalizable for users with different playspaces or ambulatory abilities. Users can travel across large virtual spaces, and users do not experience the fatigue associated with physical locomotion like walking and running. Although artificial locomotion strategies tend to be easy to use, they are often unfamiliar at the start, which means training may be necessary, and interaction reminders may need to be available. Artificial locomotion tends to have lower plausibility than physical techniques (since artificial motion techniques in general do not exist in the physical world), and occasionally artificial locomotion can lead to coupling of tasks, since a controller or gesture may be used for both moving and interacting, or a movement may be tied to an interaction or vice versa.

Artificial strategies can be broken down into **continuous motion** methods, which allow the view to change smoothly as the user drifts through the virtual world, and **discrete motion** methods which make the user's view jump from location to location or direction to direction. Additionally, these methods include options for whether the user is in control of the motion or not and how the motion is explained in the narrative.

**Inverse Locomotion**

While the majority of artificial locomotion strategies are framed as moving the user's viewpoint within the virtual space, there are sometimes when it can make conceptual sense to imagine the space itself being moved, rather than the user's point of view. This is called **inverse locomotion** and can take many forms. In some cases, inverse locomotion can be perceptually identical to regular user-centric locomotion, and although the user is controlling the movement of the land rather than the movement of the avatar, they can't tell the difference (See Section 4.1.8). If the user can control more than just the position of the viewpoint, inverse locomotion becomes more useful as a concept. With the use of two hands, the position, orientation, and scale of the world can be modified. In some implementations, the environment can be continuously moved by alternating grab-and-pull actions with each hand, much like flick scrolling through a document on a touchscreen device. This can be effective for experiences involving data manipulation and visualization, or rapidly exploring areas of interest from arbitrary viewpoints, for example when issuing commands to units on a battlefield in a strategy game. Developers must be cautious, though, because the unique mechanics required for inverse locomotion can carry a higher learning curve.

## 10.3.1 Voluntary Continuous Motion (VCM)

The user's viewpoint moves smoothly through the virtual world, and the user is in direct control of that movement. VCM can be suitable for VR experiences where exploration of a vast environment is necessary, such as an open-world platformer, or for experiences where the user's movements must be precise, such as a first-person combat game. Advantages include ease of use and familiarity, especially when the input is a joystick, as this button mapping is likely similar to that of countless flat-screen video games the user may be familiar with. Disadvantages include moderate risk of inducing VR sickness, although the increased level control delegated to the user can mitigate this, and reduced biomechanical symmetry depending on the method of implementation. This may force certain tasks to be coupled by the same action, which decreases intuitiveness to the user. Some examples of VCM implementations are listed here:

**Gaze-directed VCM.** The direction of the user's gaze specifies the forward vector for motion. In other words, pushing the joystick forward will move the user in the direction in which they are currently looking. This should be combined with the ability to *strafe* or move along the left, right, and backward vectors, based on the position of the joystick. There is usually no need for the input device to control rotation or vertical translation, as this can be handled by any HMD with six degrees of freedom. Indeed, if rotation is controlled both with gaze direction and with the joystick, this can add to user confusion. Gaze-directed

VCM is a familiar metaphor for experienced gamers, especially if motion is constrained to the two horizontal axes, and it does not require any peripheral hardware. Its primary weakness is the fact that the user is unable to look in one direction and travel forward in another direction. As such, gaze-directed steering may not be suitable for tasks requiring movement relative to objects in the virtual environment.

**Hand-directed VCM.** The orientation of the user's hand or controller specifies the forward vector for motion. This can be more natural than gaze-directed VCM because the user can look around the virtual world while travelling in a different direction. The user's sense of proprioception can inform them on the direction in which their hand is pointing—even if the HMD occludes explicit vision of it. Hand-directed VCM mitigates the coupling issue that was described for gaze-directed VCM and is generally more flexible as well. Hand-directed VCM has the potential to induce strain on the user's hand, wrist, and shoulder due to prolonged stretching. The other challenge appears when a user must use an object while they are travelling: if the user attempts to throw an object or place it in a precise location, their travel direction may be affected, even if using the other hand. In an extreme example, the user may need to aim a tool or weapon with one hand and dictate the direction of travel with the other hand. Since both actions involve precisely extending and orienting an arm, the user's cognitive load may increase in such experiences.

**Torso-directed VCM.** The orientation of the user's torso specifies the forward vector for motion. Typically, a tracking device is attached to the user's waist, and the forward orientation of this device is relayed to the VR system. This decouples gaze direction and travel direction, while also leaving the user's hands free to manipulate objects, but requires an additional controller to detect the direction of the hips or torso. An alternative (called "Lean-directed VCM," see also "Human Joystick" in Section 10.4.3) allows the system to measure the direction in which the user is leaning, and use that to indicate the direction of travel. This can lead to instability in the user's stance and can make it difficult for the user to reorient their direction of view more than a few degrees while travelling.

**Hardware-directed VCM.** A steering prop is integrated into the virtual environment to specify the forward vector for motion. This typically occurs in flight simulators and other experiences that simulate vehicles controlled by hardware, but can also be used in other experiences with standard VR controller hardware. The direction of the user's motion is influenced by the manner in which the user operates the external device. Cockpit-based steering props can simulate driving a car, being at the helm of a ship, or flying an aircraft. Delegating the control of movement to a dedicated hardware device can add realism (since sensorimotor contingencies are more accurately supported) as well providing haptic and restive feedback to the user, depending on the hardware. Such hardware interfaces can be expensive, and the physical interface is well aligned with the virtual interface only in scenarios that are supported: driving a car with a hands-on throttle and stick (HOTAS) is likely to be non-intuitive, especially if the virtual avatar is holding on to a steering wheel.

It is worth noting that many VR developers have attempted to recreate such steering props in a purely virtual manner. These virtual steering devices may assist users in understanding the interface of a vehicle, but are generally much more difficult to control due to their lack of proprioceptive force feedback. Nonetheless, the inclusion of a realistic interface for a vehicle in virtual space is useful in preventing VR sickness, as the interface is a constant frame of reference for the user.

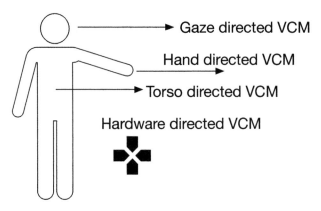

Figure 10.2: Options for controlling voluntary continuous motion.

### 10.3.2 Involuntary Continuous Motion (ICM)

Rather than the user controlling their movement, the user is passively moved through the virtual environment without the intervention of input or agency. Since there is no input from the user, this method is easy to implement and highly accessible. Although ICM can be thematically appropriate for cinematic experiences or experiences where the user is (for example) a passenger in a vehicle they are not controlling, this method has a high risk of inducing VR sickness, since not only is there conflict between visual and vestibular input, but the user cannot anticipate the motion, only react to it. Consistent linear ICM can be fairly comfortable or be adapted to quickly, but rapid changes in direction and high rates of speed can lead to the onset of VR sickness. Common mitigation techniques (discussed below) can help, including reduced field of vision and visual context cues.

**VR Roller Coasters**

When a VR enthusiast wants to convince one of their friends that VR is amazing, they will usually select a short, easy experience to show off the technology. Often, this experience is a virtual roller coaster. It seems ideal—the user does not have to do anything or be taught any controls; all they have to do is sit and experience the wonder. A track extends in front of them, and they ride around a fantastical coaster that snakes its way through alien landscapes or a dense jungle of skyscrapers. The VR novice sits down and puts on the headset and is amazed by the visuals, but as soon as the ride starts, they are very quickly nauseous. The VR enthusiast, of course, has developed a resistance to VR sickness over many hours of gameplay, but as a first experience, a roller coaster is almost guaranteed to induce VR sickness if the user is prone to it at all. It is somewhat ironic that what seems like a great first experience may in fact be discouraging people from experimenting further with VR.

### 10.3.3 Discrete Motion

While continuous motion is more conceptually straightforward, the fact that it often can lead to VR sickness has caused many developers to consider discrete techniques, where the user's viewpoint jumps from place to place. The most common implementation of this technique is **teleportation**, where the user specifies a destination within the virtual environment, via some input device, and is instantly or near-instantly transported to the new destination. Although initially developed to avoid continuous motion that leads to VR sickness, teleportation can be an effective locomotion technique in itself, especially when considering the challenges of traversing vast virtual environments.

There are two design decisions to be made when implementing teleportation: how to choose a destination and how to transition to the destination. Selecting a destination can be done using any pointing technique (see Section 11.4.1.2), and teleportation targets can either be individual points on the landscape or the entire surface in front of the user. Targets may also be range limited, if it is important for the situation that users not be able to travel too far. An alternative could be to select the destination by choosing a direction and a distance or even to select a direction and then to jump a standardized distance in that direction. Some options for destination selection are shown in Figure 10.3.

Usually, the orientation of the user's view is maintained between the origin and the destination of the transition; however in some cases it may be useful to allow the user to reorient as they transition. Jumping behind an enemy is not as useful if you then have to turn around to face them, but if you can turn around as you are jumping, you can be both in the right place and facing the right direction. Figure 10.4 shows the difference between teleportation with and without a rotation.

Once a destination has been chosen, the user's viewpoint is then shifted to the new location. This shift in view can itself be discrete or continuous. The simplest and quickest transition is to immediately change the view with no indication or delay, often called a "snap change." This works well for rotating in place (a snap turn), but can be very disorienting for teleportation. A "blink" is a slightly delayed transition, where the user's view is momentarily occluded, often by fading out and back in again. Allowing the user to maintain their view during the transition can significantly reduce

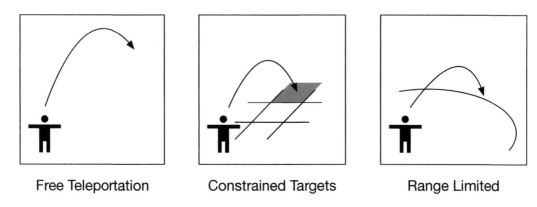

Figure 10.3: Options for selecting a destination for teleportation.

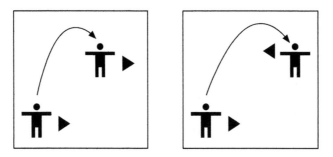

Figure 10.4: Teleportation without rotation (left) is restrictive, but teleportation with rotation (right) requires additional control and can be disorienting.

disorientation, because the user can see where they were and where they are going; however, this method becomes very similar to ICM and can lead to VR sickness. A faster transition, with smooth changes, can mitigate these challenges. Another clever solution to the problem of transitioning the user's viewpoint is **portalling**, where the user can see the view as it will be from the new location as they prepare to teleport. Portalling sometimes requires a surface to transition through, with a portal on the surface revealing the new location behind it; alternatively, a spherical portal can be placed showing the viewpoint of the new location from any direction around the portal. Portalling removes the requirement for transitioning from the old location to the new location, but can add complexity to both implementation and interaction.

While teleportation can be a versatile and comfortable alternative to continuous motion, it comes with a few drawbacks. It can be difficult for a user to accurately control the destination of a teleportation, especially if the target is far away (See Fitt's law, Figure 11.24), and it can be disorientating, especially if the method of transitioning the viewpoint is not carefully considered. Teleportation can also lead to reduced sense of presence, since teleportation is unlike any method of locomotion used in the real world. It can be seen by the user as implausible and takes away from the feeling of being in a realistic world. Many developers make a special effort to justify the existence of a teleportation system in-world, in order to allow users to suspend their disbelief. This can be achieved by giving the user a teleportation tool, like a handheld beaming device or a glove; however, such a justification can add additional design criteria which may conflict with the usability and comfort criteria described above.

## 10.4  PHYSICAL LOCOMOTION STRATEGIES

Physical locomotion encompasses methods of travel in which the movement of the avatar within the virtual world is directly tied to movement of the player in the physical world. In some cases, this can be as simple as allowing the user to walk around and have that change in location reflected in the virtual space; this can also be as complicated as full body tracking to calculate the speed and direction the avatar should move based on how the user is moving in the physical world.

Physical locomotion strategies are both highly intuitive and highly plausible, since the user is employing very familiar actions already conceptually aligned with getting from place to place. Additionally, physical locomotion strategies are (usually) much less prone to VR sickness because stimulation of the vestibular system is more closely aligned with what the user sees as they travel. These methods are constrained, however, by the physicality of the user, and therefore can be less versatile and accessible and contribute to fatigue or balance issues. Additionally, if walking in VR is tied to walking in the real world, the range of travel is bounded by the size of the playspace. Some physical locomotion strategies require expensive or bulky hardware that may be impractical from a consumer perspective, and these methods tend to exclude to non-ambulatory users.

Physical locomotion strategies can be categorized as **gait-direct** techniques, in which the user walks around a physical space and that motion is translated into motion in the virtual space; **gait negation** techniques, in which additional hardware like treadmills or low-friction surfaces allow the user to walk somewhat naturally in-place; and **indirect** techniques, where some other aspect of the user's motion in the physical world is translated into movement in the virtual world.

These strategies can also be considered based on their ability to mitigate VR sickness. In general, any technique that involves physical motion will lead to a reduction in the conflict between the vestibular and ocular systems, but the more closely aligned the motion of the user, the lower the likelihood of experiencing VR sickness. Gait-direct techniques tend to mitigate VR sickness most completely, because the motion of the user's physical body is most closely aligned with the changes in the user's vision as a result of motion in the virtual world. Gait negation techniques can also work well, but are highly dependent on the responsiveness and implementation of the negation technique itself. Indirect methods are highly variable, depending on the techniques as described below. All physical motion techniques are effective in mitigating VR sickness to the extent that the technique fulfils these criteria:

- The user is in direct control of the direction and speed of travel.

- The physical motion matches the virtual motion.

- The locomotion is perceived as natural and plausible.

Plausibly is important here because the user will be more comfortable with a particular technique to the extent that they can use it without thinking about it, and therefore their motions will become more natural, and hence more closely aligned with their expectations in the virtual space.

Each technique has benefits and drawbacks, and developers may benefit from considering modifications to their planned experiences to enable the use of more natural techniques. For example, if a virtual space were the same shape and size as the physical space a user is in, gait-direct techniques may be applicable in all circumstances, and the user's experience would greatly benefit. Not all users share the same size playspace, however, and thus it is usually appropriate to implement a variety or combination of techniques.

### 10.4.1  Gait-Direct Implementations

The most natural and comfortable methods of locomotion are the methods that are most familiar. Most people walk to get places, and walking creates motion in the user's headset that is easily translated to well-aligned changes in the visual field of the virtual environment. Walking also requires no training, no controller, no decision-making, and no conscious effort. We must remember that not all users are ambulatory, and some may have challenges walking for long periods of time, but in general, walking is close to an optimal locomotion technique for VR experiences, assuming the user has the space for it.

**Room-Scale Walking.** The user walks through the virtual environment. Real-world displacement is directly mapped to virtual displacement, which unfortunately means that the locomotive range of room-scale walking is limited to the user's play area. As well, room-scale walking is less accessible to users for whom walking may be a problem, than most artificial strategies. Room-scale walking is one of the few strategies that appropriately stimulates the vestibular system, meaning there is little to no risk of VR sickness. The walking metaphor is also advantaged with respect to intuitiveness, accuracy, sense of bearing, and presence. On its own, room-scale walking is best suited for small virtual environments; however, if combined with a reorientation strategy, it may be a viable choice for larger environments as well.

**Modified Walking.** The user walks around their playspace as in room-scale walking, but their movement in virtual space is not directly aligned with their movement in the physical world. Small changes to the user's perception of virtual space encourage them to stay within the bounds of their physical space. There are a wide variety of redirected walking techniques, some examples of which are listed here:

**Scaled walking.** The user's motion in virtual space is different from their motion in physical space. Usually, small steps in the physical world are translated to larger steps in the virtual world, which can increase the range of travel but reduce plausibility

**Redirected walking.** The user's direction in virtual space is different from their direction in physical space. A user may walk in a straight line in virtual space, but the virtual view is subtly changed to encourage the user to change the direction they are walking in the physical world, orbiting around the centre of their physical playspace. Users quickly lose directional reference while in VR and can be convincingly redirected by the virtual space without losing plausibility.

Figure 10.5 shows an example of redirected walking. A user is presented with a virtual world, and they begin to walk forward. The virtual world shifts its orientation very slowly and subtly, requiring the user to turn their head in the other direction in order to continue walking in the direction they perceive as forward. The result is that the user is redirected in a curving path around their room, while in the virtual space, they feel as though they are walking in a straight line beyond what their physical space would allow. Because the changes to orientation are gradual and subtle, the directional sensing of the vestibular system has low fidelity compared to the visual system, and thus the body can be tricked into changing direction.

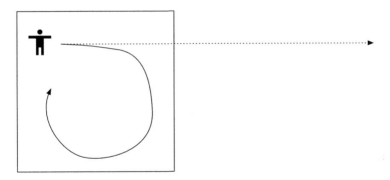

Figure 10.5: Redirected walking.

**Contextual Redirection.** The user is prevented from walking beyond the physical bounds of their playspace by events or objects in the virtual world. These events can then distract the user while the virtual world shifts subtly around them, allowing them to continue to walk after the event, allowing the virtual world to seem larger than the physical playspace.

**Portalling.** The user walks to a doorway which opens into another room, but the doorway encourages them to turn around, thus expanding the size of the virtual space while continuing to restrict motion within the physical space.

**Walking in Place.** The user moves their feet to simulate walking while remaining in the same location in their playspace. There can be some disagreement as to whether this is a gait-direct technique or an indirect technique, since the user isn't actually walking, and depending on the implementation it may even be considered a gait negation technique, since the user is walking but not moving. Regardless of the classification, the technique is popular because it is almost as natural as room-scale walking, without requiring a restriction or modification of the virtual space. Walking in place can be difficult to implement, however, since most VR equipment does not track the feet. If a user is considering adding foot tracking to implement walking in place, a more comprehensive gait negation technique could also be used without too much extra effort. Without additional hardware, walking in place can be identified by the up-and-down movement of the headset, and a more aggressive walking technique (like marching) can be encouraged to improve the reliability of this tracking. The direction of motion must be manually determined, since walking in place does not result in any actual motion. Similarly to VCM, the direction of motion can be dictated by the user's gaze, torso orientation, pointing direction, or controller input.

### 10.4.2   Gait Negation Implementations

When a user walks, the natural human gait results in forward motion. Walking in place restricts that motion but changes the user's gait. Gait negation[2] is any technique which attempts to remove (or *negate*) the forward motion of a user's walking without unnecessarily modifying the user's gait. Gait negation usually requires specialized hardware that allows a user's feet to travel past the ground rather than pushing against the ground. The most common and familiar hardware that accomplishes gait negation is the **treadmill**.

**Simple Treadmills.** The simplest way to negate forward motion of the human stride is to use a treadmill. Basic treadmill locomotion in VR is straightforward to implement, but has significant limitations. First, a treadmill allows forward motion but does not provide any mechanism for direction, orientation, strafing, or other non-forward motion, and so the developer would need to apply techniques from continuous motion to provide direction. Second, the treadmill controls the speed of walking, rather than the user, and so this basic treadmill locomotion suffers from poor plausibility. The user must manually adjust the speed of the treadmill to walk faster or slower. Treadmills are more likely to be found in users' homes, however, and walking on a treadmill while using a VR experience can improve cardiovascular health.

**Alternative Treadmills.** Treadmills are most commonly found in exercise gyms or in home workout areas, but other machines that simulate motion can also be found there, including rowing machines, stationary bicycles, and stair climbers. Any of these devices could be connected to a virtual experience to improve the experience of exercise or to improve the experience of travel within a VR scenario. Additional features can be added to such treadmills (and to simple

---

[2]It is not really the gait that is being negated, rather the motion resulting from the gait. The term is somewhat awkward, but it is in popular use and has a nice verbal symmetry to it, so we will continue to use it.

treadmills to further improve plausibility), such as a fan to simulate the feeling of wind as you cycle through France.

**Omnidirectional Treadmills.** Simple treadmills only provide forward motion, but in a VR scenario, it is reasonable to expect a user to be able to walk forward, backward, left, and right. An omnidirectional treadmill allows motion along both horizontal axes. Such treadmills may be passive, relying on the user's mass and momentum to move, or active, being directly controlled by the VR system which moves the surface of the treadmill whenever a change in the user's direction is observed. Passive omnidirectional treadmills are typically constructed with a low-friction surface and concave structure and may require the user to don special low-friction footwear, as well as motion trackers on their feet. These treadmills are often called "socks-in-a-bowl" and also require a frame and gantry to support the user as they lean in whatever direction they are virtually travelling.

Active omnidirectional treadmills look more like simple treadmills, but have a surface that can move left and right as well as forward and backward. These treadmills attempt to anticipate the motion of the user and move the surface accordingly, but often suffer from latency and balance issues, as adjustment of the treadmill's surface is a mechanical process. A harness or safety railing is often present to prevent users from losing their balance.

In general, omnidirectional treadmills demonstrate promise in the area of enabling unrestricted "walking" in virtual environments. Such devices enable a walking cycle that is very similar to our natural gait and, depending on the durability and construction, can support running, crouching, and jumping as well. These devices are typically large and expensive, require a dedicated space, and may be restrictive on who can reasonably make use of them.

### 10.4.3 Indirect Implementations

While gait-relative locomotion techniques attempt to replicate human walk cycles in some form or other, indirect locomotion techniques make use of other motions in the physical world to create travel in the virtual world. Almost any trackable physical motion can be translated to virtual locomotion, but some common techniques are presented here.

**Human Joystick.** As the name implies, this technique reinterprets the users' upright body as a joystick, and the user can lean or shift in one direction or another to invoke travel in that direction. The system keeps track of the relative position of the user's head, using this information to control horizontal direction. The more the user leans or shifts, the faster the invoked travel. This technique is compatible with small play spaces and can work even when the user is seated, increasing accessibility. While the natural mapping of direction of lean to direction of travel can increase presence, this method is prone to VR sickness, since the user sees motion but does not feel it. User agency reduces

(a) A passive omnidirectional treadmill supports the user's centre of mass. *Maurizio Pesce, CCBY2.0*

(b) Users wear low-friction footwear with motion trackers. *Maurizio Pesce, CCBY2.0*

Figure 10.6: Passive omnidirectional treadmill.

VR sickness somewhat, but other mitigation techniques as described below may be necessary. Additionally, if the user takes a step rather than just leaning, the VR sickness effect can be reduced. A challenge with this method is that for the user to stop, they must return to the location the system considers the "centre" of the "joystick." Hardware joysticks use springs to automatically centre when released, and if a hardware joystick malfunctions and doesn't return to the centre, the system experiences drift. With a human joystick, there is no automatic centring, so the user must seek the centre manually; to make matters worse, people usually perform such local navigation tasks visually, and the whole point of this system is to move the user's viewpoint to another area. Finding the centre again can be very difficult, so a large dead zone may be necessary; otherwise users may experience involuntary motion as a result.

**Arm Cycling.** Related to walking in place, this technique replicates the upper body motion of walking without requiring the feet to move. Hands are commonly tracked in modern VR systems, while feet are not, and so arm cycling can be accomplished with standard hardware rather than requiring additional third-party equipment. Forward motion is applied to the user's viewpoint when the user swings their arms, moving the VR system's tracked controllers (or employing the system's hand tracking). Turning can be accomplished using any of the techniques described for VCM. Alternatively, the direction of travel can be indicated by the vertical displacement between the two controllers at the apex of motion, or the difference in amplitude or speed between the motion of the two controllers.

Arm cycling is quick to learn and easy to use and is surprisingly effective at mitigating VR sickness, since the user is not only in control of their motion but also experiences some vestibular displacement as a result of the arm motion—users naturally tend to bounce up and down a bit when they swing their arms. As with other physical methods, the increased physical effort can improve cardiovascular health but can also lead to fatigue and be a barrier for persons with physical disabilities, but this technique can also work well when seated, increasing accessibility. One additional problem with arm cycling is that it can restrict the utility of other interactions a user might need to do while they are travelling. It's hard to aim a tool or a weapon or activate a switch or look at a wrist display, while you are swinging your arms about. One-arm swinging may need to be temporarily invoked, which may change the utility of different steering mechanisms

### Non-Walking Locomotion

Although most locomotion techniques discussed here replicate the process of moving horizontally across a landscape, many experiences have been developed that use artificial or physical locomotion strategies to move in different ways. Rock climbing simulators allow a user to reach up with one hand, grab the side of the wall, and pull themselves up to the next handhold. Kayaking and rowing simulators make use of paddles or oars to propel a boat along a waterway. Other types of unusual locomotion involve control of a vehicle like a sailboat or a parachute, which require detailed hand motions that serve as controls to a motion technique, one step removed from actual locomotion. A person may swing through the jungle on vines, or through the city on spiderwebs, or skateboard along a street or snowboard down a mountain. In each of these cases, specific actions by the user serve as direct or indirect control to the user's viewpoint moving through the virtual space, and whenever the viewpoint moves through the space, consideration must be made for usability and to mitigate VR sickness.

## 10.5  QUANTIFYING LOCOMOTIVE EFFICACY

With a diverse collection of locomotion techniques available, it is worthwhile to consider how a developer might choose between them. In the descriptions above, we have noted some advantages and disadvantages of each, but what follows is a collection of metrics that can be used to evaluate these techniques and others based on the constraints of the specific VR experience being considered for a locomotion mechanic.

### 10.5.1  Locomotive Range and Scope

In the previous section, we explained that the major drawback of room-scale walking and walking-adjacent travel in VR experiences is that its range is limited to the size of the user's play space, which results in two common problems. First, users sometimes overstep the boundaries of their play area when walking through a virtual environment, which causes presence breaks at minimum and potential injury or property damage at worst. Secondly, long-distanced travel is impossible without the inclusion of a reorientation strategy or another locomotion method. This limits the scope of virtual environments that only afford room-scale walking, as the user's overall experience may suffer if there is a disconnect between what is visible and what is accessible.

**Visible range** is the area of a virtual environment that the user can see (or otherwise sense), while **locomotive range** is the area of a virtual environment that the user can access via a particular locomotion strategy. Locomotive range varies depending on the size of the environment, but it is not dependent on the speed or control of the locomotion method in question, only by whether or not you can get there. Indoor virtual environments have small ranges (both visual and locomotive), while exterior experiences have much larger ranges. In an ideal implementation, you can go anywhere you can see, and visible range would equal locomotive range. Locomotive range might be restricted by the locomotion technique being considered; however, there are also conceptual or narrative reasons that may limit the range of where a player can travel in a world. It may not be optimal to allow a player to travel to the top of a mountain or across the sea, and indeed it may not be practical to implement accessibility to all regions that can be seen. On the other hand, **open-world** games are specifically designed to allow a player to go almost anywhere they can see, and limitations are usually narrative or diegetic, rather than mechanical—if a character has no climbing equipment, they cannot climb the large wall that is in front of them, and instead they must find another way up or around the mountain. Additionally, users may expect that every object they see be interactable, and this may be a similar challenge to the developer—either every object the user sees can be manipulated or manipulable objects need to be signified in some way. In the same way, either all locations the user can see should be reachable or areas the user can't reach should be signified in some way.

The **locomotive scope** of a strategy is the ratio of its locomotive range to the environment's visual range. This is a measure of the difference between what a user can see and where a user can go. A smaller locomotive scope means the user can see lots of areas they can't go to, which can be frustrating unless explained diegetically. When a person looks up at the sky, they generally don't assume they can visit the stars; however, if they are playing a space simulator, it might be more reasonable to assume that they can visit the stars they can see. Similarly, if the background environment of a simulation shows rolling hills, but it is made clear to the user that they can only visit locations that are within a set boundary, this is not a reduction in locomotive scope.

---

**Locomotive Scope Example**

Imagine a VR experience where the user is inside a large room, with interesting things on each wall. The experience supports room-scale walking, scaled walking, and teleportation. If the virtual room were, say, 4 metres by 5 metres, the visible range of the experience would be $4 \times 5 = 20$ square metres. If the user's physical playspace for VR was, say, 2 metres on each side, room-scale walking would give them a locomotive range of $2 \times 2 = 4$ square metres. The locomotive scope of room-scale walking would therefore be $\frac{4}{20} = \frac{1}{5}$ or 20%, meaning that a user could only experience a fifth of the room that they could see if they were walking; depending on where they started, they may not be able to access any of the interesting things on the walls at all. For scaled walking, if every step the user took in the physical world was stretched two-to-one in the virtual world, the user would be able to reach $4 \times 4 = 16$ square metres, resulting in a locomotive scope of $\frac{16}{20} = \frac{4}{5}$ or 80%. The user could get almost anywhere in the room, but there would still be a fifth of the room they couldn't get to. Finally, teleportation would provide direct access to the whole room, for a locomotive scope of 100%. The trade-offs with these methods must be carefully considered, and it may be most appropriate to implement a hybrid approach, where the user could teleport to a corner of the room and then walk around interacting with things and then teleport back to the far side of the room when necessary. Figure 10.7 shows the different locomotive scopes for each option.

---

Thus, based on the principles of locomotive range and scope, gait-direct techniques have a disadvantage over other techniques, and artificial techniques tend to be favoured when range is an issue, as they alleviate the presence-breaking disconnect that can occur between visible range and locomotive range. The trade-off, however, is that locomotion methods that are not one-to-one have the potential to induce VR sickness. Nonetheless, some gait-relative techniques like redirected walking have the potential to allow increased scope while still maintaining the high degree of presence that walking allows.

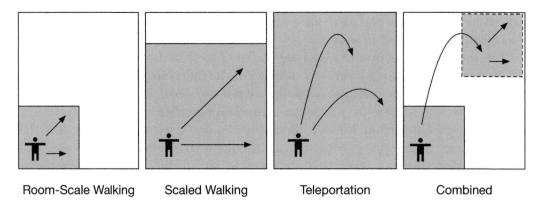

| Room-Scale Walking | Scaled Walking | Teleportation | Combined |

Figure 10.7: An example showing locomotive scope for different travel techniques.

## 10.5.2 Locomotive Utility

**Locomotive utility** refers to the overall suitability of a locomotion strategy for any particular VR experience. It can be represented as a function of performance-based characteristics that are indicative of the strategy's effectiveness and usefulness, but not directly tied to usability considerations like ergonomics or the prevention of VR sickness. The key characteristics of locomotive utility are as follows:

**Range,** described above, measures the extent of the virtual environment that can be accessed by a locomotion strategy. The locomotive range of gait-related and indirect physical strategies is directly dependent on the size of the play area, while boundaries usually need to be established on the backend of the experience for the other subcategories. In limited environments, all strategies are likely to have full locomotive range. In environments whose size exceeds that of the play space, only room-scale walking will have insufficient range, as scaling and redirection methods are likely able to alleviate the space disparity.

**Velocity** relates to how quickly travel is completed after it is invoked through a certain locomotion strategy expressed as a function of virtual displacement over time. Artificial strategies generally possess higher velocities than physical strategies, with discrete strategies being the fastest, as motion occurs near-instantaneously, and indirect physical strategies usually being the slowest, as their required motions are less intuitive than those of gait-related strategies.

**Fidelity** expresses a locomotion strategy's ability to perform small increments of travel. It is a contributor to accuracy, since small displacements enable precise error correction without affecting the user's sense of bearing. Room-scale walking has the highest fidelity, as displacement and rotation are mapped from the real world to the virtual environment one-to-one. Continuous artificial strategies generally possess high fidelity as well, while modified walking strategies may perform slightly worse depending on the sensitivity of the scaling or redirection algorithm. Non-continuous artificial strategies such as teleportation have the lowest fidelity and, thus, the least reliable accuracy.

**Adjustability** describes the extent to which the various components of locomotion can be tuned by the user, especially while they are in use. Factors influencing a locomotion strategy's adjustability include the ability to change one's position while rotating, the ability to change one's orientation while translating, the possible speeds of translation and rotation, and whether termination of travel occurs abruptly or not. In contrast to the previous three factors of utility, it is difficult to establish general principles of adjustability for each locomotive subclass. Instead, not only is adjustability strategy dependent, in some cases, it may even be implementation dependent. For example, all of the techniques described within VCM enable a variety of travel speeds; gaze-directed VCM couples travel direction and the direction the user is looking, while torso-directed VCM is more cumbersome to terminate than the hardware-controlled implementations. Thus, gaze- and torso-directed VCM have lower adjustability than the other types of VCM. Similarly, due to the latency issues present in active omnidirectional treadmills, their adjustability is lower than their passive counterparts. Furthermore, implementations of teleportation that enable explicit destination and orientation selection have higher adjustability than those with only explicit destination selection.

## The Velocity-Fidelity Continuum

A locomotion strategy can possess both high range and high velocity, or high range and high fidelity; however, high velocity and high fidelity are almost always mutually exclusive (see Fitt's law, Figure 11.24). Think of velocity and fidelity as components of a microscope. Velocity enables swift travel to the approximate area of one's destination, much like the coarse focus of a microscope is used to quickly bring an image into near focus. Meanwhile, fidelity facilitates precise correction of the subtle inaccuracies of high-velocity locomotion, in the same way that the fine focus accomplishes the necessary adjustments to bring an image into full focus. In order to ensure that both high-velocity and high-fidelity travel are possible, especially in vast environments, it may be necessary to include multiple locomotion strategies in the same experience.

Sometimes, certain utility factors are more desirable than others. For example, if exploration and searching tasks are necessary for an experience, then high range and velocity are essential. Similarly, experiences with reaction-based actions, like dodging attacks or defeating waves of enemies, are most enjoyable if their locomotion strategies feature high fidelity and adjustability. Although trade-offs between the characteristics are usually necessary to some degree, it is still good practice, as much as possible, to design for a balance of range, velocity, fidelity, and adjustability, as such versatility usually results in a higher degree of control for the user. This, in turn, can reinforce the plausibility of a virtual environment and also improve the usability characteristics of the locomotion strategy.

### 10.5.3 Travel and Presence

Presence is maximized when the user interprets the virtual environment as a real location (place illusion), and interactions within the experience as real events happening to them (plausibility illusion). A major component of interpreting an environment as a real place is the ability to move through it in a realistic manner. In the context of sensorimotor contingencies, realistic movement may involve any of the following actions while the user is fixed in the same location in an environment:

**Turning one's head** to look at a different part of the environment

**Strafing one's head** to cause parallax to distinguish foreground stimuli from background stimuli

**Crouching and craning** to look around and behind objects

In addition, the user may choose to move their body in order to take up a new position to get a better view of an object or stimuli in the environment. When the goal of the travel is to collect more information, this aspect of travel is also a sensorimotor contingency.

All of these sensorimotor contingencies have three things in common: they are invoked by physical movements; changes to one's bearing are observed continuously; and the user has full control over the speed and magnitude at which displacement occurs. Unsurprisingly, these aspects pertain to each of the sensory illusions that contribute to presence. Continuous observation of positional and rotational updates based on the user's physical movements represents validation of sensorimotor contingencies, which strengthens place illusion.

Room-scale walking, as a locomotion strategy, will maximize presence, since it corresponds directly to the user's experience of movement in the real world. Redirected walking strategies can also benefit presence if the redirection or scaling is subtle by design; for example, larger arcs are better at masking the fact that redirection is occurring than smaller arcs. Even more extreme methods like non-Euclidean geometries (Section 6.4) may also align with the user's experience of real-world walking, depending on the implementation, since although the virtual environment may not behave realistically, the act of moving through the environment does. Gait negating strategies still perform well with respect to plausibility, since although the user's vestibular system is not stimulated in a way that aligns directly with their motion in the virtual space, the motions are similar, and users can quickly get used to the differences.

Artificial strategies are widely considered to be the least realistic VR locomotion strategies, as they are not invoked by natural motions, there is no synchronization between real and virtual displacement, and vestibular senses are not stimulated at all. Nonetheless, if all other factors point to an artificial strategy being suitable, then continuous methods lead to increased presence compared to discrete methods, even though they can be more prone to causing VR sickness. Low realism is teleportation's greatest weakness as a locomotion strategy, as it performs well in the areas of accessibility, speed, range, adjustability, and VR sickness mitigation. The plausibility of teleportation as a *mechanic* can be circumvented by providing some form of diegesis or in-world justification for it, but as a *locomotion method,* it is often still difficult for users to grasp as reality.

### 10.5.4 Combining Locomotion Strategies

As mentioned previously, implementing different locomotion strategies and allowing the user to combine them can increase the range and adjustability of the experience's overarching locomotion, although it is worthwhile to consider establishing a unified interaction metaphor for invoking each strategy. If the goal is to enhance locomotive range without sacrificing VR sickness mitigation or presence, for example, then principles of room-scale walking, scaled walking, and gaze-based VCM could be combined. In this hypothetical system, the user's real displacement would only be scaled in virtual space if a particular button is held, which has potential to alleviate VR sickness because it provides extra control. Furthermore, presence can be maintained if the scaling mechanic is explained in the game's narrative—perhaps the user is travelling along a conveyor belt that they can turn on or off whenever they please, for example.

Teleportation alone usually results in the user's location changing, while all other aspects (rotation, gaze/view, status) are maintained. If a user needs to be facing a different direction when they arrive, it may be appropriate to combine teleportation with some form of rotation. Preserving the user's original orientation may assist in maintaining a sense of bearing, but requiring the user to look around before choosing their next teleport can extend the process of wayfinding. To implement this combined method, the user needs to be able to control two variables simultaneously: the location of the destination of the teleport and the rotation of the final view as compared to the current view. One possible mapping might be to have the user press the thumbstick to invoke the teleport targeting system, aim the destination by pointing with the controller, and set the destination rotation using the thumbstick. The teleport itself could then be activated by releasing the thumbstick. Such a system would eliminate the synchronization issue and also allow the user to rely on artificial actions for both translation and rotation. In teleportation systems lacking rotation, the user must break a single action into two pieces: teleport and then rotate (either physically or with a controller), which can increase cognitive load.

Combining locomotion strategies may also serve to simplify the interaction and goal forming of the user, although the specific controls may become more complex as a result. There are very few real-world scenarios in which the user will be rapidly shifting from physical motion to passive travel. As such, forcing the user to maintain and switch between multiple locomotion strategies can cause confusion and frustration.

### 10.5.5 Multi-Modal Locomotion Systems

Different users may have different experiences of locomotion. Some users are particularly affected by the physiological effects of motion in VR, while others may appreciate a more rapid and diegetic locomotion technique. For this reason, **multimodal locomotion systems**—systems in which two or more locomotion strategies are implemented and can be evoked simultaneously—enable greater creativity, customization, and expression within the user's movement. There are two main types of multi-modal locomotion systems:

**Complementary locomotion systems** are systems whose locomotion strategies are intended to resolve each other's limitations or deficiencies and are used in different situations. For example, a complementary locomotion system might include teleportation, which has high range but low fidelity, and room-scale walking, which has high fidelity but low range. This system is designed such that users will teleport for long-ranged exploration and search tasks, but walk for short-ranged manoeuvring tasks. The idea is that the deficiencies of one method are complemented by the benefits of the other method. Another example might be implementation of two different teleportation strategies, one to "nudge" the user locally and the other to allow long-distance jumps.

In complementary systems, the locomotion strategies usually map to mutually exclusive use cases, and therefore the intuitiveness of the combination of techniques is not as important. Nonetheless, design recommendations for complementary locomotion systems include simplifying the transitions between the different strategies, establishing a common interaction mechanism whenever possible, and diegetically justifying the presence of any seemingly non-realistic strategy—perhaps even going as far as explaining the connection of two dissimilar strategies in the experience's narrative.

**Supplementary locomotion systems** are systems where two or more locomotion strategies are implemented which serve largely the same purpose. In these cases, the choice of which technique to use may depend on user preference or other factors. One strategy may be preferred over the other(s) for certain types of tasks and manoeuvres. One common supplementary locomotion system is the combination of some form of VCM with teleportation. Both of these strategies have good range and reasonable adjustability, which makes them best suited for exploration and search tasks, but VCM has higher fidelity and affects presence more positively, while teleportation has higher velocity and better VR sickness mitigation. As such, the user may benefit from alternating between these two strategies if the experience suggests different types of travel tasks. Consider a VR dungeon crawler, for example, in which the user travels down labyrinths, solves puzzles, and fights enemies. For tasks that solely involve moving through the environment, the user may prefer teleportation because it is faster than VCM. However, teleportation may be undesirable for combat, since it can cause the user to lose their sense of bearing with respect to the enemy. In these situations, VCM would likely be more suitable.

An important factor to consider when implementing supplementary systems is that the user may initially struggle to understand when a certain strategy is preferred. If this occurs, then a diegetic indication of the preferred strategy may be of assistance. Of course, simply forcing the user to use a particular strategy is an option as well, but we consider this to be poor practice, as it defeats the purpose of multi-modal locomotion systems in the first place. As well, it is better to allow the user to seamlessly switch between any of the system's strategies, as forcing them to pause their session and toggle settings in a menu are both cumbersome and presence breaking. More guidelines on designing for multi-modal locomotion, including specific considerations for when the user should be using a certain strategy, can be found in Section REF.

A final consideration in multi-modal systems is that of equity in competitive gameplay. If two supplementary options are offered to allow a user to choose fidelity over comfort, for example, it may be the case that one locomotion strategy has strategic benefit over the other. In combat scenarios, both teleportation and VCM have benefits and drawbacks, and it may be difficult to balance the advantages given to one over the other. Teleportation, especially combined with rotation, will allow users to sneak behind their opponent, and so a slight time delay may be appropriate for balance. Alternatively, different leagues or leaderboards could be implemented based on which locomotion strategy is used. When multiplayer games become competitive, there is an incentive to gain any edge, and a responsibility for balance on the part of the developer.

## 10.6 PHYSIOLOGICAL EFFECTS OF MOVING IN VR

As has been mentioned several times throughout this chapter, one of the key challenges with locomotion in VR is that sometimes, when people move in VR, they feel sick. This section describes the likely causes of this effect as well as techniques for mitigation.

### 10.6.1 VR Sickness As a Result of Locomotion

In Section 4.1.8, we introduced the concept of *vection*, where a user feels the sensation of motion strictly based on visual input. Although vection can lead to uncomfortable symptoms of VR sickness (described below), vection can be beneficial for the user's experience in a VR environment, since making a user feel like they are moving can enhance presence if implemented well. A good implementation of vection typically involves synthesis of ocular, proprioceptive, and vestibular stimuli—in other words, the user sees their perspective change, infers new positions of their body parts, and perceives some type of motion via the inner ear all at the same time.

With gait-direct locomotion techniques, this sensory synthesis is essentially automatic since the viewpoint the user sees is changed relative to the position of the head as they move around. Most modern VR hardware tracks the head position sufficiently that this happens without input from the developer, although it should be noted that frame rate and refresh rate are critical to maintaining this illusion. If, as a developer, you create an experience so packed with detail that the headset fails to keep up and the frame rate starts to drop, this in itself can lead to problems with vection.

In all other circumstances, however, there will be a disparity between movement in the physical world and movement in the virtual environment. This disparity can be particularly problematic for artificial strategies, since the vestibular system senses no real-world movement that might corroborate the virtual travel that these strategies invoke. Even in gait negation and indirect physical strategies, although there is real-world motion, that motion is not aligned with the motion that would directly correspond to what the user is seeing.

For example, suppose that the user is playing through a VR experience with gaze-based VCM. If they invoke the relevant input for forward motion, then the environment is likely to provide realistic optic flow stimuli for the eyes. Consequently, the ocular system perceives that motion is occurring. However, since the user is not moving in the real world, the inner ear does not perceive motion. This sensory mismatch often leads to **VR sickness**, which has similar symptoms to motion sickness or seasickness, but actually represents the opposite physiological effect. In motion sickness, the vestibular system detects motion that the eyes do not see, usually as a result of visual obstruction—people who get carsick feel it more intensely when they are reading a book in the car, and it can be alleviated by looking out the window. Similarly, seasickness is experienced most acutely when belowdecks, and the symptoms may fade if the person comes up on deck to look at the horizon.

The physiological symptoms that VR sickness shares with motion sickness include headache, nausea, disorientation, vomiting, and perspiration. Some of its psychological symptoms that are not commonly observed in traditional motion sickness include dejection (feeling depressed), confusion, apathy, and a desire for fresh air. These symptoms are detrimental to a VR user's experience and usually result in the user quitting the experience (and sometimes quitting VR entirely); therefore, preventative measures for VR sickness are necessary when designing a locomotion system. At the same time, users who have been using VR for a long time and are familiar with locomotion can, over time, develop "VR legs" (analogous to "sea legs"), rarely experiencing VR sickness and even feeling disoriented when coming out of VR. Such users may prefer more active methods of locomotion when given the choice and may find mitigation techniques described below to be distracting. Because of this, sickness reduction methods should be provided as an option which can be turned off, and different techniques of locomotion should be offered when the narrative permits. VR games are sometimes rated on a "comfort" scale, from comfortable to intense, based on the amount and type of motion involved in the experience.

### Developer familiarity and VR sickness

VR sickness is a situation particularly prone to the challenges of developer familiarity. When a developer builds a system, they become highly familiar as a result of the experience of building it. It is often difficult to remember or imagine what it might be like for a user to experience your system for the first time. This is problematic in any usability scenario, but is significantly worse in the context of VR sickness because developers are often familiar not just with their own system but with many other VR systems and forms of locomotion. Someone who has used VR for many hours may be said to have developed "VR legs"—analogous to sea legs, when a sailor is used to living on a ship and therefore does not get seasick. In the same way, a developer with VR legs may not be susceptible to VR sickness in the same way that a novice might, and because different locomotion methods can cause VR sickness in different ways, an experienced developer may not even notice that the locomotion method they are using may make people sick. For this reason, it is very important for developers to test their system with many users regularly, to identify problems the developer may never have considered.

## 10.6.2 VR Sickness Mitigation Techniques

Although the exact physiological mechanisms of VR sickness are still being investigated, the most prevalent theory is that a mismatch between sensory inputs is interpreted by the brain as a problem, possibly interpreting this as something you ate, and the response is to cause nausea to remove the problem. This is a prevailing theory around motion sickness and seems a reasonable explanation of the cause of VR sickness; additionally, mitigation techniques based on this assumption have been successful, lending evidence to this cause.

The primary sensory mismatch in VR sickness is the mismatch between visual and vestibular stimuli. Simulating motion with vision is straightforward because vection is so effective an illusion, but there is currently no substitute method of stimulating the vestibular system, nor is there any way to prevent the vestibular system from perceiving motion—or lack thereof—in the real world while other sensory units are immersed in VR. Because the inner ear is always perceiving the user's physical motion, and comparing it to motion perceived by vision, the strategies for reducing this mismatch are focused on either mitigating the effects of vection or finding some way for the user to move in the physical world that is "close enough" for the vestibular system to not raise the alarm. Three visual mitigation techniques outlined in this section are **field-of-view (FOV) reduction**, **depth-of-field blurring**, and **reference points**, all of which present different advantages, disadvantages, and potential use cases. Motion-based mitigation techniques are also considered, but these primarily use physical motion to drive virtual motion, assuming that the physical motion will be sufficient to reduce the experience of VR sickness.

### 10.6.2.1  FOV Reduction

In FOV reduction, the user's FOV is artificially reduced during motion. The reasoning behind this technique is that visual motion is primarily perceived by the rods, and since there are more rods than cones in the peripheral field (see Section 4.1.3), restricting motion in the periphery of vision will reduce vection. Common implementations of FOV reduction include *tunnelling*, in which the space outside the reduced FOV is fully occluded with a dark restrictor, and *vignetting*, in which the brightness and saturation of peripheral objects are reduced. Tunnelling and vignetting can be implemented to always be present or to be invoked only when the user is moving.

This repeated appearance and disappearance of the tunnel or vignette can be distracting and is typically not diegetic, and as a result presence can be reduced with this technique. Additionally, information otherwise available to the user may be occluded during travel, and the feeling of motion due to vection will be reduced, meaning the user's experience may be less dynamic. This method is very effective, however, and has become a standard in VR experiences which require continuous motion of some kind.

FOV reduction strategies work best when combined with eye-tracking technology, as the visible centre of the FOV restrictor can be adjusted based on the user's eye gaze instead of their head gaze. This enables a wider area for which visual scanning is possible.

### 10.6.2.2 Depth-of-Field Blurring

In depth-of-field blurring, objects beyond a predefined distance from the user's point of view are blurred to simulate reduced fidelity of faraway objects. The technique was developed in order to combat the **accommodation-convergence conflict**, which arises due to spatial inconsistencies between virtual displays and the real world. Three-dimensional rendering presents objects at different virtual distances from the user, and when the user focuses on a specific object, the angle of their eyes change so that the object aligns with the fovea of each eye. In the physical world the eyes would also focus at that distance, by adjusting the shape of the lens, but when viewed through a VR headset, the distance from the screen to the eye is always the same, and so the two factors (eye angle and eye focus) are in conflict, which can cause VR sickness.

Depth-of-field blurring effects can lessen the strain that is caused by the accommodation-convergence conflict, reducing visual fatigue and potentially improving the quality of the VR experience. Eye movements must be tracked, and detecting the depth-level attention of the user is particularly challenging. Moreover, the user must be able to look at an object in the distance and have the focus field realign almost instantaneously, in order for the experience to not be distracting. Similar to how active treadmills must predict a user's motion before they make it, depth-of-field blurring must predict what the user will be looking at before they look. Additionally, if the transition to the new depth of field is not immediate, the failed sensorimotor contingency can lead to increased VR sickness if the effect is too excessive. The strategy works best when the blur implementation itself closely resembles what humans see in the real world.

### 10.6.2.3 Reference Points

A reference point is a fixed object or display item within the virtual environment that doesn't move relative to the user's position in the virtual space. These reference points may be spatial UI elements (e.g. outline of a helmet or glasses and firearm reticle) or relate to larger objects or contexts in the scene (e.g. cockpit of an aircraft and steering wheel of a car). The advantage of reference points is that they assist in dictating the direction of the user's eye gaze, as well as providing justification for

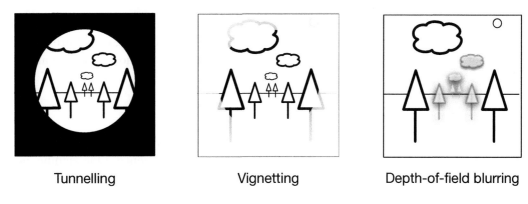

| Tunnelling | Vignetting | Depth-of-field blurring |

Figure 10.8: Methods to reduce field of view while travelling.

reduced vestibule sensation, which may reduce the intensity of sensory mismatches. Indeed, adding a virtual "nose" to the scene in the location where a user's nose would be, as unusual as it sounds, can be sufficient to reduce VR sickness.

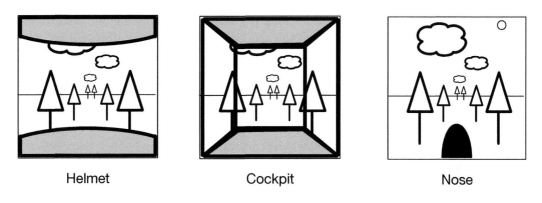

| Helmet | Cockpit | Nose |

Figure 10.9: Reference view objects.

A smaller reference object, like a helmet or reticle, is usually less effective in preventing VR sickness than a larger one like a vehicle or aircraft cockpit; however, if the reference object is too large, it may impede the visibility of other objects in the environment and sometimes detract from presence as well. Reference objects may be locationally linked to the user's head (like the nose example above) or the user's immediate environment (like the vehicle cockpit), but in either case, the key is that when the user initiates motion in the environment, the reference object stays fixed. If you fly a spaceship through an asteroid field, the motion instigated by the user is the motion of the spaceship, not the motion of the user's avatar. As such, significant pitch, roll, and yaw rotations can take place without VR sickness, if the windows of the spaceship's cockpit can be seen. If the user is floating in space with no reference, these motions are very likely to cause VR sickness. The location, size, persistence, and occlusion of a reference object are highly context dependent and can increase or reduce presence based on diegesis of the object.

Reference points and field-of-view reduction can be combined, in the example of a multi-window vehicle cabin, where only the windows you are looking out of are clear. The other windows are frosted over or blocked out, reducing vection and mitigating VR sickness.

### 10.6.3 Ergonomic Concerns

Since the motion of the body itself is an input source in VR, developers need to take into account the physical comfort of users in a VR experience. One significant ergonomic consideration for VR locomotion is whether prolonged use of a strategy can cause strain, discomfort, or fatigue. Although many developers have created VR-based fitness and workout experiences, where the goal is to exercise and an argument can be made that fatigue is a good thing, most VR experiences that involve significant motion or locomotion use unfamiliar or constrained movements, which can lead to strain or discomfort faster than expected. Many locomotion strategies require such constrained movements, and many VR experiences encourage long-term play experiences, both of which can result in ergonomic issues:

- Keeping the arm outstretched for long periods of time causes lactic acid to accumulate in the muscle tissues of the arm, which causes discomfort and fatigue. This is an important factor to consider with respect to both **hand-directed VCM** and **teleportation**. In the former, the user needs to keep their arm at a very specific orientation if they intend to travel in the same direction for a long period of time, and in the latter, the user may feel inclined to repeatedly crane their arm above their head (or contort their wrist) in order to maximize distance, increase accuracy, or teleport in rapid succession.

- **Lean-directed VCM**, as its name implies, requires the user to physically lean in the desired direction of travel. Spending long periods of time with one's back in a non-neutral position, whether sitting or standing, puts pressure on the spine and may cause back pain as a result.

- The unusual stride required for certain gait negation devices, particularly **passive omnidirectional treadmills**, can be uncomfortable for new users. In some cases, the stride resulting from the use of these devices has been found to be closer to skating than walking. As well, due to the fact that many passive omnidirectional treadmills have concave surfaces, the user's feet often land on an incline when a step is taken. This is also unnatural and may cause foot and ankle pain during a prolonged play session.

In situations where highly precise and versatile movement is required, or users of varying physical ability are expected to play through an experience, it is important to evaluate the ergonomic implications of locomotion. The user's sense of enjoyment may deteriorate if the required actions of the experience result in physical discomfort, whether in the form of VR sickness, pain, fatigue, or muscle strain. Even something as simple as sitting or standing may pose problems, as standing for long periods of time can cause fatigue, while sitting may be uncomfortable if the user is required to continuously look around the virtual environment. If the user must hold a tool in a particular way for a long time, their arms may get tired.

Nonetheless, a locomotion strategy's ergonomics is most likely to be acceptable if the action required to execute it is similar to a corresponding action in the physical world. The walking and steering metaphors are common, and individuals with experience using either metaphor may be able to translate this experience to virtual space without a second thought. When selecting a locomotion strategy or system for their experience, developers should be ergonomically conscious: to evaluate the resemblance of a strategy's invocation method to some action in the physical world and to consider the expected physical abilities and prior experience of their target demographics.

## 10.7  SUMMARY

Being able to move through a virtual world is probably the greatest advantage of VR. Seeing and hearing the world is one thing, but being able to plan a route and navigate means you are a participant in the space, rather than just an observer. Locomotion in VR is core to the experience of many scenarios, but is also highly variable in terms of the way people relate to the experience. Users should be given options to choose which style of locomotion is most appropriate for them, and consideration should be given to how users with one mode of locomotion may interact with users with a different mode of locomotion. In the next chapter, we see what we can do once we get where we are going.

# CHAPTER 11

# Activities and Interactions

In order for a virtual reality (VR) system to be immersive, the system must effectively occlude and replace a set of senses, and the replacement must be believable—the user responds as if the virtual world is real. The user will have no reason to respond to anything, however, unless there is some interaction to respond to. The things a user can do will have a significant influence on whether the virtual world feels real. Poorly designed activities can pull a user out of immersion as quickly as an inappropriately supported sensorimotor contingency, and a well-designed, appropriate, thematically consistent activity can contribute greatly to presence.

## 11.0.1 Interaction design

The design of activities and objects that enable these activities relies on a set of core principles of human interaction, each of which will be described in detail in its own section:

**Affordance:** The way an object is designed can give cues to its operation.

**Familiarity:** The way a task has been accomplished in the past can inform how people expect to perform a task.

**Mapping:** The relative location of items or objects can give cues to the results of an interaction.

## 11.1 AFFORDANCE

An **affordance** is the suggestion of an action by the shape of an object. An object *affords* an action simply by the way it is structured. Objects can suggest actions via affordances because humans are mostly the same in the way we interact with objects. When we reach out to pick up an object, we look for a way that our hand can naturally grab and lift the object. We would not expect to be able to lift a large rock with one hand, but a small rock may be lifted.

Objects designed for human use often give a hint to how they are to be used, based on their shape. Tools like hammers, saws, and screwdrivers all have a place somewhere on the tool that is the right shape and size for gripping, and when it

DOI: 10.1201/9781003261230-11

is gripped by this handle, the tool is in the right orientation for operation, further suggesting its function. A saw extends perpendicular to the handle and so affords pulling. A screwdriver extends vertically from the handle and affords turning. A hammer extends vertically from the handle, but then the action surface is at right angles, a distance away from the handle, so affords swinging. In all of these cases, of course, the function of the tool is also strongly influenced by watching other people use the tool, or by having experience with a similar tool. The design principle of *familiarity* is based on this principle and will be described later.

### 11.1.1 Functionality and Signifiers

A handle on an object indicates that it may be grabbed and used, but what actually happens when it is grabbed may be suggested by other aspects of the object. When a door has a handle, the shape and size of the handle might suggest whether the door should be pushed or pulled, and whether a knob needs to be turned, or a handle rotated, in order to disengage the latch. Doors rarely have instructions, partly because we are quite familiar with how they are supposed to work, and partly because their affordances are clear. Figure 11.1 shows examples of door handles with clear affordances. Levers and circular knobs suggest the action of turning, and the handle under the thumb press puts your hand in the right place to suggest the action of pressing with your thumb.

(a) Rotating Handle      (b) Lever Handle      (c) Thumb Press Handle

Figure 11.1: Door affordances.

Doors without latches, especially in industrial contexts, may need to be installed such that they open inward or outward, but economies of scale result in a single door model being produced that will either open away from the user or towards them. When the handle is the same on both sides, it is difficult to tell whether the door should be pushed or pulled to open. A door with a sign that says "push" or "pull," it is often because the door handle has been designed in a way that removes or obfuscates the affordance normally present. Figure 11.2 shows examples of these cases. Figure 11.2a shows a door with symmetric handles, meaning the user must guess whether the door is to be pushed or pulled. Ideally, in these cases, the door could swing both ways. Figure 11.2b shows a door which has been designed to be ambiguous, and therefore requires a label, or signifier, to be properly operated. Figure 11.3 shows an exit door which must be pushed to open, but in this case the user does not have to guess at the functionality; the bar suggests being pushed. Indeed, in an emergency, the user need not even intentionally activate the door; if they were pushed against it by accident, it would open anyway, an intentional safety feature for fire doors like this.

(a) Symmetric Door

(b) Signified Door

Figure 11.2: Industrial Doors.

Figure 11.3: Push bar exit door.

An affordance can only indicate the operation of a control; it cannot indicate the function. A light switch on a wall indicates that there is some electrical circuit that may be controlled by the use of that switch, the orientation of the switch usually indicates whether or not that control is currently enabled or disabled (although there are exceptions, such as three-way switches and incorrectly installed switches), and the shape of the switch will indicate how to activate it.

Although the existence of the switch provides lots of information to the user, one piece of information it cannot provide is what the switch actually does. For the user to know this, they must either be familiar with the context of the switch, or there must be some kind of signifier on or near the switch. A **signifier** is a type of label or other information applied to an interface element to indicate its function or mode of operation. Signifiers can indicate both the function of the interface element (what it does), as well as the state of operation (e.g. on or off). Well-afforded interface elements may include some indication of the state of operation as a component of the object itself. For example, a switch on an electrical power bar often has a light built into it, showing when the power bar is on and when it is off.

If an object has a poorly afforded interaction or is ambiguous in some way, it may require a signifier to show how it operates. A good example of this is a generic door with a generic handle that the user doesn't know if they need to push or pull. If a door needs a sign to tell you how to operate it, the affordance of the handle of that door has failed. Requiring signifiers is not necessarily evidence that your interaction design is problematic— it depends on what the signifier is intended to indicate. Signifiers can indicate the *operation* of an object (how it works), the *function* of an object (what it does), or the *state* of the underlying system connected to that object (what it is). A light switch can convey all three pieces of information without signifiers: its shape suggests how to operate it, its location suggests what it does (see Section 11.3 below), and its current state (up or down) suggests the current state of the circuit it is connected to. Chapter 12 will present a complete discussion on the display of information, including an analysis of the ways light switches can fail to signify their operation, function, or state.

Signifiers are not necessarily text or image labels. The functionality of a control can be reinforced by the physical shape of that control. In airplane cockpits, the control knob that activates the landing gear is shaped like a wheel, and the control that activates the flaps is shaped like the flaps of the wing. These controls are required to be this shape by U.S. law[1], as well as controls for mixture, thrust, and other features. The standardization of these shapes is an aspect that guarantees familiarity (as discussed below), but the shape itself becomes a signifier of the function of the knob. The knob affords an interaction, and the shape of the knob suggests what the result of the interaction will be.

### 11.1.2  Affording and signifying other senses

Affordances and signifiers are primarily visual—a user can determine the state and operation of the object based on its characteristics before reaching out to interact with it. Non-visual cues can be used to indicate the function or state of an object or control, although the association of the signifier with the control can become separated if the designer is not careful. A commercial truck, when shifted into reverse, creates an audible beacon ("beep, beep, beep") to signify to those around them that the truck may move backward. The shape of switches and knobs can suggest their function by feel as well as by sight; however, special care must be taken to ensure that the shape of the object does suggest its action. When a visually impaired person walks down the street, they sometimes use a cane to collect information about the sidewalk

---

[1]US Title 14, Chapter I, Subchapter C, Part 25.781

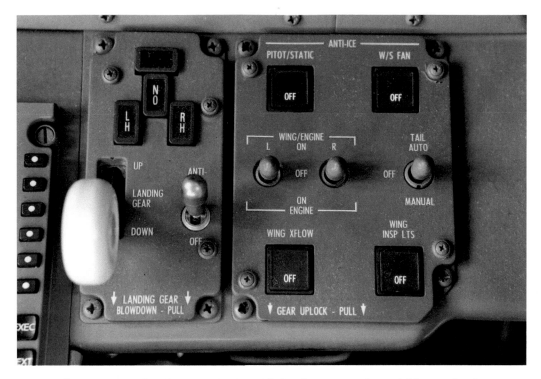

Figure 11.4: Airplane controls with landing gear shaped like a wheel.

the are walking on. A set of bumps (called "tactile paving") can be installed near intersections so the person can discover that an intersection is approaching.

### 11.1.3 Graphical Interface Metaphor as Affordance

Affordances are used in graphic user interfaces in traditional computing environments, but since the physical interaction of the user with the system is through a keyboard, mouse, game controller, or touchscreen, the displayed element must somehow convey its operation and function metaphorically rather than directly. The keys on a keyboard afford pressing, the buttons on a mouse afford clicking, the wheel on a mouse affords turning, and the joystick on a game controller affords directional displacement; but what these things actually do depends entirely on the context of the point of interaction. If a user has the mouse hovered over a button on a computer interface, clicking the left mouse button will cause the graphical button element to activate. Clicking the right mouse button will often cause something else to happen, which is a learned behaviour and not afforded by either the mouse or the software button. "Clicking" on other graphical elements will cause other things to happen, and these are mostly learned, rather than afforded.

The visual presentation of a graphical user interface button has evolved over time, as stylistic norms change, and as a result the suggestion of interaction of a button has diminished over time. We will discuss visual stylistic standards in more detail in Chapter 12, but it is worth noting that most modern styles of computer-based interfaces rely as much on familiarity and context as they do affordances.

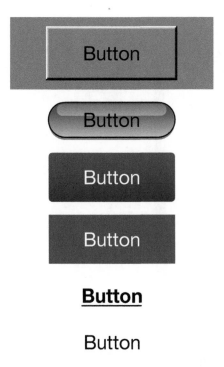

Figure 11.5: The stylistic abstraction of UI buttons has evolved over time.

Traditional computer interfaces will be discussed more in Chapter 13, but it is worth considering the user interface elements here that have been designed to suggest specific actions. Again, these elements do not immediately indicate the *function* of the operation, just what interaction is available. Figure 11.6 shows examples of some UI elements with affordances. A slider suggests the action of horizontal or vertical movement by showing the range of possible values, at the same time as signifying the current value of whatever is being adjusted. A radio button element and a checkbox element both afford pushing, the only difference in the signifier, and it is familiarity with the signifier that allows the user to recognize the difference in function.

**Why is it called a radio button?**
Even those familiar may not know why the radio button element is called a radio button—in-car stereo systems had manual radio tuners that worked by rotating a dial to a specific frequency, altering the physical components of circuits within the radio. In order to save and recall a specific radio frequency, a set of buttons were often provided which quickly shifted the radio tuner to the physical location representing that frequency. Because only one button could be pressed at a time, this one-of-many selection method became known as a **radio button**.

Figure 11.6: Some UI elements available in the operating system of a desktop computer.

### 11.1.4 Affordance in VR

While physical interfaces can make use of affordances that indicate the function of an object by their physical shape and structure, and computer interfaces must use artificial affordances in order to metaphorically represent their operation, VR allows us to combine both of these methods, using virtual affordances that appear to be physical objects. The physical shape of the object suggests the action that can be taken by that object.

A naive approach to interaction in VR has historically been to replicate existing controls in the virtual environment. If the user walks into a room with a light switch, the affordance of the switch suggests that it can be activated to turn on a light, and the context of the user suggests that the light in the room will turn on as a result of the switch being activated. A user sits in an airplane cockpit and sees an array of switches around them, each of which affords an interaction and is labelled with a function signifier. If an affordance works in the physical world, it should work in VR as well, right?

There are a number of challenges with this assumption. In the physical world, affordances are successful because an affordance suggests a course of action. A user seeing a handle on a mug plans to pick up the mug. Subconsciously, the brain creates a series of movements of the arm and hand tied to the target position of the hand, the intention to grip the mug, and the expected weight and composition of the mug. In VR, there is no mug, and so while the affordance may suggest a series of actions in the physical world, it suggests a *different set of actions* in the virtual world. There is some overlap, as approaching the mug and extending the arm will be similar, but the final act of grasping the mug will be different. In the same way, if a light switch is on the wall, the user may plan an action of reaching for the switch and turning it on; but once your hand is in the same location as the switch, the final action will be different.

If the VR system uses hand tracking, the situation is somewhat improved, but still problematic. The user may reach to try to grab the mug, but when they close their hand around the mug, they cannot physically feel any mug to grab. A sensorimotor contingency fails in this circumstance, which can have the effect of reducing presence.

A second challenge in VR is that every object that appears interactable may suggest an action, but the developer may not have assigned an interaction to every object. A tree may suggest the action of climbing, but while you could attempt to climb almost any tree in the physical world, not every tree in VR can be climbed. Developers may take different approaches to this problem. On one hand, a fully immersive world *should* make every tree climbable. You should be able to paint any wall, dig a hole in any ground, and read (or rip a page out of) any book. It is impossible to imagine every activity a user may attempt, and so-called "sandbox" worlds are therefore very difficult to make satisfying. If you tell the user that they can do anything, they will almost definitely attempt to do something you haven't thought of.

Possible actions can be signified at close range: when a user reaches out to pick up an object from a table, the developer can add a glow, outline, or other change to indicate that the user can, in fact, interact with the object. Unless explained within the narrative, however, this can lead to a reduction in plausibility: real-world objects do not glow when you hover your hand over them. Signifiers of interactability can also be added without knowing the user's intent—a glow or outline can be added to important objects in the scene that the user should notice and do something with, but this can have the same effect of loss of plausibility. Finally, users can be trained to learn which objects are interactable and which are not. Knowing that you can pick up any book from the shelf, but not the shelf itself, will allow the user to predict their actions.

### 11.1.5 Affordance Case Study: Held Object with Controls

Many control-focused objects are gripped and activated at the same time, like chainsaws, lawn trimmers, bartender soda dispensers, and most vehicle controls, such as car steering wheels, airplane throttles and sticks, and bicycle handlebars. These objects follow a similar design principle, which requires maintaining a firm and reliable grip on the object while simultaneously being able to operate controls associated with the object. The controls are typically located near the thumb or index finger, and the remaining fingers are engaged with the hand grip. There are three primary forms of operation for handheld objects with controls. Single-handed gripped objects (Figure 11.7) have a handle with controls intended to be operated by the hand that grips the controls. Two-handed gripped objects (Figure 11.8) are either a single object or pair of objects that are gripped by both hands and have controls accessible by both hands. Off-handed gripped objects (Figure 11.9) are held with one hand and operated with another. An object that is common in videogames and has interaction elements that fall in to each of these three categories is the handgun firearm. Held in one hand, several controls are activated by the thumb of the hand holding the firearm. It is often held with two hands in order to stabilize it, and there are circumstances (like charging the slide or activating the safety) that are performed with one hand while the object is held with the other hand.

Firearms such as pistols, rifles, and shotguns, are common interactable objects in VR experiences, mostly because the first-person shooter is a common context

(a) Grass Trimmer    (b) Bar Soda Gun    (c) Chain Hoist

Figure 11.7: Single-hand gripped control objects.

(a) Hands-On Throttle    (b) F1 Steering Wheel    (c) Game Controller
and stick (HOTAS)       *Ben Sutherland, CCBY2.0*

Figure 11.8: Two-hand gripped control objects.

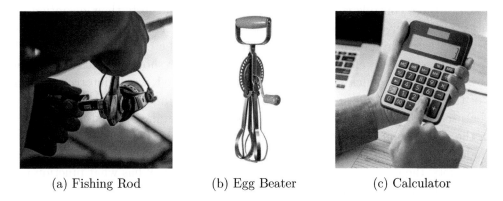

(a) Fishing Rod    (b) Egg Beater    (c) Calculator

Figure 11.9: Off-hand gripped control objects.

for gaming, and trends in VR experiences are often inspired by trends in gaming. Designing a virtual handheld weapon that maps directly to the physical VR controller is possible, but in games or training scenarios where realism is important, the handgun must appear and operate in the same way that the real-world physical object does, in order to maintain familiarity (as discussed in Section 11.2 below). If a user learns to operate an object in one context and the controls are in a different location in another context, the learning does not translate and the skill does not transfer.

Most firearms have a set of common controls near the grip that can be activated by the hand holding the firearm: the hammer, the safety, the magazine release, the trigger, and the slide. Revolvers, shotguns, and other classes of firearm may have different controls. All of these controls are mechanical and are afforded in their operation and by their location with respect to the hand holding the firearm. Figure 11.10 shows a common example, the M1911, also known as the Colt 45 Government Issue. The magazine release is a small round button, usually textured, that affords pressing by the thumb; the safety and the slide stop are thumb levers that afford rotation; the hammer is a lever that affords pulling back by the thumb; and the trigger is a lever that affords pulling by the index finger. The slide has texture on each side that suggests that it can be gripped, and the shape of the slide and its operation suggest that the slide can be manually pulled by gripping it on either side.

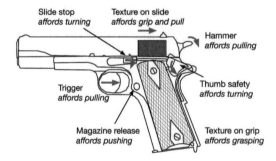

Figure 11.10: M1911 pistol, with affordances indicated.

Each of these controls is constructed in a way that suggests their *operation*, but the user must receive training to learn the *function* of each of these controls. An experienced user may be able to infer the function of the controls of an unfamiliar firearm. For example, a close look at the slide stop lever shows a notch on the slide nearby, which might indicate that the lever, when engaged, would interrupt the motion of the slide. The safety, similarly, is near a notch in the slide that suggests it can be used to lock the slide. The safety also has a signifier—a red dot will show when the safety is off, meaning the firearm is ready to fire; and engaging the safety will hide the red dot, indicating that the firearm is safe. Even with these affordances and signifiers, the primary way that users know what control has what function is by training to develop familiarity.

### 11.1.6   Hand controllers in VR

As shown above, there are many common real-world objects that may be simulated in VR. The affordance of the object suggests how the hand will grip and operate the object, but in VR, if the object isn't present, the sensorimotor contingency of reaching out to grab the object will immediately fail. The solution is to have a real-world physical representation of the object for the user to hold in their physical hand. This object would need to be tracked in its position, in the same way that VR headsets and controllers are tracked, and the wide diversity of possible hand-controller objects means that it would be impractical to have physical representations of each object. The compromise is to have a single handheld controller that can, more or less, represent any held controllable object.

VR hand controllers are designed in the same way as held controllable objects: to fit comfortably in the hand, with buttons readily available to the fingers and thumb without losing grip of the handle. VR controllers usually have two triggers, one for the index finger to replicate trigger controls and one for the other three fingers (or more frequently just the middle finger) to indicate that the user has gripped the handle. When the user squeezes the secondary trigger, the system is informed that the user intends to grip whatever object is contextually relevant, and when the user releases the secondary trigger, the object being held is dropped. Of course, a developer can remap these controls for other functions, such as using a button on top to initiate a grip instead of the secondary trigger, but this disregards the affordances built into the controller, which may result in much confusion on the part of the user.

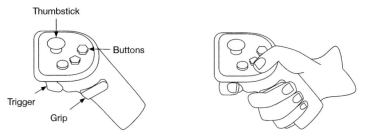

(a) Parts of a VR Controller        (b) Hand Grip for a VR Controller

Figure 11.11: Typical VR controller.

The VR controller also usually has a thumbstick and buttons for interactions similar to a gamepad thumbstick. The hand controller itself and each of the controls have affordances, too. The shape and size of the grip suggests that the controller can be picked up and held, and the orientation of the controls near the respective fingers and thumb indicates that they can be pressed or moved.

The key challenge in the design of handheld objects in VR is that the object being held in the physical world (the VR controller) has one arrangement of controls, and the object being held in the real world is likely to have a different set of controls (unless the developer uses a model of the VR controller). Because of this, *the affordances the user sees do not match the activities they can perform*. One solution to this problem is to make the virtual object have the same controls as the physical object (a technique that will be discussed in Section 11.3.4 below) but when the virtual object is intended to resemble a real-world object, this cannot be done. In addition, the relationship between the hand controllers is also often relevant. Objects that are held with two hands serve to set a constant distance between the hands; VR hand controllers are independent, and therefore the user's hands in the physical world may vary in distance, while their hands in the virtual world must stay the same distance apart. A device held with one hand and operated with another poses an even further problem—if you bring your hands together in VR, the controllers you are holding are likely to collide, which is distracting and can interrupt tracking.

Imagine being in a virtual world and picking up a flashlight. The flashlight has one control on it, which affords pushing and turns on the light. You reach out your thumb to where you know the control is, but your thumb only feels the smooth plastic of the controller (a failed sensorimotor contingency). Then you remember that you are holding a VR controller and not a flashlight (a reduction in the plausibility illusion), and you feel the controls of the VR controller with your thumb. You feel three buttons, and you wonder which one is the button that turns on the flashlight. Then you remember that, so far in this game, the "A" button has been used to activate or interact with held objects. Because you can't see the buttons on the VR controller, and they all feel the same, you try to remember which one is "A," but you can't, so you press a button at random. You press "B" by mistake, and something else happens. The system then recognizes that you are having trouble (or you remember the gesture that brings up the help) and a model of the VR controller appears in your hand, showing you which button is which. This help menu, the image of the VR controller superimposed on the virtual object you are holding, is a signifier that does help you find the necessary function, but at the cost of further reminding you that you are in VR.

There are several ways to address the challenge of aligning mismatched controller buttons. You can teach the user where things are, developing their familiarity, or you can put the virtual button in a place that is more closely aligned with the button on the physical controller, improving the mapping. Both of these techniques are discussed in Sections 11.2 and 11.3.

## 11.2 FAMILIARITY

When a user reaches out to flip a light switch, they know that the switch will activate a light. The function of the switch is suggested by the fact that the user has used light switches before—when a switch appears near the door to a room, that switch usually controls the lights in that room. **Familiarity** is when the operation or function of an object is suggested by past experience with that object. Familiar objects can suggest their operation by affordance, but when a user is familiar with an object, they rapidly understand its operation even if the affordance may be obscure. Further, while affordance can only suggest the operation of an object, familiarity can suggest the *result* of the operation. The gulfs of evaluation and execution are reduced when a user knows what to expect, because they can formulate a task plan more easily, and they have a better idea of what will happen as a result of executing the task.

Familiarity is developed by experience and by context, and a user's intuition about an interface is built on prior experience. When a user sees an object they are familiar with, they can infer how to use it. A person familiar with a hammer will know a hammer when they see one, and how to use it, even if the shape and other attributes may be different. If a user sees an unfamiliar tool near a hammer, they can make some assumptions about its use or function based on its proximity to the hammer—it's probably a tool for woodworking or hardware, rather than a tool for preparing food or cutting hair.

### 11.2.1 Example: QWERTY, Dvorak, and Alternative Keyboards

Some objects and interfaces are common enough that a degree of familiarity can be assumed. Most people using a computer today have used a QWERTY keyboard, named for the first six letters of the top row. The development of the QWERTY keyboard has an interesting history, and several alternatives have been proposed; however, the main benefit today, and the reason most people use it, is *that* most people use it. Its familiarity (and ubiquity) is the principal benefit of the layout and is sufficient justification to choose that over some other arrangement of letters.

Much discussion and study have been made regarding the optimal keyboard layout for computer interfaces. It has been suggested that QWERTY was originally designed to slow typists down to avoid jamming the machine and that other keyboard layouts may be better. Regardless of the original design intent (more likely to do with Morse code than jammed armatures), and whether other layouts might be faster or easier to learn, the principle argument for keeping QWERTY is that it is already ubiquitous. Learning a new layout, even if it were faster, would require unlearning QWERTY, and the familiarity and muscle memory are very hard to shake. Re-learning another layout would take more time, and most people forget how long it took them to learn a skill like typing. It is difficult, especially without the neuroplasticity of youth. Finally, many computer interfaces are intimately tied to the QWERTY layout in subtle ways. The fact that CTRL-C is the shortcut for copy makes some sense, but CTRL-V for paste is only rational because V is next to C on the keyboard. Many games use WASD for movement because those four letters sit nicely under the left hand, based on the keyboard layout.

Interestingly, many streaming service search interfaces do not use a QWERTY layout for their text interface, instead using an alphabetical layout in a specific grid, as shown in Figure 11.12. The QWERTY layout is primarily horizontal, and a need to redistribute screen space may have lead to this design decision; additionally, although QWERTY may be more familiar than an alphabetical grid, that familiarity primarily manifests as *muscle memory*, in that a user's fingers will remember where the letters are without the user having to consciously consider the location of each key. When interacting with a streaming service via a remote, the actual activity is different—the user is using directional buttons (up, down, left, and right) to select a letter rather than typing a letter with a discrete finger.

Because text entry is such a common task in computing, every computer system, from laptops to phones to streaming services, supports a way to enter text.

| A | B | C | D | E | F |
|---|---|---|---|---|---|
| G | H | I | J | K | L |
| M | N | O | P | Q | R |
| S | T | U | V | W | X |
| Y | Z | 1 | 2 | 3 | 4 |
| 5 | 6 | 7 | 8 | 9 | 0 |

| 1 | 2 | 3 | 4 | 5 | 6 | 7 | 8 | 9 | 0 | - |
|---|---|---|---|---|---|---|---|---|---|---|
| Q | W | E | R | T | Y | U | I | O | P | / |
| A | S | D | F | G | H | J | K | L | : | ' |
| Z | X | C | V | B | N | M | , | . | ? | ! |

    (a) Alphabetical Grid          (b) QWERTY Grid

Figure 11.12: Alphanumeric grid for directional search and selection.

Section 13.2.4 presents a deeper discussion of how text is used in traditional and VR systems. When these text entry systems are well aligned, familiarity is preserved. Any laptop purchased in North America will come with a QWERTY keyboard built-in, although one can request an alternative keyboard at the time of manufacture, and many countries where English is not the official language may have standardizations of keyboards that reflect their alphabet, or the most common diacritical marks in their use of the Latin alphabetic characters.

### 11.2.2 Standardization and Jakob's Law

Standardization is one route to familiarity, but it is a challenge for organizations attempting to protect intellectual property, because standardizing to a single manufacturer requires sharing of trade secrets or admission that your particular implementation of a common activity is, perhaps, not as unique as you might claim. Control of the definition and evolution of the standard also provides benefits, which gives developers incentive to make their implementation of competing systems different enough to resist standardization. A common example is video game controllers. There are three major manufacturers of video game consoles: Xbox, PlayStation, and Nintendo, and each has exclusive titles and a standardized controller layout. All three layouts have strong similarity, with a directional pad on the left side and a grid of four buttons on the right side, but the labelling of the four buttons is different between platforms. On the PlayStation it is on the bottom, on the Xbox it is on the left, and on the Nintendo it is on the top, as shown in Figure 11.13.

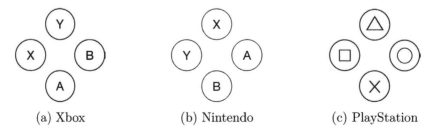

    (a) Xbox          (b) Nintendo          (c) PlayStation

Figure 11.13: Button layout of three video game controllers. Note the different positions of the "X" button.

The problem with this comes when a game instructs the user to "press X." If the user only plays on one platform, they may recall which button is X but they are likely to have to take their eyes off of the game to look at the controller, unless they have a high level of familiarity with the controller. A user who plays on two or three platforms would need to remember which platform they are playing on in order to remember which button is "X" without looking. Further, the conceptual function of the buttons is more likely to be known by the user, rather than their labels. Each game is different, but a player soon learns which button does what and associated the *function* of the button (jump, duck, interact, etc.) rather than the label.

Although developers of game systems may see an advantage in ensuring that their button layout is somewhat unique and may indeed be required to make the layout unique to avoid intellectual property action by competing manufacturers, the effect on the end user is confusion. If there is a common way of doing things, you should do things that way. Jakob Nielsen, a usability expert in web design, noticed the same phenomenon in the design of websites. Many web developers were making their sites stylistically and functionally different, for many reasons but primarily to be distinct. **Jakob's law** states, "Users spend most of their time on other sites. This means that users prefer your site to work the same way as all the other sites they already know."

This observation, that developers do not build things in isolation, but rather design for a user who also uses other things, is fundamental to the principle of familiarity. Not only do people understand better how to use a thing if they have used it before, but people develop that familiarity by using the products and services of your competitors. Standards of usability evolve and develop over time, but diverging from a known standard just to be different will lead to frustration among your users.

Standards can emerge from convergent solutions to interaction challenges or can be instituted centrally when interoperability between suppliers is required. Light bulbs are manufactured by many different companies and come in a variety of shapes and sizes, but they must all conform to the E26 (Edison screw, 26 mm) standard, and they must all operate properly in electrical conditions expected by the wiring connected to the home. Circuit breakers must conform to the standards set by government bodies; otherwise fire or electrocution may occur.

## 11.2.3   Malicious Implementation of Standards

The other consequence of standardization is that users come to expect certain outcomes and become complacent to the risks of using a system if standards appear to be implemented. Early in the development of the internet, a standard emerged that blue text with an underline would represent a link to a different website. In general, the text would describe what page the link would take you to, and you could be reasonably confident that, even if the link took you to a different page or an unintended page, the worst that would happen would be that you would waste a bit of time or discover something new. As internet traffic became a measure of the quality of a website, and therefore its priority as a location of a search, web developers began to develop methods to change the target of a link in order to trick a user to navigating to a different site. Over time as graphics replaced text links, and graphical ads became popular forms of financing otherwise free websites, nefarious developers would build advertising content that appears the same as or similar to functional content on the website. If you navigate to a website with a "download" button and you see four buttons that all say "download," you won't know which one to click on. One of the buttons is the authentic download button, and the other three are links to other, possibly malicious, websites.

### 11.2.4 Jakob's Law and in Virtual Reality

Although VR is a relatively new medium, some standards are beginning to emerge, and developers have a choice as to whether to adhere to the processes that are becoming common or to develop new interaction processes. Just like with the early days of the web, people will spend most of their time in other developers' VR experiences, and it is therefore worthwhile for the VR developer to at least consider making their common interactions similar to the way other VR experiences implement these actions. Examples from locomotion and object gripping are given here.

**Locomotion.** In Chapter 10, we discussed several modes of locomotion, including teleportation. In the early days of VR, developers attempted many different techniques to facilitate teleportation and made these techniques available to users through several different interface structures. Common teleportation methods included the following:

- Aiming a controller and pressing a button
- Looking in a direction and pressing a button
- Aiming the thumbstick in a direction
- Throwing an object at the desired location
- Using diegetic teleportation device

As development proceeded and more games came to market, a standard teleportation method emerged, based in part on the ease of implementation of a freely available framework. Individual developers either adopted this method directly or created a method that was intentionally different in some way. Some methods resulted in increased usability or functionality, but when a user is used to getting around the play area using one method in most games, the friction of using a different method must be compensated for in some way and the user might need to be reminded of the teleportation method more often. The key reminder here is that other systems exist and developers must take this into account.

**Object Gripping.** Another example that has become ubiquitous is the mechanism of gripping an object. Again, there have been many different implementations of grabbing mechanics in VR applications, and even in the simplest circumstance (when the user's hand is near the object), there has been dispute as to which button to press. Over time, a consensus has been reached that grabbing objects should use the "grip" button, if available, to grab an object and use the "trigger" button to activate the object. This interaction isn't necessarily the most obvious or affordable, but it is inherited from the interactions with firearms, where a person holds it by the grip and activates it by the trigger. One aspect of this interaction that is different between experiences is whether or not releasing the grip button should drop the object or not. On the one hand, it is more "natural" to have to hold the object the entire time it is being used; on the other hand, the user is holding the VR controller the whole time anyway, and requiring pressure on the grip button can lead to fatigue. Depending on other aspects of gameplay, developers may choose to default to using the grip button as a toggle (press once to grab; press again to drop) or a state (press and hold to grab, release to drop) and possibly allow the user to choose which they prefer. In this case, the different ways this control is used may lead to the user accidentally dropping the object, or not being able to drop it when they want to.

### 11.2.5 Learning and Common Experience

Familiarity can be learned by active training and education; in fact it is easy to forget that when we discuss things that are familiar to us, these are by definition things that we have learned. Throughout childhood and adolescence, our primary goal as humans is to learn things and become familiar with the cultural, linguistic, technical, and academic processes that surround us. Much of what we learn when we are young becomes interconnected with our personality and identity, and it becomes difficult to imagine that others would not know the same things that we know. As we grow, learning transitions from a passive experience to an active experience, requiring dedicated study and active activity selection in order to learn more complex tasks and concepts. School presents a formulated set of subjects and tasks that all students learn together, creating a shared common experience. Everyone who went to school at a particular time and read a particular book in English class can use that book as a point of reference when discussing other media or situations, and anyone who has not read that book will not understand the allusions being made. When we say someone has "opened pandora's box," for example, we understand the allusion to the Greek myth and the release of problems which cannot be put back. Critically, however, we also expect others to *share our understanding* of that reference. We rely on a shared experience to be able to communicate complicated ideas to each other.

These shared experiences also permeate user interactions. In the early days of the first graphical user interfaces, there was an understanding that people would not know how to use these systems. Each new computer that came with a mouse also came with a training program that assisted people to learn how to use the mouse. New users were trained to make the association between moving the mouse on the table and seeing the cursor move on the screen. Users were trained on the difference between a click, a drag, a double click, and played games to practise these new skills. Today, children learning to use computers do not play these direct games; instead they are presented with a computer, told to click and drag, and must figure it out for themselves. The teacher or parent will quickly show them what they mean, and the child will develop the skills without the direct educational programs or practice sessions required to develop these skills. Typing is another example of a learned skill that develops over time, either formally or informally. People studying for clerical work would take formal typing lessons, much like music lessons, and be examined on their speed and accuracy. Today, everyone types, and children are exposed to keyboards early in their life and expected to develop the typing skills informally over time, rather than taking active training later in life. As customs, activities, and knowledge become more commonplace, the time when they are learned moves earlier in a child's life.

The same thing has happened recently with touch screen devices. When first made available to the public at large, touch screen devices required training and affordances, and each activity or interaction was detailed so users could learn how it worked. Because there are two primary touchscreen platforms (android and iOS) with slightly different user experience expectations, we have an opportunity to observe directly the differences in expectations as users become familiar with a user experience over time. Android phones always have a "back" button, which either returns to a previous screen or menu or cancels the current activity. iOS devices do not have a back button, and as a consequence users of this platform do not develop the expectation that there would always be a way to return to the previous activity. Instead, iOS users learn to press the "home" button to return to the first screen of the interface. Both of these interactions provide methods to exit the current activity, and neither is objectively better from a usability standpoint, but the expectation of what happens when you exit the current activity is different for users of each platform, and the frustration that a user feels when changing platforms comes primarily from the difference between their expectation and their experience. As developers we must remember that some design decisions may not speak to a user's experience in the same way that it speaks to your experience.

Touchscreens have evolved significantly as technology has advanced, and while early phones had buttons that were available and labelled to indicate functions, most phones today are a sheet of glass with no buttons. As the number of physical controls has been reduced, the functionality of the devices has increased, and additional gestures and interactions have been added to the user interface. As each new gesture is added, the interface has been modified to include affordances and signifiers for these new functions, and opportunities for the users to learn these new functions. When iOS removed the home button from the bottom of phones, it was replaced with a gesture to swipe up from the bottom of the screen, as seen in Figure 11.14. This gesture was initially afforded by adding a visual signifier in the graphical interface to indicate to the user that they can swipe up. The location of the gesture in the interface reminds the user of the button that used to be there, and the function of that gesture is therefore tied to an assumed familiarity with past functionality. As users emerge who have not used a home button, but learn the interface as it is, the signifier and the gesture will become familiar and the signifier will no longer be needed. At that point, the familiarity with the functionality, and how to access it, will be assumed. "Everyone knows you swipe up to go home, it's obvious!" and users who have trouble may need to consult external reference material to be reminded of how to make use of the functionality that has been hidden from view.

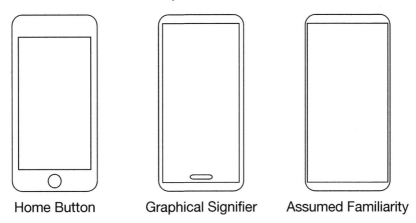

Home Button      Graphical Signifier      Assumed Familiarity

Figure 11.14: Evolution of controls and affordances in a phone.

These same evolutions are currently happening with the interfaces that are becoming standard within VR software systems. Developers of VR hardware include software that assists the user in learning the common activities and gestures of the system, since it is reasonable to assume that most users of the system will have little to no understanding of the expectations of interaction. This is similar to when mouse-equipped computer systems came with tutorials to help users learn to point and click. These VR interactions are also signified by showing the VR controller and buttons within VR, along with labels and functionality for each button. Over time, these signifiers will be removed, but will still be able to be invoked again by the user if they need a reminder of the expected interactions. The challenge with VR, of course, is that consulting a reference that is external to VR requires the user to remove themselves from the VR scenario entirely. For this reason, it is very important for developers to include reference assistance and an easy way to access it. Most VR platforms today have a dedicated help button on one of the controllers that presents a menu or reference document for the user about the VR scenario they are currently using. A second button takes the user back to the starting scenario associated with the headset (a main menu, loading lobby, or construct). As hand-controlled gestures appear and become more common, the removal of signifiers in VR will mirror the removal of signifiers in phone design, and users will be expected to know what to do to invoke commands or launch scenarios. "Everyone knows you touch your right finger and thumb together to exit reality!" But what if you forget?

## 11.2.6 Training

When we know that a user is likely to be unfamiliar with a method of interaction within a system we are building, or when we know that it is very important for a user to get an action correct, we can offer or require training to ensure that the user is able to correctly operate the system. The earliest personal computer systems came with large and complicated manuals, often taking up more volume than the computer itself. Users had to read and understand the manuals before they were able to make use of the computer, because the interface of the computer assumed that people would be trained in order to use it. As the design of computers integrated more and better usability principles, the need for large complicated manuals was reduced over time, but because this coincided with more people knowing how to use computers, it is not clear what portion of learning can be attributed to the better interface and what portion moved earlier in a person's experience, came from getting help from other users, or continued to reside in the reading of manuals.

The trade-off between usability and training is subtle and challenging. As discussed in Section 12.1.1, if developers know users will be trained, there can be a temptation to not worry as much about making the interface easier to use.

Training scenarios and manuals must be designed with attention to usability in the same way as the activities they are meant to inform. Boring or difficult-to-process training scenarios can result in individuals not learning the information or skipping the training. At the same time, training must be aligned with the experience of the user being trained. Early video games trained their users in their controls by **exposure**: players were dropped into a new scenario with no information, and they would just figure out what to do. This is a practical training technique when the stakes are low (no consequence for failure) and the number of things to learn is small (it is easy to figure out what to do). Each level that introduces a new mechanic is carefully crafted to promote discovery of that mechanic and understanding of its functionality and use. Modern video games often use **tutorial** levels in place of exposure training, where the early levels are designed to explicitly train the user in the mechanics of the game and not permit the user to proceed until they have demonstrated that they are able to successfully execute the activities in the scenario. This type of training is appropriate when the stakes are high (failure is dangerous or frustrating), and the number of things to learn is large (it is difficult to figure out what to do). The challenge with tutorial levels in game design is if a user plays the game again, the system does not know they are an experienced user and requires the player to complete the tutorial levels again, in order to prove their competence in the game mechanics. In the speedrunning community, the biggest challenge is often finding a way to bypass the initial tutorial levels, since they are usually time-consuming and contain unskippable cutscenes. The prevalence of tutorial levels in modern game design has led some to conclude that modern games are too easy, to "hand-holding" and earlier games were more hardcore and challenging. The truth of the matter is likely that earlier games had simpler mechanics and less to learn; however, modern games with clever and careful tutorial level design are often more satisfying to play, especially a second time through.

When a person starts a new job or activity, they are trained in that activity in a number of ways. Employees are given a manual and expected to read and understand it, they are also expected to attend training seminars to learn processes, and they are expected to learn on-the-job as activities occur that the manual or the seminars have not addressed. There are two types of knowledge acquired in this context. **Explicit knowledge** is knowledge that is written down and communicated to new individuals directly, through training or documentation. This constitutes the common known and understood information associated with the activity or organization, and it is assumed that all associated individuals have access to this information. It can be consulted in reference documents, and the act of amending or modifying this information or the associated processes is usually participatory, and consultative (although not all stakeholders are consulted). In contrast, **tacit knowledge** is that collection of knowledge expected to be understood by associated individuals, but is communicated informally and in unorganized pieces, if at all. This is knowledge contained in the memory of individuals associated with the organization or activity, but not passed to others in any structured way. "It is the way we have always done it" is a phrase used to justify tacit knowledge or processes. Tacit knowledge is discovered accidentally, when an activity emerges that requires it, and an individual with that knowledge is nearby to impart the knowledge. It is unreliable and can easily be lost from the organization, which is why organizational documentation is developed—to formalize and regularize the transfer of institutional knowledge to new individuals.

### 11.2.6.1 Jargon and Wizards

There is a risk in situations that require training that the act of accumulating and regularizing knowledge in order to teach new users (employees or stakeholders) can have the side effect of further isolating or excluding those who have not been trained. As systems (both systems of interaction and systems of knowledge) become more complex, more training is required to understand them, and as new processes are developed, new language is invented to efficiently describe these systems. As discussed in Section 13.1.1, terminology was invented for emerging computer systems that helped new users understand and discuss operational topics, but this language served to exclude individuals who had not learned it and made these processes appear even more obscure and confusing. **Jargon** is the term given to technical language specific to a domain, but the term is also used to describe needlessly complex or obfuscating language. Individuals who learn the domain must learn the new jargon, and those who don't know the jargon find it more difficult to learn the processes just by watching trained individuals perform the tasks. Over time, an air of mystery or prestige can emerge around individuals skilled in specific processes who are fluent in the jargon of those processes. Untrained individuals can feel less empowered to undertake these activities, even as the activities themselves become easier to use or to learn or more automated. Computer usability has improved significantly over time, especially in the domain of personal touchscreen devices, but many are still intimated by these devices at least in part because they don't understand the language used when experts discuss these devices. When an expert uses special language and performs complicated activities quickly to produce impressive results, it can seem like magic, and the people who can do these amazing things can seem like wizards.

### 11.2.7 Familiarity as a Hint to Function in VR

Although one of the advantages of VR development is that the developer is not tied to reality, building reality-based virtual experiences has two benefits in the context of familiarity. First, users who know about a particular real-world object or phenomenon can expect that their familiarity with the physical version of the object might inform their interactions with the virtual object it is modelled after. If I see a telephone in VR, I might expect that I should be able to pick it up and put it to my ear and be able to talk to another person somewhere else. The specifics of that interaction may be different (how do I dial a call, how do I grip the receiver, can I cradle the receiver on my shoulder, etc.), but the activity suggested by the object will be informed by the user's familiarity with that object. Drawers can be pulled, books can be opened, bats can be swung, and balls can be thrown. This expectation is so pervasive, in fact, that if a user sees an object they are familiar with in a virtual environment, they may *expect* that it should be interactable. Unless you want to implement interactions for every object in your scene, you may need to *signify* interactability to the user, as discussed in Section 11.1.1.

A challenge here, of course, is that some virtual versions of objects *cannot* be interacted with in the same way. A virtual chair cannot be sat in. A virtual cane will not support your weight. A virtual tree cannot be climbed. A virtual doughnut can be virtually eaten, but the result will be the same as a certain cookie-eating monster—virtual crumbs everywhere, and no actual calories consumed.

The second potential benefit of leveraging familiarity in VR is the use of VR as a training medium for the physical world. Many researchers and developers have seen the potential for virtual experiences to build experience in situations that might otherwise be dangerous or expensive. Simulators have been used by the military for decades to train pilots and astronauts, but virtual experiences can be used for more mundane training tasks like company onboarding and safety training. Moving these training scenarios to VR has several additional benefits, including reducing the requirement to travel to a training location, reducing the time required by the trainers or facilitators, and implementing evaluation metrics within the VR scenario to ensure training compliance and success.

If specialized hardware is available, like a virtual steering wheel or virtual HOTAS, certain interactions may be more intuitive and natural, like driving a car or flying an airplane. The degree of alignment between the virtual object and the physical object will have some impact on how easy it is for the user to interact with the physical object and its virtual counterpart as if they were the same object. Much like the rubber hand illusion (Section 2.4.3), the user's mind will attempt to align the sensations from the visual system and the preoperative system, and unless the sensations diverge in an unusual way, the illusion may be maintained. This relies on a careful alignment of the virtual controls to the physical controls, so that when the user looks at a virtual button under their virtual thumb, they also feel a physical button under their physical thumb. The alignment of the a control with its expected outcome is called *mapping*, and it constitutes the third key method for helping users understand what the result of an interaction might be.

## 11.2.8 Metaphor and Analogy

If a user is not familiar with a use case in a system they are to use, and traditional training is unavailable, inappropriate, or would reduce user engagement, an option is to build the system in such a way as to leverage existing familiarity. This may seem counterintuitive at first, since if they are not familiar with the system, how can they use familiarity to improve ease-of-use outcomes of the system? If the system is made to look similar to a system they are familiar with, then they can leverage existing knowledge to "short-circuit" the process of discovery and learning required to use the new system.

The classic example of the metaphorical user interface is the desktop, where computer storage units are like paper files, the background work surface is like a desk top, the list of incoming tasks is like an office inbox, and the file deletion process is like a wastepaper basket. The metaphor is so ubiquitous at this point that much of computing terminology is taken directly from the office scenario it imitates, from opening folders to sending mail. Desktop computing is a bit of a mixed metaphor, of course, because along with a desktop there are menus (a metaphor taken from restaurants) and palettes (taken from painting), as well as cutting, copying, and pasting (taken from newsprint shop processes).

Some metaphors are more successful than others. Microsoft Bob, a famously failed operating system, attempted to reinvent the computing metaphor as one of a house with rooms specific to tasks, and while the intention was to make computing more user-friendly, the result was a cluttered interface with functionality that was difficult to find, and signifiers that were difficult to distinguish from ornamentation.

Most VR experiences are literal, since the intent is to replicate the functionality being simulated, and the principle benefit of VR in this context is that you can give the user direct access to the functions and activities implemented, rather than requiring a proxy to operate it and a metaphor to understand it. Metaphorical interfaces can assist VR as well. Many multiplayer games have players first enter a staging area where they wait to be matched with a group to start a game. The purpose of this area as well as the expected activities within it can be communicated to the user by framing it as a "waiting room," a familiar concept to most people. It could be a large open area where users can experiment with their abilities before spawning into the game stage, or it could be a classic waiting room with white walls, uncomfortable chairs, and old magazines.

The key with metaphoric interfaces is to understand what you are trying to communicate to the user via the metaphor, to ensure that the analogy between the actual interaction and the metaphoric interaction is close enough that the metaphor is not communicating erroneous information or causing a user to be more confused, and to ensure that the familiar experience of the metaphor is sufficiently universal as to be a useful shorthand for the interaction or information being communicated.

## 11.3 MAPPING

When indicating the function of a control or interaction, the physical or conceptual location of the control can provide clues to the user. As with the light-switch-in-the-room example, the function of the light switch is assumed to be the lights in that room, and it would be unusual (and frustrating to the user) if the switch controlled the lights in a different room, or the heat in the house, or something else. In houses with gas heat, it is important to be able to turn off the gas to the furnace in an emergency, and a switch is a common element to do so, because its function is familiar. The switch should be central to the house, so the user does not have to run to the furnace to turn it off (especially if the furnace is dangerously malfunctioning), but the result is a light switch that doesn't seem to do anything. If a user is confused about the function of the switch and turns it off by accident, the user may not know that the furnace has been turned off, because the result of the action is also not obvious. A change in a far-off sound and an inability for the furnace to produce heat later in the day are mismatched effects of the switch. The first solution to this problem is to add a signifier to the furnace switch so the user can directly perceive its function, but since accidental activation is potentially quite serious, these switches are often put in slightly unusual places, for example on the wall of a stairwell, a few feet above the light switch for the stairwell. Having two switches on the wall allows the user to confirm that the switch is for something other than lights (since the light switch is present), and having the switch in an unfamiliar place makes the user reconsider its function. The new location of the switch is a **mapping**, an alignment of a characteristic of a control (usually its relative location) with its function

### 11.3.1 Mapping Case Study: Stove Controls

When a collection of similar controls exist to operate a collection of similar functions the mapping of those controls is critical. A classic example of the benefit of good mapping (or the drawbacks of poor mapping) is the arrangements of controls on a four-burner stove. The burners are arranged in a grid, but sometimes the controls are arranged in a line, as shown in Figure 11.15a, because it is preferred by the designer either aesthetically or functionally. These controls can appear at the back of the stove, or in front, but being at the back has a secondary drawback—that the user must reach their hand over a hot stove to activate or deactivate the stove. Although the controls on the right are likely to activate the burners on the right, the linear mapping means the user does not know which right-hand control activates the front burner and which activates the back burner. Stoves like these usually have a signifier, showing the grid of burners and which one is activated by the control. Figure 11.15b shows a much more direct mapping of the controls. The grid arrangement of burners is reflected in the identical arrangement of the controls, and there is no confusion regarding which control activates which burner. Further, the controls are clustered in one location, meaning the user can activate any burner with the same hand gesture, and the size of the controls reflects the size of the burner. While this last design choice is probably not necessary and may lead to increased manufacturing cost, problematic ergonomics (the size of the controller is dictated more by the size of the hand that uses it), and less-than-desirable aesthetics, it demonstrates that mapping can occur in many features of the controls, beyond their physical arrangement and layout, although it could be argued that the size of the control in this case is a signifier rather than a mapping feature.

Complicated environments like the cockpit of the Apollo spacecraft are particularly challenging for mapping. The physical locations of the controls are arranged as

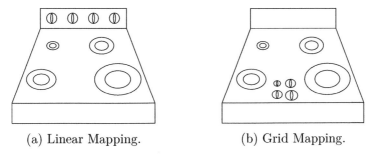

(a) Linear Mapping.        (b) Grid Mapping.

Figure 11.15: Mapping of controls on a stove.

much as possible to their relative functions, if there is such a logical arrangement, but mostly the controls are arranged conceptually, with clusters of controls organized by function. Figure 11.16 shows the control layout of the Apollo spacecraft, with the function of each cluster of controls indicated. The complexity of the controls, combined with the obscure functions and importance of quick responses, means the astronauts had to rely on mapping, affordances, signifiers, and familiarity, in order to be able to push the right button at the right time. Section 12.3.1 details organizational principles of information that can assist in communicating a specific mapping to a user.

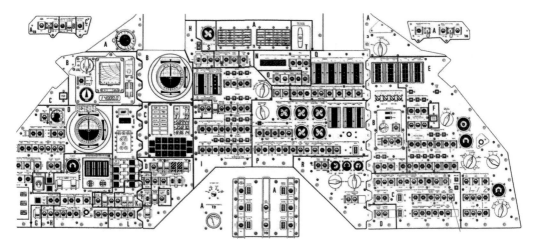

Figure 11.16: The control panel for the Apollo command module. *NASA, public domain.*

**Articulatory directness** is the degree to which the motion suggested by the control is aligned with the effect of the control. If there is a knob on a computer interface, it suggests turning, and the effect of the control should be related to turning in some way. Conceptually, the temperature of a stove element can be set on a scale from off to as hot as it can be, and although the scale is linear, the articulation of the dial corresponds to the amount of gas or electricity provided to the stove and is reasonably articulatory direct. Users are familiar with the dial on the stove

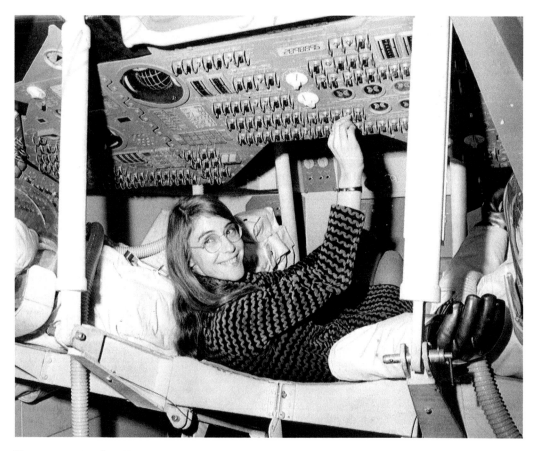

Figure 11.17: Apollo programmer Margaret Hamilton with the Apollo control panel. *NASA, public domain.*

because it is ubiquitous and common, but a linear temperature selector may be more articulatory direct. The type of information manipulated can also relate to the directness of the control. A phone number is an integer, but setting the value of that integer with a slider would make little sense and be frustrating; while a volume control is also an integer, the user should not be required to type in a number to set the volume each time they want to change it. Phone numbers are discrete and independent, while volume controls are continuous and relative. Finally, the action taken by the user should also align with the action suggested by the control. Dials are familiar and compact and therefore often presented as a way to control a number on a computer interface. In the physical world, a dial can be actuated by gripping the dial and rotating, but in a mouse or touchscreen computer system, rotation cannot easily be translated from the user's hand to the system, so dials are often controlled by clicking and dragging, or by rotating the mouse wheel. This a direct contradiction of articulatory directness, since the interface suggests a rotating action, but the actual interaction required is linear.

## 11.3.2  Mapping in VR

There are two ways in which mapping can improve usability in VR. The first sense is how mapping is used in the physical world: the arrangement of controls lends a clue to their function. If a virtual cooking simulator needed a stove, the same mapping principles would apply as for a stove in the physical world—when many similar controls are available, their arrangement should reflect an aspect of their function. In VR, you won't be burned if you hold your hand over a virtual stove element, so the absolute location of the burner controls may matter less, but if they are in a line instead of in a grid, the same frustrations may apply. Further, signifiers may be difficult to see in VR especially if they are small, and adding labels can affect the style of the experience.

Another option in VR is to remove in-world controls altogether and allow a user to activate an object directly. If you need to turn on a stove element, you can first select the stove, either by pointing at it or holding your hand near it, and then activate the element by pressing a button on the VR controller or making a gesture with your hands. The interaction is not as direct (the user must remember or be reminded of the button or the gesture), but if there are no controls, there is no need for mapping those controls to their results.

If the controls are intended to replicate an object or interaction in the physical world, for training purposes or to increase realism, the arrangement of interactions should, of course, resemble the physical object as much as possible; the challenge here is that although the user will know (or learn) where a control is, have its operation afforded, and have its function signified, the actual activation of the control will always be different in VR than in the physical world, because the user will not have access to the physical interaction of flipping the switch or pushing the button. If a user is flying the Apollo spacecraft in VR and reaches out to press a button on the console, their hand will pass through the virtual console. Not only will the user be frustrated because they cannot touch the button they want to press or lean their other fingers on the console for support, but presence will be reduced because the user is reminded that they are not in the Apollo spacecraft, but are still sitting in their basement. The only way to effectively replicate the feeling of operating a switch on the console of a spacecraft is to have a physical representation of that switch in the physical world, aligned with the virtual representation of that switch, such that when the user reaches out their virtual hand, it touches a physical object. Because the variety of switches, knobs, and controls that can exist in the physical world is almost unlimited, a custom piece of hardware would be required for every experience in order to have the highest fidelity. In practice, VR developers building flight simulators or other complex environments have three options:

- Present the interface as-is and require the user to interact with an element by selecting the control (by pointing or reaching) and pressing a button on the VR controller.

- Simplify the controls significantly so that it is easier for the user to select and activate the controls.

- Require the user to have a physical representation of the object in their playspace.

### 11.3.3 Mixed Reality Object Alignment

The simplest and most effective form of mapping to accomplish in VR is when the object the user sees in VR is the same as the physical object the user can feel. The creation and distribution of virtual assets is reasonably simple, but the creation and distribution of the corresponding physical asset is significantly more difficult. There are several ways that this physical-virtual alignment can be achieved. The first way is to mass produce a physical object corresponding to the virtual object and require the user to acquire this object. This is problematic and impractical for many reasons. Requiring the user to purchase a physical object will significantly reduce the user base of your experience. If your experience is intended for a specific target such as a training facility, there may be a justification for a budget for manufacturing and distributing these physical objects. Additionally, once the physical object is distributed, no changes can be made to the general arrangement of the virtual object it is meant to align with. If the physical object is a standard object, such as a medical or construction tool, a firearm, a piece of sporting equipment, or a vehicle control system like a steering wheel or HOTAS, the physical object may be applicable to more than one scenario and the overall design of the object is less likely to change.

The second approach is to develop and distribute a set of plans for a physical object to be mapped to the virtual object in your experience. The physical object could be constructed using electronics and 3D printing, which is becoming more accessible to hobbyists, but the average user may not have the capabilities of manufacturing the object themselves. The advantage of this approach is that the physical object can be changed, both in the plans for the physical object that are distributed and in the construction of the physical object itself, even after it has been created. The disadvantage is that the developer has less control over the quality of construction of the physical object, and therefore the user experience may suffer if the constructed object breaks or otherwise fails.

A variant to this approach is to provide plans for a 3D printed object to augment the physical VR controllers that users already have. As VR hardware systems become more standardized, developers can assume that users have VR controllers that adhere to a particular shape. As a result, an object can be designed and manufactured which connects to that virtual controller, changing its shape and making it feel more like the virtual object it is meant to represent. For example, it is possible to download plans for a ping-pong paddle, a golf club handle, or a pistol grip (Fig 11.18), as well as two-handed gun stocks, finishing reels, and other objects, all of which are designed to connect to the VR controller and provide a more satisfying and usable alignment of the feel of the virtual object in the user's hand. It should be noted here that this does not change the orientation or arrangement of the *controls* on a VR controller, only the overall shape of the physical object itself. If the virtual object has no controls, or if the controls are only used out of the context of using the object (for selecting menus or other meta-interactions in the VR experience), this will not be a significant problem, but if the virtual object has controls that are different from the physical object, mismapping can occur.

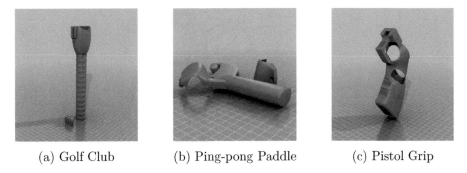

(a) Golf Club          (b) Ping-pong Paddle          (c) Pistol Grip

Figure 11.18: 3D printed objects to augment a VR controller.

### 11.3.4    Mapping physical objects to VR controllers

Section 11.1.5 showed several examples of handheld objects with controls; the affordance of those controls is tied to the handling of the object, but if the physical object has controls in one set of affordances and the virtual object has controls in a different arrangement, the misaligment of these controls can lead to frustration and errors. As an example of this, consider the earlier study of the affordances of the M1911 handgun (Figure 11.10). The physical object has three things that the user can do with the thumb of the hand which holds the object: they can pull back the hammer, they can release the magazine, and they can toggle the safety. The VR controller also has three buttons which can be activated by the hand that holds it; the question is, which button does what? Figure 11.19 shows an alignment of the virtual object (the M1911) with the physical object (the hand controller). The trigger and grip are well aligned, and if the user looks at the virtual object, the trigger will be afforded correctly; but no matter how the user looks at the virtual object, they will not be informed as to the way in which those three thumb controls will be activated by the three buttons on the physical VR controller. Even more problematically, since there is no natural mapping from the buttons to the interactions of the handgun, any VR experience which implements the M1911 may map these controls differently, which makes learning and remembering the mapping almost impossible. Jakob's law would only apply if a standard mapping emerges from the developer community, but this mapping would only apply to the M1911, unless a *conceptual* mapping were to emerge, where button "A" is always safety, button "B" is always magazine release, and button "C" is always pulling back the hammer. The user's only option here is to practise to develop familiarity or press a button that invokes a help menu to remind the user of the operation of the object. Regardless, the advantages of using a model of a real-world object may be outweighed by the disadvantages of a failed mapping.

It should be noted that the two-handed interactions in this case are also problematic. Holding the firearm in one hand while supporting it with the other hand should work well, but the action of pulling back the slide to charge the firearm may

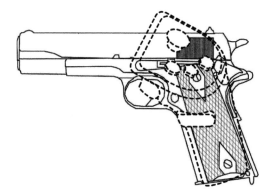

Figure 11.19: M1911 handgun aligned with VR controller.

be challenging to accomplish. First, the hands must be brought close together, which may mean the VR controllers collide, which may break presence and reduce tracking fidelity, and second, the action of gripping the slide may or may not have a natural mapping to the control options available on the VR controller. It makes conceptual sense to use the "grab" trigger on the handle of the VR controller, since the actions are similar, but this grabbing action is not directly analogous with either the index finger or the middle finger and is more of a full-hand grip, depending on the experience of the user. Again, because the M1911 is a popular firearm, it is likely that the firearm will be present in multiple VR games and experiences, and because there may be disagreement on what the "best" mapping might be, different experiences are likely to implement this action differently, leading to confusion, frustration, and errors.

If a VR experience *must* have a virtual version of a real-world physical object, great care must be taken to develop mappings that are as natural and reasonable as possible, and the user should be given every opportunity to learn (and relearn and be reminded of) the mappings the developer has chosen. If the user requests a reminder, simply showing the button names is likely insufficient. A full rendering of the VR controller they are holding should be implemented, with clear indicators, both with labels and linkages, to what each button does.

### 11.3.4.1 Case study: finger tracking and virtual musical instruments

Musical instruments are a class of physical objects that at once seem a perfect fit for VR, and also a very difficult implementational challenge for developers. Musical instruments are used with the hands, not with VR controllers, so hand tracking or haptic gloves are required for a realistic experience. The interactions of the hand with the physical instrument are deeply subtle and specific. The accuracy required to place a finger on a violin string and create a note that is in tune is less than a millimetre. Wiggling your finger back and forth a fraction of a millimetre will add vibrato to the sound, but requires subtle control feedback between your finger and the fingerboard. Often, with musical instruments, your fingers are close together and in unusual poses compared to the expected pose and gesture of hand tracking systems, which means finger tracking for virtual musical instruments may be more susceptible to tracking errors as well.

Some musical instruments, like brass or woodwind instruments, consist of specific physical valves or linkages that are activated by a finger. In these cases, the finger tracking required is much more forgiving, because as long as the valve is depressed, the instrument should register the change in the note. Sensors could be placed on the physical instrument to inform the VR system when a valve is pressed, allowing the system to know what note to produce.

Other musical instruments, like drums, require larger gestures of the arm and body, which are much easier to track. Developers have built VR systems that attempt to replicate the experience of playing drums, allowing users to place drum skins in any location and hit the drum with a virtual drumstick aligned with the controller held by the user. These experiences are engaging for novice users but can be frustrating for people who know how to play drums because, although the large exuberant motions of the drummer's arms and body are what the audience sees, subtle movements of the fingers holding the drumstick are what allow the drummer to play. Indeed, the grip of the drumstick as it bounces off of the drumhead is what allows skilled drummers to produce a "drum roll," and in VR this is impossible. There is no drum skin to bounce off of, and no stick to do the bouncing, so instead, the drum sound is activated when the user passes the virtual stick near the virtual drum. In the same way that "guitar hero" does not teach you how to play guitar, virtual drums will not teach you how to play the drums. The experience may be enjoyable and satisfying, and it would be possible to develop new VR instruments that build on the advantages of VR without the limitations of the physical world, but whenever a physical world experience is translated into the virtual world, especially one with the subtleties of music, the limitations of the VR technology will result in a less-than-perfect translation.

### 11.3.4.2  *Virtual controllers from physical controllers*

Where VR is used as a tool for accomplishing a specific goal, like drawing, sketching, sculpting, or designing, the narrative of the experience is not tied to any virtual world but is instead linked to the activity being accomplished. As such, the controller in the virtual world can be an exact replica of the physical hand controller, with the same affordances for buttons and other controls. Signifiers can float with the controller to indicate what each button does, and different tools can be selected with modal switches. Because the object model can be changed to clearly indicate the mode, concerns of modal interactions are less problematic.

As long as the user can perceive the controller in the virtual world and the buttons and triggers are mapped to the same location in the physical world, the shape of the controller itself is not important. Developers can allow the buttons to float or embed them into a framework that more accurately reflects the style of the world they are constructing or can attach a tool or actuator onto a virtual model identical to the physical controller. Allowing the buttons to remain in the same location provides the advantage of reminding the user of where the buttons are and what they will do, and showing a model of the user's hand interacting with the virtual control surface allows a closer mapping and improved plausibility. Figure 11.20 (a) shows an example where the virtual model of the original controller is augmented with a tool, which the user can swap out for other virtual tools. This technique is common in sculpting and drawing scenarios. In Figure 11.20 (b), the original hand controller model is replaced by a virtual wrist-worn controller in order to allow the virtual hand to appear empty, improving the illusion that the user can reach out and pick up objects. The buttons on the controller are maintained in their original locations so the user can still see the buttons and be reminded of their function, and the wrist portion can be further augmented with a display for the user.

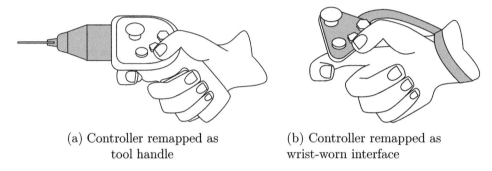

(a) Controller remapped as      (b) Controller remapped as
tool handle             wrist-worn interface

Figure 11.20: Virtual hand controls mapped to button locations on controllers.

One challenge with this approach of mapping virtual control buttons to the location on the physical controllers is that it assumes all users will have the same physical controllers. As VR hardware changes, VR controllers will also change, although controllers produced by each VR hardware company will likely retain the same button location and layout. Games or experiences that use controller mapping will require a separate asset pack and mapping procedure for each hardware system they run on, as well as a way to operate if the user employs hand tracking or haptic gloves instead of controller access. Figure 11.21 shows a set of three common controllers available in 2022, from three different manufacturers. In each of these cases, although there is a general similarity in the collection of buttons available to the user (thumbstick/pad, thumb buttons, and trigger, grip), the arrangement and shape of these buttons are different between platforms. Any VR software making use of controller mapping will need a separate model for each hardware platform they plan to support. Affording interaction with a button in a different place, or a button that does not exist, is problematic for the user.

### 11.3.4.3 *Mixed Reality Mundane Object Mapping*

The other way to approach this challenge is to alter the physical object the user is interacting with in order to more closely align with the virtual object that appears in your experience. If the user is interacting with a common physical object, like a computer keyboard, a piano, a game controller, or a pencil, the VR developer can make use of several tricks to align the virtual version of the object with the physical version of the object. This mixed-reality approach may require some initial manual

(a) HTC Vive          (b) Oculus Quest          (c) Valve Index

Figure 11.21: Different button layouts on popular VR controllers.

alignment on the part of the user, but needs no expensive or complicated tracking system for the object— ordinary physical – world objects will suffice.

As an example, if the user will be typing on a keyboard, the developer can create a virtual keyboard model that is similar in shape and size to a physical keyboard. The system would need to perform some basic steps to align the virtual keyboard with the physical keyboard that is in front of them, but once those alignment steps are performed, the user would be able to reach out with their fingers, type on the physical keyboard, and see that typing accomplished on the virtual keyboard.

The alignment would require the system to be able to visually detect and align the keyboard; otherwise the user would need to see both the virtual and physical keyboards at the same time to align them, which would require a headset that supports pass–through mixed reality. This activity would also require high-quality hand tracking. Note that camera-based visual hand tracking can be particularly challenged when the fingers are interacting with real-world objects.

Even though the set-up is complicated, the advantage is that the user's fingers feel a realistic interaction with the physical keyboard, and the user's eyes see the virtual keyboard which then can be modified in any way the developer chooses. A typing tutor could highlight particular keys to be practised. The keyboard could be remapped to any language instantly or re-imagined with any key doing almost anything. A similar scenario could be imagined using mixed reality to augment a piano keyboard. The same finger tracking and alignment challenges would occur, but once aligned, the visual presence of the keyboard could be modified in any way, while the tactile feel of the keyboard would remain familiar.

Almost any physical object could be aligned to a corresponding virtual object in this way, as long as the system could reliably identify and track the location of that object in the physical world. The user might have a collection of arbitrary shaped objects on their desk, and when they reach out to grab one, the VR system would make that object appear to be anything they use or wanted (Figure 11.22). A plain white cube in physical reality could become any number of varied interaction devices in VR. This technique is often called **augmented virtuality**.

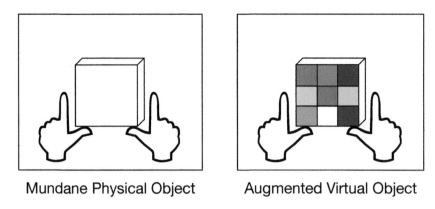

Mundane Physical Object        Augmented Virtual Object

Figure 11.22: Augmenting a physical world object in VR.

### 11.3.4.4 Virtual Hand Representations

Another decision to be made by the developer is what will be the virtual object that is used to represent the location of the user's hand in physical reality. If a user is holding an object and they hold the object in front of their face, they should see some representation of the act of holding that object. Although it may seem intuitive to make this representation as accurate as possible, there are design decisions to be made here and there are advantages and disadvantages to each. There are, in fact, five possibilities for the visual representational mapping of the user's hand:

- A virtual hand holding the controller

- A virtual hand holding the object

- The controller without a virtual hand

- The object without a virtual hand

- A virtual hand without the object or controller

Each of these options may be appropriate in different situations. For example, a new user learning the controller may be advantaged by seeing a virtual representation of that controller, complete with signifiers for each button, so the user can quickly and easily be reminded of which buttons are available and what they might do. Showing the user's hand on the controller may add a form of articulatory directness, but the hand model is likely to occlude parts of the controller that may be important. Showing the controller without the hand model may, at first, seem like it is a less direct mapping, but once the user moves their hand and sees the controller moving exactly the same way, the alignment will be very clear and obvious because of the successful sensorimotor contingency. Similarly, showing the object the user is virtually holding allows the user to articulate that object and direct it towards a particular goal, by aiming it at a target or moving it close to some other object they wish to manipulate. In this case, whether or not to show the virtual hand depends, in part, on the content of the virtual experience you are creating. In some cases, it may make more sense to have a hand model holding an object—if there are many objects to consider and the user is routinely picking up one object and letting go of another; in other cases, the hand model may be redundant and add unnecessary complexity—if the user selects one object and then uses that object for a period of time. Showing a virtual hand by itself may be a more direct mapping, especially if the VR system is using hand tracking or a haptic glove and may also encourage more direct interaction by the user—the user may feel they are able to reach out and interact with buttons and levers if they can see their hand directly.

### 11.3.4.5 Motion Mapping

In the same way that it can seem obvious that a virtual representation should be as similar to the physical world as possible, the way that representation moves, on first analysis, should be as similar as possible to the way the real-world object moves. If I hold my hand in front of my face and I move my hand, it seems obvious that the representation of my hand that I can see should move in exactly the same way. Indeed, sensorimotor contingencies may be broken if I move my hand in one way and the visual representation of my hand moves in a different way. However, there are some circumstances where the mapping of the motion should not necessarily be directly one-to-one. In the physical world, when I hold a small, light object, it is easy for me to move that object around through space. If, on the other hand, I am holding a large, heavy object, it is more effort for me to move that object around. The object has momentum, and I feel that momentum through the object's interaction with my hand. I need to work harder to make that my object start to move, and it may take longer for other objects start moving. I may even have to drag that object across the floor if it is very heavy. Virtual objects, however, have no weight—unless they are associated with a real-world mixed reality proxy of that object. In general, If I am holding a virtual pencil or a virtual sledgehammer, the relative movement of those virtual objects will be identical. This is a situation where altering the motion mapping can add an illusion of weight to a virtual object. If I hold a sledgehammer by the end of the handle and am able to smoothly wave it through the air, it will feel more like a balloon than a heavy tool. If the hammer includes a simulation of momentum, the weight of the tool can be communicated to me visually, as shown in Figure 11.23. I move the handle, and the head is delayed for a moment, angling the handle backward before it starts to follow the motion of my hand.

This technique is commonly used in sword-fighting games—imbuing the sword with a sense of momentum or inertia can make it feel far more realistic. A similar technique may be applicable to situations where a user is pointing at an object from far away. If the user holds out their hand and points a laser beam from their finger, the end of that laser beam amplifies any tiny movements in the user's hand, because it is so far away. A small shake or uncertainty on a part of the user's hand will translate to a large variation in what the user is pointing at. Artificially dampening that movement, while apparently reducing the directness of the mapping of the action, leads to a more satisfying experience because it increases the directness between the *intended* action and the outcome. The user wants to point at something specific, faraway, and the shaking imbued by the user's hand is involuntary[2].

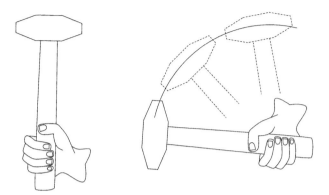

Figure 11.23: Motion of a weighted object. A slight delay in the motion can add a feeling of momentum.

The alignment between the motion the user makes with their hand and the object they see moving as a result of their hand motion is reminiscent of the rubber hand illusion described in Section 2.4.3. If there is commonality between the user's intention and the perception of the result of that intention, the user will build an association between their physical hand and the virtual object representing it, even if that object is not a virtual model of a hand. Moving the object they are holding will lead to the same illusion, and providing it with appropriate illusion of weight will increase plausibility of the interaction. The user will perceive the virtual hand as their real hand as long as sensorimotor contingencies are preserved. Modifying this mapping slightly can provide improved presence even if the user is not holding a tool or object— or they are tired, or under the influence of hypnosis or a drug, making the user's hands move differently than expected can be a compelling clue. If you want the user to believe they are a giant, making their hands move slowly can make them feel large and slow.

## 11.4   COMMON INTERACTIONS IN VR

When developing interactions for VR scenarios, it is important first to decide whether your system will be as close as possible to expected interactions in the physical world, or whether the interactions the user will engage in will be abstracted from reality. The **interaction fidelity** of a system refers to how similar to the physical world are the activities and actions within the system. Although conceptually similar to sensorimotor contingencies, interaction fidelity engages at a higher level. Sensorimotor contingencies relate to how we expect our sensations to change as a result of our actions, and interaction fidelity refers to how we expect our actions to affect the

---

[2]Some neurological disorders, such as Parkinson's disease, can lead to significant involuntary muscle movement. Mediated motion mapping may be used to provide satisfying experiences in these situations.

world. Interaction fidelity need not always be high— abstracted worlds where very unusual things happen can be entertaining and engaging, but if the intent of a VR scenario is to train a user in operation of a device in the physical world or help the user overcome an anxiety rooted in the physical world, a higher level of interaction fidelity may be more appropriate.

A key indicator of interaction fidelity in VR is the idea of **object compliance**: whether or not an object behaves in the expected or learned way. Some compliances emerge from natural experience with the physical world, while others are learned from experience. Interactions can be compliant as well, based on the expected interactions. When a driver grips the steering wheel and turns it to the left, the expected reaction is that the car will steer to the left. Flying an airplane with a joystick also adheres to such directional compliance—if you pull the stick back, you expect the airplane to nose up. This compliance is in direct conflict with a second similar compliance, however, which is the movement of a targeting reticle. If you are controlling the aiming of a weapon with a joystick, pulling the stick back will result in the reticle moving down, since in this case the compliance mapping is related to the linear movement of the joystick compared to the linear movement of the reticle. If you are flying a plane and using a targeting reticle, these two compliances are in conflict, which is why games involving flying often allow the user to select how the stick should behave. A similar compliance conflict exists in the interfaces of traditional computers, based on the direction a scroll wheel should move content. Before touchscreens, the scroll wheel was conceptualized as moving a frame over a static piece of content—thus, scrolling "down" would make the content move upwards. Since touchscreens have become ubiquitous, a more direct conceptualization has emerged, where scrolling the wheel moves the content past a fixed frame, so scrolling "down" makes the content move downwards.

In each of these examples, a decision must be made regarding which is the "natural" direction of motion based on the user's input, but the choice is between compliances which are reasonable. If a user pulls back on the stick and the airplane banks to the left, this is an example of **non-compliance**, where an outcome is different from what is expected. If you move your hand to the left and the hand model in VR moves to the right, this is an example of non-compliance, and while there are situations where this interaction may be desirable, learning may be required on the part of the user.

**Nulling compliance** refers to the expected behaviour of an object when the user is no longer controlling it. If a user picks up an object and then releases it, what should happen to it depends on the physics of the scenario, the interface aspects of the interaction, and the likely next interaction with the same or a different object. If the user is stacking blocks to make a tower, letting go of a block should allow it to interact with the physics of the world and the other blocks in the tower. If the user is looking at a display on their wrist, that display should disappear when they turn their wrist away; however, if the user is looking at a spawned display screen for inventory, that screen should stay where it is placed in order to allow the user to interact with the inventory and only disappear when the user indicates that they are finished with the inventory task. If the user releases their grip on a weapon, should it drop to the floor or return to the user's holster? Should the user be required to continue to grip the weapon while they are using it or should the user be able to press a button to grab the weapon and then press another button to release? These design decisions will reflect the ultimate usability of the system.

Nulling compliance also comes into play when considering what happens to an object that is connected to the rest of the world. When you pull on the launch knob of a pinball machine and then release it, it is pulled back into its original position by a spring, launching the ball into the machine. When you pull on the arm of a slot machine, it springs back into its original location. When you push against a door handle and walk through the doorway, the door may swing back after you pass, it may stay open, or it may continue turning (if it is a revolving door). What happens to objects when we release them is as important as what happens when we grab them.

When interacting with and manipulating an object in VR, a user must first choose which object or objects to interact with and then modify characteristics of that object via rotation, scaling, or positioning. In the physical world, there are only a few ways of interacting with objects—you can reach out with your own hand, or you can project your agency with some tool or process. Similarly, on flat-screen user interfaces, there are only a few ways of interacting with objects—direct selection with a cursor or pointer or collecting a set of objects locationally or conceptually. In VR, on the other hand, many alternative methods for selection and manipulation are available.

Selection, for example, is a fundamental activity for any computing interface where multiple objects are available. We select text in a text editor in order to change, move, or augment it; we select areas of an image to modify; we select menu items to activate; and we select files to interact with. The act of selection in traditional interfaces is so familiar and fundamental that it can be easy to forget that it is, in fact, heavily mediated. We move a mouse on a table surface, which moves a cursor on a screen, which is collocated with the objects we wish to select. When the cursor is near the object we want, we press the mouse button, which causes the selection to occur. Anyone of these mediated interactions can lead to a frustrating interruption. If the mouse doesn't move properly on the table, the crusher can skip. If the cursor disappears, we don't know where we are selecting. The problem is further exacerbated in three-dimensional interfaces projected on two-dimensional screen. Interacting with a 3D model using a mouse is unpredictable and difficult: which axis will it rotate on? Which items under the mouse will be selected? If I drag a rectangle around a 3D model, will it select all points on the model or only the ones I can see? A touchscreen has similar limitations: if I want to select an object on a touchscreen, I simply reach out and touch it with my finger; but if I want to then move it, will dragging my finger move the object or will it select more objects? Again, the target interaction is mediated by the screen between the user and the content.

VR has the potential to remove these proxies of interaction, but for direct selection and interaction we only move them down one level. In order to grab an object in VR, the simplest approach is to simply reach out and grab it, this act of selection, however, depends on whether the user has a controller or is using hand tracking; with a controller, the user needs to know how close to place their virtual hand and which button to press. Pressing the wrong button will lead to a different interaction than intended, and affording the correct button can interrupt plausibility if not implemented naturally. If hand tracking or a haptic glove is to be used, the user must make an appropriate hand gesture, but if the gesture is not recognized, the object will not be selected. Using hand tracking can increase presence because sensorimotor contingencies involved in moving the hand and articulating the fingers are reflected visually, but these reinforcements set up expectations about what will happen when the user attempts to grip an object—when the virtual hand closes around the object, but the user's actual hand feels no such resistance, the illusion can fade.

Developers have collected a set of common patterns for interactions in VR, which are listed and described below. Selection methods, as described above, involve choosing which object or objects to interaction with, and modification methods involve changing characteristics of the object. Some taxonomies of interactions like these also include viewpoint control techniques; however, these are discussed in Chapter 10.

## 11.4.1  Selection

### 11.4.1.1  Direct Selection

As described above, the most straightforward selection method in VR is to reach out with your hand and grab something. This pattern exemplifies the challenges with any design pattern, since it seems straightforward on first conceptualization, but is fraught with complexity and opportunities for failure. Any hand interaction method must be thoroughly tested, especially with people who have not been involved in its development, because hand interaction appears strictly intuitive. A developer will say to a user: "pick up the ball," and the user will not know which button to press, how close to be, or how to get closer, and both developer and user are frustrated. Direct selection requires clear instruction and opportunity for experimentation in order to be reliable. Because it is ubiquitous, many VR experiences will implement it, and because developers differ in their approaches, many different implementations will be presented to the user. Jakob's law (Section 11.2.2) applies here as well.

When the user cannot reach the target object from their position, action-at-a-distance is required. Many options are available for this situation. Simplest, perhaps, is to allow or encourage the user to move to a place where they can interact with the object. If the character is hungry and there is an apple on the ground, the character can simply walk over to the apple, pick it up, and eat it. Depending on the physical situation of the user, however, bending over to pick up a virtual object off of the floor may be impractical. In these cases, even though locomotion to the target may be intuitive, action-at-a-distance may still be required.

An extension of direct selection can be made which breaks compliance but may be useful in some scenarios. If the user is able to "project" their hand away from themselves and then use the hand to interact with the object at a distance, the simplicity and intuitiveness of direct selection can be maintained, and distance action can be permitted. The challenge with this interaction technique is how to control the location of the hand, or the distance away from the character. Natural, intuitive interaction requires a mapping of the motion of the user's hand to that of the extended hand, as well as a way to extend the hand outward and retrieve it when the interaction is complete.

### 11.4.1.2 Pointing

If an object is too far away for the user to reach, an alternative is to allow the user to point at the object to select it. This is a common pattern for menus, keyboards, and other controls, as they allow selection from a large collection of options with minimal hand movement. Usually, pointing consists of an indicator beam emerging from the user's hand, although the same pattern is used in laser sighting features of some weapons. In addition to pointing with a finger, pointing can emerge from an object (like a weapon or a tool), or from the user's head (via gaze-based selection). Depending on the distance to the object being indicated, the dexterity of the user, and the size of the target, pointing can be difficult to accomplish accurately. As the distance increases, small variations in the direction the user is pointing translate to large variations in the end of the beam, and if those variations are larger than the object being selected, the user will be unable to make the selection. **Fitt's law** states that the time required to accurately seek a target is related to the distance from the target and the size of the target. If a target is far away, but large, it is easy to move to somewhere in that target to activate it. If the target is far away and small, however, it is more difficult and it will take longer for the user to acquire that target. If the user is required to point at something far away, the target should be made large in order to make pointing easier, or additional features like target magnetism or flashlight pointing can be added to increase the conceptual size of the target.

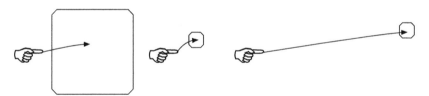

Figure 11.24: Fitt's law. A close, large target will be easy to reach, but a small, far target will take longer to acquire.

The user may also select an object by looking at it. In this case, the system should somehow differentiate between looking at an object and selecting that object or allow the user to select the object being looked at with a control input. Augmented reality often uses head look selection to add an informational overlay to any object being examined by the user. Head look selection can become overwhelming if every object being looked at is selected, but simple highlight signifiers can let a user know when an object they are looking at may have further information or interactions associated with it.

If the target is the ground or another flat surface, the **fishing pole** technique can be employed—the user establishes the direction, and the beam arcs to the target from the user. This method is common in pointing for teleportation. **Spherecasting** can be used to enlarge the target at the end of the pointing beam—as the beam gets farther away, the sphere gets larger to compensate for the increased difficulty of pointing at long distances. A more practical example of spherecasting is the use of a flashlight to highlight and interact with an object, although this technique can also be extended to the selection of multiple objects, if the size of the sphere or flashlight beam can be adjusted by the user. If selecting a single object using a flashlight, a signifier should be used to ensure that the user knows which object within the flashlight is or will be selected. Figure 11.25 shows some examples of pointing techniques.

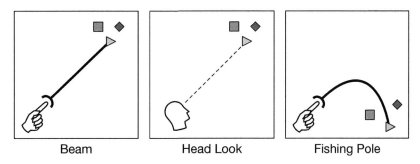

Figure 11.25: Examples of pointing techniques.

### 11.4.1.3  Assisted Pointing

In the physical world, when an object is far away and a person wants to interact with her in some way, they will often use some kind of tool or assistance to make that interaction easier or more effective. A classic example is an artist who will hold their thumb at an arms; length when sighting a real role reference in order to establish scale or block parts of the object to make the drawing more accurate; or a filmmaker who will hold their hands outstretched with each thumb and forefinger in the shape of an "L" to create a frame, which helps to imagine the boundaries of a shot. An astronomer aligning a telescope will often look through a small rangefinder to get a rough direction, before fine-tuning their telescope viewfinder. A navigator may use a sextant to find the angle of a celestial body above the horizon to assist in determining their location on the earth. And each of these cases, do user is augmenting their ability to see at a distance. VR, methods like these can be extended to augment action at a distance. The user might employ a tool, like a viewfinder, or they may use their hand as a reference or selector. An **alidade** is a two-piece viewfinder used to aim another device at a target. Firearm sights are a form of alidade, where the user looks between a slot at one end of the barrel and lines it up with a point at the far end of the barrel to ensure that the direction of the barrel is aligned with the target. Advanced alidades also include adjustments for distance, wind offset, and trajectory drop due to gravity. Because these techniques involve looking at two different objects at two different distances, users will often close one eye to avoid complications of parallax. Examples of assisted pointing are presented in Figure 11.26

**Magnetic pointing** or snap-to-target allows the end of the beam to snap to selectable objects when they are near, effectively increasing the target area. The object can be highlighted in order to indicate that it is the target of the point, and the beam itself can be made flexible so that the user's direction of pointing is not compromised. The "attraction" of each object must be carefully designed, however, so that users can point away from an object as easily as they can point towards an object.

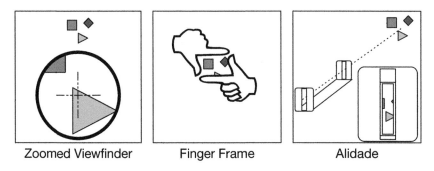

Zoomed Viewfinder    Finger Frame    Alidade

Figure 11.26: Examples of assisted pointing techniques.

**Action at a distance in popular culture**

VR developers can get an inspiration from the numerous examples of "action at a distance" that permeate popular culture. In the physical world, a person's sphere of influence is tightly constrained, and so it makes sense that fantasy and imagination often consider what might happen if our sphere of influence were extended. Whether implemented by magic, superpowers, or technology, the implications of these abilities are well explored in media and often investigated in VR.

- Slinging webs from your wrists, or cables from your back, to swing from the tops of buildings

- Extending your hand across the room to grab an object using a robotic or flexible arm, or a magical floating hand

- Using telekinesis or to lift a latch on the other side of a door

- Freezing your opponent with mind control or a freeze ray

- Controlling an element of nature or a swarm of small robots to build structures or attack your enemies

Developers should not restrict their "action at a distance" implementations to fantastical themes, however. A grappling hook allows a character to climb a wall, a bow and arrow or a firearm allows a character to direct physical force a distance away, and even a long stick can be used to exert influence outside a character's direct location.

### 11.4.1.4  Selecting multiple objects

Usually when selecting an object to interact with, the intent is to interact with a single object; in some cases, however, it may be desirable to select multiple objects to interact with. In this case, there are three considerations—how to select multiple objects at once, how to add or remove objects from a selection, and how individual objects will interact with each other during manipulation of the group. Selecting multiple objects can be as simple as an extension of the selection processes for a single object—a user might point a flashlight-style beam at a collection of objects, and any object hit by the beam is included in the selection. A user might establish a finger frame within their view, and all objects within that frame would be selected. If a user requires more discrete control over the distance of the object selected, a volumetric approach may be more appropriate—for example casting a sphere or other volume away from the user and using that to select a collection of objects. If the objects are nearby, the user may be able to draw a circle around them or draw a box between two points which include a collection of objects. Multiple object selection techniques can be further categorized as acting locally or at a distance, and as using fingers or using some assistive tool. Figure 11.27 provides some examples of selecting multiple objects.

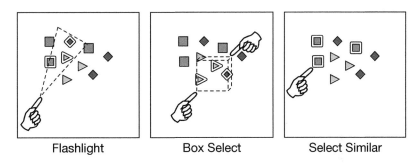

|   Flashlight   |   Box Select   |   Select Similar   |

Figure 11.27: Examples of selecting multiple objects.

## 11.4.2  Modification

After an object or objects have been selected, the next interaction is usually to modify that object in some way. This could be as simple as using the object as intended, or changing its position, or it could be as complicated as altering the shape, size, features, or function of the object. When the characteristics of the modification are mirrored in the tool being used to affect the modification, this can be accomplished directly. When more abstract features or characteristics are to be changed, activities must be made available to the user which allow these modifications to be made.

### 11.4.2.1  Direct Modification

The simplest of the modification methods, direct modification, corresponds to the case where the movements of the user's hand translate directly to the movements of the object being controlled. Once the object has been selected, the model of the object can be integrated with the hand model or tool being used, or the object can replace the hand model or tool. Care must be taken when considering the physics of the object to be manipulated. If the object is tethered to the world, either via physics interactions or by a physical connection, the user's hand should conceptually be similarly constrained. Since this user's hand is in the physical world, and the constraint or connection is in the virtual world, these constraints must be simulated and can be challenging to make convincing. As discussed in Section 11.3.4.5, in order to add a feeling of weight, the object should resist motion or even drag the user's hand towards the ground. If the user is manipulating a steering wheel, the wheel should turn on its axis but the axis should be constrained to its location in the virtual world. When the user selects the wheel, the hand model can connect to the wheel model, but as the user moves their hand, the hand model, constrained to the wheel, may move away from where the user predicts their hand would be. If the object is selected at a distance, via pointing or another technique, the object must be manipulated remotely as well, unless the user is given the ability to bring the object towards the character and place the object within the character's sphere of influence. Manipulating an object remotely can be challenging for the user, especially if the object is far away and there is no nearby frame of reference.

Direct modification can inherit well-understood interaction activities from touch screen interfaces and other traditional interfaces (see Section 13.2). Grabbing two sides of an object, one with each hand, and moving the hands separately will result in the object being rotated and scaled based on the relative position of the hands. As with many of these techniques, affording this interaction can be challenging. Manipulation handles placed on the object can indicate that it can be changed in this way. It is also important to establish any constraints that may be relevant for the specific interaction being considered. For example, must the object remain upright? Must the object be scaled proportionally on all axes or can it be stretched or bent?

### 11.4.2.2   Proxy Modification

When the object to be manipulated is far away or within another context (like behind a screen or within an interface), the user can be presented with a model representing the object, and the manipulations of this model can serve as a proxy for the manipulations of the actual target. Proxy modifications can be based on interactions with a small copy of the target object in the virtual world, or they can be related to a real object in the physical world, the motions of which correspond to the motions of the object in the virtual world. VR controllers are a type of physical proxy object that can be generalized to represent different objects in VR, and while these usually represent objects held by the character, they can also be used to proxy-manipulate objects outside of the user's sphere of influence.

### 11.4.2.3   Tool Modification

The act of using a tool to manipulate another object is a common pattern in the physical world as well as in the virtual world. The advantage of using tools in the virtual world is that a tool need not be constrained to its own functionality. Put another way, a virtual tool can be built with a strictly interaction-driven design, since a virtual tool contains no implementation of the manipulation facilitated by the tool. Tools also provide the opportunity to manipulate a virtual object beyond simply changing its location or orientation. A tool allows the user to change hidden parameters about the object like its size, shape, colour, or classification.

Tools need not completely replace the interaction, however. A **jig** is an assistive tool that allows the user to constrain certain aspects of their interaction. Most commonly associated with carpentry, a jig allows the user to accurately cut or connect pieces of a construction. A ruler used to draw a straight line is a jig. Drawing and modelling scenarios can use jigs to constrain symmetry, bind interactions to surfaces, objects, or contexts, and generally increase the accuracy and repeatability of activities.

## 11.5 SUMMARY

Developers should design for usability first, since to users, the *interface is the product*. When something goes wrong with a user interaction in your experience, the interface is the first point of failure, and although users may blame themselves for the failed interaction (which they usually do), an improved interface may reduce these errors. Developers often joke that the users are the biggest problem with most systems, but without users, the system has no purpose; every user error is an interface error. Developers should incorporate usability concepts from the beginning of a project and keep users involved. Regular user evaluation should be performed in order to ensure that the interface works for a range of people and not just for the developer.

# CHAPTER 12

# Information Display

In Chapter 11, we learned how to design good activities for the user. This chapter will present details on how to appropriately display information to the user, so that they can understand the state of the system and choose their actions accordingly.

## 12.1  INTRODUCTION

The flow of information from the system to the user is highly dependent on the design of the interface between the system and the user. It is not enough to provide an interface, nor to provide opportunities for the user to find the information they need; this information must be presented in such a way that it it can be interpreted and understood, taking into account the ways in which users collect and process information. Recalling the five E's of usability design from Chapter 8, we can see the risks inherent in poor information display. If the user cannot find the information they need, the user may

- Be unable to make a decision or take an action;

- Take longer to decide or act than would be appropriate;

- Become frustrated with the system;

- Make an error;

- Be unable to learn how to use the system.

The design of activities and interactions has a significant impact on the way users collect information from a system, and there are systems which display no overt information—good interaction design, following principles of affordance, familiarity, and mapping, can solve many of these problems, and in some cases interaction design alone may be sufficient. The state of a system can sometimes be inferred simply by the state of the controllers that activate the system. In other cases, however, an activity is sufficiently complex and unfamiliar that the display of overt information is required. In these cases, the ideal situation would be for users to receive training to develop familiarity, but leaning too heavily on user training can give a designer permission

DOI: 10.1201/9781003261230-12

to overlook poor information design. Most importantly, there are situations in which just-in-time information is the only information available.

Consider the case of and automated external defibrillator (AED). These devices provide a shock to a patient's heart in order to interrupt abnormal heart rhythms during a heart attack and restore normal heart function. Defibrillation is critically time sensitive, and although defibrillators are installed in ambulances, the time it takes for an ambulance to arrive to the scene of a heart attack is often too long to save the life of the patient. In 2012, the Canadian Government began an initiative to install AEDs in public places. The intent of the initiative is to have AEDs available much sooner for a person suffering a heart attack.

This is a particularly challenging usability design problem. Although AEDs are designed with sensing technology that allows the device to deliver the appropriate level of shock automatically, it is still a complicated piece of medical equipment that must be attached directly to the patient in the correct way. Because AEDs are installed in public spaces, they will almost certainly be used by someone who has never seen one before, although training for local staff has been made available. A heart attack is an extremely stressful situation, and so the person using the device is likely to be flustered and unable to think clearly. Canada is a diverse country, English is not the first language of many citizens, and the device may even need to be used buy a child, so the instructions should be visual when possible, but should also be available in detail in many languages, increasing the perceived complexity of the device; but some devices use voice prompts, which by necessity can only be in one language at a time. The device must be used only when indicated and should be used differently on a child than an adult—using the wrong setting, or using it when it shouldn't be used, could cause serious harm. Because seconds count, the defibrillation must happen as soon as possible, and defibrillation is only one step that may or may not be needed in the process of attempting to save a person suffering from a heart attack: an ambulance should be called first, and CPR (cardio-pulmonary resuscitation) should also be administered before and after the shock. Because heart attacks are uncommon, these devices will sit unused for years and must work at a moment's notice. There are likely to be millions of these devices, created by several different manufacturers, with different interfaces and procedures, and millions of dollars of public money will be spent to design, develop, and install these devices. Figure 12.1 shows examples of different AED information design.

What this means is that a complicated, dangerous, unfamiliar, expensive device must be used very quickly, in a life-or-death situation, by an untrained user under high levels of stress who may or may not be able to read the language the instructions are presented in. VR information design is unlikely to be so high stakes (although VR systems could be developed to train users on a variety of AED devices, in realistic scenarios, without them having to have access to a physical device), but it reminds us why closing the gulfs of information and interaction is important, and what the role of information display can be.

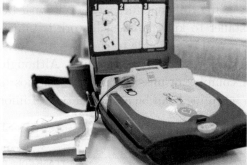

Figure 12.1: Differing AED interface designs and instructions.

### 12.1.1 Trade-off: Efficiency versus ease of use

When designing interfaces and information, especially for somewhat complicated systems, there is sometimes a decision to be made about whether to ensure the system is as easy to use as possible, or as efficient to use as possible. The AED is an extreme example—it must be both efficient and easy to use, although a small reduction in efficiency is preferred if the device can be made easier. In general, if the device is likely to be used by novices, designers should favour ease of use over efficiency. It is better if a task takes a bit longer if the user can figure it out quickly, especially if that task may be rare.

If users are expected to act quickly and do the same or similar tasks frequently, the information and interaction design should instead optimize for efficiency and require or assume training or familiarity. The interface for an air traffic controller workstation is complicated and difficult to learn, but allows operators to quickly understand information and quickly make and communicate decisions. Indeed, the language patterns used to communicate between pilots and ATC operators are highly structured so each party can quickly transmit and assimilate information, even over a noisy radio channel in a stressful situation.

If efficiency matters less, because the interface will rarely be used in a stressful situation, it can be tempting to abandon efficiency or ease of use in favour of simplicity of design. A home furnace needs to communicate its state to an installer, but the installer is paid by the hour and is well trained, so (the argument goes) the interface design doesn't matter. These considerations should not be abandoned altogether, though, because ease of use and efficiency can also influence whether an interface or information display is prone to errors. There is a domestic furnace that uses a single red LED to display diagnostic codes to the user for troubleshooting proposes. This system was likely inherited from earlier models where only a few diagnostic modes were possible, but as furnaces became more complicated, more information needed to be delivered through that single LED. In the user manual for this furnace, there are 25 separate pieces of information listed to be transmitted to a user or installer through this single LED, as shown in Figure 12.2. The installer must sit and watch the LED, counting flashes, for several seconds. This is highly inefficient and highly error-prone. Granted, the interface will likely only be used by a trained professional, but there are many different furnaces, each with better or worse interfaces and expecting an installer to know how each work is unreasonable. It is not enough to simply make information available to the user. It is critical that it be presented in a way that the user can reasonably understand. Although some training can be expected, especially for complex or mission-critical scenarios (see Section 11.2.6), relying solely on users to be trained can be an abdication of information design.

| Ignition Control Board Diagnostic Codes (Red LED) | |
| --- | --- |
| FLASH CODE (X + Y) | STATUS/ERROR DESCRIPTION |
| FLASH CODE DESCRIPTIONS | |
| Pulse | A 1/4 second flash followed by four seconds of off time. |
| Heartbeat | Constant 1/2 second bright and 1/2 second dim cycles. |
| X + Y | LED flashes X times at 2 Hz, remains off for two seconds, flashes Y times at 2 Hz, remains off for four seconds, and then repeats. |
| Pulse | Power on – Standby. |
| Heartbeat | Normal operation – Signalled when heating demand initiated at the thermostat. |
| FLAME CODES | |
| 1 + 2 | Low flame current – Run mode. |
| 1 + 3 | Flame sensed out of sequence – Flame still present. |
| PRESSURE SWITCH CODES | |
| 2 + 3 | Low pressure switch failed open. |
| 2 + 4 | Low pressure switch failed closed. |
| 2 + 5 | High pressure switch failed open. |
| 2 + 6 | High pressure switch failed closed. |
| 2 + 7 | Low pressure switch opened during ignition trial or heating demand. |
| LIMIT CODE | |
| 3 + 1 | Limit switch open. |
| WATCHGUARD CODES | |
| 4 + 1 | Watchguard – Exceeded maximum number of retries. |
| 4 + 2 | Watchguard – Exceeded maximum number of retries or last retry was due to pressure switch opening. |
| 4 + 3 | Watchguard – Exceeded maximum number of retries or last retry was due to flame failure. |
| 4 + 5 | Watchguard – Limit remained open longer than three minutes. |
| 4 + 6 | Watchguard – Flame sensed out of sequence; flame signal gone. |
| 4 + 7 | Ignitor circuit fault – Failed ignitor or triggering circuitry. |
| 4 + 8 | Low line voltage. |
| HARD LOCKOUT CODES | |
| 5 + 1 | Hard lockout – Rollout circuit open or previously opened. |
| 5 + 2 | Control failed self check, internal error (control will restart if error recovers). |
| 5 + 3 | No Earth ground (control will restart if error recovers). |
| 5 + 4 | Reversed line voltage polarity (control will restart if the error recovers). |
| 5 + 6 | Low secondary (24VAC) voltage. |

Figure 12.2: A single LED is used as information display for a furnace control board.

### 12.1.2  Light Switches, Again

If a light switch is in the "down" position, usually that means that the light it operates is off. Since a light switch is usually near the light that it activates, the state of the light can be understood by the amount of light in the room. However, if a user is vision impaired, or if the switch operates a light in a different room or operates a furnace or other piece of equipment not obviously present, the state of the system must be inferred exclusively from the state of the switch. This is further complicated by the existence of three-way switches, which allow two switches on two different walls to operate the same light. The problem this is meant to solve is that, in a larger room, there may be more than one place where it would be appropriate to control the lights. Maybe there are two entrances to the room, each of which has a light on the side of the doorway. In these cases, flipping the switch doesn't force a state on the light; it *toggles* the state—if the light was off, turn it on, and if the light was on, turn it off.

Two-way or single-pole switches operate the same way, but because the operation of one switch corresponds to the operation of one light, the user forms a mental model that the switch is a state directive, not a toggle. The user believes that regardless of the current state of the world, if I flip the switch up, the light will go on. This model is wrong, but useful, since it is almost always true. If a light switch is installed upside down, the rule will be reversed, but still predictable: if the switch is down, the light is on. Indeed, switches are installed sideways in some cases as well, and in this case the switch becomes a much less reliable indicator of the state of the circuit, since humans remember left-right differences less than they remember up-down differences. Regardless, for a single switch activating a single system, the state of the system can theoretically be read off of the state of the switch.

In a three-way switch circuit, the state of the system can be changed on either switch, which fundamentally breaks the user's mental model that the state of the system can be read off of the switch. Each switch in the circuit must be able to independently change the state of the circuit, so changing one switch from down to up might turn the light on or turn it off depending on the current state of the light. The switch itself can no longer indicate the state of the system. Because switches are unreliable indicators of state, systems for which it is important to know the state of the switch may have another signifier, like a light, which shows the state of the circuit controlled by the switch.

The designer of a system must understand when controls themselves are sufficient indicators, and when more information may be needed by the user. The constant challenge here is that the designer is familiar with their system because they designed it. Of course you have to flip this switch before that switch will work! It's so obvious! Users don't know what you know, and they will build a different mental model than the one you have. You must provide the information necessary for them to build the most accurate model they can, knowing again that all models are wrong, but some are useful.

## 12.2 CAUTIONARY TALES

The usability of any system is contingent on the appropriate presentation of information to the user who will make decisions and implement those decisions on the system. Too often, the design of systems assumes too much of the user. Users are expected to understand the limitations of the system, as well as the causes and implications of errors made when using the system, and users often blame themselves for errors that could have been avoided by better information display or interaction design. When we, as designers, understand that the user is part of the system and that the success or failure of the system depends on how well the user can interpret information maintained by the system, we understand better our responsibilities to make the system easier to use and make the information presented by the system accurate, appropriate, and actionable. There are many examples throughout the history of the development of interactive systems where inappropriate, incorrect, or missing information has led to failures of the system as a whole. In many cases these failures are fixable, but occasionally, errors in design in mission-critical scenarios can lead to significant loss or even death.

- The Mars Climate Orbiter mission failed, at a loss of hundreds of millions of dollars, because one component of the system used imperial units and another component used metric units.

- Millions of dollars were spent to repair computer systems which may or may not have failed when the two-digit year rolled over from 1999 to 2000, and a similar problem will occur in 2038 when Unix time, a 32-bit number representing the number of seconds since January 1970, rolls back to zero.

- A passenger airplane redesign led to failures and crashes when a hidden automated stability system overcompensated and forced the nose of the airplane down, even when the pilot was pulling up.

- A medical radiation system (the Therac-25) incorrectly displayed the results of dosages and gave vague error messages, leading technicians to radiation overdoses causing death.

- A COVID-19 close-contact tracking team used a spreadsheet to record and track cases. The spreadsheet had a maximum size of 65565 rows ($2^{16}$), but no error was given when importing more than the limit, and thousands of positive cases were not tracked.

In these and many other cases, the appropriate display of information, during development, testing, and deployment, as well as documentation of the likelihood and consequences of possible errors, could have saved money and lives. If we learn lessons from these failures, we may avoid similar errors in the future.

## 12.3   PRINCIPLES OF INFORMATION DISPLAY

Humans collect and organize information from the world through our senses, and we have evolved to allow different senses to collect different types of information. Our eyes see specific bands of electromagnetic waves, our ears hear specific frequencies of pressure waves, and our fingers are able to detect physical features of objects we touch, like texture, temperature, and composition. We have evolved to use these senses to create a mental model of the world around us, but at the same time, we evolved methods for inserting our own information that others (with the tools to do so) might decode and understand. Language, gesture, and human contact are ways in which we produce information that will be collected by another to pass knowledge and experience from one person to another. We shape our world not just to make it easier to live in, but easier to understand.

Designing an information display must take into account how the user senses the world, because after it has been designed, the designer is unable to add information on how to use it later. The user of the display cannot ask the designer for clarification; they must understand what the display is telling them about the system they are using. Training and familiarity can help, but when information about a system may change over time, the way that information is displayed should be clear and unambiguous to reduce errors and make the system enjoyable to use.

### 12.3.1 Gestalt Organization

Humans are pattern-finding machines. Our brains are constantly seeking order in the information they are bringing in and expecting to find order in noisy or cluttered signals. When a tiger might be hiding in a bush, the difference between a twitch of a leaf caused by the wind and the twitch of a leaf caused by a tail can mean life and death.

The term **gestalt** means "form" or "structure" and refers to the understanding that the brain can perceive within patterns of objects a larger whole, and structure among patterns can lead to the perception of connections between objects that may form groups, the rapid detection of outliers within those groups, and the conceptual relationships between those groups. As is often the case, the examples of these organizational principles will be primarily visual, but the principles extend to other senses as well. We hear a melody in a song as a single line rather than discrete notes, because the notes form a relationship between themselves and are seen as separate from the rest of the music. We feel the individual dots of a braille character as a unified shape because they are closer to each other than they are to the neighbouring characters.

There are many individual gestalt principles that lead to the perceptions of groupings, which will be discussed here in isolation, but in the real world these groupings are often reinforced with several principles at the same time. The core static gestalt principles are similarity, proximity, continuity, and closure. Principles that relate to the foreground and background are area and symmetry, and principles that relate to motion are common fate and past experience. The list below gives definitions of each of these principles, and Figures 12.3 and 12.4 show examples of each.

**Similarity.** Objects that have similar features are perceived as belonging to the same grouping.

**Proximity.** Objects that are closer together are perceived as belonging to the same grouping.

**Continuity.** Objects are perceived as belonging to groups with smooth or predictable contours.

**Closure.** Groups are perceived as complete even when parts are missing.

**Area.** Smaller objects are perceived as foreground, and larger objects are perceived as background.

**Symmetry.** Objects which are symmetrically similar to each other are perceived as being members of a group.

**Common Fate.** Objects which move together are perceived as members of the same group.

**Past Experience:** Objects which evoke a familiar pattern are perceived as belonging to a group that fits that pattern.

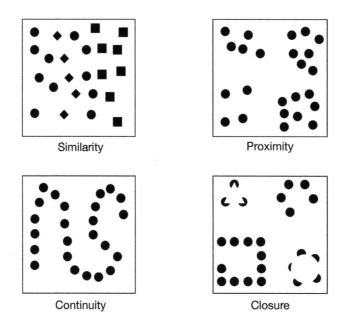

Figure 12.3: Examples of gestalt principles of similarity, proximity, continuity, and closure.

Considering the examples given in Figure 12.3, we can see the first half of these principles at work. These gestalt principles relate to the way individual elements of an image (or objects in a scene) relate to each other, and how our brain automatically detects patterns in the groupings of those objects. When objects exhibit *similarity*, like the diamonds or squares in the "similarity" figure, they naturally form subgroups even though a diamond may be closer to the circles than to other diamonds. When objects are closer together, as in the *proximity* figure, we see them as individual clusters even though they are all the same shape and size of circle, and some circles in separate groups may be closer together than those in a different group. The group of four in the bottom left are somewhat spaced apart, while on the right, the closest circles between the top and bottom group are actually closer together than some of the circles in the cluster of four to the bottom left. The principle of *continuity* means that our brain sees objects that form a path as belonging to a single group. This is closely related to the principle of *closure*, which shows how objects which seem to make up part of a recognizable whole tend to cluster into the perception of that whole, and our brain fills in the missing details. This manifests when observing objects that overlap with one another, because the brain interprets an occluded object as being continuous even though it is hidden behind another object. In general, these gestalt organizational principles can be summarized as a sort of "Occam's razor" for the perception of ambiguous objects. The simplest consistent interpretation is the one that the brain uses.

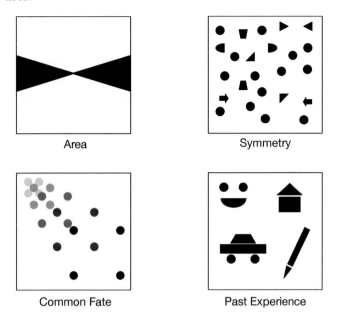

| Area | Symmetry |
| Common Fate | Past Experience |

Figure 12.4: Examples of gestalt principles of area, symmetry, common fate, and past experience.

While the first half of the gestalt principles discuss how the brain interprets objects as they relate to each other, the second half (with examples in Figure 12.3) concerns the relationships of objects with time or context in some way. The principle of *area* says that objects which are larger tend to be interpreted as background, and objects that are smaller tend to be interpreted as foreground. In the example given, the two black triangles are seen as objects of interest, and the two white pentagons are seen as background to those objects. The principle of *symmetry* says that two objects which are mirror images of each other tend to be seen as related in some way, even if they are farther apart than other objects. In the figure, the pairs of related objects can easily be picked out of the collection of circles. A classic text example of the use of symmetry to help disambiguate is the use of brackets: when paired in one way, they form groups of close-together pairs:

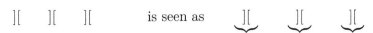

but when brackets are placed at the beginning and end of that sequence, they form enclosed groupings between the pairs of brackets, even though the distance between the pairs of inverted brackets is the same:

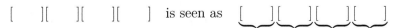

and indeed, complicated sequences of brackets can be parsed reasonably easily as long as the pairs of brackets are different enough, even in size, to be identified as symmetric pairs:

$$((()((()())())))  \text{ is harder to understand than }  \left[() \left\{\left(()()\right) ()\right\}\right]$$

The principle of *common fate* relates to the motion of objects over time. If two objects begin by being close together, and over time they move farther apart, as long as their motion is similar enough, they will continue to be perceived as members of the same group. If the motions of these objects diverge, the membership will also diverge. The motion need not originate close together for this illusion to emerge. In a random arrangement of dots, if a collection of those dots begin to move in the same direction and speed, in a way different from the rest of the dots, they will be perceived as having shared membership in some group. This effect can be perceived in audio as well. When multiple instruments in an orchestra play the same sequence of notes, they are perceived as a single construct. Indeed, a pipe organ often has multiple separate sources of sound, but if the sounds follow the same sequence, they will be perceived as one instrument rather than a set of separate pipes.

Finally, the principle of past experience is closely related to the previously discussed principle of "familiarity." When elements of an image appear in an arrangement that reminds us of an object we recognize, even in an abstract way, we tend to see that object rather than the individual shapes. A rectangle and a triangle together may form an abstract house, or an abstract pencil, depending on the arrangement and relative shape, but in both cases it is the brain adding the higher level of interpretation onto these primitive shapes. Two dots may either be the eyes of a face for the wheels of a car depending on context and past experience.

## 12.3.2  Gestalt and usability

Each of these gestalt principles can appear in isolation or together, and when they appear in conflicting ways, they might infer different group membership of the same objects, and optical illusions may occur. For example, the classic face-vase illusion shown in Figure 3.1 occurs because features of colour, symmetry, area, closure, proximity, and past experience are competing to form one of two interpretations of the figure, and the evidence for each interpretation is similar enough that the brain either perceives both at the same time or rapidly flips between the two interpretations. The face-vase illusion can be countered by making the faces somewhat less face-like, by making the vase black and the faces white, by removing the outline around the faces, or by otherwise pushing information in the direction of the interpretation that is desired. The same competing gestalt principles that form optical illusions can also form ambiguous sources of information for the user of a system. If a user can't decide which category an interface element belongs to, they may misinterpret the function of such an element or they may make a mistake about the interpretation of information they are trying to understand. Being intentional about the use of gestalt principles that appear in a display of any kind can help remove ambiguity for the user.

These gestalt principles are often used in textual language to reinforce rapid understanding. Indeed, the serifs of typeset text exist to draw the eye along the line of text, make groupings of words more clear, disambiguate characters like "l," "I," and "1," and make it easier, in general, to read. Sans-serif fonts should be used when text lines are short and large (like in a projected display or sign), and serif text should be used when text lines are long and small (like in a line of text in a book). Text are particularly difficult to read in VR, and best practices for display of text are discussed in Section 13.2.3.

When competing gestalt principles occur in a text, humorous results (or intentional misreadings) may occur. A classic example from the television show "the walking dead" occurs when a room full of zombies is barricaded and a desperate survivor writes "Don't open! Dead inside," but because they write the first half of the message on one door and the second half on the other door, it may be read as "Don't dead, open inside." In another case, a sign on an automatic door suggests caution, but may be read as "Automatic Caution Door." A third example attempts to be inspirational by saying "You matter! Don't give up" but instead, the sign may be interpreted as "You don't matter. Give up." These examples are shown in Figure 12.5

Figure 12.5: Examples of text groupings where competing gestalt can lead to multiple interpretations

The organization of interfaces makes use of gestalt principles of organization. Buttons all look the same and do the same thing. Radio buttons in a list are all related.

### 12.3.3   Abstraction

When representing information to the user, clarity and accuracy are paramount, but in some circumstances, a clear and accurate representation of all information made available to the user may be overwhelming. Users must be able to quickly and efficiently understand the information presented to them, and when that information may be informed by familiarity, a representation of the information may be sufficient. An **abstraction** is a simplification of an idea or concept, often pictographic, which allows increased information density. Icons on a desktop are abstractions of the files or folders they represent. Buttons on a menu are abstractions of the functionality that they offer. Abstractions are commonplace in environments where many different functions or pieces of information must be available at the same time, and the user must rapidly assess information in order to support activities or decision-making. Abstractions allow the designer to assemble a lot of information in a small space, but this transfers responsibility for interpretation of the abstraction to the user. If the user is not familiar with the representation, or the representation is not recognizable, then the abstraction can fail. As such, abstractions must be designed with care, but may also require training.

A classic example of abstractions is the use of symbols on road signs. Drivers must be able to quickly gather the information that the sign represents, and decisions affecting the safety of the driver, passengers, and others on the road may come from correct or incorrect interpretation of these signs. The abstract shapes that are easily identifiable as road signs (Figure 12.6) rely on familiarity and training: there is nothing directly connecting a red octagon to the concept of "stop" except our shared cultural association; still, we can rely on this shared cultural association because it is universal. Similarly, the use of arrows to indicate direction is a form of abstraction, but the context surrounding an arrow can alter the meaning, as shown in Figure 12.7. The curving arrows here indicate that the road ahead will curve, but the context of the sign is a learned abstraction that indicates whether this curve is an option that is required, an option that is permitted, or a warning.

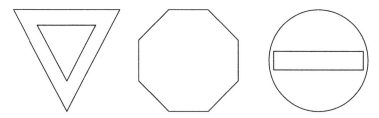

Figure 12.6: Abstract shapes as road signs: (from left) yield; stop; do not enter.

Figure 12.7: Arrows are abstractions that mean different things in context: (from left) you must turn, you may turn, and warning: a turn is approaching.

Although abstractions may be designed to be universal and easily recognized, different representations of the same concept can lead to confusion. If a barrier is approaching in the road, a sign usually accompanies to indicate that the driver should be aware. In some jurisdictions, the sign represents an abstraction of the approaching barrier and the path the driver should take to avoid it (Figure 12.8a) but in other jurisdictions, the sign exists to draw the driver's attention to which side of the barrier they should pass (Figure 12.8b). Both of these abstractions represent the same information, but they do so in different ways, and depending on which you are familiar with, the other may be confusing.

(a) Keep Right          (b) Keep Left

Figure 12.8: Two different abstractions indicating the same concept ("Squeeze" or avoid the barrier approaching).

Abstractions exist in many situations where information must be communicated in a small space or in a small time. Laundry instructions on clothing exist in the form of abstractions (Figure 12.9) because the tags on clothes are small and detailed textual instructions would be difficult to read. The context of the label helps to identify the abstractions beyond simple shapes, but the symbols can still be confusing and most people end up washing most clothes on "normal" cycle anyway.

Figure 12.9: Laundry symbols: (from left) wash, bleach, dry, dryclean, and iron.

Abstractions are common in user interface design because of the limited screen real estate and large number of functions that must be made available. An email program may have icons that represent functions of creating a new email, filing an existing email, selecting a specific mailbox, checking for new mail, adding attachments, flagging an email as important, or marking it as spam. A few of these icons are shown in Figure 12.10. Some of these abstractions are straightforward and based on long-established usability metaphors from the early days of computing, but some novel functionality has required new iconography, which has been represented by a variety of abstractions before settling on a common familiar UI set. Although the abstractions serve as a quick reminder and signifier of functionality, most abstractions must be learned, and it is easy to forget that not everyone understands the representations of iconography that developers or dedicated users understand.

Figure 12.10: UI abstract icons for an email program: (from left) check mail, calendar, trash, inbox, unread, file, flag, and archive.

Indeed, many of the abstractions we use today are taken from metaphors intended to assist learning when the functionality could not be assumed to have universal common experience. When computers were first becoming popular, the metaphor of the desktop was used to assist learning the interface, and that metaphor has persisted. Many abstractions that emerged have come to represent commonly understood functionality, even though the metaphor of that abstraction may no longer be relevant. Figure 12.11 shows some examples of abstractions that have become common even though the underlying metaphor may no longer be strictly relevant.

Figure 12.11: UI abstractions based on metaphor. (from left) Save, Cart, Battery, Telephone, Palette, Cut, Security, Cloud

The "save" icon represents an old-style floppy disk, because the act of saving a file usually meant picking up a physical disk and inserting it into a disk drive. Modern computers use solid-sate memory, and physical spinning removable disks are no longer commonplace, but the icon has remained. The shopping cart and battery icons are relevant, although most devices with a battery icon do not have a removable battery. The telephone receiver is an iconic shape, although most people have not held a physical receiver of that shape and size for decades. The palette represents selections even thought most people have never used an artist's palette. The cloud is an abstraction that represents an abstraction—it is a way of talking about decentralized networked storage infrastructure.

Jakob's law is relevant when considering abstractions for a user interface—if an icon or abstraction exists on some other system or context for a certain functionality, it is usually better to make use of that existing abstraction rather than developing your own. You may have found an icon or arrangement that more clearly indicates the information you are displaying, but abstractions must be learned, and the process of unlearning an existing association and re-learning your new association may lead to frustration on the part of the user. This can happen if you use a different icon or abstraction than is common for the functionality you are considering, and it can happen if you use a symbol that is common in another context. For example, a five-pointed star can be used to represent many different ideas. In the context of a set of five stars, it represents a 5-point rating. Alone, it can represent a favourite item. Within a shield, it can represent authority. If you choose to use a symbol that already exists in a different context, you may need to provide training to the user to learn the meaning of the abstraction, as well as opportunities for reminders of what the abstraction represents. A help menu which lists the icons and their meanings, as well as an optional tooltip setting, can assist interpretation of new or ambiguous abstractions.

**Skeuomorphism** is a term given to objects that retain ornamental but non-functional elements of previous design elements. It can be thought of as the opposite of abstraction—while abstractions attempt to reduce complexity to facilitate rapid understanding and fit more information or function in a small area. Skeuomorphism increases complexity by adding aesthetic elements that remind the user of the functionality of previous versions of a tool or interaction. Skeuomorphism became a more commonly understood term when it was used as a stylistic choice for early smartphone software, particularly the iPhone. The calendar app was given graphic elements to represent a coil-bound desk calendar; the contacts app was made to look like a leather-bound agenda by using stitching around the icon, and the notes app was given the look of a classic yellow legal pad, complete with a bit of paper left from the last page torn off of the pad. Skeuomorphism can also be found in decorative elements of clothing—when decorative buckles are added for style but do not themselves serve to fasten the clothing, and home decor—when chandeliers are made to look like gas lamps or wooden banisters are carved to look like wrought iron. Skeuomorphism can serve to aid usability of software when new products are introduced, by reminding users of the interaction modalities of products intended to be replaced, but can also serve to limit the adoption of new technologies, since the advantages of the new interaction may be hidden by the attempt to make it look like the old way of doing things. Skeuomorphism has gone out of style in interface design, replaced with simplicity and sparse interfaces, although some features of this design philosophy have survived in the form of emoji representing functionality, as shown in Figure 12.12.

Figure 12.12: Examples of skeuomorphism in emoji design, compared to abstracted icon counterparts.

### Skeuomorphism in VR

VR developers, too, are relying on the visual representations of familiar objects in order to communicate functionality to the user. When a user sees an object that looks like something from their real-world experience, they know how to pick it up, how to hold it, or how to operate it. Whether this is skeuomorphism or realism is a somewhat semantic debate. Skeuomorphism represents the visual aspects of an archaic function to suggest current functionality, while realism suggests the function of an artefact based on contemporary understanding. An example of skeuomorphism in VR may be an object that looks like a handgun but in fact operates like a futuristic beam weapon, or a control interface that looks like an old-style video switcher but in fact operates a high-tech editing studio. If the style of the interface is nostalgic or reminiscent of an earlier interface, skeuomorphism may be an appropriate term. If the virtual object matches the functionality of the real-world object it represents, this is more appropriately called realism rather than skeuomorphism.

### 12.3.3.1 Abbreviations

**Abbreviations** are a form of abstraction that represents a short string of characters for a longer phrase. Abbreviations assume domain knowledge and are often ambiguous, so rely heavily on familiarity to provide information. With familiarity, abbreviations can significantly speed up the transfer of information between a system and its user (or between two people). As an example, the Apollo program had abbreviations for most of the workstations in the mission operations control room (MOCR) including FiDO (flight dynamics officer), GuiDO (guidance officer), CAPCOM (capsule communications), and GNC (guidance, navigation, and control). Each part of the mission had abbreviations as well, including the parts of the spacecraft (CSM = command and service module; LM = lunar module) and the types of missions (EOR = earth orbit rendezvous; TLI = trans-lunar injection). Without knowing the context, these abbreviation (or any others) are meaningless. On the Apollo command module control panel, many labels are spelled out in full rather than abbreviated to avoid misunderstanding. Abbreviations should be employed when the phrase being abbreviated is long and used often, and the user can reasonably be expected to know what the abbreviation means without consulting a reference document. Abbreviations can simplify an interface, but if a user does not know what the abbreviation stands for, it will not function as an abstraction. Relying on training for interpretation of abstractions is equally problematic, since time spent training is time spent not doing. The use of an abstraction is a trade-off between simplification and familiarity and should be approached with caution.

Abstractions are always context dependent and rely on the user remembering the meaning of the abstraction or being able to guess the meaning of the abstraction. When abstractions make use of language, they require specific literacy on the part of the user, and, as discussed in Section 8.5.4, users from different locations and contexts will speak different languages and use language differently. Abbreviations are inherently language dependent, such that countries with multiple official languages often have duplicate abbreviations. The Canada Revenue Agency (CRA), the Canadian government organization responsible for taxation, is called the Agence du revenu du Canada (ARC) in French. DNA, the English acronym for deoxyribonucleic acid, corresponds to acide désoxyribonucléique (ADN) in French. Any user interface element relying on an acronym will need to either be translated when the experience is localized or rely on the assumption that a user with another first language will be able to understand and interpret English acronyms. Information presented as acronyms that must be used by individuals speaking different languages necessitates compromise. International communication systems used by individuals from multiple countries, like air traffic control systems, either pick a single language and require all participants to use that language or require a language negotiation at the beginning of each interaction. All airline pilots and air-traffic control operators must speak English, but most also speak the local language and can address each other in either language. Acronyms used for air-traffic control (like VFR for "Visual Flight Rules") and are therefore based in English and are used in the same way even in other languages. Some acronyms are constructed assuming they will be used by multiple languages, like "UTC" for universal coordinated time (English) and temps universel coordonné (French). The acronym is a compromise in both languages, but with sufficient familiarity, a common acronym is better than separate acronyms in different languages. In some cases, there are enough phrases that need to be shortened that a separate set of code abstractions are developed which are completely separate from the phrases they are meant to represent. This can also happen if one party wants to obfuscate the meaning of information that will be heard by an opposing party, although most codesets like this will quickly be made universally available and will therefore provide little or no security. Two examples of these arbitrary abstractions are the ten-codes used in police radio and the Q-codes used in aviation. Ten-codes have entered the cultural lexicon via police procedural television shows, and many people know that "10-4" means "acknowledged," and when someone on the radio says, "What's your twenty," they are referring to a ten-code as well—"10-20" represents "your location." Somewhat less well known, Q-codes represent a large collection of three-letter codes used in radio communication. QNH, QNE, and QFE are examples of Q-codes used in aviation ATIS (Automatic terminal information service), representing specific settings required for an airplane altimeter to correctly read 0 on the ground. These fairly esoteric values (QNH = "What should I set on the subscale of my altimeter so that the instrument would indicate its elevation if my aircraft were on the ground at your station," for example) are commonly used and therefore need a rapid and unambiguous way to be communicated.

### 12.3.3.2  *Misrepresentation*

Abstractions can lead to misinterpretation in situations where the developer believes the abstraction infers one piece of information, but the user either misinterprets or fails to interpret the abstraction. This can happen when abstractions are specified by one party, but implemented by another. An example of this is the implementation of emojis by different technology companies. The set of emojis to implement is decided by the Unicode Consortium, and individual organizations are free to decide what each emoji looks like. In principle, emojis are an excellent example of abstraction: simple images that represent a core idea, emotion, or object. Emojis are used to indicate abstract ideas that maybe difficult to explain in a short piece of text and to qualify ambiguous text with a signifier of the sense the user intended (for example, to indicate sarcasm, humour, or emotions that would be clear if spoken in person, but may be ambiguous in text alone). There are two challenges with emojis, however, that can lead to misunderstanding. In one case, people may use emojis to indicate a concept other than the concept originally intended by the imagery itself. Otherwise benign images may come to represent somewhat risque or off-colour sentiments, such as the eggplant or peach emojis.

The second way generalized abstractions like emoji can lead to misinterpretations is in the differences between platform implementations of a centralized standard emoji. The "woman frowning" emoji is an example of different platform's interpretation of the same concept. Figure 12.13 shows a collection of different emojis meant to represent the concept. Because users select emoji based on what they look like not by the textual label, the word "frowning" does not impact the decision of whether to use this icon or some other image. Two of these images are sad or sympathetic, and two are angry or frustrated. A user chooses the icon on their platform based on what they see, but the information that is sent to the other user is just the label of the emoji itself, and it is reinterpreted on the other end of the communication with the stock image of that emoji from the local platform. A user may intend to show sadness or sympathy, but instead come across as being angry instead.

Figure 12.13: Four interpretations of "Woman Frowning".

### 12.3.4 Dashboards and Heads-Up Display (HUDs)

An example of the principles of information display in action is the glanceable display. These represent clusters of key information, usually passive, that is presented continuously for the user to consult when a need arises. Deciding what information to make available in a glanceable display is a challenging information representation problem and incorporates gestalt organizational principles and principles of abstraction.

## 12.4 INFORMATION DISPLAY IN VR

Representing information to the user in VR is constrained in several ways. First, although the intention for the experience is to occlude and replace senses with representations that lead to presence, the differences between the way VR presents to the senses and the way the physical world presents to the senses are still sufficient that representational models that work well in the physical world may or may not work well in the virtual world. Reading in VR is particularly difficult—screen resolutions remain reduced compared to the resolution of reality; the memory required to represent crisp text as an image is high, and because the focus of the eye is at one distance and the angles between the eyes are at a different distance, looking at objects close up in the virtual world can result in eye strain and fatigue. Developers should avoid requiring their users to look at objects close up for long periods of time. Additionally, because interactions in VR may also be constrained, the normal ways in which we collect more information (by holding an object closer or moving closer to it, or by holding it up to inspect it) may or may not work as expected in VR experiences. There are ways to adapt text to be readable in VR, which will be discussed in Section 13.2.3, but in general, the ubiquitous ways we present information in the physical world may need to be adapted to work well in the virtual world.

Further, being within a VR experience may change our information-seeking behaviour as well. Even considering the ways in which interactions may be different, as discussed in Chapter 11, the types of behaviours that we invoke when information-seeking fails may also not be available. We can't just grab our phone and look up an answer; we can't go online to look something up; we can't even place a finger on a book we are reading to keep our place. Some of the most detailed and subtle actions we take are related to the collection and assimilation of information, and if these activities are not quite right in VR, the information-seeking behaviour will be unsatisfying. As such, the presentation of information must be adapted in order to ensure users have access to the information they require.

The benefit of presenting information in VR, however, is that we can augment objects or activities in order to supply contextual information when it is needed most. In the physical world, seeking additional information about an object requires the use of a separate information-seeking device. If I want to know how much battery is left on my wireless headphones, I need to connect my phone and check the app; but in VR, I might be able to make a simple gesture, by holding my hand near the headphones, or by turning them over, to provide an overlay of additional information directly aligned to the object I am interested in. Augmented reality holds the promise to provide contextual just-in-time information about the world around us, and in a virutal world, everything can be augmented.

## 12.5  SUMMARY

The way we represent information in our systems allows the people that use these systems to quickly understand and make decisions, although we must keep in mind that misinterpreting displayed information is one of the most common errors that people make when using systems. Information in VR is limited by the quality of the sensory presentations made available by the hardware, and must be complete since removing your headset to look up something on your phone is immersion breaking and problematic. VR developers have a responsibility to ensure that the way we present the world allows the users the best chance of making good decisions and avoiding confusion in complex scenarios.

# CHAPTER 13

# Translating Traditional Interfaces for VR

Although a virtual environment presents many possibilities for new forms of interaction, there are some activities, experiences, and contexts where traditional interfaces may be worth implementing. The primary benefit here is that a level of familiarity can be assumed with a traditional interface, where a new interface must be intuitive or be taught, and we as designers often overestimate the intuitiveness of our designs and the ability or interest of our users to learn a new thing. From "don't reinvent the wheel" to "if it ain't broke don't fix it," we have many tacit and intuitive motivations to doing things the way they have been done, and these should not be ignored. However, virtual reality (VR) is a different medium than traditional user interfaces and is also different from the real world. As much as VR tries to replicate immersive 3D experiences, it remains a mediated experience, and as such some interactions we may expect to be intuitive or familiar may fail because of the subtle differences between VR and traditional computing interfaces, and between VR and the real world.

In this chapter, we will begin by analysing some of the traditional interface modes of computing that we are all familiar with, including command-line interfaces, window-icon-menu-pointer (WIMP) systems, and touchscreen interfaces common to tablets and smartphones and explore how they may or may not translate well to VR. We will then discuss the challenges of displaying and interacting with text, best practices for scrolling through options, and interacting with menus.

## 13.1 A SUMMARY OF TRADITIONAL UI

Although user interface standards have changed over the years, the evolution of these interfaces has landed on two "standard" methods as the defaults for interacting with computers. Graphical user interfaces are ubiquitous in workstations, like desktops and laptops, while smartphones and tablets use a touchscreen and a "grid of icons" as the base interface design. Word processing, web browsing, and other common tasks require applications that are launched to add functionality to the system, but the basic interface elements should remain familiar to the user.

In some cases, it is beneficial to replace the operating system completely with a new interface. Integrated development environments, media consoles, and video games are common use cases where the software, when launched, replaces the system with a different interface, depending on the interactions required and activities available. When a computer is used as a media console, the text is often enlarged, and the interactions are assumed to happen with a remote control rather than a mouse or trackpad—as a result, most interface elements for this purpose are presented in a grid format that are accessible with directional buttons. The information displayed and options available for selection are simplified, as the interface tasks are often significantly reduced (e.g. pick a piece of media content and play it). On the other hand, for software such as integrated development environments and game engines, a large number of activities must be simultaneously available, and the user must have access to many pieces of information and controls to change parametres, all in real time.

In traditional interfaces, significant information is often tied to a specific location on-screen. A menu bar may always appear at the top or bottom of the screen, a tool palette may always appear to the left or to the right, and the *desktop*, a layer of files, often arranged in a grid, tied to screen locations, is available at a keystroke. These anchored items are not always present, in the case of video games and other full-screen experiences, the screen anchoring is replaced entirely by a new interface. It is unusual, however, to have a situation where no information is tied to the screen location. Fullscreen media playback is one of these unusual situations, and in this case any activation of an interface device, like wiggling the mouse or pressing a button on the remote control, will bring up screen-tied controls for media playback.

When it comes to implementing a common computing task in VR, it is tempting to replicate existing models from the physical world, and while some will translate well, others will hold challenges.

### 13.1.1 Command-Line Interface

When computers were first developed, the interface was designed in the same way that interfaces were designed for other machines—functional elements that provided their operation but not their function. A bank of switches allowed a user to enter a command into the memory of the machine, but the user would either have to remember or reference the specific commands to execute the intended function. As computers developed, programming languages allowed the computer operator to string together collections of instructions to be executed one after the other, but the operator still needed to memorize or look up the instructions. Operating systems allowed the computer to automate significant portions of the administrative operation of the machine, organize collections of files, issue commands to background processes, and secure operation against unauthorized activities which could compromise the operation of the machine. The interface between the user and the computer remained opaque, since computer operation still required significant training. The command-line interface is the way in which operators would issue commands to such computers, and it was the interface in common use when computers began to be used by the general public. The first "personal" computers made use of command-line interfaces, and they are still associated with highly competent programmers, hackers, or old-style computer experts. A classic command-line interface would consist of a blank screen with a simple prompt, as shown in Figure 13.1.

Figure 13.1: Command-line interface

When considering the human-computer interactions inherent in a command-line interface, and with reference to the gulfs of execution and evaluation, a command-line interface places the responsibility of closing those gulfs entirely outside of the machine. The user must remember or refer which commands exist, which might be possible in the particular context of the machine at this moment, which command will perform the task the user wants to perform, and how to spell the name of the command. Not only are commands complicated, esoteric, and domain specific, the developers of these early machines delighted in choosing stylistic or unusual names for these commands. For example, a process running in the background of a computer, making decisions and keeping track of information, is called a "daemon." To use a machine like this, not only would you need to know that there exists a background task, but that it is called "daemon" and not "demon" and remember the particular string of characters that would invoke this daemon in the right way to make the thing do what they want it to do. The burden of the gulf of execution is placed entirely on the user. See Section 11.2.6.1 for a discussion on the exclusionary aspects of technical jargon, the training required, and the position of privileged that trained users can take.

Additionally, the state of the system is entirely opaque unless you know the commands to gather information from the system. The blank screen with the single prompt is all the information that is available to you, and if you don't know which command to run to gather that information, that information is unavailable to you. In fact, even the commands available to search for how to use the computer would be complicated and difficult. On Unix shell systems, the command to find out how to use a command isn't "help"; it is "man" which is short for "manual." If you wanted to find out which process or daemons are running, the command "ps" would list all currently running processes, or "top" would list the processes using the most resources. To display the contents of a file, the command "less" is used, because the person who built the text display software based it on an older version called "more" which would display a file one screen at a time—the user would say "more" when they wanted the next screen of the text file.

The benefit with command-line interfaces is that although the user is responsible for all activities and information gathering, the complete set of functionality that the machine is capable of is available in one place, at the user's locus of attention. A skilled user (sometimes in this case called a "power user") can be more efficient with an interface like this, because they do not have to spend time hunting through menus to activate the command they know exists. The downside is that the machine does not help the user, and if the user forgets a command, they must consult external reference documentation.

Within the context of VR, command-line interfaces are mostly stylistic. The challenges of textual input (discussed in Section 13.2.4) apply uniquely here, since typing text into a screen is the exclusive method for completing activities available in a command-line interface. Further, command-line interfaces often make use of small, dense, low-contrast text, which can be difficult to read in VR. As an affective choice, however, command-line interfaces can effectively represent a very specific aesthetic. Cyberpunk, hacker culture, 80's retro-futurism, and the so-called "used future" all can make use of command-line interfaces to represent a computer system that requires skill to operate. Players may discover information about a scenario in pieces, represented as disks that they must find around the space, and as each disk is inserted into the drive, information is presented to the user scrolling up in a hazy and abrupt green font. If a command-line interface will be part of a VR scenario, the reference documentation required to operate it must also be available within the virtual world. Expecting a user to memorize and recall all available functions may be challenging, but since note-taking is also very challenging within the context of VR (the user must either enter text, which is difficult, or write on a whiteboard or notepad, which is awkward, or remove their VR headset, which breaks presence), the simplest implementation would be to have a set of buttons below the screen, each of which represents one of the commands that can be entered on the console. This then becomes a form of menu interface, since the user must search for the function they need rather than typing it in, and the style of the command line interface is all that remains.

### 13.1.2  WIMP interface

WIMP is an acronym which stands for windows, icons, menus, pointer. It has come to represent the standard graphical user interface on most laptop and desktop computers. The key feature of this model is that selection activities are mediated between the user and the computer using a mouse or other pointing device. The user holds the mouse in their hand and moves it on a tabletop surface, and a pointer, or cursor, moves on the screen in a similar way. The mapping between the mouse movements and the pointer movements are not necessarily one-to-one, and the user can lift the mouse to readjust the position of the pointer.

Commands are made available through menus, which is in direct contrast to the command-line interface, where commands must be remembered (or looked up) and spelled out. Menus list a collection of thematically related commands, and the user first navigates to the menu bar (which may be on the top or bottom of the screen or somewhere on a window or invoked contextually with a right click or a modifier click), selects one of a set of menus, invokes the menu with a mouse click, examines the options available, selects the option that is relevant to the task they are trying to accomplish, and invokes the task by clicking on that menu option. If the user forgets which menu a task is in, it may take several tries to find the command they are looking for. Information is presented in windows, which may be scrolled up or down when there is more information to display than will fit in the window.

The trade-off with WIMP interfaces is that although users do not have to remember and manually type each command, they do need to move their attention (and their pointer) away from the task they are working on in order to invoke a command. Contextual menus allow selection of commands nearer to the user's locus of attention, but only a small number of commands can be invoked in this way. Navigating a menu structure requires training, since although the commands may be listed in categorical menus, not all commands can be cleanly categorized and may be in a different menu than the user expects. To mitigate these challenges, WIMP interfaces often have **hotkeys**, short keystroke combinations which represent common commands. Control-C represents "copy," and Control-V represents "paste," for example. Users can increase their operational efficiency by learning these keystrokes, but these represent an *abstraction* from the command the user is looking for, and while some keystroke abstractions are intuitive, like C (representing copy), some can be abstruse—V means paste not because it represents the word alphabetically, but because C is next to V on the keyboard and pasting often comes after copying. Although WIMP interfaces are very familiar to most computer users, it is worth remembering that the design and implementation are somewhat arbitrary and require familiarity and training to become efficient.

Many software applications add to this interface model, using tool palettes, dashboards, pop-ups, and other additions. **Tool pallets** are a way to use abstractions to represent a large collection of common activities at the same time (see Figure 13.2). Each function has an icon, which serves as an abstraction to the function, and the tool palette as a whole serves to remind the user of the functions available in the current context. Tool palettes are also often associated with "tool tips" which provide a short description of the function of the tool when the user hovers over the icon representing that tool.

Figure 13.2: A tool palette

Dashboards (discussed in Section 12.3.4) are collections of information presented to the user to allow quick glanceable information content to be available at any time. Pop-ups and popovers are small windows that appear, usually in the user's locus of attention, to give additional information or to request an interaction from the user. These features of WIMP interfaces extend the functionality and provide, as much as possible, a complete set of functionality (for a given task) on a single screen. Users can quickly change between applications, invoking a completely new set of functionality based on the task to be performed, but most applications on desktop and laptop computers use the same metaphor.

Although very familiar to most users of computer, the accuracy of mouse movements is limited. As children grow, they develop fine motor skills required to draw with a pencil, paint with a paintbrush, model with clay, and generally manipulate objects with great detail. A mouse allows movement in two dimensions, primarily constrained with the wrist instead of the fingers. Drawing or printing with a mouse requires a different set of fine motor skills than drawing or printing with a pencil, and while these skills can be learned, most users tasked with signing their name with a mouse would not produce a satisfying result the first time they do so.

### M-dimensional Interfaces for N-dimensional Objects

Some applications of WIMP computing involve the creation and manipulation of three-dimensional objects. Animation, modelling, game design, and scientific computing are all examples of such applications. A two-dimensional screen can only display a projection of a three-dimensional object, creating the illusion that the user can see length, breadth, and depth. Because most WIMP interfaces do not use special glasses to simulate 3D displays, other features of the image trick the user's eye, like parallax, depth, shading, motion, and occlusion. Since VR is, by nature, a three-dimensional display, the interaction with 3D objects is more natural and intuitive. Further, it is reasonable to consider the possibility of projecting a four-dimensional object into the 3D space of VR, using a set of illusions similar to those that allow a flat screen to show depth. Non-Euclidean spaces and higher dimensional objects are discussed in Section 6.4

The advantage of considering a WIMP interface in a VR scenario is that it will almost definitely be familiar to the user. This familiarity will allow the user to quickly understand how to interact with such an interface. WIMP interfaces in VR are often presented as computer terminal screens, and the user would approach the screen and know, conceptually, how to interact with it. As with other traditional interfaces, however, the representation may or may not translate well to the virtual world. Selection via pointing is familiar to us, but is necessary only because the screen in a WIMP interface can (usually) only display information, not serve as an interface itself. The physical object we use as a proxy to the interaction we are targeting is itself mediated by the screen representation of the pointer. The mouse moves the pointer, the pointer moves the object on-screen, and the object moves the representation of that object in memory. In VR, this three-step proxy is not only unnecessary, it would be very difficult to implement. In VR, a user holds a controller or makes a gesture with their hands. The controller does not feel like a mouse and is not constrained to a desktop like a mouse. Moving a virtual mouse would require the user to hold their hand in space, rather than resting the palm of their hand on the desk while moving the mouse. Some features from WIMP interfaces translate well into VR, like menu selection and scrolling collections, but these must be adapted to work with direct selection available in VR rather than the mediated selection available with a mouse and pointer.

Manipulating a 3D object takes different forms depending on the interface modality available. WIMP interfaces require several layers of mediation, as discussed above. Touchscreen interfaces (discussed below) require only a single layer of mediation, but the objects being controlled are still projections onto the screen, and the interaction still happens exclusive at the screen boundary. VR allows users to directly manipulate objects; however, as discussed in previous chapters, even this interaction is mediated by the controller or hand gestures available to the user. Figure 13.3 shows these three forms of mediation.

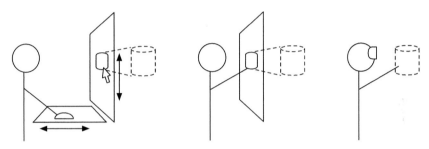

Figure 13.3: Interface mediation: (left to right) mouse and pointer; touchscreen; VR.

### 13.1.3 Touchscreen Interface

Touchscreen devices have rapidly become the primary way that people interact with software systems, and touchscreen devices use a different set of standard UI methods than WIMP interfaces. Because the screens are small compared to desktop and laptop computers, screen-anchored content is significantly reduced or even removed. There may be a small status bar that indicates common information like battery level or connectivity, but these indicators are also available in a separate status/settings application or portion of the interface, accessible via a swipe or gesture. With touchscreen devices, the range of different experiences is much greater, and most software fully replaces the baseline interface, which exists primarily to allow for the selection of an app. Although there remain standard interface practices, each app develops their own interface style, affordances, signifiers, and display of information. Jakob's law applies here as well, since most of the apps on a user's phone are not the app you are developing, it is worthwhile to at least be aware of existing commonalities between typical interaction tasks and information displays, before making yours different for the sake of different.

As discussed in Section 12.3.3, skeuomorphism is the use of visual artefacts from a previous implementation of functionality in order to assist understanding of a new technology. Early smartphones made use of skeuomorphism to allow users to understand the functionality of the calendar, notepad, telephone, and other aspects of the new user interface. As the interface matured and a wider proportion of the population became familiar with touchscreen interfaces, skeuomorphism fell out of favour and became an unpopular stylistic choice, replaced by minimalist designs which rely heavily on familiarity over affordance. In modern smartphone design, the difference between a text label and a text button may only be the colour or the context of the text, and many interactions (like gestures) are not afforded at all. Skeuomorphism, and the stylistic trend from more representative to more abstract, is not exclusive to touchscreen interfaces—skeuomorphic interfaces have often been used as an aid to developing familiarity when new modalities are first introduced to the general public. Early WIMP graphical user interfaces were skeuomorphic and have also become more abstract as they have become more familiar.

Even as the stylistic elements of touchscreen interfaces have changed over generations, the primary form of the interface is more or less unchanged from the early versions of smart phones. Fundamentally, a touchscreen computer is a grid of icons, each of which launches a small application or app. Each app completely replaces the interface with whatever touch-based controls are required for that function, making use of whatever affordances, gestalt organizations, and functionality are appropriate. The fundamental conceit of a touchscreen device is that the developer can present a graphical representation of a control on the screen and the user can reach out their finger to touch that graphical control. While multitouch interactions are common place today, the development of multitouch interfaces were a significant advance in the technology of touchscreen devices. Placing two fingers down on a single screen and then moving them in relation to each other allows the user to pinch, zoom, and rotate whatever object they are interacting with. A user can zoom in on a map or an image and can rotate or otherwise interact with any other interface element that the developer enables. As touchscreen phones and tablets became more popular, certain fundamental gestures became ubiquitous and therefore un-afforded. Users are expected to know that dragging down from the top of the phone opens a control panel or that dragging up from the bottom of the phone brings the user back to the home screen. New users may have to learn these gestures and may be given no visual reminders that the gestures are available.

One of the challenges of touchscreen devices occurs when a user must interact with a device without looking at it. You need to know where your fingers go when using detailed devices, and with a touchscreen, your fingers cannot feel where to go. When we type on a keyboard, play a musical instrument, or use a familiar tool, our hands are the primary way in which we gain information about that device, making sure the fingers are hitting the right keys or playing the right notes. A virtuoso musician does not need to look at their instrument to play their instrument. If, on the other hand, your instrument consists of a flat piece of glass, your fingers would have no way of knowing whether they are touching that piece of glass in the right place or not. Keyboards on touchscreen devices are notoriously difficult to use, and although many apps have been created that turn a phone into a musical instrument, the use of these for virtuoso performance has been limited to primarily demonstration purposes.

Smart phones can also make their way into a VR experience. As with WIMP interfaces, the primary benefit is that the user is familiar with the operation of a smart phone, and the primary challenge is that a smart phone in a VR experience will not function in the same way that a smart phone in physical reality will function.

In the real world, a user would reach out with their finger to touch the screen, and feel the pressure of the screen on their finger. This registration of a finger touch allows the user to have detailed control of the movement of their fingers on the screen. That detailed control is unavailable in VR, when a user reaches out their finger and mines the action of touching the screen, without actually feeling a screen underneath their finger. Phones can be used as a display object, where the user may invoke the action of reaching in their pocket to retrieve their phone, and the system would, at that point, display certain information on this virtual phone which may be relevant to the VR world being presented. In the same way that a user may turn their wrist to check their watch, they may also raise their hand to check their phone showing the time, or a mini map to a location, or some other piece of information. Since the primary interactive benefits of touchscreen devices are not available in typical VR experiences, the use of a phone becomes simply another way to display information. If thematically relevant, it may be appropriate, but the familiarity benefits may be outweighed by the expectations of the user for interaction that is not available.

## 13.2  TRADITIONAL INTERFACES IN VR

Although the promise of VR is to enable access to tasks and activities that are not possible in traditional interfaces, in many circumstances, traditional activities may still be required. Although you are flying through space in an unimaginable spaceship, in order to determine the address of the next star you are jumping to, you may have to type some text into a window or select a star from a menu of options. Fundamental interaction activities are commonplace on all traditional user interfaces Because they represent fundamental information interaction activities that humans pursue. In the section, we will present a collection of fundamental informational activities and provide constraints and best practices for enabling these activities in VR.

### 13.2.1  World Screens

The simplest way to enable fundamental activities in VR, as discussed above, is to use a familiar interaction from a traditional user interface. Developers need not insert a complete copy of a command-line, WIMP, or touchscreen interface directly into VR, but selecting particular elements of one or more of these interfaces may provide a clean and easy-to-use display of information within a virtual world. A **world screen** is a flat collection of user interface elements in VR intended to be viewed from a particular distance. Often, world screens are invoked by the user and presented to the user at an appropriate viewing distance, but sometimes world screens are presented diegetically, and the user must approach them in order to be able to read them. The intended viewing distance of the screen informs the size of the screen, the density of its content, and the method of interaction with the screen.

When using a world screen, the screen should be presented far enough away that the eye can naturally focus. Screens presented too close to the user will lead to eyestrain and difficulty in reading the content. Users may be inclined to walk away from the screen, possibly leaving their play area, resulting in larger problems. The natural viewing direction of the human eye is slightly below horizontal, and we can look up or down about 30° from this baseline comfortably. The eye has a 35° lateral range of movement, which provides stereo vision out to about 60°. These ranges are shown in Figure 13.4 and provide a square of comfort for placing elements on a screen assuming a constant head direction. A larger screen may be possible, but this requires the user to move their head around to see the entirety of the world, which may result in neck strain or discomfort. The listed angular specifications allow a large variety of screen sizes based on the distance from the user. Very small screens like wrist watches or a HUD can be presented quite close to the user, while large screens like movie theatres should be presented far away from the eye and in order to maintain the same comfortable angle of viewing. Figure 13.5 shows the relative sizes of a screen which are possible given a comfortable viewing angle. These different screen distances can be simulated in VR, but recall the vergence-accommodation conflict: although the angle between a user's eyes may be larger or smaller depending on the distance to the object they are observing, the focus distance to the physical screen in the VR headset remains constant—therefore looking at very close or very far objects for a long time can contribute to fatigue or VR sickness.

**Dynamic Screen Placement**

If you need to show a user some information on a screen, the placement of that screen should fall within the user's locus of attention. If the user looks away, there may be a need to have the screen follow their line of vision, or the screen may need to be locked in place in space. Follower screens are popular for studio logos at the beginning of a game, and as the user looks around, the logo may follow their gaze. This following behaviour should be slow, so that the user can subconsciously confirm sensorimotor contingencies as the experience loads. If the screen appears directly in the user's line of sight and moves exactly with the user's line of sight, the user may have the experience of a glitched VR display, where the scene view does not change with head movement.

### 13.2.2 Wrist displays

Wrist displays are very common in VR because they can be invoked with a simple gesture of raising the wrist, and this is a common and familiar gesture in the physical world as well. Wrist displays, when invoked, can present as a dietetic surface on the user's arm, like a wristwatch, or they can create a floating display locationally bound to and tracked with the wrist, but floating above it. Such displays provide quick access to important information like a user's health or ammunition, the time of day, the direction to a location or task, or any number of glanceable data points. Because wrist displays are typically small, information there should be kept compact and abstract, and because it takes an intentional action to invoke a wrist display, information there is usually conceptually time specific and local as opposed to global

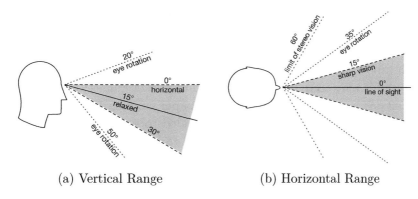

(a) Vertical Range        (b) Horizontal Range

Figure 13.4: Angular ranges of vision.

Figure 13.5: Screen size is related to intended viewing distance

or static information that could more appropriately appear in a menu or inventory screen, or settings panel.

### 13.2.3  Text and Detail Display

The size of the screen on which to present information is the only one factor in designing the way information will be presented to the user. The amount of detail that the eye can resolve at a particular distance is related to the angular size of that information. A large screen at an appropriate distance with very small text will not be discernible, and users presented with this information will likely invoke some action or activity in order to try to increase the size of the resolution or bring the screen closer to them. For this reason, it is important to make text and other screen-displayed elements a reasonable size for the distance away from the user. On the page of a book, 10-point font is standard, and users can hold the book at an appropriate distance from their eye to allow the text to be comfortably read. Fonts smaller than 5 point will be difficult to read at this distance, and users may need to bring the book closer to their eyes in order to make out the text. Headings and titles are displayed in larger fonts to draw the eye and facilitate understanding at a glance from slightly further away. Computer screens are used at arm's length, and typically use a font size of around 12 points, although individuals often customize their text size to balance between how much information can be presented on the screen and how readable it is. As people age, their visual acuity tends to be reduced, and the ability of the eye to adapt to different distances quickly is also reduced—therefore older people tend to use larger fonts on their phones and computer screens.

Text fonts are measured in points, and one point is $1/72$ of an inch or 0.35 mm. Text read on a computer monitor in 12-point font is 4.2 mm, and if the screen is 1 metre away, this gives a measure of 4.2 dmm. Similar readability in a book held at arm's length (about half a metre away) would be 2.1 dmm or 6 point font. On initial consideration, this may seem unusually small, but pocket guides and references books may have fonts as small as 4 point, and newspaper running text fonts are typically 4 or 5 points in size. These font sizes are intended to squeeze as much information onto the page as possible, and readers may need to hold the page closer to their eyes to be able to make out the text.

Text on a road sign is necessarily larger than that in a book, because it must be quickly read from much farther away. At that scale, "points" are not a useful measure, and fonts are instead measured in linear distance (centimetres or inches). The word "stop" on a stop sign is 25 cm (10 inches) tall. The absolute size of the text to be read relates to how far away it is, and a more useful measure of this relates to the angle of an object at a particular distance. The distance-independent millimetre (Figure 13.6) provides a simple angular measure appropriate for maintaining reasonably constant size of objects in the visual field. A distance-independent millimetre (dmm) is the angular size of an object 1 mm in size seen at 1 metre distance. Other standard angles can be converted to dmm: 1 dmm is equivalent to 0.573 degrees or 0.001 radians. The utility of dmm as a measure is that when building VR worlds, the developer often chooses the size of the object directly and places the object at a specific intended distance from the user. Having an understanding of readability at different dmm sizes allows the developer to adjust the size of the object in an intuitive and direct way, rather than having to calculate viewing angles based on size and distance.

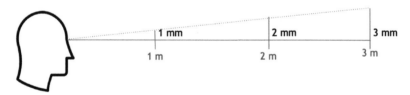

Figure 13.6: Distance independent millimetre

Design guidance varies significantly on the selection of font size for a given application. In general, larger text is easier to read, but less information can be conveyed in a given space. Although VR hardware continues to improve, many headsets still have challenges with visual resolution, and so larger fonts should be preferred when possible. Reading long passages of text in VR can lead to fatigue, not only because of the accommodation-vergence conflict, but also because reading on a screen in general can be exhausting due to the brightness and directionality of the light from the screen.

Another factor in the choice of text size is the time available for the user to understand the text. Road signs and billboards must be able to be read quickly because the user is often passing by the sign, so it is only available for a few seconds, and the user (if driving) only has a limited amount of attention to give to the sign. If the words are unfamiliar, like a street name in a new town, the person may need to read the sign twice in order to fully acquire the information on the sign. User interfaces in VR that must be read quickly and therefore need large clear type are the same interfaces that must be read quickly in the physical world: glanceable displays, like object identifiers, dashboards, or HUDs.

The choice of font to use also depends on the context in which a person will read the text. Large fonts to be read quickly—such as road signs, book titles, and chapter headings, are typically written in a sans-serif typeface, so that each individual word is seen as a separate object and can quickly be understood. Smaller text intended to be read in a continuous way typically use serifs to guide the reader along the line of text across the page. A serif is a small tab on a glyph that serves to reinforce the line of the text across the page, making use of the "closure" principle of gestalt organization (see Section 12.3.1). The shape of the font, or the glyphs used, can also change with font size. A glyph is a letter symbol within a font and is used to describe the general shape and size of letters as graphical objects. Smaller text typically uses wider and thicker glyphs, compared to tall, thin glyphs used in situations where the text will be printed in a larger font size. Modern computer fonts usually do not modify the glyph based on the size of the font, but professional typeset systems may have multiple glyph sets for a single font, based on the size at which the text will be read. Figure 13.7 shows examples of font shape as a function of font size, as well as other features of font glyphs to consider.

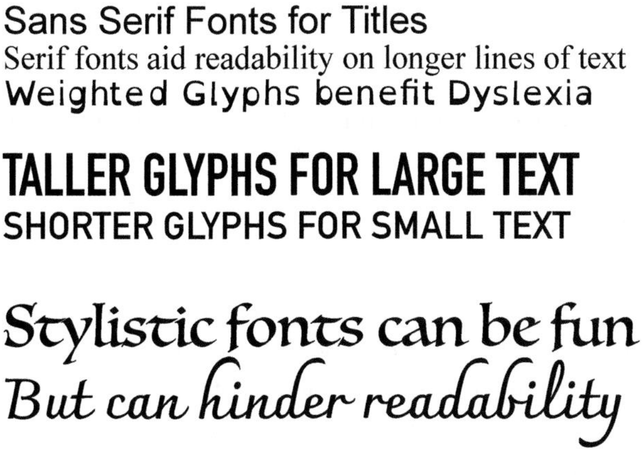

## Sans Serif Fonts for Titles
Serif fonts aid readability on longer lines of text
**Weighted Glyphs benefit Dyslexia**

## TALLER GLYPHS FOR LARGE TEXT
### SHORTER GLYPHS FOR SMALL TEXT

*Stylistic fonts can be fun*
*But can hinder readability*

Figure 13.7: Some features to consider when selecting a font

Font colour must also be considered when displaying text for readability. High contrast colour combinations are usually best to support rapid recognition of words and lines, with black-on-white or white-on-black text being the easiest to read. Whether black should be used as the background or the text colour depends on the ambient light of the room in which the user will read the text. In brightly lit contexts, black text on a white background is best, while in dark rooms, white text on a black background will be easier to see. A coloured background can be used to indicate context for a sign that must be understood quickly. For example, road signs use colours to indicate whether they describe the name of the street, the destination of a road, or an instruction to the driver. The contrast with the text on the sign must be maintained, however, and if the colour of the text is too similar to the colour of the background, the text can be difficult to read. Additionally, individuals who are colour blind may have specific difficulties reading certain colour combinations between the text and the background, or understanding the information that is included in the colour of the background or the text. Coloured text can likewise convey significant information, and many software development environments use different colours to indicate different conceptual ideas related to the text being written as computer code. Variable identifiers may be one colour, reserved words may be another, and structural punctuation may be a third colour. Figure 13.8 shows how readability can change with the colour of the text and the background

Figure 13.8: Impact of font and background colour on readability

**Dark mode**
A recent trend in graphic organization for computer screens is the emergence of dark mode. Dark mode significantly reduces the brightness of screen displays, as well as reducing the power consumption of those displays in some circumstances. The primary benefit, for those who prefer dark mode, is that text displayed on backlit screens in dark environments is easier to read. Since most modern computer systems, by default, provide white text on a black background, dark mode support for individual software applications is something developers have recently had to actively implement. It is interesting to see how these stylistic decisions and trends change over time. Command-line interfaces in the early days of computing were almost exclusively dark mode—often displaying text in a bright green or yellow colour, depending on the technology of the cathode-ray tube (CRT) connected to the computer to display text. The advent of computers that could display black text on a white background was seen as an advancement from the archaic display of white text on a black background.

### 13.2.4 Text Input

When a user puts on a VR headset, they occlude their senses from the physical world. Because of this, even though a computer keyboard may be available in front of them, most users will not be able to use that keyboard in VR. Even users who have learned how to touch type will have difficulty, because they may be unable to locate the keyboard once they have walked away from the desk—users quickly acclimatize to an understanding of the geometry of the virtual world instead of the geometry of their physical world that may include a physical keyboard. In the absence of a physical keyboard, users required to enter text can either use speech recognition or will require some form of in-world virtual keyboard. The activity of typing on a keyboard is a significant, learned, fine motor skill that makes use of direct tactile feedback between the physical keyboard and the user's fingertips. This interaction is unavailable in VR, unless a physical keyboard with responsive keys is made available, and even then, a virtual representation of that same physical keyboard should be provided to the user so they can find it, align their fingers to the keys, and begin typing. Although this form of augmented virtuality is becoming more common, as of yet, most commercial systems do not include the ability to track real-world objects.

Implementing a virtual keyboard depends on the characteristics of the virtual world in which the keyboard will reside, as well as the interaction modes that are available to the user. If the user is holding a controller, the system will not know enough about the position of all fingers to allow full eight-finger typing. Instead, the user might point to individual letters with one or two fingers or use a virtual probe, tool, or mallet which can activate the keys remotely. These options are shown in Figure 13.9. In each of these cases, the ability for users to enter text is significantly slower and less accurate than that same user's ability to type text on a physical keyboard. Text entry with a virtual keyboard can approach 30 words per minute (wpm) for a user familiar with the system, while proficient users on the physical keyboard average 50 wpm and may approach 80 wpm. Users will also become fatigued more quickly when using a virtual keyboard, because their hands are not resting on a desk and their fingers do not make contact with the keyboard.

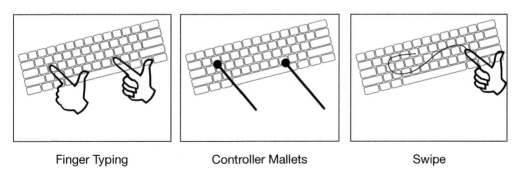

Finger Typing          Controller Mallets          Swipe

Figure 13.9: Options for traditional keyboards in VR

Finger tracking VR systems offer an alternative, where each individual finger might interact with a set of keys on the keyboard. Aligning the virtual keyboard with a flat surface like a desk gives tactile feedback and allows the user to rest their hands on the desk, even though the fingers do not directly sense any keys. Care must be taken here to provide an opportunity for the user to align their fingers with the keyboard, and if the user is not looking at the keyboard, their finger positions may drift away from the correct alignment over time. Similar to the errors that can happen when typing on the glass screen of a smart phone or tablet, typing on a flat desk with a virtual keyboard can be challenging.

Depending on the context, alternative keyboard and text input methods may be appropriate. If the user is holding a controller with a directional pad or joystick, directional text input as discussed in Section 11.2.1 may be an option. Smartphones sometimes allow text input via swiping, where the user traces their finger over the layout of a keyboard, drawing a pattern connecting the letters of a word, and the system makes a best guess of the word they were trying to type. Such swipe systems can also be implemented in VR systems. Alternative layouts, swipe systems, or other unfamiliar methods for inputting text will need training and familiarity for the user. A developer may be tempted to make text input as familiar as possible in order to aid understanding and suggest interactions, but a keyboard that looks familiar but does not function as expected may end up causing frustration. The trade-off between suggesting actions via familiarity and frustration that those actions do not operate as expected will have to be carefully considered.

The other consideration of virtual keyboards is that due to the error-prone nature of typing in VR, the user should have what they are typing displayed prominently as they are typing it. This direct visual feedback should appear in the users locus of attention (Section 8.3.2) as much as possible.

### 13.2.5 Scrolling

Traditional interfaces presenting information too large for the display will allow the user to scroll through the information. The mental model is either of a frame scrolling up and down across a larger page of content or of the page of content scrolling up and down behind the frame. Although conceptually similar, the activity itself is reversed, and as touchscreens have become more prevalent, it has become more common to manipulate the content below the frame rather than manipulating the frame over the content. The act of "scrolling down" has therefore become somewhat ambiguous, because although the conceptual action is to move downward through content, the physical action is to use your finger or the scroll wheel to move the content you have already seen up and out of the way. Grabbing the content and moving it in the desired direction also relates to zooming and rotating, but involves two locations of control rather that the single point of control required for scrolling. Scrolling is both heavily constrained (the content moves only in one direction) and heavily regularized (users are familiar with the concept of scrolling and the interactions required for it).

Scrolling in VR requires special consideration, because the divergence between moving the content and moving the frame over the content matters more when the content takes up a large portion of the view. On desktop or mobile applications, the content to be scrolled often takes up the entire view of the device, but in VR, if the content being scrolled takes up even a portion of the main view, it is possible that the act of scrolling can induce feelings of motion. If I scroll a page upward, I can feel like I am falling downward, especially if the view takes up a significant portion of my vision. Because of this "scrolling-falling" illusion, many VR developers have instead chosen to implement horizontal scrolling rather than vertical scrolling. The horizontal movement may feel like rotation, depending on how much of the view is taken up by the content being scrolled, but this is a more straightforward motion and less prone to nausea and disorientation, at least in part because rotation in VR is a very common activity and falling in VR is so uncommon.

Scrolling in VR is also typically performed in discrete steps rather than continuously. Rotation of a user's view is also typically performed in discrete steps (although options for continuous rotation are usually offered and should be presented to the user based on their motion comfort level), and scrolling in discrete steps mirrors this interaction, increasing familiarity and reducing the triggers of simulator sickness. The second key reason scrolling in VR should be done in discrete steps is that it is easier to control. As discussed above, selection targets become more challenging to acquire and interact with when they are smaller, and although the content itself is usually a very large and close target, grabbing the content only allows scrolling within the frame (unless momentum-based "flick" or "fling" scrolling is implemented). Scrolling outside of the frame is typically implemented using a *scroll bar* which serves as both an indicator of the current view of the frame within the larger context of the content, as well as a method for grabbing the frame and moving it to another location within the content. Scroll bars are typically small compared to the content and can be difficult to accurately select and move. Discrete movements can be performed with controller buttons or gestures and are more reliable.

## 13.2.6 Menus

In traditional interfaces, menus provide a collection of (usually) related functions hidden behind a set of semantically related categories. Menus allow users access to a larger set of functions without having to remember that the functions exist or how to access them. Menus in traditional interfaces typically appear either in a dedicated menu bar affixed to the currently active window or to the desktop itself, or contextually when invoked in relation to specific actions required of some content. Examples of traditional menus are shown in Figure 13.10.

Menu selection patterns in VR are common and familiar ways to select from a collection of options; however, the traditional formats of menus must be modified somewhat to align with the ways that people interact with virtual worlds. The fine motor control available with a mouse on a desktop or a finger on a touchscreen is not available in VR since the user is holding the controller or their hands in empty space in front of them. Small targets are much harder to access in VR. Further, dedicated screen space locked to one location is not a common practice in VR scenarios; therefore global or local windowed menus are not recommended. Instead, menus should be invoked within contexts that require them. Inventory screens or interaction panels can have traditional menus, but the control challenges still apply—therefore tabbed

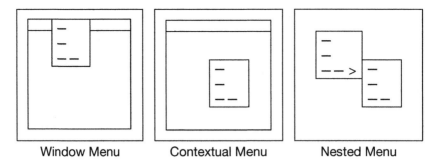

Window Menu       Contextual Menu       Nested Menu

Figure 13.10: Traditional menu structures

interfaces may be more usable than traditional menu systems. In contexts where a panel presentation is not available, contextual menus can be invoked from objects, or from the user's person, connected to a wristwatch or tool, as shown in Figure 13.11.

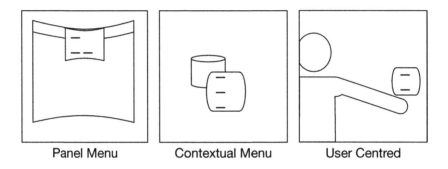

Panel Menu       Contextual Menu       User Centred

Figure 13.11: VR menu structures

The form that these menus take in VR must also be considered. A linear list of options may be difficult to control and select from, but the familiarity of this pattern should not be discounted. Other options that provide similar functionality and the potential for improved usability in VR recognize that actions are initiated from a point in space, and the most controllable action from a point in space is a radial selection from that space. A menu can be invoked with a controller, presenting a wheel of options, and the directional pad or thumbstick on the controller can be used to select one of these options. As an additional benefit, if the options are always in the same location, the act of invoking the menu and selecting an option can be learned and therefore does not require direct attention to the options to be invoked. Variations on the circular menu abound, and some examples are the following:

**Pie menu.** A set of options are presented as wedges around the point of invocation. The user can move outward from the point to select the relevant menu item.

**Ring menu.** A set of options are presented as segments on a ring encircling the point of invocation. The user can select the ring segment corresponding to the relevant menu item.

**Wheel menu.** A set of options are presented around a wheel. The user can turn the wheel to highlight the relevant menu item.

**Sphere menu.** A set of options are presented as tiles on a sphere. The user can rotate the sphere to highlight the relevant menu item.

Each of these options can also be combined with or enhanced by diegesis. If the collection of options available is integrated with the object being controlled in a way that makes sense within the context of the world, the selection of options may make more conceptual sense and be easier to understand and invoke. Objects from the physical world with inherent menus may contain a grid or array of buttons, much like a tool palette. Many real-world objects also have small screens to display options, and although this can be used as a diegetic method to convey information to the user, keep in mind that the physical and conceptual limitations of real-world objects, as discussed previously, can lead to problematic usability. Bringing familiar objects from the real world into VR can improve outcomes in the short term, but these objects should not be limited by their real-world implementation limitations. If the screen on an interactive object is small and the text is hard to read, consider projecting that screen or a conceptual representation of it to the user in order to aid readability and interaction.

## 13.3 GESTURES

In most traditional interfaces, the gulf of execution is limited somewhat by the implementation of mechanisms to constrain actions. A button can be pressed in many ways, but the system responding to the button will only ever see the button as pressed or not pressed. These constraints of action have the effect of ensuring that no matter what variation there may be in the user's action, the system will always perceive the exact intention of the button press. Video game controllers, pilot cockpits, and other collections of controls are a way to bring together a large number of specific actions and allow the user to activate any action at a given time and to ensure that the action is not misconstrued by the system. Of course, when button functionality is ambiguous, or modal, or multiple buttons can be pressed at the same time, or the context of the system dictates the function of the button, then the result of the button press may be unknown, but the state of the button (pressed or unpressed) will always be agreed upon by the user and the system.

A button, however, can only indicate one bit of information: the choice to do a thing or not do a thing. Many contexts require more subtle levels of control from the user to the system, and controls that allow a range of responses have become popular. Video game controllers often can tell not only that the user has pressed a button, but how hard or how quickly the button was pressed. Any control that has a range of responses rather than a simple on-off can be used to communicate significant subtlety to the system, as long as the system is in a position to receive and respond to that subtlety. Musical instruments are a core inspiration to such variable controls. A piano will respond differently depending on whether a key is struck softly or forcefully, and digital piano keyboards are designed to register this difference in pressure and translate it into a variable called *velocity*, relating to the speed at which the key moves from one position to the other.

When a user has continuous or variable control over a characteristic of input, there is the potential to communicate discrete information based on a pattern of movement. A **gesture**, in this context, is a unified movement of a control, identified by the system as a single action. Our understanding of gestures can be informed by their use in personal communication, although some of these gestures are culturally specific and many are contextually dependent. When I wave my hand at a friend, it is a complex motion interpreted as a single action with a specific meaning: I am saying "hi." When I show my fist with a thumb extended, it indicates agreement or assent (except in some cultures where it is a rude gesture), but if I show a different finger extended, it might indicate anger, aggression, or displeasure. Holding a fist in the air can indicate pleasure in success, or a threat. Holding two fingers in the air can indicate a sign of peace or victory or can be a very rude gesture if the hand is held palm-in, and the fingers are moved upward.

Sign language is made up of motions of the hands and body, some of which are static and some include motion. In order for a person (or a system) to understand a hand sign, it must be able to identify the position of the hands, track their motion, and distinguish between the end of one gesture and the beginning of another—a particularly difficult problem since one gesture often leads into the next, in much the same way that one spoken word naturally blends into the next word, with no space or gap between words. Our understanding of the break between spoken words is entirely semantic, and the same is true for breaks between gestures.

In computer systems, any input that can have a variety of values can be used to communicate a gesture. A continuous button can be pressed hard or softly to indicate a specific action. A thumbstick or joystick can be turned in a circle to indicate that the character should change their tool or their armour. A user might shake the mouse to find the cursor, and the system might detect this shaking and enlarge the cursor as a result.

In VR, gestures are central to the experience of users, but remain difficult to implement. Early generations of VR hardware required the use of external controllers like a keyboard and mouse to deliver input to the system, and as progress developed, game controllers and eventually handheld motion controllers became commonplace. In each of these cases, the primary way to deliver input to the system was still to press buttons. Button presses are more consistent, easier to learn, easier to remember, and easier to interpret by the system, so even as motion controllers became prevalent and the system could detect the hand position of the user with reliability, higher level interpretations of the path of motion of the hands, as would be required for gestures, were still rare. Hand position gestures are reasonably easy to detect, since hand controllers can often detect where the fingers are resting on a button in addition to whether the button is pressed, but these are still discrete on-off controls. If the user is touching the grip button but not the trigger button, the system interprets this as the user pointing their index finger. The challenge with this, besides being limited to a small number of gestures, is that the system is not attempting to interpret any of the actual finger positions; it is only measuring presence or absence of contact.

Users can wave their hands around, and the positions are tracked in real time, but most VR systems do not identify when the user is moving their hand in a specific way over time.

By their nature, motion-controlled gestures are not guaranteed to be successful. If the system allows the user's hand to move in a circle to indicate a specific interaction, the user may not successfully indicate that gesture if they move the hand too fast or too slow or don't quite close the circle. Gesture recognition systems must be implemented with some tolerances or allowances in order to ensure that users making slightly inaccurate gestures can be successful, but at the same time, if a user makes a somewhat random motion that the system interprets as a gesture and incorrectly invokes an action, this can be frustrating as well. For this reason, gestures are sometimes trained, in that a user can show the system what their version of the gesture looks like, and the system can employ statistical techniques to create a model of the gesture for recognition later. Training techniques were popular in the early days of speech recognition, but the requirement to train a system before it can be used served as a usability barrier for many. Similarity, if a VR system needs to be trained before it will recognize a user's gestures, this can be seen as a limitation. Humans have no problem identifying gestures of other humans, so it stands to reason that it must be possible for a VR system to be able to reliably identify instances of gestures while rejecting false positives.

Although gesture recognition is still diverse between VR scenarios and even claimed specifically as a feature or virtue of some games or experiences, there are a few simple gestures that are becoming commonplace in VR scenarios. Games that include weapons that need to be reloaded often implement a gesture to allow the user to perform the reload without pushing a button. In archery games, the user might reach behind their back to grab another arrow; in games with firearms, the user might point the weapon upward or downward to reload or they may reach for their belt to grab a clip. In order for gestures to be intuitive, they should map reasonably closely to the expected motion of an activity in the physical world, although some gestures in the physical world may not map well to the virtual scenarios.

Broad gestures with the arms are straightforward to implement, since the location of the hand is known from the location of the hand controller, and the location of the arm segments can be inferred using inverse kinematics. Gestures that make use of fingers are more difficult to detect, depending on the finger tracking technology being used. If the system detects fingers based on whether or not they are resting on sensors on the controller, a limited number of discrete gestures are available. If the system detects fingers using a tracked haptic glove, the position of each finger should be detectable with some degree of precision. If visual or infrared cameras are used for direct finger tracking without a glove, some gestures can be particularly difficult to detect, especially if the fingers are pointing away from the camera or if two fingers (or both hands) are close together. In these cases, the visual finger tracking technology can have errors of detection, leading to user frustration.

## 13.4 SUMMARY

Although VR provides opportunities for a wide diversity of alternative interface modalities, in some cases there are benefits to using interpretations of traditional interfaces our users are familiar with. These interface must be modified for the virtual worlds we are creating, because traditional interfaces are built for the real world. There are innumerable new interfaces enabled by VR techniques that waiting to be developed, but we must be conscious that every new interface must be learned, and that some may be easier to understand than others. The activities and experience enabled by VR present a vast new landscape of opportunity for developers, as long as we take into account that the human is always at the centre of the experience.

# Bibliography

[1] J. Anderson, D. Bothell, M. Byrne, S. Douglass, and C. Lebiere. An integrated theory of the mind. *Psychological Review*, 2002.

[2] P. Anderson, B. Rothbaum, and L. Hodges. Virtual reality: Using the virtual world to improve quality of life in the real world. *Bulletin of the Menninger Clinic*, 65(1):78–91, 02 2001.

[3] S. Baase. *A Gift of Fire: Social, Legal, and Ethical Issues for Computing Technology*. Prentice Hall Press, USA, 4th edition, 2012.

[4] R. Baraas, F. Imai, A. Yontem, and J. Hardeberg. Visual perception in AR/VR. *Optics and Photonics News*, 32:34, 04 2021.

[5] L. Barfield. *The User Interface: Concepts & Design*. Human Computer Interaction. Addison-Wesley, 1993.

[6] J. Blascovich and J. Bailenson. *Infinite Reality: Avatars, Eternal Life, New Worlds, and the Dawn of the Virtual Revolution*. William Morrow, 2011.

[7] J. Blascovich and J. Bailenson. *Infinite Reality the Hidden Blueprint of Our Virtual Lives*. William Morrow, an imprint of HarperCollins Publishers, 2012.

[8] K. R. Boff, L. Kaufman, and J. P. Thomas. *Handbook of Perception and Human Performance*. Wiley, 1986.

[9] C. Bohil, C. Owen, E. Jeong, B. Alicea, and F. Biocca. *Virtual Reality and Presence*, chapter 59, pages 534–542. SAGE Publications, 01 2009.

[10] D. Bowman, E. Kruijff, J. J. LaViola, and I. Poupyrev. *3D User Interfaces: Theory and Practice*. Addison Wesley Longman Publishing Co., Inc., 350 Bridge Pkwy suite 208 Redwood City, CAUnited States, 2004.

[11] D. Bowman and R. McMahan. Virtual reality: How much immersion is enough? *Computer*, 40(7):36 – 43, 08 2007.

[12] J. Broderick, J. Duggan, and S. Redfern. The importance of spatial audio in modern games and virtual environments. *2018 IEEE Games, Entertainment, Media Conference (GEM)*, pages 1–9, 2018.

[13] J. Carroll and M. B. Rosson. A case library for teaching usability engineering: Design rationale, development, and classroom experience. *ACM Journal of Educational Resources in Computing*, 5(1):1–22, 03 2005.

[14] N. Chapman and J. Chapman. *Digital Multimedia*. Wiley, 2014.

[15] S. Coren, L. M. Ward, and J. T. Enns. *Sensation and Perception*. John Wiley & Sons, 2004.

[16] J. E. Cutting and P. M. Vishton. Perceiving layout and knowing distances: The integration, relative potency, and contextual use of different information about depth. In *Perception of Space and Motion*, 1995.

[17] A. Delazio, K. Nakagaki, R. Klatzky, S. Hudson, J. Lehman, and A. Sample. Force jacket: Pneumatically-actuated jacket for embodied haptic experiences. In *ACM Conference on Human Factors in Computing Systems (CHI)*, pages 1–12, 04 2018.

[18] A. Dix, J. Finlay, G. Abowd, and R. Beale. *Human Computer Interaction*. Pearson Education Canada, 2006.

[19] W. Galitz. *The Essential Guide to User Interface Design: An Introduction to GUI Design Principles and Techniques*. Wiley Desktop Editions. Wiley, 2007.

[20] A. Gallace, M. Ngo, J. Sulaitis, and C. Spence. Multisensory presence in virtual reality: Possibilities and limitations. *Multiple Sensorial Media Advances and Applications: New Developments in MulSeMedia*, pages 1–40, 01 2012.

[21] M. Garau, D. Friedman, H. Widenfeld, A. Antley, A. Brogni, and M. Slater. Temporal and spatial variations in presence: Qualitative analysis of interviews from an experiment on breaks in presence. *Presence: Teleoperators and Virtual Environments*, 17(3):293–309, 06 2008.

[22] J. J. Gibson. The senses considered as perceptual systems. *Oxford England: Houghton Mifflin*, 1996.

[23] J.-C. Golovine. Experimental user interface design toolkit for interaction research (IDTR), 01 2013.

[24] D. Gomez, G. Burdea, and N. Langrana. Integration of the Rutgers Master II in a virtual reality simulation. In *Virtual Reality Annual International Symposium*, pages 198 – 202, 04 1995.

[25] B. J. Harris. *The History of the Future: Oculus, Facebook and the Revolution that Swept Virtual Reality*. Dey St., 2020.

[26] D. Heeger. Perception lecture notes: Depth, size, and shape, 2006.

[27] A. Henderson. *Interaction Design: Beyond Human-Computer Interaction*. John Wiley & Sons, Inc, New York, NY, USA, 03 2002.

[28] C. Hendrix and W. Barfield. Presence within virtual environments as a function of visual display parameters. *Presence: Teleoperators and Virtual Environments*, 5(3):274–289, 08 1996.

[29] K. Hirota and M. Hirose. Simulation and presentation of curved surface in virtual reality environment through surface display. In *Proceedings of the IEEE 95 Virtual Reality Annual International Symposium (VRAIS)*, pages 211–216, 1995.

[30] L. Jacquey, G. Baldassarre, V. G. Santucci, and J. K. O'Regan. Sensorimotor contingencies as a key drive of development: From babies to robots. *Frontiers in Neurorobotics*, 2019.

[31] J. Jerald. *The VR Book Human-Centered Design for Virtual Reality*. Morgan & Claypool, 2016.

[32] K. Kilteni, R. Groten, and M. Slater. The sense of embodiment in virtual reality. *Presence Teleoperators & Virtual Environments*, 21(4), 11 2012.

[33] K. Kilteni, J.-M. Normand, M. Sanchez-Vives, and M. Slater. Extending body space in immersive virtual reality: A very long arm illusion. *PloS One*, 7, 07 2012.

[34] R. Konrad, A. Angelopoulos, and G. Wetzstein. Gaze-contingent ocular parallax rendering for virtual reality. *ACM Transactions on Graphics*, 39(2), 2019.

[35] S. M. Lavalle. *Virtual Reality*. Cambridge University Press, 2019.

[36] J. J. LaViola, E. Kruijff, R. P. McMahan, D. Bowman, and I. Poupyrev. *3D User Interfaces: Theory and Practice*. Addison-Wesley, 2017.

[37] K. M. Lee. Presence, explicated. *Communication Theory*, 14(1):27–50, 01 2006.

[38] G. Makransky, L. Lilleholt, and A. Aaby. Development and validation of the multimodal presence scale for virtual reality environments: A confirmatory factor analysis and item response theory approach. *Computers in Human Behavior*, 72, 02 2017.

[39] M. Martens, A. Antley, D. Freeman, M. Slater, P. Harrison, and E. Tunbridge. It feels real: Physiological responses to a stressful virtual reality environment and its impact on working memory. *Journal of Psychopharmacology*, 33, 07 2019.

[40] A. Maselli and M. Slater. The building blocks of the full body ownership illusion. *Frontiers in human neuroscience*, 7, 03 2013.

[41] D. R. Mestre. Cave versus head-mounted displays: Ongoing thoughts. *Society for Imaging Science and Technology*, 2017.

[42] P. Milgram, H. Takemura, A. Utsumi, and F. Kishino. Augmented reality: A class of displays on the reality-virtuality continuum. *Telemanipulator and Telepresence Technologies*, 2351, 01 1994.

[43] D. Nitz. A place for motion in mapping. *Nature neuroscience*, 18:6–7, 12 2014.

[44] J. Noble. *Programming Interactivity.* Oreilly and Associate Series. O'Reilly Media, Incorporated, 2012.

[45] I. A. Nordin, J. Ali, A. Animashaun, J. Asch, J. Adams, and P. Cairns. Attention, time perception and immersion in games. In *CHI Extended Abstracts on Human Factors in Computing Systems*, pages 1089–1094, 04 2013.

[46] D. A. Norman. *The design of everday things.* MIT Press, 2013.

[47] M. North and S. North. A comparative study of sense of presence of virtual reality and immersive environments. *Australasian Journal of Information Systems*, 20, 02 2016.

[48] A. Noë. *Action in Perception.* MIT Press, 2004.

[49] E. Pangilinan, S. Lukas, and V. Mohan. *Creating Augmented and Virtual Realities: Theory and Practice for Next-Generation Spatial Computing.* O'Reilly Media, 2019.

[50] M. Parger, J. Mueller, D. Schmalstieg, and M. Steinberger. Human upper-body inverse kinematics for increased embodiment in consumer-grade virtual reality. In *Symposium on Virtual Reality Software and Technology*, 11 2018.

[51] T. Parsons. Virtual reality for enhanced ecological validity and experimental control in the clinical, affective, and social neurosciences. *Frontiers in Human Neuroscience*, 9:660, 11 2015.

[52] R. Pausch, D. Proffitt, and D. Williams. Quantifying immersion in virtual reality. *Proceedings of SIGGRAPH97*, pages 13–18, 08 1997.

[53] J. Perret and E. V. Poorten. Touching virtual reality: a review of haptic gloves. In *ACTUATOR 2018*, 06 2018.

[54] M. Pharr, W. Jakob, and G. Humphreys. *Physically Based Rendering:From Theory To Implementation.* Morgan Kaufmann, 2018.

[55] D. Pittera, M. Obrist, and A. Israr. Hand-to-hand: An intermanual illusion of movement. In *Proceedings of the 19th ACM International Conference on Multimodal Interaction*, pages 73–81, 11 2017.

[56] J. Preece, Y. Rogers, and H. Sharp. *Interaction Design: Beyond Human-Computer Interaction.* John Wiley & Sons, 5th edition, 2019.

[57] S. Pritchard, R. Zopf, V. Polito, D. Kaplan, and M. Williams. Non-hierarchical influence of visual form, touch, and position cues on embodiment, agency, and presence in virtual reality. *Frontiers in Psychology*, 7(1649), 10 2016.

[58] M. Pyasik, G. Tieri, and L. Pia. Visual appearance of the virtual hand affects embodiment in the virtual hand illusion. *Scientific Reports*, 10, 03 2020.

[59] J. Raskin. *The Humane Interface: New Directions for Designing Interactive Systems.* Addison-Wesley, 2000.

[60] K. Reinig, C. G. Rush, H. L. Pelster, V. Spitzer, and J. A. Heath. Real-time visually and haptically accurate surgical simulation. *Studies in health technology and informatics*, 29:542–5, 01 1996.

[61] G. Robertson, M. Czerwinski, and M. Dantzich. Immersion in desktop virtual reality. In *Proceedings of the 10th annual ACM symposium on User interface software and technology*, pages 11–19, 01 1997.

[62] M. B. Rosson and J. Carroll. Scenario-based usability engineering. In *Proceedings of the 4th conference on Designing interactive systems: processes, practices, methods, and techniques*, 12 2002.

[63] C. Rouby. *Olfaction, Taste, and Cognition.* Cambridge University Press, 2005.

[64] M. Sanchez-Vives and M. Slater. From presence to consciousness through virtual reality. *Nature reviews, Neuroscience*, 6:332–9, 05 2005.

[65] A. Sankar. Immersive data visualization with virtual reality. In *Conference on Human Factors in Computing Systems (CHI)*, 2015.

[66] J.-C. Servotte, M. Goosse, S. Campbell, N. Dardenne, B. Pilote, I. Simoneau, M. Guillaume, I. Bragard, and A. Ghuysen. Virtual reality experience: Immersion, sense of presence, and cybersickness. *Clinical Simulation in Nursing*, 38:35–43, 01 2020.

[67] D. Shin. Empathy and embodied experience in virtual environments. *Computers in Human Behaviour*, 78, 09 2017.

[68] R. Skarbez, S. Neyret, F. P. Brooks, M. Slater, and M. C. Whitton. A psychophysical experiment regarding components of the plausibility illusion. *IEEE Transactions on Visualization and Computer Graphics*, 23(4):1369–1378, 04 2017.

[69] M. Slater. A note on presence terminology. *Presence Connect*, 3, 01 2003.

[70] M. Slater. Place illusion and plausibility can lead to realistic behaviour in immersive virtual environments. *Philosophical transactions of the Royal Society of London. Series B, Biological sciences*, 364:3549–57, 12 2009.

[71] M. Slater. Immersion and the illusion of presence in virtual reality. *British Journal of Psychology*, 109(2), 03 2018.

[72] M. Slater, M. Usoh, and A. Steed. Depth of presence in virtual environments. *Presence*, 3:130–144, 01 1994.

[73] M. Slater, M. Usoh, and A. Steed. Taking steps: The influence of a walking technique on presence in virtual reality. *ACM Transactions on Computer-Human Interaction (TOCHI)*, 2:201–219, 12 1995.

[74] L. Squire, D. Berg, F. Bloom, S. du Lac, A. Ghosh, and N. Spitzer. *Fundamental Neuroscience*. Elsevier Science, 2008.

[75] J. Stevens and J. Kincaid. The relationship between presence and performance in virtual simulation training. *Open Journal of Modelling and Simulation*, 03(2):41–48, 01 2015.

[76] A. Sutcliffe. *Human-Computer Interface Design*. Springer New York, 2013.

[77] S. Tachi, H. Hoshino, R. Hirata, and T. Maeda. A construction method of virtual haptic space. In *Proceedings of the Fourth International Conference on Artificial Reality and Tele-Existence*, pages 131–138, 1994.

[78] M. Usoh, C. Alberto, and M. Slater. Presence: Experiments in the psychology of virtual environments, 06 1999.

[79] N. Wade and M. Swanston. *Visual perception: An introduction*. Psychology Press, 2013.

[80] A. Waggoner, E. Smith, and E. Collins. Person perception by active versus passive perceivers. *Journal of Experimental Social Psychology*, 45(4):1028–1031, 07 2009.

[81] B. G. Whitmer and M. J. Singer. Measuring presence in virtual environments: A presence questionnaire. *Presence*, 7(3):225–240, 06 1998.

[82] Y. Zang, D. Kong, and Y. Zhang. Study and implementation on stereoscopic display in virtual reality. *Communications and Information Processing*, 289:25–36, 01 2012.

# Index

9781032198699